Mestizaje in Ibero-America

Mestizaje in Ibero-America

CLAUDIO ESTEVA-FABREGAT

Translated by JOHN WHEAT

THE UNIVERSITY OF ARIZONA PRESS
Tucson & London

The University of Arizona Press

Original edition copyright © 1987 by Claudio Esteva-Fabregat
Translation copyright © 1995 by the Arizona Board of Regents
All rights reserved

This translation of *El mestizaje en Iberoamerica* is published by
arrangement with Alhambra Longman, Madrid, Spain. The
present edition has been translated with the help of a grant
from the General Administration for Books and Libraries of
the Ministry of Culture of Spain.

♾ This book is printed on acid-free, archival-quality paper.
Manufactured in the United States of America

99 98 97 96 95 94   6 5 4 3 2 1

Library of Congress Cataloging-in-Publication Data

Esteva Fabregat, Claudio.
    [Mestizaje en Iberoamerica. English]
    Mestizaje in Ibero-America / Claudio Esteva-Fabregat ; translated
by John Wheat.
        p.   cm.
    Includes bibliographical references and index.
    1. Ethnology—Latin America.   2. Miscegenation—Latin America.
3. Latin America—Population.   4. Latin America—Social life and
customs.   I. Title.
GN562.L34E8713   1995
306.84′5′098—dc20   94-18731
                                                                      CIP

British Cataloguing-in-Publication Data

A catalogue record for this book is available from the British Library.

CONTENTS

MAPS

FIGURE

TABLES

TRANSLATOR'S NOTE

Translation is often a balancing act, a compromise between the thoughts and phrases of the original and what most accurately and legibly conveys the original content to readers in another language. The present work involves several such situations, most of which are discussed in the translator's notes in the text. A few terms, however, merit special mention here because they will bear on the reader's initial understanding of this work.

First and foremost is the term *mestizaje,* the title and central concept of Professor Esteva's work. On an elemental level, *mestizaje* refers to the mixing of two races, specifically of Spanish and Indians in the New World context. Yet, the term has broader meanings embracing both the biological and cultural aspects of mixture, as this work makes abundantly clear. Although the term *mestizo* is part of the English lexicon, its derivative, *mestizaje,* is not; the term needs translating for the general reader. With all these considerations in mind, I decided to translate *mestizaje* throughout generally as "racial mixing," except where the context specified either biological or cultural mixtures.

The original text employs such ethnic terms as *caucasoide, negroide,* and *europido.* While these might be valid terms, my ear has led me to adopt "Caucasian," "Negro" (or sometimes "black"), and "European" throughout. I have glossed and retained *criollo,* however, to avoid confusion with the English concept of Creole.

Finally, the term *América nuclear,* or "Nuclear America," appears several times in the original.[1] Although this reference to the centers of the great pre-Columbian civilizations is known in anthropological literature, it is not one that is immediately clear to the general reader. Thus, I have rendered *Nuclear America* as "the populated centers of America" throughout, mindful of its pre-Columbian context and of the fact that the term has more than a purely demographic meaning. It is hoped that the compromises outlined above will serve the interests of the general reader and the area specialist alike.

As a final point, in translations, Esteva-Fabregat's insertions in quotations for explantory purposes are enclosed in parentheses, while my own are enclosed in brackets, as in other places in the text.

John Wheat

Translator

Mestizaje in Ibero-America

Concepts

Throughout this work we make rather frequent use of basic concepts that refer to identities both racial and ethnic, springing mainly from the historical and cultural context of the American continent, especially in the Hispanic and Portuguese regions. The concepts that we wish to emphasize most are the following: Ibero-America, Spanish America, Indian, white, black, mestizo, mulatto, and *mestizaje* [racial mixing], among others. For precise discussion, they should be defined at the outset.

The concept of Ibero-America today includes Spanish-speaking America, which begins politically at the United States–Mexican border and extends to Tierra del Fuego on the continent, as well as Brazil and the Spanish-speaking Antilles. It thus excludes the English-, French-, and Dutch-speaking regions of both the mainland and the islands, in the latter case the Lesser Antilles. The territories north of the Mexican border are designated by the term *Anglo-America,* although one should recognize the existence of strong Hispanic communities, whose roots extend back to the late sixteenth century, in the states of New Mexico and southern Colorado, especially the so-called Hispanos [people descended from early Spanish settlers who retained Spanish culture but who were cut off from Mexico by Indians and who call themselves Hispanos]. Additionally, it is equally clear that these Hispanos, especially in the states of Texas and California, have seen their cultural identity reinforced by the incorporation of groups of modern Mexican ethnic origin, such that they constitute ethnic minorities governed, on the one hand, by the national political and economic system of the United States, and on the other, by customs that are truly Mexican, including the so-called Hispanos.

Nevertheless, the concept of Anglo-American is also valid for these ethnic minorities to the extent, at least, that they are bilingual in Spanish and English and tend to use the latter as a language of social integration, particularly in economic life, and as a symbol of their gradual pragmatic adoption of the culture of prestige: the Anglo-American. Beyond that, we must exclude the province of Quebec from the concept of Anglo-America and place it historically in the sphere of what could be called Franco-America, that is, the eastern region of Canada, French Guiana, and the French Antilles. Yet, Caribbean Franco-America would be racially and culturally less "French" than Canada, and in a sense should be designated as Franco-African, particularly when we consider the statistical weight of its racial demography, in this case one of great African predominance.

The same distinctions could be made for the British Antilles. In each case, nonetheless, dominant political traditions certainly appear in this region: the French and the British. The African masses of the population, cut off from their ethnocultural origins, have assimilated the dominant cultures of prestige. This allows us to consider these masses as culturally submerged populations within the larger dominant political system and its corresponding institutional structures and organizations. It is thus easy to see that island, or Antillean, Anglo-America and Franco-America have undergone a process of racial stratification more rigid than that which occurred in Ibero-America. Consequently, Anglo- and Franco-America have developed racial forms of African origin that are more sharply defined, or less mestizo and more mulatto, than those that are recognized in Ibero-America, because in the latter the speed of miscegenation was faster and the process of social and cultural capillarity was more open, or rather came to produce a more profound and dynamic osmosis.

To a lesser degree, there have been Dutch influences in very small areas (Guiana/Surinam) of the mainland and in some Antillean islands. But given the sparse cultural dimension and its present tendency for historical withdrawal, we do not feel it important to elaborate a concept of a Dutch-America, since in the historical reality of the American continent it has disappeared as a significant geopolitical entity.

On the basis of the regional or Ibero-American character that we apply to this work, Anglo-America and Franco-America acquire only a statistical value and do not form part of the dialectic of the specific process of racial mixing that interests us.

Ibero-America thus includes the territories dominated linguistically by Spanish and Portuguese. The specific regions that form the respective Spanish and Portuguese communities reflect a cultural history of synthesis among the Spanish, Indian, and African, in one case, and among the Portuguese, Indian, and African in the other. However, these syntheses occur within a framework of predominant cultural systems in which the Spaniard and *Luso* (Portuguese), whose institutions and corresponding territorial, political, religious, administrative, economic, and educational organizations, in general, have shaped the respective Hispanic-American or Luso-American character or qualities by means of which we may define common histories overlying pre-Hispanic indigenous traditions. That is, Hispanic-America and Luso-America constitute histories united by common initial factors: discoveries, conquests, foundings, colonizations, and Spanish vice-royalties as a society with shared institutions in one case, and the Portuguese society, with its peculiarities, in the other.

Similarly, when we focus on Spanish-speaking countries, we make a distinction: we refer to them with the concept of Hispanic America. Besides, the concept of Latin America is totally foreign to the ingredients that define the cultural-historical and biological form that distinguishes the countries south of the Río Grande. Latin America is an incongruent notion, a careless distortion in specifically anthropological studies, whose use can be contained only in terms of historical ignorance or of interests that are marginal to a truly systematic conceptual focus on the questions involved in the formative process of the Ibero-American countries. Of course, none of these countries either speaks Latin or writes in this language.

The concept of *Indian* designates those individuals descended from indigenous or native lineages of pre-Columbian America, who are thus racially distinct from Caucasians and Negroes. Since this distinction is difficult to establish biologically when there is no rigorous classification of the individual, the concept of Indian is also applied to individuals who are members of tribal societies or ones that are politically autonomous from the national societies in whose territory they live.[1] In this sense, anthropometric and serological research, on the one hand, and ethnic-cultural research, on the other, allow us to designate as Indians large masses of the individuals who live tribally, in some instances, as occurs in jungle or isolated communities, or whose ethnic identity appears separate from the national identity of the state to which they belong. It is also common to designate as Indians groups of peasants who speak only indigenous languages, who live in a communal or local form, who are called such by members of the national society, and who refer to themselves in a manner distinct from what is properly the identity of the state. Such natives we do not consider here as Indians, and ethnically, they seem to be in a process of acquiring a consciousness of the nation or state. In this sense, their children are already bilingual and include themselves within the national identity.

Nevertheless, in no case are the principles that we mention absolute in character, since within each Indian group there are mestizo individuals, and even other racial categories that we could locate only by turning to genealogical research, which, in many cases, it would be impossible to undertake or even to control sufficiently. Thus, the concept of Indian presents us with two variants: one biological, the other cultural. The former amounts to a useful generalization when applied to human groups about whom we have evidence regarding their pre-Columbian ethnohistorical connection; the latter is also a useful generalization applicable only to the lifestyle manifested by certain human groups in Ibero-America. In some cases, the generalization is valid, biologically and culturally, for certain individuals. In others, it applies to only one of these aspects. In addition, the *Indian* concept assumes, in either case, the recognition of no biological or cultural antecedent, either separate or in specific combination.

When we mention *white,* the concept includes individuals of European origin in their several Caucasian varieties. The concept of *black* refers to the racial group of African origin whose morphological characteristics describe individuals of this origin, distinguished by the black color of their skin, kinky hair, thick lips, and a broad, flat nose, among other perhaps less evident features (see Comas 1957, 552). In general terms we include as Negroes the several varieties of black individuals who are equivalent to *African.* With the concept of *mestizo* we are referring to the hybrid resulting from the biological mixture of a white man and Indian woman or of an Indian man with a white woman. When we speak of the concept of *mulatto* we understand it to mean the hybrid of white and black. And with the concept of *zambo,* we refer to the hybrid of the mixture between an Indian man and a black woman, or, less frequently, between a black man and an Indian woman.

We shall also speak of *mestizo culture* or the integrated or functional mixture of lifestyles of different ethnicities, in this case, of the mixture of indigenous traditions with European and Negro ones, and of their different combination within their respective ethnic or national contexts. When we use the concept *criollo,* we refer only to the product of the union of two white or European progenitors who has been born on American soil. This concept of criollo is often used to designate Negro persons born in America from the union between two Africans. This occurs in certain Africanized areas, but has no general application. Nonetheless, here criollo will have the meaning given in the first sense: the child of white parents who was born in America, particularly of Spanish or peninsular whites, that is, from the Iberian peninsula.

We shall make frequent use of other concepts. These include acculturation, recombination, and syncretism. Each of these helps determine the qualities and character taken on by cultural patterns resulting from historical pressures having their origin, fundamentally, in first the encounter, then in the implantation of indigenous features and cultural complexes mixed with Spanish and with African ones, in alloys of the three among themselves, or in separate combinations of two, but which in any case—and in the reality of cultural mixing—often reflect a predominance of Spanish cultural modes, or Portuguese modes in Brazil, over the indigenous and African.

On the one hand, acculturation is a phenomenon resulting from the addition to an already existent cultural system of one or various elements of another, or other systems; these additions appear in the form of isolated traits or of complexes that, upon joining the system, modify the ingredients of social action and thus the cultural system without necessarily transforming its political and social structure. Examples of acculturation would be the incorporation of new cultigens without changing the techniques and strategies of land cultivation; the adoption of different clothing without changes of status; or the addition of new foodstuffs and the expansion of dietary resources without modifying the economic system.

These are phenomena of acculturation that may signify the substitution of some elements for others without their becoming effective agents of a transformation of the social structure and of behavioral values within the various institutions. At the most, in an early stage, cognitive references can undergo changes and under favorable conditions, can lead to the examinations of new solutions and cultural strategies. In this way, a society may be acculturated without simultaneously modifying its political, religious, military, economic, and institutional administrative structure and its organization of status. Likewise, a structural change could result when the cultural design that is introduced has a strategic nature, for example, automation in the context of industrial systems.

The Spanish in America were acculturated when they adopted elements of the indigenous diet and vocabularies of the languages, especially those referring to fauna, flora, and the landscape. Nonetheless, that did not necessarily mean the transformation of the institutional structure that they imposed upon groups of indigenous Americans. The greatest changes were in the dietary practice of the Spanish and the cognitive references that allude to its ingredients. The Indians were acculturated when they entered into Spanish-American society, and also when they acquired beasts of burden from the Spanish, new cultigens, the horse, sheep and clothing made from them, in addition to numberless other cultural elements brought from Spain.

The concept of cultural recombination explains conscious use of elements of two or more cultures within a single personal behavior for the purpose of carrying out a more efficient social action. It denotes a dynamic of cultural selection and implies the use of a flexible institutional structure and of a social organization continually open to the adoption of new lifestyles. It refers more to individuals than to groups. For example, for a bilingual, bicultural individual,[2] recombination assumes the use of two specific permanent structures, one that the individual uses to communicate with the members of his or her group of origin, and the other that he or she uses in the course of his or her activities within the group of adaptation. This would be the case of indigenous Americans, who, upon using Spanish culture, nonetheless avoided renouncing their own; they enjoyed both cultures without distinction and assumed the permanent recombination of their elements. As they were acculturating through social adaptation, they were recombining their new elements of experience. In this sense, all recombination is a conscious process, characteristic of learning strategies.

We shall here understand the concept of syncretism in the sense of behavioral characteristics of one social structure absorbed by a similar one, but one of different ethnic and cultural origin. For example, the appearance of the Virgin of Guadalupe at Tepeyac (Mexico) was beheld by an Indian because it corresponded to a similar symbolic line of thought: that of the mother of life. Offerings to the divinity and libations were as much aspects of indigenous ritual in the high cultures of the Americas as they were of Catholic liturgy. Likewise, they were part of the same conceptual structure. In any case, syncretism pertains to the sphere of symbolism and concepts more than to that of ergology and social organization. It assumes acculturation and recombination and eliminates formal cognitive contradictions through the substantiality of its symbolic representation. Syncretism is the most complete intellectual manifestation of cultural mixing.

Of course, these three concepts represent shades of processes that took place at differing intensities within the racial, ethnic, and social communities of America. Each of them appears manifesting a historic or specific behavior in a given space, and each represents a significant unit. That is, each is equivalent to an adaptive cultural dimension, in this case, fundamentally, of Spanish culture with respect to the various indigenous ones. In such circumstances, if acculturation does not necessarily presuppose a structural transformation, and if recombination implies adaptability to opportunity, and, as in card games, assumes opportunism in its practice; and if syncretism assumes a fusion of different cognitive forms into a common symbolic formation, the three concepts are, nevertheless, aspects of the responses made in America by the different racial, ethnic, and social groups according to the circumstances of their adaptation to the mutual pressures that emerged throughout the diverse processes of formation of unique local, or territorial, societies.

Acculturation and Racial Mixing

Within the context in which we are working the study of acculturation, understood as a dynamic phenomenon of the evolution and transformation of lifestyles, constitutes a dialectical aspect of modern anthropological theory. The concept and methods that explain these issues have been argued in different and varied discussions,[1] and each of them has shown a concern with the creation of models that might serve to guide field research. Some of these discussions represent valuable contributions, but in certain instances they are mere formulations of concepts more than they are methods. In addition, each time we undertake concrete research—ethnohistorical or field work, cultural or biological, according to the circumstances—we note an enrichment of the issues and the emergence of new concepts. This characteristic of research assumes the expansion of the existing conceptual apparatus, at the same time that new arguments emerge that lead to the imposition of methodological adaptations. All of these elements create the need to produce constant reformulations of the theory and method of acculturation.

With regard to their effect on the discussion of the processes of racial mixing in Ibero-America, the dialectic of acculturation touches upon interracial and intraracial social relations in two ways:

First, the Indians, Spanish, and Africans were relatively associated with one another, because their relations were socially and historically asymmetrical. That is, the dominant political position of Spanish culture over that of Indians and Africans assumed that the Spanish had a greater capacity to transform the way of living of the other racial groups than the others had to transform the Spanish. Wherever Spanish culture appeared along with military and political dominance (and that was common in this history), its capacity for acculturation was decisive, to the extent that the Spanish way of living became a valid institutional model for all those individuals who formed part of the social structure and, in any case, of its cultural system. For this reason, the Spanish were acculturated significantly less by the Indians than the latter were by the Spanish. And of course this also happened with the Africans, for they acted in cultural isolation, socially and politically subject to the Spanish. On occasion the Africans managed to re-create parts of their aesthetic culture and of their primary social organizations in those instances where they lived as fugitives. Even under these conditions, however, they tended to use Spanish culture to a greater extent than their own, precisely because the heterogeneity of their origins carried with it the need to communicate to one another through a freely circulating instrumental medium, and in such a case the Spanish model filled this role to a larger degree than could be foreseen from the Africans' cultural origins.

Second, it is also important to recognize that the Spanish, considered individually, did not have a uniform social capacity to acculturate the natives because that capacity depended upon the status they had in relation to the Indians and to the social structure in which they functioned, and from which they came. Thus, for example, a soldier could not have the same impact on the Indian as a missionary would, and a Spanish artisan situated in an urban context acted in a capacity different from that of a landed family of *encomenderos*[2] in charge of Indians or of entire Indian villages. The important thing here is to realize that the phenomena of acculturation had different intensities according to the status position of the Spanish with regard to the Indians and Africans.

Depending on these variables, the adaptive responses were different; the processes were relatively faster or slower, and syncretisms and recombinations took on asymmetrical cultural forms and influences, especially with reference to the volume of influences received and to the dominant configuration in behavioral structure.

At this point we shall concern ourselves with certain methodological problems related to Ibero-America. At the same time we shall point to the need to carry out studies of acculturation and of cultural mixing based on assumptions that take into account the principle of the existence of a great number of variables whose interaction and products are conditioned by historical-cultural as well as ecological and sociological factors, or are associated with the functions of the social organization of the ethnic groups involved. Furthermore, the dimensions of acculturation that most concern us are those related to the study of recombination and syncretism, although it is obvious that in many cases certain associations of the phenomena with the incidence of biological mixing have to do with the different combinations that derive from the number of individuals who take part in the mixing processes and from the particular force of the imposition of their culture upon those of the dependent societies and individuals. From this standpoint it is evident that the processes of acculturation created in Ibero-America responded to the spread of Spanish culture through contact, interaction, and imitation. Furthermore, they were the result of imposition (a) through missionary preaching of the Gospel introduced into Indian villages, or later, through the settlement of Indians, by which means a direct or more systematic political control was established over their way of life, including the transformation of their cultural system and social structures, or (b) through the civil government over the Indians, whether it might be from the economic use of the Indian as a labor force, or through the access of young Indians to Spanish education, in that the latter included the ideological transformation of new generations of Indians and their individual development within the Spanish society.

The acculturation of Indians and Africans did not follow a single path, particularly because individual circumstances were so diverse and because relations between each racial group had alternatives and obeyed equally diverse strategies of opportunity. Therefore, the most important quality in the process of acculturation occurring in Ibero-America throughout the various formative processes, and with regard to indigenous groups, was asymmetry. That is, it consisted of the fact that the dominant political and cultural mode had varying capacities of diffusion and implantation according to the relative receptivity of the Indians, their demographic numbers, the number of Spanish and Africans who took part, the social pressure and prestige that they exercised on indigenous cultural systems, and within the latter, on indigenous social structures.

Asymmetry was as true for the Indians as ethnic and racial groups subject to political pressure as it was for the Spanish and Africans who lived together or in indigenous communities and who depended for their subsistence on native production. In this sense, the acculturation of Spanish and Africans was especially significant in the realm of foodstuffs, whereas it was very slight with regard to ideological influences, to a worldview, to technological culture, and to the institutional organization of society. Spanish and Africans absorbed indigenous influences more at an individual than at a group level, except with regard to the consumption of foodstuffs and the adaptation that they had to make to the indigenous world when economic and social dependencies of a permanent nature were established.

In this context the historical process of acculturation was parallel to that of racial mixing, although at the outset it was easier to mix than to acculturate, especially when we reflect that if sexual relations lacked social stability and involved only opportunistic encounters, the culture of each side absorbed very little of the other, except for whatever might prove useful and visible, including artifacts and material culture. By way of language, ideas, and a worldview, acculturation called for a more complex intellectual theme as well as for a rational design, both of which were impossible to integrate without the prior existence of social stability and the institutionalized coexistence of each racial entity within the context of a common social structure.

Of course, under these conditions, acculturation and racial mixing were not necessarily parallel phenomena, because whereas the former made indispensable from the outset the existence of a nationalistic pragmatic utility, the latter required only a sexual impulse and the opportunity to satisfy it. Acculturation appeared inevitably in the same way that racial mixing did: through contact between racially different individuals. The first vehicles were individual and appeared as spontaneous acts. That is, the Spanish in the phase of conquest made no attempt to acculturate; what they sought was to dominate and to establish themselves as the masters of the Indians in the latter's territories. Meanwhile, the encounter with Indian women produced racial mixing.

Under these conditions, the natives were being acculturated by rudimentary imitation, basically of Spanish technology, of tools, and above all, of Spanish usage of animals, weapons, and clothing, to the degree that horses and mules represented a system of power symbols and transportation more efficient than their own traditional ones, while weapons and clothing represented imitations, respectively, of prestige and efficacy. Nevertheless, these cultural practices were acquired gradually because they called for training and social participation or internal coherence within the systems of everyday motivations and objectives of each culture. Comparatively, racial mixing lacked this initial process of rational or selective design. If man is a categorizing animal, it is also clear that in the heart of the conquest Spanish men categorized Indian women according to those aesthetic and physical qualities that coincided with Spanish preferences, but the resulting sexual relation was not necessarily equivalent to a systematic plan of acculturation by means of sexual intercourse. This unsystematic acculturation constitutes one of the first perspectives of the matter that concerns us.

When this lack of system concerning the study of acculturation and racial mixing is posed within complex cultural contexts, as happens with the Ibero-American historical process, the analysis in terms of purely cultural models becomes a significant problem. The starting point to emphasize here is that of the need to turn to analyses that can establish the distribution and interaction of cultural components in terms of the social groups who use and transmit them, that is, to analyses made according to the organization of roles and status revealed within specific social structures. This type of analysis will tell us about the relative permeability of social groups within the culturally pluralistic societies that make up Ibero-America. It will also tell us to what degree acculturation and racial mixing acquire a different frequency, not only as a function of certain ethnicities, but also according to the relative forms that the social structure adopts, that is, in accord with the specific adaptations of role and status in social activities.

In addition, the principal difficulties that we face when we regard Ibero-American acculturation deal with the great number of variables involved in each specific process, as well as their stratification and their relative volume and frequency of interaction. Furthermore, these variables represent inter-actions that vary regionally according to their cultural and ecological com-binations. This fact obliges us, methodologically, to turn to the adaptation in situ of the principle of the relative intensity and frequency of each of the variables involved in each combination. According to this, the great diversity of data to which we turn in order to comprehend the processes implicit in the nature and situation of each variable with a specific complex of inter-actions, makes some of our traditional tools of operation inadequate.

To study acculturation in terms of the mere formal description of cultural elements is insufficient, especially when, as is frequently the case, the func-tions of each cultural element within the institutional complexes of the social process are not well established. Description is inadequate, moreover, be-cause it overlooks the relative distribution of cultural ingredients according to their specialization by social groups and in terms of role/status systems. With regard to Ibero-America, studies of acculturation have been set forth without taking into account the presence of such systems. The prevailing tendency has been to consider cultural components as self-explanatory.

In many aspects, anthropologists[3] have tended toward a certain ignorance with regard to the establishment of the internal functions of cultural traits within concrete societies, revealing themselves to be more interested in dis-covering formal historical relations than in studying the position that these functions have within specific sociocultural systems.

The fact we wish to stress here is that the study of acculturation is not just a question of showing the relative origin of cultural traits in the sense often presented by diffusionists,[4] nor is it sufficient to limit ourselves to defining the morphological characters, but it is also necessary to highlight their spe-cific activity in terms of their internal connections. Thus, more than a prob-lem of simple cultural diffusion, we are dealing with a problem of the inter-action of cultural variables, indigenous and foreign, whose combination is peculiar to each circumstance and whose process, therefore, is also specific to the sociocultural system where it appears. Since the historical process of the Ibero-American countries is not uniform, and since there are great regional variations in the cultural content of their national organizations, it becomes necessary to formulate acculturation studies based on the principle that, since the cultural variables involved are different, at least with regard to their relative strength and relative frequency of occurrence, and since the social organizations that relate and integrate them are similarly diverse, it is also true that the resulting cultural combinations are different.

With regard to the study of racial mixing, it is not only a valid principle that where there are diverse racial variables, combinations among them produce different results, but also that the ecological adaptations achieved by each variable and by each one of the phenotypes derived from the exchange of genes among them are also different. In any case, the exchange process, as well as the relative strength and frequency of occurrence of each variable in that process, constitute complex functions that cannot be determined with just a morphological description of individuals but demand studies capable of showing the interaction in ecological, genetic, and sociocultural terms. As in the case of acculturation, the observation and study of racial mixing must be more an analytical structural-functional study than a descriptive one. In this sense, observation of the behavior of the several variables involved in the phenomena of acculturation and racial mixing forms a proper basis on which to build a truly dynamic analysis.

The Study of Acculturation

In the study of Ibero-American acculturation and racial mixing, we begin with the assumption that all the ethnic groups of that continent are now acculturated, although in different degrees and proportions. Acculturation has been progressive and continuous in some groups, and sporadic and discontinuous in others. The latter are the least in number. In each case, acculturation has depended on the relative access of the Spanish, and secondarily of other ethnicities, to native areas, and on the specific exchange that they might have sustained in the course of that contact. This access has been rapid in those cases where geopolitical and economic interests have predominated. In such cases, acculturation has turned out to be an intensive process involving a great number of individuals. The most characteristic examples are those of the conquest of the populated centers—Meso-America and the Andean region—and of the Antilles. Later, other regions of the Americas proved attractive, such as southern South America—the Río de la Plata, for example. In each of those cases where conquest had a geopolitical importance—in addition to the economic and spiritual—acculturation and racial mixing took on a progressive and systematic character.

We refer here to regions that were initially attractive for their geopolitical, economic, and spiritual importance, but where the results are culturally different according to the relative activity of the indigenous, Hispanic-

Portuguese, and Negro variables—*demographic density, social system, cultural system, and ecological system*—at the moment of the conquest, each of them facilitating or hindering acculturation and racial mixing. Furthermore, the marginal regions of the tropics remained outside intensive acculturation and racial mixing precisely because of their lack of geopolitical and economic attraction and, therefore, because they did not constitute urgent objectives. Such is the case of the southern tip of South America and the Orinoco and Amazon Basins at the time of the first contacts between natives and the Spanish and Portuguese. The exploration and settlement of these regions were more acts of individuals or very small groups than a collective and systematic activity. Thus, it follows that acculturation and racial mixing in such marginal areas had a sporadic and discontinuous character, though there were direct or indirect contacts of some kind.

It is important to keep in mind, however, that acculturation does not necessarily imply racial mixing, even if the incidence of the latter is more common in those areas where some kind of cultural exchange or transmission took place than where the potential receiver group has remained isolated. Such isolation would occur very rarely. It could happen, then, that acculturation might be produced by intermediaries of the same racial variety, without the direct intervention of individuals carrying other racial genes. In such a situation, there is no racial mixing, though it remains potentially feasible, since acculturation is in itself, deeply, the result of a social attitude favorable to genetic exchange. Once the conditions for acculturation are present, those that promote racial or genetic exchange occur easily. Thus, it is most probable that where acculturation processes, and therefore relations between groups, have existed, genetic exchanges also appear to a certain extent, with greater or lesser stability according to the relative proximity of the populations involved.

In accord with such assumptions, it is clear that we are dealing with populations where acculturation and racial mixing emerge as phenomena to be considered in terms of their relative intensity or frequency in each specific ethnic group. In the case of acculturation, this intensity refers to the number of cultural traits introduced by the contributing ethnic groups and the relative integration of those traits with the system of culture or the system of institutionalized behavior of the individual members of the receiving society. In the case of racial mixing, the frequency, which refers to the relative number of individuals resulting from miscegenation and their specific characters and adaptations, whether physiological, psychological, or ecological, is at issue. Thus, in both cases the problem is viewed from the perspective of the specific social system and in terms of the internal functional stratification, that is, in terms of that which derives from the system of roles and status into which the individuals and groups of each society are organized.

The Study of Racial Mixing

With regard to biological mixing, we must begin with an assumption: all ethnic groups in Ibero-America feature at least some individual antecedent of mixture. This antecedent might be proportionally great or small in its relative incidence and its continuity, depending on the historical-cultural circumstances in which the specific racial contact may have occurred as well as on the frequency of the flow of genetic exchange. There are even times when racial mixing can fail to appear phenotypically, for example, in those cases where many generations have passed since the first incidence and the hybrids could have been reabsorbed by ecological adaptation or by ethnic endogamy, thus reestablishing genetic predominance. This question is clearly an aspect of physical anthropology and calls for the use of methods proper to it and to genetics in its serological flow. Nevertheless, cultural anthropology, particularly ethnology and linguistics, has much to say about these problems, especially with regard to the identifying of cultural traces that describe interethnic contacts and interdependence between these sciences.

When we think, for example, of racially pluralistic societies as complex as those of Trinidad and as some of those found on the Ibero-American coasts of the Atlantic and the Caribbean—where there is evident mixing of European, indigenous, Negro, Syrian-Lebanese, Hindu, Chinese, Japanese, and other genes derived from combinations and mixtures—it is clear that we must have genealogies or antecedents of the individuals participating in the formation of concrete lineages as well as of the historical and sociocultural conditions under which the genetic exchange took place. In addition, today we know how difficult it is to define racial groups when there are not only phenotypical, anthropometric, or genetic variables involved, according to each case, but also adaptive ones. There is no doubt that it has now become important to study the effect of ecosystems or physiological human adaptations, as has been demonstrated especially for the Andean region by Monge (1953) and his associates. In this case, they have shown the importance of studying phenomena relating to adaptations in their functional aspects by establishing the specific interaction between ecosystems and the physiological traits of each individual in particular, or of the ethnic-social groups in general. Thus, we know how relative many of the criteria used to measure racial mixing have been and continue to be, especially the cultural ones, but this relativity should disappear when we use anthropometric criteria, for which we must have available definitions that result from the agreement on certain data to be considered as sufficiently descriptive and definitive for the purposes of classification. Beyond the necessary typologizing, it is absolutely indispensable to gather samples of representative Ibero-American populations, both for their degree of specific purity and for their relative degree of racial mixing.

The effort to characterize the population of Ibero-America anthropometrically is in itself one of physical anthropology's most important tasks, but in studies of racial mixing this effort becomes one of the principal areas of research to which physical anthropology can aspire as a truly dynamic anthropological science. The problem we are considering in this case is not just one of characterization, but of adaptive processes, of ecological specializations, of determinants and conditioning, and of degree and frequency of internal reproduction for each group or racial variety.

With regard to its scientific utility, the study of biological mixing is the touchstone against which modern physical anthropology can test itself, because in a large sense this subject is the true test of a dynamic anthropology, since for the most part current physical anthropology is no more than descriptively anthropometric and largely static in its results as well as in its concepts. The study of racial mixing simultaneously as a process and a phenomenon—at the moment when the mobility of human populations has increased, and at the moment when cultural determinants act upon biological life in incomparably greater measure than at any time in the past—should become one of the pillars of the new physical anthropology. Factorial analyses, joined with characterological description, are the type of research we need from physical anthropology if we hope for it to help us complete our understanding of acculturation and racial mixing.

The Formative Ethnicities of The Ibero-American

We shall consider the problem of biological mixing, then, in terms of a study featuring various interdependent but methodologically isolatable aspects, such as: (1) the relative racial homogeneity of each ethnic group in its origin and during the time in which contact or exchange with another group or groups takes place; (2) the relative homogeneity of each culture in its origin and at the time in which the relation with another or other cultures takes place; (3) the relative transmission of cultural features and complexes carried out by Hispano-Portuguese and Negro groups who established relations with the American indigenous cultures; and (4) the participation and cultural interaction of each ethnicity with respect to another or others, as well as the relative cultural syncretism or syncretisms produced once sociocultural interaction implies the adoption of new models of behaviors.

With regard to the process of cultural change in Ibero-America, we cannot speak of sociocultural homogeneity with reference to the Hispanic group, because the latter features three significant variables: (1) as a racial group the Hispanic is diversified and represents different Caucasian varieties, and furthermore, it is composed largely of types resulting from racial mixing among those varieties; (2) as a cultural group it is also diverse, in the sense that the Iberian Peninsula features different cultural traditions, although the cultures of the first settlers in America were more similar to one another than would be the cultures of the ones who arrived later; and (3) as a social group, up to recent times, it features a marked internal stratification based on aristocratic principles, which are reflected through organization into social classes.

With regard to the indigenous peoples, we also cannot speak of sociocultural homogeneity in a universal sense, such that the three variables indicated for the Iberian group are applicable among them; that is: (1) there seems to be no racial homotype, and although this is still a debatable point, for that reason ecological adaptations of native Americans to acculturation do differ, as do the results; (2) there are a great many cultural differences among the thousands of ethnicities that constitute or have constituted native American societies, and this cultural diversity is also valid for Anglo-America; and (3) the internal social structures of each indigenous society doubtless show as important differences, both with regard to the kind of receptivity that they offer to acculturation and to social change, and with regard to the type of cultural model that results from exchange with other groups and with specific individuals from those groups in terms of social structure and of its function within that structure.

With regard to Negro groups, relative sociocultural homogeneity is proposed under the same or similar assumptions, since in their origin (1) there seems to have been no absolute racial homogeneity, although initially the ecological adaptations of Negro groups were more uniform than those of American Indians, because, whereas the latter represent a great ecological mosaic, the Negro groups came largely from tropical or subequatorial regions; (2) the Negro cultures transplanted to the New World were not homogeneous, although they did feature less differences among themselves than did the American indigenous cultures; and (3) in Negro societies there were internal stratifications that caused some groups to adapt better than others to certain cultural changes, and in turn caused some to be more successful than others in transplanting their institutions and way of life to Ibero-America.

The three great formative groups—Iberian, Indian, and black—feature their own internal variables, which allude to the cultural and to the racial when we limit our inquiry to the formal study of acculturation and racial mixing. However, the consideration of these variables becomes insufficient when we study the problem in terms of groups and social classes that form the social system of Ibero-America after the consolidation of the conquest; that is, after those groups and classes had created a definitive political, social, economic, and religious organization—a social system made up of associations and of individuals operating within a recently constituted Ibero-American society by means of role and status functions. When we consider the study of problems of acculturation and racial mixing in terms of a dynamic anthropological theory, it becomes evident that both are largely conditioned by the *social system* factor. While this factor defines the spheres of action of individuals and social groups and the structure of their mutual relations, it also gives us the structural-functional reference for that society.

The *social system* variable thus has vital importance in the studies of acculturation and racial mixing in Ibero-America and cannot be overlooked when we seek to understand their dynamics. In this sense, the Hispanic variable is particularly significant in relation to the other ethnic variables because, due to the predominant political and social position of the collective Spanish group during at least three centuries, this variable determines the macrostructural forms of Ibero-American society and establishes the system of roles and status by means of which different social groups are related to their specific cultures. With regard to racial mixing, the system of roles is a behavior indicator that tells us to what extent the sociocultural exchange between individuals belonging to the different coexisting ethnicities and races is limited or facilitated, but it also tells us how visible the genetic exchange is between these same groups.

The Hispanic Variable: The Social System and Its Interpretation

Upon determining the character of this social system among the Spanish, we observe that its organization reveals a rigorous social stratification, especially after the consolidation of the conquest and the stabilization of a well-defined social system. The basic principle accounting for the stratification of Hispanic society, and thus for that of the Ibero-American collectivity—Spanish, Portuguese, Indians, Africans, and other ethnicities—was an aristocratic one. This aristocratic character was more prominent among the Hispanic groups of the center and south of Ibero-America than among those of the north and east, which presumes the existence of a certain range of intensities when we speak of the organization and structure of social relations in situ, according to whatever specific ethnic influence and proportions might apply. Thus, we are dealing with a social stratification made up of specialized cultural or class adaptations that would then lead, among the Spanish themselves, to different ways of living.

In this sense, the group of conquistadors and high officials of the Crown were gradually forming an upper social class, increasingly separated from their other compatriots by differentiated notions of class and socioeconomic interests, and from the other ethnicities—indigenous, Negro, and mestizo— by notions of class and caste; the groups of settlers who join the American population after the consolidation of the conquest, by contrast, represent a more flexible and less exclusivist social class that, because it is in more direct contact with non-Hispanic ethnicities, is also more inclined toward exchange and racial mixing with them, and thus is also the social class that largely influences the process of acculturation of those ethnicities. Here, instead of their superimposing their culture, like the conquistadors, who continued living in the Spanish way, the less exclusivist settlers engage in a functional mixing that influences the formation of new cultural forces among the native and other non-Hispanic ethnicities, as well as among the settlers, whose role and status cause them to interact more frequently with these ethnicities than did conquistadors and officials. In effect, as a social group, the colonists were the ones who created the most extensive and direct linkages with the natives.

Fundamentally, in Ibero-America two forms of Hispanic acculturation take shape, acting as agents of change. The first form is sociopolitical and economic acculturation, the former referring to the function of territorial and administrative organization, and additionally, to the formation of a new social stratification, and the latter to the establishment of the great agrarian domains, or *encomiendas*.[5] In each case, this form of acculturation is an immediate consequence of the conquest and concerns a geopolitical concept, that of the Spanish state, conducted and administered by its trusted men. With the triumph of the conquest, the great Indian empires and chieftaincies were broken, replaced, or modified in each case by new forms that we will not attempt to describe, much less analyze, now.[6]

This acculturation, derived from the exercise of Spanish political power, refers, on the one hand, to the organization of new territorial, administrative and economic, and local and regional models, and, on the other, to the modification of equivalent indigenous structures, in each case leading to institutional adaptations in situ. This is an acculturation that affected above all the structural-functional organization of both the pre-Hispanic society and the newly constituted Hispanic one. Its formal institutionalization should be considered through the study of the role of the Spanish ruling class, that is, of the conquistadors and high officials of the Crown. The mixing of this group with the indigenous populations was of the type we call "frontier mixing," or concubinage, in many cases, and a "prestige mixing," which refers to the matrimonial alliances made by the conquistadors with Indian women of elevated lineage and status.

The second form is socioeconomic, referring to the transfer of Hispanic forms of culture to the natives and other non-Hispanic ethnicities by colonists or immigrants, with significant expansion in the area of the peculiar socioeconomic organizations that they established, such as those created by different religious orders—Jesuits, Augustinians, Dominicans, Franciscans, and so on—in various indigenous zones of America. In each case, lay people and clergy served as a direct vehicle of acculturation. Because of their direct contact or daily coexistence with the native and non-Hispanic ethnicities, this was the main type of acculturation that spread Spanish culture throughout America. The study of acculturation created by both Spanish groups—colonists and priests—makes us aware of the processes of cultural syncretism carried out on that continent, with the realization that the ethnic exchange was intense. Racial mixing between the secular colonizing group and the natives and other ethnicities was more stable than that carried out by the group of conquistadors and officials. Thus, the genetic exchanges between the secular colonists and the natives and other ethnicities were continuous and allowed for a systematic sociocultural interaction between them. The sociological study of these groups thus leads to an understanding of firsthand acculturation and racial mixing in the case of secular colonists, and to an understanding of mass acculturation, in many regions, in the case of religious orders.

Let us say, then, that the first form of Hispanic acculturation, that of the conquistadors and officials, is more macrostructural and affects the socioeconomic and political organization of the new society;[7] whereas the second one is microstructural and affects particularly the basic sociocultural organization—family and local communities—of the native societies. The second form of acculturation modifies the indigenous system of internal relations, but especially modifies the contents and values attached to those numerous cases where the natives join the new social organizations derived from the Spanish sociocultural system. Because the cultural relations and systematic interpersonal exchanges between the Spanish and the Indians and non-Hispanic ethnicities were carried out through colonists and priests, thus forming mixed societies through direct coexistence with them, it is therefore certain that the most effective agents of acculturation were these two groups. As for racial mixing, once the conquistadors and officials had become a social group that was sexually self-sufficient, the secular colonist group was the one that related in the most stable manner with the indigenous and non-Hispanic ethnicities, particularly because, unlike the other Spanish groups we have mentioned, it was not sexually self-sufficient. It is through this group that we may observe the development of racial mixing and acculturation in a continuous form, and it is among these relations where a mestizo ideology evolves.

Thus, whereas the *criollo* group is a continuity of the conquistadors and officials, the *mestizo* group is a continuity of the colonists exchanging with indigenous and Negro groups on a cultural and genetic level. The popularization or spread of Spanish culture, that is, its penetration of and integration with the Indians' cultures, involves the colonists and priests more than it does the conquistadors and officials. In both cases, the nature of the phenomenon is different, and we must study them in terms of these social relations. In general, these relations emerge above all from the social system, the organization of roles and forms of status, and derive their specific content from the functional culture that each social group—conquistadors, officials, colonists, priests, natives, and non-Hispanic ethnicities, including their own internal stratifications—utilized for the fulfillment of its role and for the achievement of social interaction.

The Spanish sector acted as a basic acculturator, but the type of culture that it transmitted systematically constituted a function of the specific social group. According to this process, the frequency and intensity of the social exchange carried out by each Hispanic group with the Indians and other non-Hispanic ethnicities determined the importance and qualities of the acculturation, and additionally, of racial mixing. Clearly, then, direct exchange contributed a basic condition for acculturation. During the conquest phase, the characteristics of the acculturation clustered around the culture of the conquistadors and of the officials, as well as of the missionaries. Once the conquest was consolidated, acculturation became a phenomenon whose process of integration would involve the colonist group, those Spanish who acted socially, economically, and spiritually in the cities and in the countryside as individuals, in the case of the secular colonists, or autonomously, in the case of the missionaries. Because the group of conquistadors soon became stratified as an upper social class, it quickly lost its direct contact with the indigenous and non-Hispanic populations, and its place was taken by other classes of Spanish—colonists, artisans, soldiers, and missionaries—who maintained a close relation of exchange with non-Hispanic groups in urban centers and in the countryside.

After the conquest, once native social and territorial organization had been destroyed on a political level, and the most important indigenous territorial units had disappeared as national or macropolitical entities and were becoming, as Steward points out (1958, 60) local political or segmented organizations, there emerged in Ibero-America not only a clearly rigid stratification but also a characteristic cultural specialization for each social class. In time, each social class developed its own cultural traditions. Thus, when Ibero-American society crystallized into a highly stratified structural model, often referred to by some writers as characteristic of a caste society, some social classes were more receptive and flexible than others to both acculturation and racial mixing.

The cultural variables that resulted from the social system emerged initially from the Hispanic, indigenous, and Negro sectors, but each of them had, as we have said, their own internal variables. While the Hispanic variables are related to their different regional traditions, we must consider similar variables for indigenous and Negroid groups. Later, new migratory shifts in European and Asiatic groups would in turn produce other ethnic variables whose importance has not been well established. In addition the combination of different cultural variables and subvariables with different social variables and subvariables contributed to the expression of a greater number of traditions, such that the process of cultural segmentation was still more intensified in many cases.

For these reasons, when the Spanish conquest of America was consolidated and a stable socioeconomic structure had been established, we can observe that America became what Nash (1957, 826) has called a "multiple society with a plural culture." Given these circumstances, and in pure methodology, we must ask, with regard to culture and to racial mixing, the same question that Spindler and Goldschmidt (1952, 80) ask with regard to the psychological: To what extent does sociological differentiation imply cultural differentiation? In that case, to what degree does a differentiation in role/ status imply the formation of different cultural models? We have answered this question in the affirmative in other places, especially when, as in the case of Ibero-America, we contemplate the development of a structurally multiple and culturally pluralistic society.

Studies of Role/Status: An Example

Given this proposition about the relationship between role/status and the formation of cultural models, whose arguments center around the importance of studying the social system, seen as an indicator of acculturation and racial mixing, we must specify this study of social system in the realization that when we operate methodologically we depend upon data from the social system, which makes it indispensable to study the functions of groups, as well as those of individuals in terms of their social class and sex, and, to a lesser degree, of their age, since this last factor is diluted within the general indicators for behavior. Because it is of interest to us as an example of the application of the concept of role/status to studies of acculturation and racial mixing in Ibero-America, we can assess the role of the Indian woman—a greater one in any case than that played by the Spanish woman—in the mixing process, and therefore, in acculturation.

In this specific case, we emphasize the need for many studies regarding the status of native women in their society and in the Hispanic one. It also is indispensable to determine their cultural specializations within each context, especially to understand their relative influence in concrete processes of acculturation. They become more important when we consider the scant demographic number of Spanish women in the early phases of Ibero-American society. We know very little about the degree to which native women were acculturated by the Spanish, because in many cases the former appear not only as agents of biological hybridization, but also as shapers of the socialization and the formation of the basic personality structure of their mestizo children. Native women even play the role of acculturators of the Spanish, at least in the culinary sphere. This acculturation is clearest where the union between the Spanish and the native was stable. For the rest, there is no doubt that there was, and are, changes in status for the native in cases of social union with the Spanish. We can also note certain types of changes in recent years when we observe such a union in terms of social organization, where the functions and values of prestige took notice of the ethnic status of the spouses. If we begin with this last assumption of prestige acknowledging, we recognize how enormously important it is for us to examine problems of role/status as a function of sex and of one's ascribed culture, above all in stratified societies, as in some of the Indian ones and in the Spanish, where the sexual division of labor constitutes an indicator of significant sociocultural differentiation.

The values ascribed to each role/status are, furthermore, indicators of the comparative receptivity of each sex to acculturation and racial mixing, and it becomes useful to study role/status when we observe the specific resistance of the women of each ethnicity to coupling with men of different ethnicities. The different role/status position in the social system of the man and woman of each ethnicity was a factor of considerable importance in acculturation and racial mixing. Historically, those qualities have been modified according to the continual changes in social organizations and in the contents and values that regulate the functions of each role and its recognition of specific prestige and status.

The appreciation of this type of problem leads to the study of significant variables in the process of individual and group integration and evidences the relative social possibilities of each acculturation in terms of concrete roles and status within the social system. To define these roles and the culture or contents that correspond to them calls for attention to the very dynamic of acculturation and racial mixing.

One of the advantages of this type of research, seen from the perspective of ethnology, lies in the fact that it is presented in the form of given phenomena. This means that we can determine, not only the consequences of a sociocultural process, but also the circumstances from which it sprang. Such is the case of Ibero-America, though it is clear we have yet to gain sufficient knowledge regarding the data that characterize the problem in its concrete interactions. We know that acculturation and racial mixing took place, but we know little about how it was consummated in specific instances and about which factors facilitated, interrupted, or prevented it in terms of the indicators of role/status that we have mentioned. Thus, to say that there was acculturation and racial mixing is obvious, but the consideration in analysis of social groups and ways of living that proved more susceptible to a specific exchange, as well as the mechanisms of transmission that made possible, according to the case, a sporadic or systematic exchange between individuals and between groups, is not obvious.

Cultural Selectivity and Syncretism

Of course, if we study this problem of the cultural differentiation in the form of ethnic and sociological variables seen as the causes of different traditions, we are also obviously thinking of the incidence of greater acculturation in some social groups than in others, and of societies of Spanish monolingualism more than of those of native monolingualism. This differential acculturation is also true with regard to racial mixing. In addition, the relative speed of this acculturation would have been greater among urban groups than among rural ones. Furthermore, the crystallization of Hispanic syncretisms is greater among rural groups even today than among contemporary urban groups, since among the latter, we should consider a greater frequency of exchange with other modern national groups, especially European or Western, than among the former. For the most part, this exchange should be considered in the form of influences derived from internal and external migratory movements, each one of which modifies individuals and even specific groups in their traditional behavior to at least some degree.

We are considering, then, a historical-cultural process that at the present state of its development should be studied in terms of a great number of influences, some of them entering as new variables in the process of acculturation and racial mixing in Ibero-America, as is the case with the incorporation of new European and Asiatic groups. This fact has made the study of the problem of acculturation and racial mixing more complex when we consider it in its contemporary version. Thus, for example, in Trinidad, though it is somewhat marginal to what we consider strictly Ibero-American, the study of these questions has proved extremely difficult, because there are frequent cases of individuals and groups miscegenated by way of very diverse racial and cultural antecedents (Crowley 1957, 820). In effect, it is very difficult to evaluate acculturation in a family where the mother is of Hindu and Portuguese descent and the father is of black and Chinese descent, while one servant is a native of the island of Grenada, and another is from the island of St. Vincent. Added to this number of variables is the fact that the son of their marriage attends a Catholic school run by an Irish priest and, at the same time, receives the influence of the greater Trinidad society, where the culture of interaction consists of even more variables of cultural traditions and racial varieties.

Due to the incidence of diverse variables, although the nucleus of sociocultural integration in Ibero-America is basically Hispanic-Indian, there are cases that reveal cultural spectra as complex as the one we have just mentioned. This complexity helps us to understand that at this advanced stage of historical development, we cannot study this type of problem by relying on just one social or cultural segment, or through a single ethnicity, although we can recognize the decisive nature of the Hispanic contribution in the sociocultural sphere and of the indigenous ethnicity in the sociocultural sphere from a microstructural perspective. Nonetheless, both contributions being central, they must be considered to be influencing and shaping new cultural traditions.

These integrations or syncretisms that deal with material culture constitute studies of great importance, above all in affirming the conclusion that macrostructural forms were created around the axis of Hispanic organization, whereas the exchanges that resulted in syncretisms correspond more to the cultural than to the social system. In Yucatán, for example, agricultural and culinary technologies revolve around the native complex of corn and beans, but the political and religious organizations are largely centered around Hispanic influence (Redfield 1944, 120). Wissler (1920) revealed a similar fact when he pointed out that, whereas the white man in North America adopted all the traits of the material culture of the Indian corn complex, he did not adopt their ceremonial associations. In Yucatán this tells us that although there was certainly an acculturation among the Spanish with regard to the culture of animals and plants and of certain techniques, including military and culinary—as well as with respect to the adoption of indigenous materials occurring traditionally in situ, and even to the adoption of non-Hispanic vocabularies—the Spanish do not appear to have changed with regard to the

structural aspects of their social organization. This leads to an important conclusion: While it is relatively easy to acculturate a conquering group with
regard to the transmission of the traits of native material culture, it is very
difficult to acculturate it concerning native social and political systems;
whereas the relative capacity of the conquering group is undeniably greater
when attempting to achieve a similar social and political acculturation in the
native society. In general, that is what seems to have happened in Ibero-
America, because, while the Spanish were destroying the native sociopolitical
system and were acculturating the indigenous societies with contributions of
all types of material culture, the native and non-Hispanic ethnicities acculturated the Spanish only in the latter sense. From this perspective, the different cultural traditions derived from the mixtures of different variables are
united by means of a Hispanic macrostructural model. Language and the
spiritual and organic expressions of Catholicism contribute the great axes of
conceptual and ethical nucleation for this model, while the political, territorial, and administrative organization and the large outlines of socioeconomic
orientation, both urban and rural, correspond to the structural model of the
Hispanic tradition during at least three centuries.

Basic Monographs

The problems that we have just discussed and that referred largely to the
study of the social system and to cultural specializations suggest the necessity
of doing ethnohistorical monographs on structural-functional research. We
also need to typologize. Currently, we have attempts at Ibero-American
typology that describe and analyze sociocultural forms of the present and
even of the pre-Columbian era (Redfield 1944), but basically, these studies
seem to ignore the formative antecedents that have intervened in the elaboration or process of said typologies. Fundamentally, these studies ignore the
concrete or regional sociocultural systems that were characteristic of the
Spanish conquistadors and settlers of the formative era of Ibero-America. In
that case there is a marked fundamental historical gap, at the least, from the
late fifteenth century through the seventeenth century.

Thus, it can be said that ignorance of the specific social and cultural systems of the Spanish and Portuguese regions relating to the formative period
of Ibero-America is nearly total. The same can be said for the African tribes
and regions from which came the black groups who arrived in the New
World as slaves or forced immigrants. In this sense, we lack studies relative to
Hispanic, Portuguese, and African ethnohistory because (1) there is no real
ethnohistory with regard to the fifteenth, sixteenth, and seventeenth centuries for certain regions of Spain, especially for Andalucía, Extremadura,

Castilla and León, or for Portugal, and, in Africa even more recently; and (2) there are great gaps in the ethnohistorical background of those anthropologists who devote themselves to Ibero-American studies with reference to problems of acculturation and racial mixing.

These gaps deal particularly with knowledge of the Hispano-Portuguese sphere, on the one hand, and of the African Negro sphere on the other. Furthermore, we shall even ignore here the possible acculturation produced in undetermined aspects by the Asians brought to America by the Spanish, as when we consider the fact that already, in the early years of Lima, there were Asians—Chinese, Japanese, and Portuguese Hindus—who contributed a significant demographic contingent in that city.

We do not, then, have a sociocultural typology for the Portuguese, Hispanic, and African populations for the aforementioned centuries. Above all, we lack monographs that describe the ways of living in representative Portuguese and Hispanic towns, *villas,* [8] and cities, in their contexts as well as in their segments, and the same must be said for black African groups in their distinctive structural flow. This work should be undertaken by ethnohistorians equipped with a solid background in the theory and methods of acculturation, and it requires, furthermore, a solid sociological base, since to study and work with the social system is a prime necessity in this type of research.

There are modern efforts in this direction, such as that of Foster (1961), yet, though his study is very useful from a comparative point of view, it is insufficient from a functional point of view because it represents a generalization in some cases and fails to integrate cultural data in terms of sociostructural segments in specific populations: villages, towns, villas, and cities. Furthermore, while his data for Spanish rural culture tend to explain other current data in Ibero-America, we do not know to what degree they applied to Spain during the centuries we consider significant in terms of formative integration. For purposes of acculturation we are interested in the form of the traits as well as their functions in the new societies, and in this sense it is as important to know their origin as to know their relative integration in indigenous and Ibero-American cultural traditions. [9]

Therefore, problems such as those set forth by Spindler and Goldschmidt (1952, 80), in asking to what extent similar socioeconomic and political structures have produced like personality structures when we know there were differences in the cultural contents of the formative societies, represent research of the greatest interest, which we can make dynamic when we have properly interpreted sociocultural systems, either in situ or through adequate documentation.

It is thus clear that we must have sociocultural genealogies capable of identifying the antecedents of each tradition and the character of each combination, with their specific results. The study of these problems assumes the use of a truly genetic approach (see Esteva 1984), and to this approach we should add a structural-functional analysis proper to current sociology. This means that we need not only to arrive at the formulation of a cultural typology of ethnic and social groups in their mestizo or hybrid version, but also to consider their development in terms of the participation on the part of each ethnicity and each concrete social group.

Contemporary Acculturation and Racial Mixing

In addition to the problems of studying acculturation and racial mixing mentioned above, there are others that refer to the process of transformation of Ibero-American political conditions and to subsequent changes in the demographic components of ethnicities. The most important one to consider is that of the mass incorporation of Italians, Germans, French, Slavs, and other Europeans into some Ibero-American countries, especially into those of the Atlantic coast of South America and in Chile. It is clear that all of these ethnicities have been assimilated by the Ibero-American cultural model, especially on the levels of macrostructure, as defined. Nonetheless, in general, and except for some Brazilian studies, anthropologists have ignored research into the processes and characters assumed by acculturation and racial mixing among Europeans of recent immigration and among the ethnic and social groups involved in the interaction. Without a doubt, there is a large number of problems in this respect still to be clarified.

In the United States, for example, Spiro (1955) and Ianni (1958) have criticized the lack of interest of that country's anthropologists in research about acculturation and racial mixing, and their abandonment of it in favor of what Spiro calls an interest in the purely exotic. Although Ibero-American anthropologists cannot be accused of such an absolute disinterest, they often fail, nonetheless, to set forth seriously a systematic investigation of these problems.

In addition, in Mexico it is still possible to study problems of acculturation and racial mixing with regard to two important national minorities: the North American minority of the past fifty years, and the Spanish minority of the last twenty-five years, particularly that which resulted from the exile brought on by the course of the Spanish Civil War. It is certain that the latter group has exerted a great sociocultural influence in Mexico. Because of the nature of the Spanish as a selective cultural minority, this research would reveal very valuable data for identifying such issues as the specific effect caused in an open and changing society, in this case Mexican society, by the incorporation of a politically oriented national group that brings with it prestigious occupations and knowledge. The research would also reveal the effect upon this group and upon particular members of it of their relative assimilation into Mexican cultural models.

Studies of this type have been made in recent years,[10] but the perspective that they have adopted has referred more to intellectual contributions than to the social life of their protagonists among Mexican groups and the effects of this interaction in an anthropological sense, including not only the mixtures resulting from their unions with Mexican men and women but also the behavior and cultural integration of their descendants.

Of course, for those cases we have certain methodological advantages concerning the data: (1) we can control the contact in time and space; (2) we can establish the cultures of origin and their social systems in terms of the role/status of these individuals in their origin and in the receiving society; (3) we can observe the relative selectivity of their adaptations during the process of interaction with Mexican groups; (4) we can control the results of each cultural difference as we see social differences; and (5) we can consider the frequency of racial mixing and the values involved in the course of genetic exchanges.

When we think that the Mexicanization of this group is a phenomenon closely related to the length of their residence in Mexico and the degree of exchange that its individuals maintain with Mexican society, it is evident that pointing out the conditions that control this process constitutes an important theoretical contribution toward the study of the problem. In this sense we are thinking of such questions as To what degree are cultural syncretisms stable when they appear in the first generation? And to what degree is the maintaining of a cultural society, that is the functioning of a cultural minority, a function of the value system of origin in contrast with that of the new society—the Mexican social system in this case—seen in terms of role/status categories? These and other questions suggest answers whose study is an eminently anthropological task.

What is certain in the type of research we are discussing is the fact that we know very little about the specific influence of urbanization, seen as a universal cultural *mode* to which the individuals are susceptible, whatever culture they may have come from, or whether this influence can be assimilated without trauma only by those individuals who, independent of their historical-cultural tradition, were already members of urban societies. This problem is not posited as just a contemporary issue, since it is also applicable to the study of the processes of acculturation following the conquest of America by the Spanish. The study of the relative urbanization of the society of Spanish origin, of which many of its officials and conquerors were interpreters, and the determination of the degree to which the processes of acculturation and racial mixing differed according to the factors of the specific urbanization of the groups involved in exchange, is a question that clarifies ways of living and explains in terms of different ecological and sociocultural contexts part of the process of cultural formation that took place in Ibero-America.

→   →   →

Another aspect to consider is the degree to which anthropological studies centered on the investigation of a single community are capable of satisfying the demand for a dynamic explanation of the process by which acculturation is produced. Actually, if we think only about the descriptive or static aspects of acculturation, it is enough to make an inventory of cultural traits and of their origin in a given community or in a group of them. Generally, this has been the aim implicit in ethnographically oriented studies of acculturation. Since this should not, however, be the ultimate purpose of the research we are advocating, but rather a means of classification for analysis of the problem, we think it important to emphasize, in the phenomenon of acculturation, the *factorial,* on the one hand, and the *adaptive,* on the other. Thus, in the first case the importance of the macrostructural concept emerges, by means of which we consider interaction between one community and others in terms of interdependence, each community thus constituting what we have come to call a segment of the larger society.[11] Additionally, we can appreciate this interaction, which makes certain communities interdependent according to the specific individuals who affect the sociocultural contact or exchange. This means that the culture carried by said individuals represents specialized conceptions of their role/status. The performance of culture through the social function of human individuals and the interaction of the community on a plural or macrostructural scale are, grossly speaking, the factorial aspects of acculturation. In the adaptive case, the aspect that we see is the functional, because it refers to the localized, or in situ, interaction of acculturation according to the sociocultural relations that produce it.

We must point out that the methodological principle under which we are operating emphasizes the macrostructural side of social relations, especially of political relations, emerging from the fact that the majority of the acculturated communities of Ibero-America, including many of those we call indigenous, constitute sociopolitical, educational, religious, and also economic segments of the larger or national societies.[12]

From this perspective the sociocultural variables of each acculturation are functions of the *systems* discussed previously. In that sense, little has been said up to now with regard to the urban or rural *mode,* for example (whichever the case), of the Hispanic cultures that modified the indigenous cultures and that created new societies, or with regard to the effects that the relative continuity of contacts might have produced in the specific homogeneity of a given cultural region. According to what was stated previously, it is certain that contemporary Ibero-American communities—rural or not—represent segments of a larger society, for the purpose of a macrostructural interaction. For this reason, the study of the diverse segments that represent qualitatively the larger societies constitutes the means of representing the phenomenon of acculturation as a process. In addition, the study of the various cultural segments representative of the society is a way of relating structural and functional information. Thus, such a study is the only means of establishing the dynamic of cultural change in such cases.

The study of several communities situated on a synchronic level is, thus, the basic ideal for the research we are advocating in the area of acculturation. In any case, the study of several communities representing the different segments of a larger society really implies working with the total culture in interaction with the total society. This is, in our view, the way in which it will be possible to make a correct interpretation of acculturation in Ibero-America, which assumes our considering acculturation also macroculturally. No community thus represents the total culture of a society, nor does one individual represent the total community. For this reason, the dynamic interpretation of the phenomenon of acculturation consists of following it within a larger context than that of the community itself. Otherwise we may speak only of a *case* of acculturation according to a local *mode,* without being able to establish the sources and the dynamic or factorial elements of the process of interaction, especially if we think that every acculturation should be seen as an internal adaptation as well as a relation with external factors.

This methodological conception assumes the need to resolve problems relating to the formation of teams working simultaneously within a regional, or macrostructural, framework, when it comes to field work aimed at establishing contemporary acculturation. Furthermore, though many of the methodological problems set forth are different, the study of acculturation in its ethnohistorical dimension offers a similar theoretical conceptualization.

To racial mixing we can apply similar methodological concepts, since for the factorial aspect we consider (1) that studies of individuals in terms of communities, for the purposes of the determination of origins, represent the morphological description of other individuals pertaining to other communities, and in this case the description means establishing the degree and frequency of the interactions that have occurred among those individuals; and (2) that studies of individuals pertaining to certain communities constitute research with reference to ecological specializations, and in a certain way are segmented expressions of diversified forms of adaptation to local circumstances. This means that the individuals constitute adaptive variants—in the morphological and physiological sense—of an ecological conditioning, on the one hand, and microcultural and macrostructural conditioning, on the other.

Such examples, given by way of their relative importance in the study of acculturation and racial mixing in Ibero-America, constitute methodological indicators that tend to integrate our problem within certain conceptual limits. Without a focus that takes account of the functions of the described systems acting as interdependent variables, we shall not succeed in interpreting Ibero-American acculturation and racial mixing in dynamic terms. This has been a point of departure, then, which we shall apply immediately.

Historical Overview

The Spaniard who came to America for the conquest and colonization was, culturally and biologically, a Euro-mestizo, though more specifically European than mestizo. In the late eighteenth century, the Spanish who
were emigrating to America were predominantly of the Andalusian ethnic
type, whereas earlier arrivals in prior centuries seem to have been more blond
and of taller stature (Hollanda 1956, 75).

Whatever the character and specific circumstances that concern us, certainly the attitude and predisposition of the Spaniard toward racial mixing
were positive, that is, flexible. Such an attitude could be considered reinforced, or rather abetted, in America by the development of certain specific
social and material conditions, which we can summarize throughout their
initial context into three fundamental historical components: (1) the absence
of Spanish women in the early stages of the conquest and colonization of
America; (2) the existence of factors of prestige and position favorable to the
mating of Indian women to Spanish men; and (3) the scant number of families of Spanish origin established on American soil during the early stages of
Spanish or general Iberian colonization of that continent.

The first factor, more than any other, led the Spanish to establish their
sexual unions with Indian women. Thus, according to data obtained from
the first years of the conquest, the greatest proportion of Spanish women to
Spanish men never rose above 10 per 100. In Chile, for example, around
1583, there were only 50 Spanish women for 1,150 Spanish men (Konetzke
1945). Furthermore, it has been shown that the Spanish woman did not adapt
well to the tropics, or to the Andean high plains, which fact, in addition to
other sociopolitical and military strategic factors, contributed to her absence
from the initial settlement of America. Thus, the problem of biological adaptation appears as one of the reasons why not until fifty-three years after the
conquest was a criollo born in Potosí (Bolivia), a city situated at 4,300 meters
[13,022 feet] of altitude.

In this respect, Lizárraga (1968, 62), referring to Cuzco and in particular to the difficulties in adaptation experienced by the Spanish in their first encounters with the altitude of that region, confirms these reports when he says that reproduction on the part of Spanish conquerors and settlers was very difficult in this region. He states the following: "The climate is cold and harsh, and after the Spanish had settled, no purely Spanish child was born." Further on, and for the same Cuzco area in later times, Lizárraga states, "now they are born in quantities." Elsewhere, when he mentions these vicissitudes endured by the first Spanish and the comparative degree to which they reproduced in Potosí, he adds:

> the children of the Indians multiply here amazingly; to the Spanish one or another is born and these are defective and soon die. The Spanish retreat to a warm valley, 12 leagues from Potosí, where they remain with their children three or four months, until the child acquires a little more strength, though, since the weather has moderated a bit, they now begin to be born and to propagate, but they are strange. (Lizárraga 1968, 89–90)

Given the conditions of the Andean milieu, these first European generations faced adaptive difficulties, and the second generations were more apt for biological reproduction (Konetzke 1952, 81–82). Thus, it is clear that the criollo did not survive easily, and peninsular Spaniards scarcely reproduced with Spanish women in the Andean altiplano. On the contrary, the mestizo reproduced easily because in him a favorable genetic contribution had emerged. In this sense, mestizos adapted harmoniously to Spanish culture, and while they tended to prefer it for its prestigious identifications, they also spread it through their demographic proliferation and mobility throughout their social and political association with the Spanish.

Torre Revello (1943, 130), in mentioning a letter report of the cleric Martín González, sent in 1575 to the Council of the Indies, recounts that he said, "in the city of Asunción alone there are five thousand mestizos, the children of Spanish and Indian women, and probably more than three thousand of them are 18 years or older, and there are nearly another five thousand mestizo women." Torre Revello also adds that this cleric commented on the fact that against the ten thousand mestizos, "the Spanish were no more than two hundred eighty, and of them, a hundred were useless and the rest were old."

The second factor accelerated the formation of multiple unions of an informal polygynous nature among the Spanish men and Indian women during the early periods. This situation was facilitated by the fact that the Indians offered the Spanish, especially military officers, women of good lineage for the purpose of linking up and forming kinships with the conquistadors. The spread of pluralism was such that it was to be denounced openly by some

Spanish missionaries, scandalized by the sexual conduct of their countrymen (Konetzke 1946). By polygyny, a companion of Bernal Díaz del Castillo, a Spanish conqueror of Mexico, had thirty children in three years, while another comrade had fifty. By the mid sixteenth century, some Spanish in Santiago de Chile who were married had thirty or more concubines, and likewise in Chile, some of the hundred soldiers of J. Alvarez de Luna accounted for up to sixty children in a week's expedition. In Paraguay, contemporary sources indicate that each Spaniard had twenty to thirty concubines, such that one of the results of this sexual behavior was that, in that country in 1575, the mestizos could muster an armed force of three thousand men, whereas the Spanish could provide only two hundred.

The political fear created by the great demographic disproportion between mestizos and Spanish caused Hernando de Montalvo, a royal officer, to write the king in 1579 regarding the need to send a greater number of peninsular Spanish to Paraguay, given that "the children of this land increase daily, both criollos and mestizos, and four out of five people are the latter and each day their numbers increase" (Pérez de Barradas 1976, 211).

This was the general attitude in the Indies. Easy sexual access to Indian women burgeoned from the onset of the conquest, and the results emerged in the form of great numbers of mestizos. In the latter half of the sixteenth century, they were already a majority with regard to the Spanish. Every writer of the period agrees on this demographic preponderance. About Buenos Aires, for example, Montalvo himself wrote in 1585 that "out of every five parts of the inhabitants of the jurisdiction, four and a half were field laborers, and these were calculated to total a thousand" (Torre Revello 1943, 130).

The aforesaid demographic tendency became patent during the Spanish founding of towns and *villas*. For example, according to Garay in a letter to the king of 20 April 1582, the foundation of Santa Fe (Argentina) in 1573 was accomplished with seventy-six settlers, of which only seven were actually peninsular Spanish. In addition, the same Juan de Garay reported that he had founded the city of Trinidad with fifty men born in the (new) land and ten peninsular Spanish (Torre Revello 1943, 131).

Of course, with the multiplicity of unions between Spanish men and Indian women, it is obvious that the mestizos soon overtook the Spanish in numbers. In Chile, as late as 1810, the demographic proportion of mestizos constituted three-fifths of the total population, and in the province of Buenos Aires, mestizos and criollos represented 80 percent of the census.

There is no doubt, thus, that racial mixing constituted the most important genetic phenomenon of this first period, nor is there any doubt that, apart from the relative sexual opportunity that the Indian women offered to the

Spanish, massive miscegenation was also abetted by the social character of the natives, which was highly permissive in these matters, and by the lack of Spanish women, whose presence in insufficient numbers in the expeditions increased the sexual role of Indian women. In this sense, it is known (Konetzke 1952) that in the expedition to the Río de la Plata, of a total of fifteen hundred persons there were only eight Spanish women. Additionally, since Spanish women usually did not take part in military expeditions and ended up living in urban centers, the foci of racial mixing were intensive in the rural and indigenous areas. This means that the behavior of the Spanish, beyond the social control of the moral values of their Catholic culture of origin, was basically polygynous without carrying out this relation in an institutionalized matrimonial form.

In these terms, and these examples will suffice, the situation was very clear in the context of the initial periods of the conquest: the Spanish mated quite permanently with the Indians, despite religious prohibitions to the contrary. Thus, we read that an expedition commander (*adelantado*), Pascual de Andagoya, reported that:

> Speaking of the Sixth Commandment, an Indian turned to a captain, who was his master, and asked him: How do you have three wives? And the master, wishing to avoid the issue, did not reply because I had not understood. When he explained again, I understood and I gave (the Indian) to understand that they were not his wives, but servants, to which he replied: Then why does he have children with all three of them? (Fernández de Navarrete 1963, 2:258)

And certainly it was not just a question of obtaining women by force, because Américo Vespuccio, in referring in 1497 to Venezuela and its coastal regions in particular, said with regard to the relations of Spaniards with Indian women that "We rested there (on the coast) that night, and with total openness they offered us their women, who sought us out with such insistence that we could scarcely resist it" (Fernández de Navarrete 1964, 2:137).

Under friendly conditions, the Indians considered these relations as part of their hospitality toward the Spanish, and thus we are told by the same Vespuccio source when he adds that "Their greatest and most indicative sign of friendship is to offer both their wives and their daughters to their friends to do with them as they wish. In this, both the father and the mother feel very honored and favored if one of their daughters, though still a virgin, is received and taken off by someone to use her, this being one of their principal means of achieving mutual friendship" (ibid.).

In addition, the systematic miscegenation of the Spaniard with the Indian women occurred in the areas where sedentary indigenous culture was practiced, as well as in the gathering and hunting areas. It was simply a question of establishing a contact relation with these societies, whatever their level of cultural evolution might be. Nevertheless, racial mixing in the indigenous areas that practiced agriculture had a more stable character, precisely because the Spanish made the Indians into their tributary labor force and were in a position to use Indian women at their will. This stability is why the greater proportions of mestizos resulting from Indian women and Spanish men were created in the populated centers of America.

Despite this ratio, while stability of residence was an important condition for the permanence of relations with Indian women, the instability of conquest, paradoxically, also favored such relations on occasion, and in greater and quicker measure than occurred in the populated centers of America.[1] The differences would come from the fact that the somewhat correct control or measure of the numbers of children produced by mixture was easier to obtain under conditions of stability of settlement than under those of conquest, because in the latter case, the abundance of sexual unions—in the camp of the Spanish or in the course of their passing through the territory— did not necessarily imply control and knowledge of the lineages that resulted from these relations.

Under conditions of social stability, however, the Spanish began to receive Spanish women from the peninsula and therefore began to lose their formal interest in Indian women in terms of marriage, although in many cases the opposite was seen, when some Spanish men preferred Indian women after the women had created with them more or less permanent households and had taken responsibility for their mestizo children. For the rest of the Spanish men, and in defiance of the institutionalized formalities that followed upon the founding of Spanish settlements in new lands, the reproduction of their culture did not occur necessarily—as we have seen—through marriage to Spanish women. When the reproduction of culture occurred it was frequently in union with Indian women, and later with Africans. This means that the process of racial mixing was never interrupted, although the first stage was the most intensive and uncontrolled one, whereas the second was either more furtive in character, or on the contrary, laden with formal obligations to contract marriage because of the increase in social control imposed by Spanish civil society.

In addition to such assumptions, there also occurred a high degree of racial mixing in the regions of America where the Indians were subjected to *Reducciones*,[2] because in many cases these led to closer contact with the Spanish. Nevertheless, we must point out the exception that once the indigenous population had begun to shrink, the lack of Indian women was filled with the arrival of black women, especially in the tropical zones, where the African was employed in the labor force. In the Antilles, for example, Spanish coexistence with the Indians was relatively brief (Zavala 1958, 895), and for this reason, very soon the exchange between the Spanish and black women gave rise to the emergence of another product of mixture: the *mulatto*. In any case, and further given the scarcity of black women, the Africans turned to the Indian woman as an object of sexual relations (Aguirre Beltrán 1972), sometimes exclusively where their own women were lacking. From this union, the *zambo* was born.

In Mexico the process of racial mixing was also quite rapid. Thus, in 1545 New Spain was populated by only 1,385 Spaniards. In 1810, at the onset of independence, there would have been three times as many Indians as mestizos. In contrast, twenty years later the Indians only doubled the mestizos, whereas in 1900 the latter were already double the number of the Indians. Now there are nine times as many mestizos as Indians, and even more if we consider that the process of miscegenation affects the bulk of the Mexican population and that few groups will have managed to remain untouched by it. In spite of everything, in the late eighteenth century in Mexico there were few individuals who could claim to be of unmixed blood (Borah 1954). For the rest of the Mexican population, the phenomenon of the union between Mayas and Spanish was nearly universal in the nineteenth century (Williams 1931). And of course, when we consider that biological mixing was often submerged within a racially stratified social classification, it is enough, evidently, to recognize the unbridled sexual tendencies of the Spanish in the early stages of the conquest and settlement in order to conclude that real mixing was always greater than the formal mixing accepted in the official censuses. This is especially so when we realize that the social immersion of mestizos, often in indigenous groups, also constituted a trait of viceregal society to the extent that Spanish parents could contract only monogamous marriages and were obliged formally to ignore those children born outside of these exclusive, Catholic, unions. In fact, furthermore, racial mixing in campaigns of conquest and camp situations was as intense in Mexico as it would be in other parts of America. Thus, in reality, the fact that so many more Indians appear in historical accounts than do mestizos reflects more a single trait of ethnic classification than an index of racial taxonomy.

Considering the third factor indicated as important in the development of racial mixing, we must note the fact that, for historical reasons, the unequal proportions of Spanish men and women were influential in the comparatively few marriages that took place between Spaniards. This suggests that they were barely able to create a nucleus of Spanish families sufficiently numerous and stable to become self-sufficient. Due to this social scarcity of Spanish women, the first familial or household phases were between Indian women and Spanish men. These unions and their resultant mestizo progeny acted dynamically against the tendencies toward crystallization of a criollo caste, because mestizo interests came to outweigh demographically and socially even those of the European criollos, until finally displacing them from the rule and sentiment of Ibero-America.

Of course, it is also true that with regard to racial class, the criollos inherited economic power from the peninsular Spanish, though not necessarily political power in every case. That economic power began to wane slowly as their mestizo cohorts lent social strength to the new American societies. Meanwhile, it also was true that when the parents of mestizos decided to make their offspring criollos and proclaimed them such, mestizos easily became criollos; being closest to the criollos in racial character, mestizos were also the most likely to ascend socially, whereas the criollos soon lost their initial, unstable political strength. This was especially so in the countries of the great civilizations, where indigenous masses, but particularly their elites or ruling nobilities, had given the Spanish their first great numbers of mestizo descendants, the latter enjoying the prestige both of their noble Indian ancestry and of the simple antecedent of being the child of Spanish conquistadors or settlers, whichever the case might be.

4

The Process and Context of Racial Mixing
in Ibero-America

When we contemplate a physical map of America, what most amazes us is the great variety of climates and topography that it offers. Of course, it can be said that in America racial mixing forms part of the general traditions of its racial history, since its most primitive inhabitants indicate the presence of differentiated human groups (Pericot 1962; Comas Camps 1967), in turn bearers of their own cultures.

In modern times, or since the Columbian discovery, there has emerged in turn a new process of intensive racial mixing that is practically concluded in some countries of contemporary America. Yet several countries are still carrying out this process, which allows us to deduce that the phenomenon of racial mixing does not constitute a final integration for the whole of that continent. This continuing phenomenon makes it evident that America should be considered a great human entity of multiracial character where conditions are optimal for the development of a coherent society of mestizo nations.

Accordingly, if we cannot conclude that a complete racial mixing of the American continent has been achieved, and given that we are not postulating here that contemporary American populations are racially homogeneous, we can, however, comprehend, that racial mixing constitutes the prevailing tendency in Ibero-America; it prevails precisely because in this part of the New World racial relations are more open than in Anglo-America, and because the breach through which the individuals who strive for status can enter into social mobility is relatively wider. Furthermore, although in every country of America there are white groups or minorities that practice racial discrimination on a greater or lesser scale (Comas Camps 1961) and hold attitudes and values that greatly impede the achievement of intensive racial mixing, it is clear that in the totality of the American continent—though to a lesser degree in Anglo-America—we can see a lessening of structural rigidity with regard to socioeconomic organization. As a consequence, social exchange between various racial groups is more frequent. As a result, we see a greater mobility and circulation of those individuals and groups traditionally situated on the lower levels of American societies—especially indigenous and black. But miscegenation is more rapid and intensive today because in the countries of America, through processes of urbanization and industrialization, great population movements are being created, consisting of individual but massive migrations that are in themselves the seed of a growth in racial exchanges.

In each case, yesterday and today, the encounter and consequent exchanges between different races have assumed the development of new racial and cultural forms. Due to the various regional adaptive traditions, both historicocultural and historicoracial, these forms are expressed through regional nuances and modes. Such regional differences thus constitute the expressions of ecological adaptations and, furthermore, are historical results of the ethnic groups that manifest them. But in their origin these formal regional differences should be attributed additionally to the relative numbers of each racial group that has intervened in the genetic exchange with other groups, as well as to the selective qualities of the socioeconomic structure acting as a specific dynamic agent of contacts and exchanges among different racial groups. Furthermore, and as Esteve Barba (1965, 6–7) has made explicit, we cannot speak of cultural homogeneity either, because the indigenous cultures at the moment of the Spanish conquest were not uniform. We can state, then, that the processes of biological race mixing and of cultural syncretism vary in intensity and frequency (a) according to the ecological adaptations and the demographic number of racial groups involved; and (b) according to the sociocultural structure of the ethnicities and races who have carried out the modifying processes since the Columbian discovery, both in terms of their relative capacity to adapt to relations of racial exchange and in terms of their relative capacity to constitute together a single sociopolitical structure.

This first evidence indicates that racial mixing was a generalized phenomenon from the very moment in which the aforesaid process had become open for the entry of the different groups of our type. This fact, as we have said, is seen with the first prehistoric populations that successively, and in various immigrant waves, occupied American territory. Therefore, when Columbus discovered those first Lucayan Islands,[1] America was both somatically and culturally pluriform.

By somatically and culturally pluriform we mean that throughout America's history biological miscegenation and cultural syncretism have been carried out; and if the mixtures resulting from the exchange between, for example, Mayas, Toltecs, and populations of northern Mexico, and between jungle and highland Indians, have meant the appearance of new products of mixture, then the apparently common racial heritage of the individuals of these populations, the American Mongolian, has relatively diminished the political and symbolic significance of biological race mixing, while it has increased the significance of cultural mixing. The historical significance of the mixes produced during the different pre-Hispanic periods refers to cultural diffusion, to the constant emigration and territorial relocation of groups in movement, and finally to the institutionalization of some societies and cultures over others, and in that context of some ethnicities over others, through political domination and the rights of conquest. Thus, there are numerous pre-Hispanic examples where wars of conquest led to the creation of great empires—such as the Mexican and Inca—and where it is evident that with the formation of great empires, miscegenation was also occurring between the people who formed part of them, whatever their ethnic and social condition might be. The Mexican and Inca upper classes for example, were polygynous, and at the same time, the capture of women was a general characteristic in the wars among Native Americans of every evolutionary degree. This implies the existence of a permanent process of sexual exchange and miscegenation in pre-Columbian America. In any case, for the pre-Hispanic eras we have recognized some mixing between individuals of slight racial contrast, perhaps with greater reference to products derived from the mixture between persons adapted to different altitudes and climates, but remains of individuals belonging to different races have also been discovered. Nonetheless, given the massive volume of population that the Mongolian American group represents, it is most certain that we are dealing with small interferences that ended up being submerged in the heart of the dominant race. Of course, pre-Hispanic populations were not uniform in terms of stature, corporeal volume, physiological rhythms, or even facial coloration, because in those, environmental factors had a decisive influence.

The historical context of this long and continual process of racial mixing in America began to change after the Columbian discovery, when successive groups of Spanish conquistadors and settlers engaged in intensive and multiple sexual exchanges in various parts of the continent. This change gave rise to the development of miscegenation between different racial stocks, such as the Indo-American, the European, and the African. The fact of mestizo biological products' being accorded different recognized status on the basis of origin and physical characteristics implies that racial mixing carries with it not only values related to the adaptive qualities of the mestizos, but also political and ideological values largely associated with power interests and with institutions of domination.

As a phenomenon of massive and simultaneous participation by all races, racial mixing takes on its most universal dimension in America in the Spanish period. This is the moment during which the mestizos become important populations. Furthermore, we do not know to what extent anatomical mixtures in pre-Hispanic times might have carried stigma and social discrimination, and from our own data we have no such evidence. While we assume, on the one hand, the importance of political alliances between different lineages for the purposes of control, we do not assume, on the other hand, that such unions had racist or discriminatory significance in pre-Hispanic periods. If they did have significance, possible discrimination against mestizos (?) should not have resulted from somatic differences, but from their specific position of status within political and economic relationships of domination.

The reality that we are considering for the Spanish period is that [discrimination] did have relevance. It is evident that it played an important historical role in the processes of institutionalization of mestizos in the bosom of the Spanish social structure and of its culture. If mestizos and the different products of mixture were the objects of legislation by the Crown and of opinions and controversies regarding their moral and physiological qualities; and if this concern does not seem to have occurred in the pre-Hispanic era, or at least we lack any evidence of its involvement, it seems proper to recognize this dual problem—biological and cultural—throughout the Spanish period and even through much of the independent period up to our day, in many cases.

After the entry of the Spanish into America, racial mixing became a spontaneous choice that gradually took on organized form; that is, it occurred in accord with norms through which it was sought to establish control over race relations to the degree that racial mixing indicated a deterioration in the prevailing moral system and, in some cases, threatened the direct hegemony of peninsular Spaniards over the social structure.

At the heart of regulations designed to control interracial relations during the viceregal epoch, there was always a fear that the "pure" ideas and institutions of the Crown might be contaminated by the principles of moral disarray that accompanied the disorder in sexual unions and the illegitimacy of many of the products of mixing, not so much because those unions involved mestizos, mulattos, or zambos, but because their demographic emergence and their marginal social status were becoming problems for the stable integration of the Spanish political system in many instances. Thus, free or spontaneous choice in interracial sexual relations became the object of moral preoccupation as well as a source of political and social anxieties.

The process of controlling these unions assumed greater concern as the indigenous and African populations and their products of mixture were becoming more Hispanicized, precisely because Hispanicization itself was a weapon of great ideological effectiveness that made those persons who exercised power more vulnerable. The more accessible their techniques of operation were to different racial populations, the more fragile were those who exercised power as an organization of social control. As long as the different racial populations remained on the margin and did not master Spanish culture, because it was alien to them, that culture maintained its institutional strength and that of its groups in power, and did not lose the political control of social, in this case interracial, reality. When natives, mestizos, blacks, and mulattoes began to live like the Spanish, to learn their methods and cultural forms, to use their weapons and to ride horses, at the same time that they developed economic possibilities and obtained opportunities for status, then their Hispanicization had an inevitable effect: it diminished and even destroyed the superiority of native Spaniards through a differential in population growth, through which the non-Spanish groups began to become a political problem that was all the more dense the closer the racial image of individuals who before were Indians or blacks approached that of the Spanish.

In this sense, the proliferation of spontaneous interracial sexual unions was reduced because monogamous Christian marriage was imposed as a condition for their acceptance, and although they continued to occur in a surreptitious fashion, the controls on this point were more rigid the closer the individuals were to institutionalized power. In the middle and base of the social pyramid, spontaneity was greater than at the top. Thus, the defense of those at the top was greater the more rigidly these controls were exercised over their own Spanish populations, precisely because, at a certain point, the secret to continuity of peninsular Spanish political power lay not only in the Hispanicization of the Ibero-American demographic totality, whatever its racial origin, but, paradoxically (also) in the least possible control over the political awareness of this power, particularly on the part of the members of their broad indigenous, African, and mestizo bases in their various colorations and somatic appearances.

Independent of this problem of the effect created by the entry into political power of mestizo individuals, it is certain that while, in their totality, the base populations—natives, Africans, and mixtures derived from multiple types of sexual crossings—were acquiring Spanish culture, their individual members were also becoming aware that power was also part of their social possibilities to the extent that they dominated the status structure in their various options: military, political, bureaucratic, ecclesiastical, economic, and even professional. The development of these options introduced social mobility on scales possible only for peninsular Spaniards and for their criollo children.

Otherwise, there is no doubt that without the existence of relatively open structures that might facilitate the social spontaneity of the populations, the dynamic possibility of racial mixing would not have existed. For the racial mixing to be produced it was indispensable for different races and ethnicities to recombine their ways of living—interpreting or assimilating others—such that in this case cultural, as much as biological, recombination constitutes an intrinsic condition for racial mixing and for its fundamental processes. Thus, if cultural recombination is a permanent process in humanity, the notion of racial mixing moves historically in the direction of the genetic modification of initially different populations and of distinct cultures that act selectively and do not suspend social interaction among themselves over time.

The decisive stamp in cultural mixing was the Spanish one, precisely because it contained conditions necessary for it to manifest itself in a pre-dominant way: (1) a stable settlement of great numbers of Spanish popula-tion throughout the continent which today we know by the name of Ibero-America; (2) a predominant military, political, and social position for these populations in the historical process of implantation and institutionalization of Spanish and Portuguese cultures; (3) a dominant culture of greater prestige than the native cultures, with an enormous capacity for interethnic and in-terracial circulation accompanied by a rapid dismantling of native institutions in decisive areas, such as the military and the political; and (4) an accelerated process of sexual exchange between natives and Spaniards, and, to a lesser degree, between the latter and Africans. This process culminated very soon in the form of mestizos who, because of their very problematical condition in terms of their place in social status, immediately became aware that the use of Spanish culture was the ideal means of their social advancement, at the same time that the numerous cases of illegitimacy, based on the fact that a large number of births occurred out of wedlock, was turning them into social outsiders.

The dominant impulse of the personality toward self-realization could thus face the obstacle of illegitimacy, but the integration of the individual behavior of these mestizos into the bosom of Spanish culture and society lent to their initial illegitimacy possibilities of reacting to the system. The impor-tant thing was to acquire the techniques of controlling the social environ-ment. These techniques—Spanish culture—provided the first social and personality defenses to the mestizos, and thus, the great number of them born in the new society also created a decisive means of social pressure for ele-vating their status position a few steps within the prestige structures of the system.

From what we know, the first mestizos produced on campaigns and the children of conquistadors and Spanish soldiers had no problems of legitimacy, to the extent that their parents tied them to their persons and to their interests, giving them filial recognition. This made possible the great number of mestizos mobilized on expeditions and mentioned alongside peninsular Spaniards without significant problems of accommodation and status any different from those that arose habitually among the Spanish themselves. Essentially, the achievement of status was a question of how correctly one adapted to military duties: capacity for combat, decision-making effectiveness, personal initiative, discipline and bravery in war, and, of course, fidelity to the Crown and Christianity.

But once civil societies were founded, social control demanded personal stability and legitimacies of another kind; it was especially important for marriage to confirm the paternity of each individual. Thus the mestizos born outside marriage began to be the objects of discrimination and social alienation. Nevertheless, integration into Spanish culture gave to the mestizos and all products of mixture, as well as to the Indians admitted into Spanish societies, the instrument for controlling the action that would let them transform their position of discriminated status into a growing volume of social pressure for their normalization and acceptance within the structure. This was a question of time and structural opportunities. While, on the one hand, time and structure revealed the gradual wearing out of political and military bureaucratic hierarchies of peninsular origin, on the other, they showed the pressure of these mestizos and their creole allies determined to obtain the political control of the institutions of domination through replacement. In fact, then, mestizos and other mixtures took centuries to occupy dominant positions in the context of the power structure, but their cultural Hispanicization was the principal condition that allowed them to exercise those positions alongside the criollos.

In many ways, the dynamic of racial mixing represents a process that gradually presumes the predominance of Spanish culture over the indigenous, and while the elements of the latter slowly diminish in combinations, greater and lesser syntheses are produced according to the influences each group has exercised over the other. In its final viceregal form, Spanish culture assumed a dominant weight not only in the major institutional features, such as the political system, language, and legal, religious, and economic structures, but also in the areas of formal education and the nature of the *eidos* in the new American societies. At the outset of the wars of independence, Spanish culture was already institutionalized, and it would be the criollos who legitimized it with their victory over Spanish power.

Within these circumstances, it is easy to recognize that the Hispanicization of mestizos meant that they and other mixtures and urbanized Indians gradually absorbed Spanish culture, and this absorption was taking place to the extent that Spanish culture was practically imposed and was creating a stable institutional structure within which castes and classes were integrated accord-ing to Spanish cultural patterns of prestige and of socialization. The groups of mixture and those racially integrated within this Hispanic institutional sys-tem assumed social needs derived from their adaptation to goals and aims corresponding to the social character of Spanish life in America, or Portu-guese life in Brazil. In their history or process of incorporation, mixed bloods had the transmission, through selective exchange, of the dominant biological or cultural characteristics as an antecedent to their socialization. The cultural ones, of course, because of their weight and volume, constituted a Spanish or Portuguese version adapted to specific processes of incorporation of native or African elements, according to each case. The most important aspect of this dynamic is the institutionalized formation of a transplanted Spanish way of life, and in each case this way takes on the native influences of each region in a selective manner through recombination and syncretism.

Throughout this process Hispanicization was being imposed as the master institutional system and as a program of action. The socialization design was Spanish. In this sense, the mestizo face that could be recognized in the ma-jority of Ibero-American populations at the moment of their independence was nevertheless culturally Hispanic with specific regard to a way of living and thinking. As a form of life it cannot be considered a definitive structure, because it remains subject to the constant historical recombination of its ele-ments, whether through adaptive choice or simply through the selective sub-stitution of some characteristics for others. The world of technology and its innovations would be an example in this sense.

With the loss of the stability and historical continuity of the native cul-tures, the breakdown of their institutions of control, and after the first structural crisis, Hispanic cultural constructions and formations appeared—architecture, laws, social organization, religion, social topics and character, and language—and gradually these became the dominant mode in Hispanic societies. Once biological miscegenation and cultural recombinations had occurred, the transmission of mestizo or synthesized characters is understood here as an irreversible phenomenon, but one open to new experiences of racial mixing to the extent that the mestizo groups belong to societies that are racially open and socially inclined toward status mobility and thus suscep-tible especially to ethnic exchanges and to the integration of great European migrations.

In essence, cultural mixing follows lines similar to those of biological mix-ing. That is, there are modes respectively Indian and African, in the sense that the cultural participation of each racial group is a function of its specific weight in the formation and development of what are properly the contem-porary Ibero-American national cultures. The historical course of this cultural insertion consists of successive generations habitually using, as their own form of behavior, cultural elements that do not have their origin in the locality where they are practiced. And often these descendant populations are biologically mestizo from the generalized exchange of their ancestors with individuals of other races. This process of mixing will be equally valid for the cultural realm, but it is also admissible, by contrast, that a totally European group might be culturally indigenous, as was observed by Gillin (1961, 76) in a community of Cajamarca (Peru), where the population, of criollo origin, had remained isolated from the urban and European stream and related to the Quechua-speaking groups, for which today it can be considered as Quechua from its forms of life and identity.

Thus, not every process of racialization and biological mixing is necessarily equivalent to a cultural mixing of the same order. For this equivalence to occur it is indispensable that there be continuity in exchanges and stability with regard to the relative racial and cultural homogeneity of the populations. The most visible way of achieving this correspondence in racial and cultural amalgams consists of the different populations involved forming part of the same social structure and the latter producing opportunities for mobility in terms of status and of relative access by individuals of the different groups to the use of a decidedly common culture.

When we have validated the principle of the existence of racial mixings, more than a mixing, we have also recognized that groups biologically more homogeneous and those apparently more mestizo correspond to closed social structures in some cases, and open structures, in others. For example, urban populations produce social stratifications where individuals separately are accustomed to competing for status to a greater degree than they do in rural societies, and obviously in indigenous societies, because in these the limited occupational structure permits little individual mobility. This social circulation also has more possibilities for becoming racial circulation if the predominant political values and moral ideologies favor such a circulation. This favorable context occurs singularly when the groups exercising power are not racially different from those of the rest of the society, or therefore do not owe their power status to racial competition or to colonial domination.

The relative homogeneity of small egalitarian populations, however, also tends to translate into racial homogeneity when the matrimonial relation is based on local endogamy, and thus we see that the biological mixings in Spanish America and in Brazil had a decidedly spontaneous individual character in the early stages. But when the government and European structures were consolidated, the qualities of these mixings were modified, because from that moment on they resulted from furtive unions or from concubinage morally condemned by the Church and by legislation; or they came of consensual relations with the white man on the part of Indian, black, and mixed-race women by virtue of mutual favors or of identification of prestige and power.

According to these different situations, in Ibero-America racial mixings during the viceregal era corresponded to increasingly stratified relations, to artificial circumstances of caste, that tended to homogenize the colors of populations according to their social status, largely corresponding to the racial origins of their members. Still, biological mixings were not interrupted because a clear discriminatory ideologization between the races never existed, and because, additionally, where a certain economic fluidity and interracial coexistence was allowed, facilities for racial mixing also appeared. Furthermore, this situation did not keep mestizos, Indians, and Africans from adopting Hispanic or Portuguese culture; on the contrary: they acquired it because it offered them better instruments for personal fulfillment.

At any rate, cultural syncretism appears as a better-defined historical phenomenon than biological mixing precisely because the variables of cultural mixing can be characterized by qualitative visible forms more easily than can the biological variables, both apparent and subsurface. For example, the export to and implantation in America of European architecture, or the incorporation into said continent and islands of work animals by the Spanish, are easier to discern in their origin, distribution, and current practice than many of the physical characteristics shown by the individuals of these collective populations. It is easier to diagnose the components of an ethnographic model and of its geographical distribution than to trace, for example, the physical characteristics of a demographically complex and socially heterogeneous population. From a cultural viewpoint, the ethnographic model allows us to identify the elements of behavior that constitute a population's way of life and its social and ethnic distribution, as well as its immediate, controlled origin and its specific integration into the context of a historically and culturally verified society. Additionally, the fact that Ibero-American societies possess cathedrals, colonial architecture, Catholicism, crops and work animals, agricultural tools; and institutions such as municipalities and governors, plazas, and the Spanish language; along with pre-Hispanic foods and cooking, customs, and special medical beliefs; and economic components of native tradition, offers the opportunity to produce an analysis of the degree of racial mixing in a population in terms more precise than those that might result from a biological sample.

The ethnographic reports currently available allow us to distinguish what is indigenous, what is Spanish, what is African, and even what is Asiatic in racial mixing; furthermore, they allow us to determine the specific weight of the cultural elements in the context of the activity itself. For example, if among the Quechuas of the *altiplano*[2] of Cuzco the process of cultivating the land involves the planting of potatoes, barley, quince, wheat, peas, and even corn in certain places (canyons sheltered from the cold); and if it also recognizes the use of the *chaquitaclia,* or reinforced digging stick, the use of the Spanish plow, the use of mules or oxen for turning the earth, the consumption of *chicha*[3] and liquor, and the saying of a prayer in Quechua to the spirits of ancestors and of the mountains; and if what we really define is a truly balanced mestizo cultural structure that shows ethnographically localized recombination and syncretism, then in such a case we can state that some features are Spanish and others are Quechua, integrated into the same activity. And we can venture further in this sense when we notice that the rest of the culture shows institutions of Hispanic character, such as Catholicism and the power structure, along with organizations of purely Andean origin, such as the *ayllu*[4] and some practices associated with marriage, birth, music, and other features. In this point, we see that when we follow an ethnographic trajectory, we can observe other equally mestizo ingredients. They appear in the form of institutions or behavior that include elements of Quechua and Hispanic origin united in a specific activity.[5] And if we continue in this cultural analysis we see that in recent years there has appeared, for example, Western-style consumption in its North American version, such as soft drinks, canned food, bicycles, radios, household appliances, and a market gradually replacing the barter system.

This is a mixture in a state of readaptation and constant selectivity of cultural elements, in this sense, absorbing some and eliminating others but, in the process of interaction with the national culture, assuming new forms of experience. The cultural system is never finally definitive, and thus, while it is adaptive in its social behavior, it is equally adaptive in its biological behavior.

In these circumstances, a homogeneous community of Andean peasants may have produced a mixture of the category that we have assigned to some Cuzco communities. And at the same time, individuals who form part of the municipality and who are neither Quechuas nor peasants take on mestizo cultural experiences, such as bilingualism and indigenous elements that combine with urban Hispanic culture in origin. For these reasons, the conduct of these peasants is usually expressed as an indigenous mode of racial mixing, whereas that of other sectors with the peasants—teachers, employees, farmers, and merchants—will be shown as a Hispanic mode of racial mixing. Within this process, we may draw a conclusion: greater urbanization brings greater Hispanicization.

These modes appear as variables in a cultural spectrum that joins together in the form of different specific combinations and in partial spaces of a politically nucleate larger society, such that the different social and ethnic groups that make up its social structure represent different historical arenas of racial mixing—that is, peasants, industrial urbanites, and, in a certain sense, also forest or tribal Indians.

It is obvious, however, that we do not seek to equate cultural with biological mixing. We have already stated that when we refer to a mode of racial mixing, we do not necessarily imply that the population that stresses one cultural particularity is also biologically indigenous, as distinguished from others who are developing in the Spanish mode. What is certain is that some groups developing in the Spanish mode of cultural mixing exhibit a more Indian expression than a European or an African one. That is, their cultural and biological significances are not necessarily assimilable in the social context. Still, there could probably be a certain correlation established in populations of homogeneous origin or of European predomination, as occur in Argentina and Uruguay, where their Indian and African masses have historically been absorbed by the greater European mass since Spanish beginnings. On the contrary, where there is a predominance of a racially indigenous population, such as in the Andean region, the racial mode of mixing inclines toward the indigenous, while the cultural mode inclines toward the Hispanic. Within these observations, to the extent that the culture of domination prefigures a culture of prestige and has historical continuity, it becomes the dominant culture, as the Hispanic does in this case. Once this culture constitutes a major variable or mode of social experience, it ends up becoming the system that, through recombination and syncretism, emphasizes the Hispanic more than the Indian. Certainly, it is then that the different populations approach one another socially and become accustomed to mutual dependence and exchange, since in this way the processes of mixing in its two categories, biological and cultural, are accelerated, although the latter does not necessarily depend on the biological mass contributed to the exchange. Rather, the greater incidence of cultural mixing depends upon the degree of stable domination and prestige that has been exercised by the members of the dominant group distributed in the different areas of social significance and influence. Precisely for this reason, when the regions of high culture in pre-Hispanic times achieved their independence from the Spanish and created their modern nation states, such as Mexico, for example, they carried out their cultural mixing in a predominantly Spanish mode, especially with the onset of criollo political dominance. For the rest, northern Mexico has experienced a mixing, based on hunting tribes and Spanish groups and Hispanicized Indians, that can also be defined as a mixture of the Spanish mode. The Mexican South would be properly mestizo, and in some places the Hispanic mode would alternate with the Indian. Of course, from the Bajío[6] toward the north the development of Spanish colonization, as Jiménez Moreno (1961, 84) has pointed out, was achieved with great numbers of natives uprooted from their communities of origin. Lacking the institutional controls of their local cultures, they adopted the Spanish cultural model, which in this case was the one they were receiving in an organized fashion. In its evolution, this cultural model passed first from the peninsular Spanish to the criollos, and from the latter to the mestizo groups that were later emerging in great strength in the arena of national ways of life. For Jiménez Moreno (ibid.), Mexican national consciousness developed in these central regions because the individuals who lived there, while they were acquiring a national consciousness and taking up independence from Spain, were at the same time receiving this consciousness through a Spanish culture.

Equally certain is that the interior regions of the continent, such as Paraguay, which were occupied by a great number of indigenous groups at the moment of the Spanish conquest and colonization, adopted a large quantity of indigenous traits in their cultural mixing, precisely because the social weight of the Spanish in the different towns of this area was relatively small during the formative periods. Equally important, it occurred thus because the demographic role of the native populations was maintained in the constitution of the national conscience. Despite this role, the Spanish mode progressed and imposed itself over the Indian mode, based on its greater cultural cohesion, its prestige, and the specific continuity of its control and its power of domination. Still, the fact that the Spanish programming of native life was imbued with a strong religious sense favored the role of indigenous cultures especially, and in bilingualism, based on the Guaraní, programming retained many native elements placed within a larger Spanish system. In this sense, the zones conferred by the Spanish Crown to the care of missionary religious orders preserved native cultures for a longer time than elsewhere precisely because Spanish civil society did not penetrate there. In fact, what was created fundamentally in these missionary areas was an acculturation gradually absorbed by the larger political context of domination: that of a nation resulting from an independence conceived and designed by criollos.

→   →   →

What we have described above constitutes a process and a context for racial mixing. It implies for us the need to recognize that Ibero-America contributes a Spanish-Portuguese cultural unity with specific regional processes; that we must interpret them not only from a perspective of internal plurality, but also with the recognition of the existence of different racial hues, in general, and in basically adaptive pre-Hispanic periods when we consider the existence of a predominantly Mongoloid or Amerind homotype; and that in viceregal, colonial, and independent periods, with strong tendencies—beyond the adaptive—to create a dynamic of racial circulation and of mixtures where the various shades lend an aspect of heterogeneity, they appear in the form of a multiracial spectrum running from the darkest of the African to the lightest extremes of the European. Nevertheless, the extremes are less numerous than the multiple combinations of both in the form of racial mixtures. The continuous interaction, through time, of racial groups and varieties has meant for the American continent the assumption of new biological types whose geographic distribution, as we have indicated, responds to different historical and adaptive circumstances that have favored or hindered one solution or another, according to each case. For example, Andean types constitute a historically and ecologically conditioned racial formula different from that developed in time and space by dwellers of the pampas or jungles. This conditioning also holds true for European and African types.

We know, furthermore, in relation to historical circumstances, that the sexual exchanges between the Spanish and Indians during the early stages were very intense, but most significant is the fact that members of both groups had sexual relations with multiple partners. Thus, in a relatively short time the products of mixture were numerous. A similar situation developed in Brazil (Azevedo 1966, 76), because there the lack of Portuguese women led to a union with Indian and black women on the part of Portuguese men. Thus, by the mid sixteenth century, the Portuguese were accustomed to living in concubinage with three or four women, such that in a very short time a considerably mixed population was produced. For example, in Bahía during the second half of the eighteenth century, mestizo individuals represented 64 per cent of the total population (ibid., 79).

In a certain sense, the rapid extinction of the native populations of the Antilles should be attributed as much to the mortality caused by the armed struggle; to the massive transfer of their young men, incorporated as porters into Spanish expeditions on the continent; and to epidemics and suicides, as to the decreases stemming from the diminishing availability of Indian women to Indian men, where the former had entered into concubinage with the Spanish in large numbers. Accordingly, while the lack of women led to a decline in internal reproduction by the native group, the abundant use of these women by the Spanish increased that of the mestizos. These situations, aside from the flight of Indians escaping from Spanish control and apart from their being employed massively by the Spanish as mine workers, occurred frequently enough such that during a certain number of years a kind of monopoly was created, to the extent that there were few Indian women who did not maintain some sexual relationship with the Spanish (Casas 1965, 2:105ff.).

Although the situation was not exactly the same on the mainland, it can nevertheless be considered similar, at least with regard to the phenomenon of the so-called *barraganías,* or nonlegitimized unions. Thus, the increase in the mestizo group took place at the expense of the native group. Furthermore, the relative ease with which many Indians were becoming part of the Hispanic social structure with the status of mestizos was also a factor of some importance with respect to the formal decline in the indigenous population, and in a large sense that ease represented a significant, though little studied, factor with reference to the demographic phenomenon racially considered.

On this particular many reports agree in the sense that they inform us that, on the one hand, there was a decrease in the population of the native peoples, while, on the other hand, there was an increase in that of the whites, these being understood to include mestizos. This we learn from B. de Oviedo (1930, chapter 10) when he reports that in San Gil, Colombia, at the time of the Spanish conquest there were around a thousand Indians, but that as a result of their mixture with the Spanish, in a few years only some two hundred remained. At the same time, the Spanish, mestizos, quadroons, and *cholos*[7] totaled more than ten thousand individuals. He points out that this number had its origin in some two hundred Spanish (ibid.). This writer observes that the decrease in the native population should be attributed more to the racial classifications derived from mixing than to the consequences of epidemics and wars of extermination. Concolorcorvo (1946, 205–6) confirms this observation, stating that the decrease in indigenous populations should be widely correlated with the sexual exchange with Indian women practiced by Spanish, blacks, mestizos, and other racial categories, more than with any other factor. Concolorcorvo (ibid.) attributes this intensive sexual contact with Indian women to the lack of women that each of the non-Indian racial caste groups had in relation to its own demographic balance. Additionally, Concolorcorvo's conclusions point clearly to the fact that Indians were declared to be mestizos whenever they went into the service of a Spaniard and were dressed in the Spanish style. Offering numerous examples, Concolorcorvo points out that of every hundred individuals classified as mestizos, some ninety have been considered "pure Indians."

Cámara (1964, 64) tells us that many Mixtecs and Zapotecs in Oaxaca (Mexico) were becoming mestizos in the mid eighteenth century just by learning Spanish and adopting non-Indian cultural forms. This phenomenon of mixing, achieved through cultural recognition, has been reported by Mörner (1964, 150) in the rural population of Guatemala in the late eighteenth century, to which he adds the contrary occurrence of the Indianizing of individuals who were not Indians by origin but who became such by living among them. At the same time, Indian men, due especially to their greater geographic mobility and to their relative tendency to settle next to the Spanish and mestizos, became mestizos more frequently than did the women (Gillin, 1961, 76–77). Gillin points out (ibid.) that in a community of the Peruvian altiplano near Cajamarca, the classification of Indian is conferred upon all those who speak Quechua, despite the fact that their ancestors were criollos who had fought on the royalist side in the Spanish American wars of independence.[8]

Thus, mestizos or Indians, and even blacks, have not always been categorized by either their color or their genealogy. There are many cases where they were conferred a Hispanic status just by living in the Spanish way or by being economically strong. Indians became mestizos, and mestizos became whites, when they adopted the Hispanic cultural form. The anthropologist De la Fuente (1948, 392), in addressing the phenomena of acculturation that took place among the Zapotecs of Oaxaca in terms of their relation to the Spanish, has stressed the fact that cultural factors, especially the linguistic, constitute the source of the criteria of racial differentiation used in that region, and are considered of greater importance than biological factors. Racial characterization is thus influenced by identifications of prestige that refer to the way of life adopted by the individual, and also to the locality, ethnically defined, where he resides. That identification of prestige indicates the existence of a certain fluidity in the system of racial classification created by Ibero-American societies. In fact, it assumes the organization of a system where racial mobility is culturally conditioned. According to this system, many mestizos would be Indians or Spanish, depending on their cultural status. That is what has led Pierson (1942) to state, with reference to Brazil, that the division of classes was harder to transcend than was racial division. As a result, the definition of racial groups will depend more upon their social role and cultural status than on their color and genealogy. From this viewpoint, mestizos in any period have been *whites* to the extent that the social system has allowed them to rise in status. In the early times, as Rosenblat points out (1954, 2:133), it was enough for there to be recognition of a child by a Spanish man with a non-Spanish woman, or for this recognition to adopt the form of "legitimized mestizos" (cf. Mörner 1967, 41 and Salas 1960, 25).

Other factors have intervened in peculiar fashion in the development of racial mixing. As we were pointing out, these deal with the form of social and political organization of American societies and with the relative structure of racial and ethnic relations. These structures have varied by region, but refer to historical situations that, in their beginnings, correspond to different systems of organization in Ibero-America when, for example, they are compared to those of Anglo-America. In the first region, one fundamental organizational characteristic stands out: that of seeking to constitute, from the outset, a single society with the natives. This society would have an essentially aristocratic stratification, though with certain facilities for social advancement and ennoblement on the part of those Spaniards who acquired merit recognized by the Crown. At the same time, as Mario Hernández has shown (1963, 2:566ff.), the ideological assumptions of this viceregal society would be rooted in seigniorial values of a medieval stamp. This mark of Hispanic ideology, in force among many Spaniards at the time of the founding of the American colonies, functioned as a decisive ideological concept in the course of those societies. Social differentiation by means of the system of role/status often put Spanish, Indians, and Africans in positions of superiority and subordination very similar to those of a society composed of racial classes.

The social and political organization of European societies in what is now Anglo-America would follow a different model, because they created societies apart from the natives from the outset. The point of departure for this separation was, more than an aristocratic attitude, an attitude based on the effort to preserve the continuity of the culture of origin as different from the aboriginal. This was made possible thanks to the social and sexual self-sufficiency of the Anglos in terms of men and women. The historical effect of this development would be considerable with regard to the process of racial mixing, on the one hand, and with reference to the formation of sociocultural ethnic structures in Anglo-America, on the other, in contrast with Ibero-America. This process, although it would also occur later in some parts of southern South America, would generally distinguish Ibero-American countries from Anglo-American countries.

As Rosenblat has indicated (1954, 11), in the United States there was a model of European settlement based on the transfer of entire families, in contrast with Ibero-America, where the model corresponded to a settlement effort where the nearly exclusive presence of males predominated during the early years of the conquest, that is, before the founding of civil communities. That model determined, according to Rosenblat, that the Spanish would be submerged within the indigenous populations. In Uruguay and Argentina, the historical process was somewhat similar to that of Anglo-America, although in the early stages racial mixing was also intensive, especially in the areas of the northwest and in regions to the south of Buenos Aires, as it was in the context of the Río de la Plata. Later, however, the settlements were made with Spanish and European families that largely modified the early lines of expansion of racial mixing.

We must point out, in this respect, that the democratic structure implanted in North America refers essentially to the fact of communal equality, which reigned in the early social relations among members of the European populations that settled there. Nevertheless, this equality did not prevent gradual economic differentiation from emerging among the members of these communities, soon creating a stratified social structure. It was largely a mobile structure because it maintained the principle of acquired status, more than status based on assumption or birth, by which the social structure remained open and stimulated social fluidity. In fact, this structure was possible because the Anglo-Saxons who were settling North America, from the outset of the colonization, constituted social groups of equals. By contrast, Spanish and Portuguese societies and the great indigenous civilizations lent to the new social structures their concepts of rigid social stratification. This rigidity was broken during the cycle of conquest to the extent that the undertaking developed individual initiative as the stimulus for those—generally conquistadors—who did not possess aristocratic qualities by birth. Nevertheless, as peninsular institutions were solidified, the building of Ibero-American societies consisted of reproducing heavily stratified and ideologically aristocratic concepts and institutions. Such, at least, was the nature of viceregal society.

Social relations in Ibero-America have been dominated by these strongly hierarchical principles; nevertheless, these same principles and the scarcity of women, which obliged the Spanish to depend sexually on Indian women, not only gave rise to tendencies toward massive miscegenation, but those tendencies contributed to a relaxation of sexual restrictions, all of which contributed to facilitating sexual commitments by Spanish, Negro, and mestizo males with native women. Konetzke states (according to Mörner 1961, 30) that concubinage has a certain correlation with a social structure based on a caste system, in this case with a recently constituted Ibero-American society, whereas unions between Indian women and Spaniards in the early years would have another character, that is, they would result from prestige factors wherein the Indian women, for reasons of social ascent and attraction, would prefer a union with a Spaniard over one with an Indian or mestizo. In this way, concubinage would become a social institution corresponding to the second phase of sexual relations between Indian women and the Spanish, whereas the free or casual union would correspond to the first (Mörner, 1961, 29). The initial phase would constitute a type of open and democratic cycle; the second would be characteristically aristocratic (ibid., 30). Furthermore, as Mörner states (ibid., 31), the process of racial mixing in the Caribbean and on the coast of Brazil would be similar to the one that occurred in the southern United States, where the plantation system created relations of dominance in which the master enjoyed at will the body and sexual services of the woman.

This distinctive character of the respective sociopolitical structures assumed, with regard to the future of racial mixing in America, some different specific results and thus explains the peculiarities presented by the system of miscegenation in Ibero-America and in Anglo-America. Consequently, in the continental regions where Europeans settled as differentiated societies with respect to the natives, the majority of racial mixtures had a frontier character, and the stability of such unions was precarious. Additionally, the respective interests of these politically and racially distinct societies, European and native, soon clashed, especially to the extent that European expansion implied the occupation of native territories. This occupation caused the hostility of the natives toward the Europeans, although that hostility was insufficient as a means of resistance, since the indigenous groups that practiced agriculture and lived in permanent villages tended to establish some kind of status of coexistence with the Europeans rather than abandon their traditional lands to them. Still, resistance of nomadic hunters and gatherers to the European occupation of their territories tended to be more active. The principal causes for more active resistance were: (1) their greater geographic mobility, as well as their operation over territories which, because of their greater extent, also forced the European to spread his aggressive efforts and therefore weakened his ability to subdue the natives with ease; (2) the fact that the Europeans lived in a constant state of insecurity, because of which they lent to the relative success of native resistance, at least making it easier; and (3) the natives were not seen by the Europeans as factors of socioeconomic stability, that is, they were not useful to them, except in "Indian Reducciones," for missionary purposes and in mining centers for their economic exploitation, because of which their practical interest in coexisting with them waned.

These causes contributed largely to the rise of wars of extermination. They were offensive in nature on the part of the Europeans, and defensive on the part of the natives, although once the cycle of hostility was opened, the practices of war tended to be mutually predatory. As a peculiar trait, these wars of mutual extermination took place basically in those regions where the natives lived in a nomadic system, but in those other areas—especially in those dominated by the Spanish, and even in areas occupied by the Portuguese—where the Indians practiced sedentary agriculture and lived according to urban and civilized models, the tendency of the Europeans was to convert these natives into manual laborers in their service. This conversion was possible thanks to the formation of single societies, the viceroyalties, because in the cases where Indians and Spaniards developed under the form of separate societies, their relations were based on tribute. The factor of the natives' relative economic utility thus played a considerable role in the framework of relative stability in the process of racial mixing.

The relative stability of this indigenous and African labor force allowed the development of a permanent interaction between the different racial populations and led to the stable achievement of racial mixing during a long period. Pourchet (1963, 112) characterizes this situation in Brazil when he points out that the scarcity of blacks in Ceará, and conversely, their abundance in other areas was clearly due to the degree of economic exploitation of the natives, such that where the latter were numerically abundant and available for European exploitation, black predominance did not occur. The proportion of mulattoes would also be a result of the lack of white women (ibid.) and of the plantation system, which favored the dominant and sexually unrestricted relation of the European with black women.

The phenomenon of trihybridism appeared rapidly in the Antilles and immediately created an opportunity for Spanish and Africans especially to exchange among each other and with Indian women. Black men, who at the beginning were in a demographically unbalanced proportion with respect to the number of women of their stock participating in the settlement of America, undertook considerable sexual relations with Indian women. This disproportion between males and females was less, however, than the one existing among the Spanish. Among the Spanish it came to be one woman for every ten men, whereas among the blacks it was, as Acosta Saignes has observed (1956, 560), one woman for every three males. In such a case, and due also to the greater control exercised by the Spanish over the general conduct of blacks, these exchanges with Indian women were less frequent than those carried on by the Spanish. At any rate, trihybridation in the Antilles soon absorbed the native population.

This intervention by the black group in the process of racial mixing took place on a massive scale, especially in those regions where they replaced the Indians in agricultural and mining operations. Acosta Saignes (1956, 560) illustrates this situation for Cocorote, a mining community in Venezuela, where during the seventeenth century there was a notable sexual exchange between the different racial groups, but particularly between blacks and Indians. Furthermore, as stated by Jiménez Moreno (1961, 83), there was trihybrid racial mixing in Mexico where mining operations were set up. In that case, the considerable frequency of casual unions of Spanish men with Indian and black women, and of black men with Indian women, produced mixtures that modified the racial structure of America. As for the types derived from mixture in the Antilles and on the Caribbean coast, there emerged a process of replacement of the different native ethnicities that thus very quickly altered the nature that later syntheses would assume.

The social structures that separated some individuals from others according to their race, by means of the system of role/status, have kept the mestizo for a long time in an intermediate social position, which has allowed him to behave as an interested individual in a relation at once tied to any of the racial streams from which he has originated. In that case, as the number of mestizos has grown, the system of classes has also been weakened. This has been pointed out by Escobar (1964, 199–200) for Peru, when he states that mestizos, as a social stratum, have always tended to break the caste structure, essentially on the basis of their geographical and social mobility and their tendency to live and to carry out their economic activities in urban centers. Rosenblat (1954, 2:12) has clearly observed the dynamic of this process when he points out that while the caste system is an effect of racial mixing, the latter, in turn, is also a cause of the disappearance of the caste system. As such, the emergence of a system commonly termed a caste system would have its principal weakness in the relative strength that mestizo groups might acquire in the course of American history. Thus, to the same extent that the white groups—peninsular and criollo—became oligarchies of power and accumulated exclusive interests, the mestizos weakened this hierarchical structure through the increasingly greater sociocultural weight created by their number and their interest upon the life of the countries of America.

Turning to this question, we have indicated before that the mestizo represents in a great sense the continuity of Spanish culture viewed from the level of popularization, especially to the degree to which he has received it as a legacy from the old colonists and conquistadors, who transmitted it to him in the form of processes of socialization and by means of identifications of prestige. Thus, while colonial society was being stratified and therefore was closing the channels of social mobility, the mestizos tended to break down racial stratification, converting the caste system into a system of classes. In this case, they caused the racial factor gradually to become secondary in comparison with the economic factor. Until they succeeded in making this factor dominant, many individual members of mestizo groups must have felt like illegitimate issue, since they were the result of casual unions that enjoyed no legal recognition. The corresponding situation is stated by Escobar (1964, 201–2) when he says that Peruvian mestizos have been characterized by their tendency toward spatial mobility, and by their desire to improve economically, as much as by their propensity to escape the stigma of "illegitimacy or inferiority" that has weighed upon them in their towns of origin. Such a strong feeling of illegitimacy would have its source in the very nature of moral values based on positions of social inferiority, following upon those individuals born of noninstitutionalized unions (Mörner 1967, 55).

Nevertheless, what is certain is that the emergence of mestizos; the increase in their number; their gradual access to economic activities of prestige; as well as the development of a national ideology, that is, of a political consciousness acting on the direction of the life of some Hispanic-American countries today[9] has led the mestizos, first, to develop certain kinds of anti-Hispanic feelings and attitudes and, second, to seek among the Indians and blacks the groups upon which to rely in their aspirations related to the objective of attaining political power. In this sense, American societies are gradually abandoning classifications of status according to color; therefore, the ones to benefit mainly from such tendencies have been the Indians and the blacks, but also the mestizos. Slowly, by making the individual economic role predominate over any other concept, and by gradually destroying the values ascribed to the status of color, interpersonal relations in the urban societies of Ibero-America have entered into a social stratification featuring a greater individual mobility, all of which means that its structure and way of life has the attraction of greater individual fulfillment than in the past.

→   →   →

In order to arrive at these processes and to establish this context, it is evident that events of a certain significance had to occur, many of which we have already pointed out. Of doubtless significance was the historical supplanting of the criollo by the mestizo in those places where the pre-Hispanic native population and the demographic importance of its mestizo group and the products of mixture were very much a part of social reality and where, furthermore, they represented important styles of aesthetic and emotional values in the daily life of these societies. And not only that; the style was manifested as well in the context of the cultural habits of each national society after independence, especially in matters of diet, of crops, of practices and customs that appeared, in each case, as relative indicators of Indianness and of mestizo syncretisms recognized in the semantic foundations and in the vocabularies of the national language itself, that is, of Spanish. All of these developments contributed to the character of social communities among the majority of groups, who retained in their background the presence of indigenous genes with cultured forms attributed to this origin. To the same extent that the consciousness of a certain degree of Indianness was reappearing in the daily being and habits of American populations, there was a recognition of the mestizo quality as an ontological form and structure of the national being in the modern nations with strong indigenous demographic contributions.

Historically, in everyday reality viceregal society was unique in several aspects: in its political, military, religious, educational, administrative or bureaucratic, and economic organization. Throughout the American continent the same formal structure of the Spanish state had been implanted, making America a political continuity, although this was done outside the Iberian peninsula. Spanish institutions in America were universal, that is, they were considered equally valid everywhere, although specific ordinances were adopted that served to address local adaptations to differentiated regional contexts, especially with regard to the different native traditions and to special conditions of the landscape and of intersocial and interethnic relations that were emerging and that demanded unique adaptive measures. Nevertheless, the overall structure, the Spanish model of organization of Hispanic-American society, was universal and acted as a heavy leveling mechanism.

Each one of the Hispanic-American societies that later became an independent nation was colonial in one sense: their members depended upon decisions from the metropolis and were governed according to general laws and ordinances that the bureaucracy undertook to interpret in the service of a single system, that of the Spanish monarchy in its different cultural and social expressions. The various racial, ethnic, and social groups included in the structure or systems of control of the viceroyalties and captaincies reproduced, generally everywhere, the same organization and the same style of power, especially with regard to how they instilled similar motivations in the guise of final goals. And although, in fact, in their cultural origins such groups represented peculiar traditions, such as those expressed by Nahuas, Mayas, and Andeans—to be found also in the adaptive gradations that reflected the specific nature of their incorporation into the general process—nevertheless there existed a common dialectic imposed by the cultural, and especially political, style of the conqueror.

This dialectic appears translated in the form of a macrostructural context arising out of a similar geopolitical concept applied from the metropolis and socially valid for the entire continent subject to its control. In these circumstances, the mestizo consciousness emerged very late, when the displacement of the criollo consciousness—a profound Spanish consciousness in its personality structure and in its ontology—had already occurred.

Although the national consciousness began with the independence process, and although the criollos were the creators of this political expression, they pursued independence more in the sense of seeking their political freedom as "Americans" than, for example, as Mexicans, Guatemalans, or Peruvians. These denominations emerged linked more to the borders defined by pre-Hispanic cultures than to those imposed by a criollo awareness of such borders within what the criollos could recognize objectively in a native tradition. In reality, Spanish-American nationalities emerged as products of unconscious pressure exerted from the pre-Hispanic identities that were politically dominant at the time of the Spanish conquest and that, with respect to the civilized centers of America, were also emerging as transformed reproductions of their old identity, thus having paradoxically no possibility of returning to their cultural forms of origin or to their pre-Hispanic ways of being.

Historically, Spanish-American nationalities were acts of ambiguity or confused consciousness on the part of the criollos, and the nationalities assumed their specific identities when the criollos were freed to limit the geographical framework of their political control in accord with their true capacity to exercise it, and in accord, too, with the traditions that were based on a certain specificity in their territories. From that perspective, if the Hispanic unified on a general level, the pre-Hispanic defined on the particular. This would be equivalent to a multilinear process within a unilinear context. As such, while the Hispanic was all of America, the national in that continent was everything that could be recognized as a tradition substantiated historically in the cultural sphere and that, in such a case, was Hispano-Mexican, and so on, except in those cases where the native tradition had disappeared or was culturally or demographically insufficient, that is, it did not offer a cultural heritage capable of taking root in the new ethnic, or national, formations.

What doubtless occurs in the history of this Hispanicization of the Indian and the African is that, in many cases, as Humboldt (1962, 737) points out for eighteenth- and early-nineteenth-century Venezuela, whites and mestizos as well as mulattoes—all of them incorporated into the settlements of the interior from a coastal zone of expansion—entered into Indian villages and settled there. What had begun as missions devoted to converting and acculturating the natives were becoming Spanish urban centers where the indigenous society not only absorbed the Spanish way of life, but, as Humboldt indicates, adopted the Spanish language to the extent of losing its own. Humboldt himself (ibid., 802) attached great relevance to the fact that the replacement of the missionaries to the Indians by priests in Venezuela had contributed to the settlement of Spaniards among the Indians in considerable numbers.

The effect of these intrusions was that the Indians began to diminish as a racial class, since due to their Hispanicization and therefore to the gradual miscegenation that their groups were experiencing upon mixing with others, they were entering into the category of a mestizo, or at times zambo, class with the product of mixture derived from the union of black with Indian. Even in the case where they remained biologically "Indian," it is clear that the fact of their employment as day laborers with the Spanish contributed to their Hispanicization and to their being classified as something other than Indian otherwise.

In these circumstances, a common result in terms of the establishment of Spanish settlements in native areas was the tendency of the natives to convert to the Hispanic tradition, even though the Spanish adopted indigenous place names such as Caracas, Cumaná, Maracaibo, or Coro when they founded urban centers in these places. Humboldt (1962, 764) also pointed out, in this respect, that "the only thing Indian about these cities at that time were the names." What was happening in Venezuela also took place in Paraguay. Azara (1962, 433) makes reference there to various locales such as "El Baradero," "Quilmes," and "Santo Domingo Siriano." In these places, the fact that they were not set up as indigenous communities protected in their identity as "Reducciones" hastened their Hispanicization, to the extreme that, as Azara states, even though their first residents were of Indian origin, the circulation and settlement of Spaniards and mestizos in these locales led to mixtures of blood and the corresponding mestizo process in these villages, a process that culminated in the identification of all their individuals as Spanish and the loss of their native languages and their customs.

Azara insists, furthermore, that the Hispanicization of the Guaranís resulted not only from their constant mixing with the Spanish, but also from their living with them, since in this case not only were they held to be mestizos, but by so being they lived in the Spanish way. In referring to the historical role played by the encomienda in racial mixing, Azara (1962) emphasizes that the fact that there were few natives integrated into this social organization made it necessary, during the last quarter of the seventeenth century in Buenos Aires, to contract them from outside the province. Social circulation of this kind implied the opportunity for Hispanicization and for adaptive mobility, and within this freedom it is evident that the mestizo was the result of individual choices less controlled by moral institutions. At any rate, Hispanicization occurred not only through the direct pressure of the institutions of control, but resulted from choices that the natives considered advantageous.

In their cultural expression, these populations, first Indian and then mestizo, ended up being categorized as Spanish, not through the imperatives of a formal census but as an expression of their own cultural nature. In the fact of their racial mixture, what dominated ultimately was their Hispanic cultural identity in the context of their biological race mixture.

This last process that we indicate as conducive to the formation of a national consciousness thus was assuming, within more or less defined territorial limits, a genealogy of profound political and cultural traditions that escaped the emotional or subjective solidarity of the criollos, while the latter also acted as a racial class with respect to the other groups. Despite this separateness, the pre-Hispanic populated centers of America, especially those areas where imperialist urban formations had developed, constituted at the outset a historical reality that would reappear as an identity associated specifically with a recombination with Hispanic culture. With the general political independence what was hidden before was reestablished in the form of a different status, that is, it was manifested according to the relative strength of the amounts of content that might concern it within the context of ways of living and, in the latter, according to the corresponding new national identity. In any case, if this identity was created out of a criollo definition, the true consciousness of its internal form gave expression to a combination that was really mestizo in that it expressed a historicocultural amalgam. In fact, this consciousness expressed the cultural value of this combination, syncretized in the form of a specified political identity.

According to our understanding of the successive awarenesses that emerged as dominant in the different American historical contexts, these contexts additionally have produced their respective configurations or specificities with respect to their corresponding cultural dominances. Thus, there are pre-Hispanic dominances distributed regionally and recognized through the so-called Maya, Nahua, Toltec, Aztec, and Andean traditions and other specific indigenous traditions defined within and outside of these. And following the political-military phenomenon of the various European conquests, we perceive other cultural dominances that, for the very reason that they have been imposed as ways of living, have served to transform old awarenesses, endowing them with other identities.

Perhaps the most prolonged identity, or the broadest and most cohesive in time and space, has been the Hispanic one, since it is also the one most deeply instituted as the generally practiced way of life, not only because it appears as a cultural dominance, but also because its populations of origin spread throughout the continent and constituted a continuous political and social backbone during the viceroyalties. Those populations reproduced through their own and through mestizo generations that were gradually recognized in the form of a social consciousness integrated into what presents itself to us as a Hispanic-American mode of identity.

In the context of its historical awareness, this *hispanidad* is felt in similar measure to what happens to the person of the Iberian Peninsula, who, being from Extremadura or Murcia, also identifies him or herself as a Spaniard. In the American case, this consciousness is higher and emerges as Hispanic in the background of a historical identity which has been recognized since the assumption of nationality as a cultural recombination.

Benito Juárez, the so-called Indian of Guelatao, took the mestizo option and seized hispanidad from the criollos, giving Mexico a more indigenous race, not only in its physical characteristics but also in its culture, when he gave Mexico a more rural stamp, that is, when he reduced bourgeois positivism to a purely opportune instrumentality. The *juarista* custom was rural, and when it was installed in an urban setting it ruralized national politics, making them more colloquial and discrete in the style of its Indian origins. The political structure that Juárez used was Hispanic, as were his logistics, but his comprehension of his historical circumstances was mestizo in the sense of a Hispanicized cultural model within the reserved caution of the Indian.

The first mestizo inroad to signify a Mexican national style, which we represent with the historical figure of Benito Juárez, constitutes, we believe, the antecedent of future nationalist outbursts, implicitly revolutionary in what they contain of a political break with what remained of criollismo,[10] and thus of ambiguity with regard to a mestizo national consciousness. In this case, the revolutionary scenario does not appear as the mere destruction of traditional power relationships with the restitution—in a vindictive sense—of lands to community peasants and the adjudication to them of rights they did not enjoy before; in many ways it represents a conservative mode of thought that Juárez could find by seeking his Indian roots within a cultural mode that was also Hispanic.

In the context of our considerations, what we wish to emphasize is that because the revolutions that occur in Hispanic-America are peasant revolutions in their massive operations, they incorporate into the national consciousness large groups of natives, who, upon feeling themselves members of a national culture, identify through deep-rooted habit with the Hispanic culture now consciously mestizo through the political leadership of the mestizos' displacing the criollos from their traditional positions of power.

Hispanic consciousness is not a superficial episodic dominance, since it is more than the product of power exercised by a foreign layer of the population situated stratigraphically on top of another or others, without the dissolution of the latter. What is certain is that the Spanish-American case represents a genealogical fusion in which the female cohorts who emerged from the historical process of confrontation ended up producing mestizo combinations. By being mestizo, these combinations began dissolving the episode of historic intrusion itself. Through the instruments of the cultured organization of their space, they achieved the gradual coalescing of racial and ethnic strengths, which, if they were separated at first by the dialectic discourse of a conquest and of a position of power, later became a single discourse; that is, these strengths gradually came to create a single general identity through the dissolution of the early differences within a system of common antecedents.

From this viewpoint, the nature of the Hispanic consciousness in America does not refer to a chance form. It appears as the product of a configuration and as the result of the founding of a new great Spanish society ("New Spain," "New Granada," "New Andalucía," etc.) which, in addition to reproducing the ways of the metropolis, is reproduced in the criollo and mestizo towns to which it gave origin through racial descent and through identification. Additionally, it incorporated others, such as the natives and the

Africans, into its style through recombination and syncretism until they were at least Hispanicized in their respective cultural formations.

The Hispanic consciousness was a dominant way of being, at least in the heart of the viceregal centers. That is, all of the system that was dependent upon the institutional organization of the viceroyalties was Hispanicized. It was even assumed confusedly by the populations that were resisting it and maintaining their ethnic identity, or that simply had adapted it from the very instant in which the natives appeared established in localized "Reducciones" under Catholic spiritual guidance, and therefore organized according to a strict dependency upon the Spanish official.

During more than three centuries the Hispanic consciousness has been internalized cognitively in the form of a consciousness derived from the action of the politically dominant, and therefore institutionalized, system of culture. That is, the system is established as a recognized social context in the normal behavior of the individuals and groups integrated into this total organization. The assumed values and their moral centers, the linguistic forms, the technologies and their material products, the economic organization, the governmental structure in its various local political and military manifestations—in its controls and expansion—as well as the judicial, administrative, religious, educational, and executive foundations, all together represent a configuration of Hispanic reality. From this viewpoint, what is outside of this consciousness is out of context, and we should recognize it as a depolarized feature—different, but within the system—when referring to its dimensions of practice and when it is compared, for example, with an "indigenous" consciousness; or when it is also defined as a pre-Hispanic consciousness, as commonly assumed in the different attempts to return, by means of rebellions, to government in the native way and to a native identity to the exclusion of the Hispanic; or as was the case of the populations that lived autonomously within the system: "savage" Indians and, in a certain sense, the "resettled" Indians who preserved their languages and their native customs in sufficient proportion so as to reproduce them in their ethnic identification.

All the populations who maintained their ethnic identity within the total Spanish political system were confusedly Indian when they acted within another organization, but they were the origin of another consciousness to come, which was defined as mestizo when it was incorporated into a single national society. This incorporation took place after the success of different national independence movements and within these, as soon as the natives assumed this national consciousness, having previously lost their ethnic identity as Indians. With respect to this identity, ethnic continuity in indigenous terms is an obstacle to the aforesaid national consciousness, but when the latter appears in mestizo form, it is precisely in those nations which, in addition to featuring a heavy population density in pre-Hispanic times, also had an urban and imperialist cultural development. By contrast, those that had a high population density without the corresponding urban society appear Hispanicized more than Hispanic-American or mestizo in their consciousness and their identity.

Of course, there are degrees of Hispanic national consciousness that depend upon the permanence of the aforesaid antecedents. And thus the processes that give function to this Hispanic identity vary in intensity according to the pre-Hispanic cultural ingredients that are present in the daily inventories of their social activity; but these processes also depend upon the influence of identity exerted on their consciousness by the fact of genealogical recognition, the memory of their origins, through which they also are accustomed to outlining criteria of identity, that is, according to a reason whose design is submerged in the principles of the kinship system.

The dialectic of these cultural motives inserted into the context of the relative determination of a national historical consciousness thus appears linked to the fact of the specific capacity, in the generations that follow their political foundation, for reproduction of a way of life situated with constant reference to an integrating cultural nucleus, independent from its contributing admixtures. In the case of the Spanish-American nations, their contemporary consciousness of hispanidad passes through the experience of a prolonged period of cohesion in the order of ontological formation, that is, it goes through a process of three centuries of cultural reproduction, with no less than fifteen generations constituting networks of kinship and coexistence, gradually constituting the different local and regional admixtures—biological and cultural—on which this consciousness is based.

When these different admixtures were defined in the form of nationalities with American independence in emancipation movements, the criollos assumed the reproduction of the culture of their parents, but in this case with their own decisions about its political use. The control of the political forms of this independence by the criollos signified their re-encounter with western Europe in a direct fashion through a totally Hispanic personality. Nevertheless, this re-encounter could never achieve a permanent continuity in the relatively pure form because its historical reality was not just structural, but also consisted of an adaptive environment, the American one, which was already creating its own strategies in the form of heterogeneous populations whose loyalty to European models was more instrumental than it was existential or ontological. Furthermore, hispanidad was faithful to itself to the extent that it represented racial mixture in the heart of territorial modes of adaptation that gave definition and specific meaning to different cultural traditions and admixtures. The historical fact of Spanish expansion can be seen, therefore, as an Americanized assimilation through its foundational adaptation and through an ecologically selective process in its origins, which suggested the development of an identity based outside its European sphere of origin.

→   →   →

Consonant with what we have indicated, it is evident that, while racial plurality has remained dynamically open to exchange and to social mobility, as well as to intensive mixing, in Anglo-America it has been closed and distinguished by a more rigidly stratified racial model than the Hispanic one. Thus, when in Ibero-America the racial type tends to constitute a varied spectrum gradually homogenized through mixing, where the extremes of gradation— Indian, white, and black—represent ever-declining percentages with relation to the products of mixture, in Anglo-America those extremes, especially those consisting of whites and blacks, are the characteristic modes. In Anglo-America, the mestizo grows demographically very little in relation to the other groups.

These cultural and racial differences between the components of the populations of Ibero-America and Anglo-America, respectively, are the expression of equally different historical experiences. For one thing, the racial receptivity and flexibility of the Spanish/Portuguese group have been greater than those of the Anglo-Saxon group. For another, the nature of the crossbreeding, and furthermore, of the settlement and colonization of America carried out by the Spanish and Portuguese present the phenomenon—also different—that while the Spanish, particularly, operated in regions of relatively high population density and of an advanced level of civilization, as in Mexico, Guatemala, and the Andean area, the Anglo-Saxon group operated in regions with relatively sparse and scattered Indian populations that were clearly inferior with regard to the general cultural development of those of the South. In any case, the indigenous ethnic groups located within what would constitute the first great Anglo-Saxon tradition in America—beginning at 35° north latitude, although in certain regions, for instance California, Nevada, Utah, and Colorado, this limit could be moved further north— were, despite such exceptions as the Pueblos, demographically and culturally inferior to the Meso-Americans and Andeans.

The native population upon which the Anglo-Saxons acted did not total much over a million individuals, whereas the population of the natives to the south of the aforesaid line, including northern Mexico, probably reached twenty-five or thirty million inhabitants. These population differences would not in themselves explain the phenomenon of racial mixing if we did not also take into account other factors: (1) the values governing the racial conduct of the Spanish/Portuguese group compared with those of the Anglo-Saxon group; and (2) the forms of social and cultural relations maintained by each group with respect to Indians and Africans. With regard to the first factor, we find in the Spanish group and in the Portuguese a relatively dynamic absence of racial prejudice, if we consider the latter in terms of specific attitudes of repugnancies about carrying out sexual exchanges with other races and ethnicities. This is the contrary of what would happen with the Anglo-Saxon man, if we keep in mind that in him we find a certain renunciation of practicing sexual interaction with Indian and black women under normal circumstances, that is, under principles of social control and stable coexistence according to stimulants of attraction and fondness for these races. With respect to the second factor, we wish to emphasize certain facts that we feel are significant: (a) the conquest, as well as part of the early Spanish colonization, was carried out with a great predominance of men over women of their own kind; and (b) the unions of Indian women with the Spanish were more easy than difficult.

Given their status as the dominant group, Spanish men achieved the same relations with African women as they did with Indian women. In a large sense, the exchange took away possibilities for sexual interaction between the Africans themselves of both sexes, which also led the men of this race to seek more or less fortuitous or stable solutions, according to each case, with Indian women. All this has already been stated, and we will not carry it further.

Whatever the case may be, these unions coincided with native traditions of institutionalized polygyny and with the propensity to appropriate Indian women for sexual purposes on the part of the Spanish and, by imitation, of the Africans. In each case, Indians and Africans appeared supported by polygynous traditions, and although the Spanish practiced normal monogamy in their country of origin, in the Indies they practiced multiple unions as a function of their power and of the free run of their sexual appetites. Additionally, in the historical experience of the first racial mixtures, insofar as the power and prestige of the conqueror defined the limits of the choice, through appropriation, of Indian women, it is also true that the circulation of the latter in the context of sexual exchanges with the Spanish was ruled by the power of disposition that men held over women. This context would include the Spanish as individuals, as well as the Indians and Africans, with their cultural traditions relating to marital organization and to sexual relations, in this case and in its very institutional context being widely permissive.

In contrast to the Spanish and Portuguese settlers, the Anglo-Saxons, through the structure and environment of their colonization, greatly hin-

dered the achievement of intensive racial mixing. In fact, relations with Indian women came through the soldiers' operating in zones of conflict or
frontier control, and they were engaged in equally by adventurers without
families and by the different individuals involved in mining, the fur trade, or
exploration. Despite those contacts, the rapid creation of European communities that were socially and economically transplanted and self-sufficient
was a factor of great importance in the sexual independence of white men
with regard to Indian women. The entry of Africans into the southern regions of what is today the United States did not greatly alter the situation,
because in fact, and with few exceptions, their relations with Indian women
took place in coincidence with their social mobility, especially following the
American Civil War, when they began their westward movement. Before
that, their sexual relation with Indians was very restricted, although they
soon took advantage of the presence of their own African [slave] women. As
a consequence the mestizo, as a pressure group, never represented an important social or historical force in the process of integration of Anglo-American
society.

The accumulation of the factors mentioned above thus suggests a distinctive regionalization of racial mixings. Fundamentally, moreover, the efforts
of the Spanish were directed at dominating and occupying especially the
populated centers of America, because an effective political dominance assured a high yield for the conquest and the continuity of Spanish presence
through colonization. The Spanish policy of coexistence with the American
natives, being a combination of geopolitical, economic, and apostolic interests, was also a total symbiosis of common life within a stratified political and
social organization.

As a consequence of the lesser interest that the marginal areas offered to
the Spanish, and because of the political protection that the state gave to the
Indian "Reducciones," the natives of these areas preserved not only their
identity for a longer time, but also a large part of their cultures, such that in
these areas there were slow processes of change overseen by the religious
orders. Thus, these Indians gradually absorbed transformations, especially in
their spiritual practices and in material techniques of subsistence, for the purpose of converting them more to an urban civilization than to a communal
and Christian view of life.

It must also be recognized that a large part of the marginal groups held no
immediate interest for the Spanish Crown, because they were established in
very unattractive climatic or ecological regions, as well as because they could
easily elude the control of Spanish authorities. The very fact of their geographic mobility and the cultural distance that separated them from Spanish
ways of life, as well as from the higher pre-Hispanic culture, caused Spanish

geopolitical concerns to maintain only an indirect interest in these groups. In practice, and for these reasons, they became subjects of the missions, which in turn became cultural embassies that prepared the way for the later establishment of Spanish political and civil authority. In any case, the fact that these Indians offered little economic attraction was a good reason for the processes of Hispanicization applied to them to be gradual, as shown by the fact that interior tribes are still being discovered.

In this sense, it is true that the Spanish policy of Indian "Reducciones" contributed to slowing the process of massive racial mixing in some of the regions where they were established. Certainly, the missionaries voiced their opposition from the outset to the presence of Spaniards, Africans, and mestizos among the native populations, because they thought that interpersonal relations by natives with the other groups threatened the very objective of Christianizing them and of developing in them a deeply religious moral system. The separation of these groups held back open racial mixing in the areas of the "Reducciones." Nevertheless, it was not completely interrupted, since chance and individual relations continued to occur between native and nonnative groups, such that, fundamentally, almost no indigenous group remained aloof from some kind of interracial sexual experience.

In Anglo-America, the situation was different. There the European settlers occupied Indian lands and cultivated them directly, foregoing Indian participation except in few cases of individualized acculturation. Therefore, no seigniorial system of great haciendas founded on Indian labor was produced. Anglo-Saxon colonists settled in family groups and cultivated the land in a system of mutual cooperation but seldom employed an Indian labor force. In this way, while the Spanish were economically dependent on Indian labor and founded a social organization with them, the Anglo-Saxons organized their society without the Indians. In this sense, the Indian "reservations" reinforced the principle of racial separation and established the preservation of Indian identity in a more definite manner than among the Spanish-American groups, who tended to dissolve it through social confusion.

Of course, there are exceptions to these tendencies. They occurred both in the north and south of what is today North America: Canada and the United States. In Canada the activities of the French and the Anglo-Saxons as frontiersmen served to produce racial mixtures, biological as well as cultural, with the Indians. These mixtures were relatively intense in the early periods of colonization. Later, the mestizos were gradually absorbed by the flood of Europeans who came to these lands, while the Indians absorbed their own. In practice, only the experience of a common society made racial mixing possible on a large scale, such that in North America, Indian polycentrism and European structural separation led to a decrease in the opportunities for racial mixing.

In a certain way, the so-called South of today's United States was an exception with respect to the Africans. They constituted, along with the whites, a single society, aristocratic and based on slavery but integrated into a single system: that of its political, economic, and social organization. The form of colonization, partly urban and partly based on plantation systems, and in the latter the massive utilization of African manual labor, also produced a certain racial mixture as a result of relations between white men and black women. The cultural preponderance of the European mode within these mixtures would be due as much to the dynamic strength of its political, social and economic dominance as to the growing migratory attraction of whites to this region.

Of course, it is also evident that in their condition as a subject racial group, Africans had few opportunities to exert cultural influences over the whites, except in the fields of aesthetics—especially music and song—because the broad outlines of the cultural system and of the social structure were provided by the white groups. At any rate, this type of mixture between the white man and the black woman had a lesser demographic significance than in Ibero-America, especially because, from the beginning, the plantation system was socially aristocratic and because the dominant European group was sexually self-sufficient. Nonetheless, despite the barrier of racial prejudices, opportunities for sexual contact, in some cases stable ones, did arise between the master and the black woman, enough to create a significant mulatto population in the southern United States.

Perhaps the maintenance of strong racial discrimination and the scruples imposed by racist ideology on unions between whites and blacks has created strong tendencies toward racial polarization, that is, the tendency for great numbers of mulattoes to return toward blackness instead of becoming whites; and in this case it is obvious that mulatto racial reality is largely hidden in the very African appearance of a racially separate population, and is therefore prone to be sexually self-sufficient even as a response of dignity to white attitudes. In practice, racial discrimination has been more active when the white population is more sexually self-sufficient; but also this discrimination has provided the bases that make mulatto formation and the creation of a mestizo society in the United States extremely difficult to achieve, as seems to be shown by the scant demographic influence exerted by the populations of mixed races. Fundamentally, the Indian, European, and African racial trunks have remained more separated from one another than in Ibero-America, and have become polarized. It has been so largely since the influx of European groups. The lack of an Indian population forming a single social

structure with the Europeans has meant the paralysis of the process and context of an intensive racial mixing. The enormous numerical superiority of
the white group over the black in the area of the United States and Canada;
the political and cultural power of white society over the black, as well as
over the Indian; and the weak political and social organization of the Africans
in those countries imply that the mestizo mode has had very little influence
in those regions, although a certain presence can be perceived in terms of
folkloric, spiritual, and esthetic forms.

An economic and social phenomenon similar to that of the southern
United States occurred in Brazil. However, since the Portuguese practiced
sexual intercourse with Indian and black women, the process of racial mixing
was intensive. At any rate, as the Portuguese soon created mestizos with the
Indian women, and from early on blacks were introduced in large numbers,
Brazil became a context for massive miscegenation. In addition, on the tropical coasts and in the Spanish-American Antilles a great deal of mixture occurred, and that must be attributed to the Africans' physical adaptability to
torrid climates and to their productive capacity in agriculture, mining, and
domestic service. In any case, the greater capacity of the white for domination over the African allowed the establishment of concubinage on a grand
scale, especially in Brazil,[11] where the opportunity for consummating it was
greater than in Spanish-America. This was so especially because the plantation system and the great mass of black population involved brought closer
the physical relationship between both groups and facilitated the tendencies
toward sexual exchange with black women, particularly given the mutual
attraction that had been established.

The most important exceptions to racial mixing on a large scale, in considering its relation to demography today, have occurred in southern South
America. There, specifically in Argentina and to a lesser degree in Uruguay
and Chile, the mestizos have been submerged under the weight of an ever
larger European population, to the point that today whites constitute an im-
mense majority in Argentina, and in this respect they tend to absorb the
remainder of the mestizo and native populations living in the midst of a single
social structure. In contrast, the Plata region and south to the Pampas and
Patagonia were zones of low native population density, which is characteristic of areas where inferior groups of hunters and gatherers predominate.
In general, these have adapted poorly to the techniques of Western culture. In this sense, the reaction of the pampas dwellers and Patagonians
toward the Europeans was mainly hostile, and they were completely sub-
dued. Even late in the past century, operations of mutual extermination were
organized on both sides. This specific interaction between natives of the
pampas and Patagonia and Europeans describes a parallelism or module of

Indian reaction similar to that which occurred in North America with the Plains Indians. In the Argentine case, much of the racial mixing was between Indian men and Spanish, or criollo, and mestizo women.

The perspective that we obtain from this dynamic of racial mixing in America appears linked, in our view, to a significant fact: the stable phenomena of racial mixing are the coherent result of the continual process of coexistence between racially different populations capable of sexual exchange when they are not separated from one another by moral and ethnic repugnance by some with respect to the others. The process of racial mixing has certainly not ceased. Nevertheless, mestizos still represent statistically a diffuse racial minority with respect to the other, better-defined racial minorities, such as the Indian, the European, and the African.

Therefore, within this great process of racial mixture that we see as constant in all populations, although with different statistical incidences, we can identify a sizable number of relatively "pure" individuals, in terms of the original stocks to which their familial genealogies pertain, and in this sense many of these individuals remain racially separate and self-sufficient, that is, beyond sexual exchanges with those of other races. Nevertheless, the process of urbanization is emphasizing this exchange by suppressing—gradually and through egalitarian ideologies—the sociocultural isolation between racial groups, making them increasingly interdependent and participatory. In those countries with strong mestizo populations, this process seems to intensify, especially because mestizo interests are prevailing due to their greater effective social weight, particularly with reference to the organization of cultural systems that are characteristically mestizo or that recombine different traditions.

We must not forget, however, that if for a long time racial classes were what gave significance to social and economic structure, later, and in our time, these racial classes are manifested in the form of attitudes—at times unconscious and expressed through interpersonal disdain—that have their source in a prior racial structure that made of these notions a social obstacle for the status of the racially subject classes. Historically, the most important characteristic of the social process in Spanish America has been to transform the viceregal societies, based on racial groups containing their own internal social stratifications and featuring a weak interracial mobility, into others founded successively on the socioeconomic distribution of individuals into social classes, such that at present there has been a gradual development of individual identity with relation to one's economic position and to his or her corresponding social capacity for personality realization.

To this effect, it is also true that Ibero-American societies demonstrate attitudes by which many of their individuals refuse to admit persons of other races into their groups, even in cases where these persons have attained important economic, and even political, positions. This is especially true between blacks and whites, and more so the greater the social and economic distance that separates them. And it is also true that while many Indian ethnicities remain separated from the national identity of the state to which they belong, there are also groups that develop separate identities. In these cases as well, these Ibero-American societies define the existence of natives in groups of separate identity by considering them as an "Indian problem," by which they recognize that if, as individuals, natives can be members of a given social class, their identity as ethnic groups separates them from the structure of the national society, which is at the same time a society distributed in social classes and also a multiethnic society.

Nevertheless, to the same degree that the social mobility of the indigenous and African cultures has been diluted in the midst of the national cultures, the definition of mestizo societies is valid biologically only for groups of individuals who, independent of this biological trait, nonetheless act more as members of a social class than of a racial class. Perhaps—while Indian identities remain separated from national identities—we can recognize the existence of cultural classes that in certain cases can even be equivalent to social classes, as happens, for example, with some peasant groups established in the form of communities, sometimes monolingual in the native language, or bilingual with a separate identity.

Despite this fact, there still exist what we could call "submerged mestizo ideologies," in the sense of ideologies having appeared politically conscious such that the truly national idea is equivalent to an initial symbiosis and a successive historical recombination among the Indian, Spaniard, and African. Furthermore, those who act within this type of political consciousness represent a submerged ideology in the sense that in them class consciousness still appears mixed with the cultural heritage of a strong ethnic and social consciousness based on categorizing traditions defined by the principle of racial identity.

What is certain is that a significant part of this mestizo national consciousness assumes, on the one hand, the past racial classification of individuals in its society, while on the other, it assumes the transformation of this past through another categorizing principle: that of social classes defined more by economic functions than by racial genealogies. In fact, mestizo culture has a peculiar historical sense in that it has operated from an early perspective in incomplete social integration and even from the periphery of the bosom of a society marked ambiguously by antecedents of racial classes. Then, this first perspective dissolved and took on an economic and therefore objective character: that of social classes, which, nevertheless, still conceals a powerful submerged ideology of discrimination of racial classes.

We are dealing with a process of social equalization within the system of role-status, which seeks to remain independent of racial classifications. Nonetheless, this equalization is achieved only where there also exists a single identity and a single society. As long as there are separated Indian or African groups, a submerged ideology continues to exist. The process of racial mixing is, in this sense, a substantial part of the instruments of consciousness that diminish the role of the submerged ideology. This is the reason why those countries with a higher degree of racial mixing are also the least discriminatory and therefore are the ones that best overcome the problem of the resistant complex carried in the principle of the submerged ideology.

In our focus we will not concern ourselves empirically with the content of this submerged ideology, because our theme is aimed at establishing the historical conditions of the phenomenon and the process of racial mixing in the various categories and resultant products of mixture[12] in America since the arrival of the Spanish. Yet, these tendencies operate through apparently diffuse policies, in the sense of their enormous capacity for propagation combined paradoxically with a powerful reflective emotionality. This is a national consciousness that emerges in dispute with itself, in terms both of its relative historical necessity and of the advantage of objectifying its dialectical reasoning and its conceptual apparatus.

In its political intent, the mestizo ideology[13] incorporates a formidable will for synthesis because it combines the indigenous cultures permanently with the Spanish. Generally, this recombination emphasizes the exclusion of the African, at least as the key to an ideological dialectic. It seems as if its ideological syncretism had submerged these African contributions into the subconscious depths of what should be hidden because it is unnecessary. In this sense, mestizo ideology must be understood as the expression of a political force, paradoxically new and old at the same time. This is because its ontological bloodlines tend to be established in the context of the cultural recombination of the Indian and Spanish pasts, of the dissolution of racial differences as a factor of identity and status, and of the setting forth of political strategies of an ideologically confused nature, inasmuch as one sees in those strategies differently subjective ingredients, such as a pure nationalism[14] and a powerful will expressed in the objective transformation of the social and economic reality of their countries. In fact, this nationalist will tends, additionally, to sweep away the positivist criollo nationalist spirit, because, while the mestizo is aware that he does not represent the historical continuity of the criollos, he is also aware that he cannot exclude them because they are present in the dialectic of his national cultural formation.

In this daily reality, the submerged ideology of the powerful system of racial classes that has dominated in the past still persists. Nonetheless, the context in which this submerged ideology operates has two apparently complementary dimensions: on the one hand, it is recognized in pre-Hispanic esthetics and in a certain identification with ambiguous spiritual symbols in what is characteristically its transcendent, or metaphysical, strategy. I refer, in this instance, to the enormous influences of pre-Hispanic religions on the daily practice of the Catholic religion among great social masses of humble peasant origin; on the other hand, it is recognized in the continuity of Hispanic culture as a form of total impregnation of the historical personality of the mestizo.

This perspective historically is a process of cultural syncretisms, but it is also a process of structural changes, in one sense: in that ideological forces and economic relations have modified social relations to the point of introducing into them a background of social mobility infinitely superior to that which existed in the past. In the liberal or the revolutionary setting, according to each case, this mobility has consisted of great migrations of masses from the countryside to the cities and to industries, while at the same time it has assumed the need for an available labor force and has prepared great numbers of technicians, university professors, and craft specialists, creating, in any case, a profound restructuring of the status system. Fundamentally, it has replaced the society of racial classes with the society of social classes. This change has also reached the natives, because in most cases they have become community peasants, but ones integrated into the national system and structure and largely uprooted from their old ethnic identities, even though they retain certain ethnocentric values and monolingualisms conducive to their ethnic differentiation, especially among their older classes; that is, among those persons traditionally classified within the social order having the prestige of "respect."

Historically, the period of independence has been characterized by hastening the disappearance of local indigenous structures, and has largely developed the integration of the latter into the bosom of Hispanic culture represented by the criollos. On this point, what Spain lost politically, it preserved culturally. The ensuing historical process has served to complete the process of acculturation of the natives in Hispanic terms, while through the opening of a long period of European immigration it has brought an era of relative Europeanization. In contemporary times, this relative Europeanization can be considered as an intensive process of Westernization. In this context, natives, Africans, and mixtures of all kinds are being rapidly Westernized.

Just as the survival of Spanish culture has been confirmed by the fact of its being a part of western European culture, native culture has remained only in those partial elements it contains in the way of food and linguistic inputs, as well as in esthetic elements. In these terms, the cultural dimension of racial mixing in the midst of Ibero-American populations continues to maintain a strong dynamic: culturation is constant, and technological choices introduce significant changes in ideological, especially political, praxes. Under such conditions, biological mixing continues to be intensive because the different racial populations participate in a great social circulation.

In a certain way, racial mixing remains close to the historical destiny of the political and military power of the cultures involved, and whereas the Spanish culture is Western, and has also succeeded in the syncretism and recombinations that we have mentioned, it has managed to develop a kind of common ethos in Spanish America, an ethos, furthermore, that continues to be very powerful with regard to its capacity to assimilate peoples. Thus, in the same way that the natives' institutional structures—their architecture, their ways of counting and writing, their religions, and their juridical, military, technological, and educational systems—all disappeared under the Spanish, so, too, the colonial elements are disappearing from the Spanish cultural systems, among others, industrial techniques and artifacts, juridical forms, formal education, and children's games, with the appearance of new institutions, such as unions, political parties, ideologies and philosophies, and architectural forms, which replace their predecessors and define new formal styles and new social structures.

According to these cultural changes, it turns out that the present-day Westernization of Ibero-America constitutes a process of acculturation that is historically cumulative and successively organized upon the establishment of single national societies who resolve their contradictions and their internal cultural remnants within an already constituted *ethos*. In this sense, in the same way that the Spanish were acculturated by adopting, for example, elements of native diets, so, too, are today's Spanish-American populations acculturated by introducing into their ways of living new Western elements, such as household appliances. But in none of these cases does acculturation necessarily imply syncretism. Once a substantial ethos exists, the cultural process is limited more to assimilating them to syncretizing.

In any case, those elements related to the flora and fauna, by constituting the natural basis of American native cultures, have been incorporated into racial mixing for the most part, and these elements represent contributions of a permanent nature within the integration of racial mixing today. Many of the traditional arts referred to as indigenous are the result of the combination of western Spanish techniques and motifs reinterpreted by native artists. This occurs especially because, while on the one hand the natives lacked what Silva calls the "visual tradition" of European models, they contributed, on the other hand, their own plastic sense, represented by ornamental exuberances and by a certain solemnity derived from their very lack of cultural experiences with the European motifs that were presented to them as subjects for expression. On this point, the talent of some traditional arts are mestizo in their reinterpretations, but they show themselves to be more an adaptation of the Indian to European modes than a production based on native traditions. In such a case, we can also say that we are situated within what we have called a Hispanic mode of mixing, in this instance based on a creation produced by the Indians.

The reality that concerns us is thus one in which cultural mixing maintains a homogeneous Spanish base, in contrast to the indigenous base. Because of its evolutionary diversity, the latter appears largely heterogeneous, which gives us good cause to claim that there is more than one kind of racial mixing, and in this sense, each region and each ethnicity of native population represents specific aspects of mixture, with the understanding that this is observed to be more universal in its Spanish cultural outlines than in its native cultural ingredients. Accordingly, there would be Hispano-Maya, Hispano-Nahua, and Hispano-Andean mixtures and other specific mixtures for each cultural area.

Therefore, whereas we may define a Spanish mold for the entire continent, and whereas we may locate a common Hispanic institutional structure in Spanish America, the presence of native cultures has a more regional, perhaps less universal, character insofar as it refers only to cultures whose territorial extent is culturally more restricted.

It is within this master, or macrostructural, framework that the various indigenous cultural elements characteristic to each region or to each specific cultural tradition are lodged. Thus, with the beginning of the Spanish historical period, the native groups who retained their autonomous organization were acculturated in Spanish terms, while all those who entered as part of the new Spanish-American society were integrated into it on the basis of acquiring that part of Spanish culture which corresponded to them through their social position within the new political system and its institutional structure. They were quickly trained in the use of the Spanish language, in dressing, in the Catholic religion, and in the skills and tasks of the Spanish economic system, and were integrated into the heart of Spanish political organization.

Under these circumstances, it is in autonomous political formations that cultural mixing is produced in the form of local syncretisms in relation to religious beliefs, to agricultural implements, to cultigens and beasts of burden, and to ways of dressing and of politically organizing local communities. In these terms, cultural syncretism occurs more often among politically autonomous native groups than among natives acting as separate individuals. Rather than syncretism, what the latter produce at the outset is biculturalism and acculturation, until their descendants are finally Hispanicized, that is, they enter into the Spanish mode of racial mixing. In this way, the institutions will be Spanish, while their contents will be mestizo.

Spanish Women: Junctures of Conquest and Settlement

The scarcity of Spanish women in the first stages of the occupation of America by the Spanish is a matter recognized by all historians. Likewise, it is thought that the rapid crossbreeding of the American continent has some dynamic relation to that scarcity. This has a general reality throughout America during the sixteenth century, particularly in its first half. Céspedes (1971, 394–95) states that during the period 1509–38, the royal authorities issued some 10 percent of their permits to sail to America to Spanish women. Of these, a third were recognized as married women who were traveling to join their husbands. Many of them were accompanied by their children, whereas the rest consisted of young single women who were soon sought for marriage.

Although twenty years after this period the demographic ratio between the two sexes seems to have evened out (Céspedes 1971), due especially to the political stability achieved in the urban areas, and though there existed no legal obstacles to emigration for Spanish women of acknowledged good moral habits, it is also true, nevertheless, that the war zones continued to be a factor against the entry of these women. As we shall see, there were but few exceptional cases. In fact, and this is what is important to our theme, great regions of America were war zones where a large number of conquistadors were engaged, particularly in the lands of the so-called "savage Indians," that is, northern Mexico, parts of Central America, New Granada, Chile, Paraguay, Argentina, the eastern Andean zone, Venezuela, the Guayanas, and Brazil, in the case of the Portuguese.

Military expeditions were organized according to a similar model: they basically included Spanish soldiers, Indian auxiliaries, sometimes warrior allies, porters and Indian women servants, and other Indian women where appropriate. The latter were either assigned or voluntary, according to the case, but some of them functioned as domestic servants and carriers, others as concubines, or a combination of both.

In the case of New Spain—and let this serve as an example of this initial structure of the conquest of the American continent—the conquistador Bernal Díaz comments (Díaz del Castillo 1955, 295–96) that in 1520, in the assault on Tenochtitlán, the troops of Cortés had with them only one Spanish woman. In the words of that chronicler with reference to the retreat of Cortés on the occasion of a great battle for possession of the Mexican capital, there was among the Spanish only "one woman called María de Estrada, and we had no other woman of Castilla in Mexico but that one." And in this context of the ratio of Spanish women in that period of the conquest of Mexico, Bernal Díaz (ibid., 432) tells of the death of "six women of Castilla who had remained there (in Tuxtepec) from the forces of Narváez." Later, in an expedition to the interior of New Spain in 1524 on the occasion of the founding of a Spanish *villa,* Bernal Díaz (ibid., 550) records that in the expedition there were "forty men and four women of Castilla and two mulatto women."

Additionally, Azara commented in his time (1962) that the conquest of Paraguay was done without Spanish women, and though he admits there might have been one or two, nevertheless, the great proportion or nearly all the women involved in it were Indian. Thus, the descendants of unions between these Indian women and the conquering Spanish were individuals who were not only mestizos but whose cohorts also resulted from sexual relations among mestizos, with scarcely any mixing with other Spaniards or with persons of other European nations. The effect described by Azara consists of the fact that, in the period to which his evidence refers, the mestizos called themselves Spanish, even though they were not directly such from the first generation. An intramestizo endogamy finally produced the Paraguayan racial type, and this was done on the basis of some early multiple unions of Spanish men with Indian women who, in numbers far greater than those of the men, either accompanied them or simply happened to be in the places of conquest.

Nevertheless, there is no doubt that there were exceptions to this usual pattern among the habitual events, since Spanish women appeared in the war zones, cooperating in the conquests. Testimony about the conquest of Chile is provided by Mariño de Lobera (1960, 250): the example of a Spanish woman, Inés Suárez, born in Plasencia, who went in 1540 with the army of conquest and colonization. When the expedition found itself thirsty and exhausted, without a chance to find water, the woman had a well dug until water for everyone was found. The well kept her name in commemoration of the event. At the same time, and while she tended to the wounds of the combatants, it is said that this woman fought alongside her companions at times of general despair, serving in every case as an example of courage and strength that all the soldiers admired and remarked upon.

Likewise, and under similar circumstances of combat, Mariño de Lobera (1960, 303) recounts that during the campaign of Valdivia in Arauco, two Castilian women, the first to enter Chile according to this account, fought arduously in one of the hardest battles; and in it, Beatriz de Salazar, who was married to Diego Martinez, a Spanish soldier in the aforesaid army, killed six Indians in combat, employing a hoe with a vigor and violence unbelievable for our time, and even for that one. Likewise, the 1540 expedition of Jerónimo de Lebrón to areas of New Granada apparently included two Spanish women (Pérez de Barradas 1976, 140). Before that, in 1524, when the charters for the settlement of Santa Marta were signed, it was provided that two years after the founding of the colony at least fifteen of its citizens should be married (ibid., 135), which implied that a certain undetermined number of the women would be of Spanish origin, or in some other cases would be Portuguese women with spouses of the same nation. In no case, however, were military expeditions considered a proper place for European women.

There were other cases where women accompanied soldiers on expeditions. During one of his journeys through yet unconquered America, Alvar Núñez Cabeza de Vaca reported that some Spanish women remarked on the risks to which they were exposed when they joined their husbands' company in war against the Indians; and in this regard one of them noted that even under the worst conditions of adversity and of appearance, they were preferred over Indian women and much sought after for marriage by the survivors. Fundamentally, nonetheless, there were very few women who faced dangers from which they could scarcely be protected by the efforts of their own spouses in the course of one of these expeditions.

Those women also faced the risk of capture by the Indians, and this was a compelling reason why attempts were made to dissuade them from accompanying the military forces. Many women were captured by the Indians, especially those of the frontier areas, and from these there also came mestizo descendants. There is frequent mention of these captives in the chronicles of the Indies. Many examples of roundups of Spanish women occurred with the Araucanians. For a long time during their struggle with the Spanish conquistadors and settlers, they made a special effort to capture Spanish women. According to Pérez de Barradas (1976, 206), the Araucanians captured more than five hundred of them, of whom they returned some two hundred to the Spanish.

This situation prevailed for a long time. Even in the latter half of the nineteenth century, the Argentine writer Mansilla (1962) makes frequent mention of white women captives among the Ranquel Indians, finally noting in the midst of these groups a certain number of mestizos resulting from their unions. In this sense, the capture of white women itself became a military objective on the part of the Indians. Mansilla (ibid., 248) states this when he refers to a conversation with one of these Indians, writing:

> [T]alking with an Indian, we exchanged these words:
> "Which do you prefer, an (Indian) girl or a Christian one?"
> "A Christian one."
> "And why is that?"
> "That Christian whiter, taller, finer hair, that Christian more beautiful."

Additionally, around 1870, the proportion of white captives of both sexes to natives among the Ranquels would amount to 10 percent if, as Mansilla (ibid., 247) says of an estimated eight to ten thousand individuals, white captives probably numbered from six to eight hundred persons. Otherwise, although these Christian women were in fact aesthetically more appreciated than Indian women, this did not necessarily mean a better social position for them in the context of Indian societies. There, these women usually had a secondary status, even the minimal status of slaves with respect to that of the native women, particularly because the rules of status were adjusted to local principles of rank that related to the primary role of the first wife, based on political systems of alliance and of social obligations accompanying marriages among the Indian tribes.

This question of status would be another of the characteristics of racial mixing on the frontier. But whatever its results, the fact in itself gave warning to the Spanish about the risks they faced every time they attempted to settle frontier areas with their own women. In other situational contexts, the assumed risks took on another character. Thus, in 1534 a Spanish soldier assigned to the troops of Pedro de Alvarado took his wife and two daughters along. But Garcilaso de la Vega (Varallanos 1962, 41) relates that when these women became exhausted by the difficulty of the trek and the harshness of the climate, the soldier, unable to abandon them because of his responsibility to protect them, remained with them, and the four of them froze to death in the inclement weather. Likewise, when Bernal Díaz (Díaz del Castillo 1955, 652) refers to the vicissitudes experienced by the Spaniards who came with Cortés, and by the wives of some of them, he mentions one man who had participated in the conquest of Mexico with the following words: "he was a very good man in his person, called Pedro de Guzmán, and he was married to a Valencian woman named Doña Francisca de Valterra; he went to Peru and it was said that he and his wife froze to death."

Later, in 1543, when some conquests in Peru had become stabilized, there are records of the arrivals of Spanish women either married or intent upon contracting marriages in America with those who sought them. Nevertheless, in peaceful times, these women generally went assigned to Spaniards who were already married to them beforehand and who received them in this status after having been on expedition for some time.

Most often the soldiers took in Indian women, and in such cases did not feel so beset with the problems of adaptability of their women. The Indian women held up better in their own environs and overcame the difficulties of war through their environmental selection. Perhaps some military commanders granted themselves special permission to take in Spanish women, as in the case of the conqueror of Chile, Pedro de Valdivia, who undertook the campaign in the company of a Castilian woman, according to reports of the day (Góngora Marmolejo 1960, 102). But it was more common on these campaigns to join Indian women—those brought from home or from the point of departure of the group's expedition as well as those captured or obtained during the roundups and sweeps through the field after the end of a battle, or through the will of the Indian women themselves, desirous of joining the Spanish in other cases—and pursue with them the fortunes of the war. In cases of alliance Indian women were also received, but the results of a multiple acquisition of Indian women by the Spanish provoked great alarm and criticism on the part of zealous clergy charged with exercising religious control over the conquistadors. To this extent, their moral pressure was very active in the sense of obliging the soldiers to seek their wives as soon as possible, especially those who had remained in the rear, although those wives living in Spain were the object of demand whenever a settlement was founded and established on a permanent basis in America.

Very often it was the missionaries who, thanks to laborious efforts and risks that threatened their physical integrity, not only performed the role of converting Indians, but acted as advance agents in Spanish conquests and colonization by preparing the action against the natives, as much that they might accept Christianity as that they might cooperate with and serve the Spanish. When the missionaries converted the Indians to Christianity, or when they simply reduced them to sedentary habits, making them accept intensive agriculture and cattle raising—which they did in fact achieve, and more— it was preparing the native terrain for a Spanish civil invasion.

At this point, peace would come, and it represented a good opportunity for the entry of Spanish women. In this sense, the fact of Christianization also implied Hispanicization. Both objectives formed part of the fundamental strategy of conquest and colonization. From this perspective, the historical junctures relating to the entry of Spanish women into war zones were, in any case, more unstable in the areas of "savage Indians" than in the populated centers, or those defined by their high cultures, such as Meso-America, and the central Andean region.

In fact, the mobility of Indian hunters and gatherers greatly prolonged the special and chronological extent of the frontier period. Given this condition of instability with regard to conquests as well as to Spanish settlements and colonies, the presence of Spanish women was very precarious; in contrast, instability greatly prolonged—for several generations—the exclusive sexual relation of Spaniards with Indian women, at the same time that this relation was distinguished by its high rate of promiscuity, or rather by the multiplicity of Indian women who participated in the process of miscegenation on a large scale. That miscegenation would come to include many Indian women and few Spanish men among its antecedent progenitors, such that in this phase, on the Indian side, cultural Hispanicization was largely avoided, while a significant part of the new generations appeared biologically mixed.

Thus, in addition, although the Indians had the worst of it in the clashes of war because of their inferior military technology and their lesser cultural strength, they were nonetheless sufficiently active to disrupt the settlements and foundations of the Spanish in their territories. At the least they were capable of creating enough instability to disrupt the settlement of Spanish women.

In a certain sense, nothing could less favor the settlement of Spanish women than the frontier wars, especially because a major part of the forces of conquest who appeared in Spanish expeditions consisted of young men, or *mancebos* in the language of the time. They had scarcely contracted matrimonial agreements in the homeland and thus represented a human contingent of bachelors with a sexual hunger that, under the social conditions prevailing on the frontier, led them to excess and multiple coupling with Indian women, not only because the latter were more accessible and available, but also because that situation allowed a smaller number of moral commitments.

In reality, the frontier was the most favorable opportunity [for men] to exercise in its midst the unbridled satisfaction of their sexual impulses, which, conversely, they were obliged to repress and control when dealing with Spanish women; it was precisely in relation to the latter that the context for social control was regained, and with it the authority of the moral system was reestablished, a system that was diminished, in contrast, when dealing with Indian women.

For these reasons, only a few Spanish women dared to endure the risk of accompanying their husbands on the campaigns. And only a few of the husbands dared to have them along under conditions of constant alarm and danger. The danger of losing them through violence or sickness was accompanied by a dramatic reality, that of the war, which not only prevented the concentration of attention on family life, but also fostered confusion in individual adaptive strategies, to the degree of producing shades of ambiguity of moral behavior.

To this extent, because of their more dramatic moral significance in sexual matters, Spanish women stayed away from these first competitive experiences, at least to the degree that their presence in a frontier context could create uncontrollable factors of instability and confrontation. The social aggressiveness that might be directed toward Spanish women was reduced by eliminating them from the first episodes, and to a certain extent it was obviated precisely through their replacements, the Indian women.

In fact, not even the ensuing colonies or settlements that might follow military victories were stable. And it is also true that the expansion of personal freedom acquired during these experiences—of moral indifference and loss of the social controls that govern sexual behavior—could not easily be renounced by those so-called mancebos and older military personnel who, with their freedom of personal action, found decisive rewards, such as feeling more like their own masters when they were with Indian women than when they were with Spanish women, mostly because with the former they achieved the satisfaction of acting with a greater degree of individual choice.

Basically, moral confusion benefited or favored the satisfaction of impulses, and in this case the Spanish woman represented—in the understanding of Spanish political and ecclesiastical authorities—the continuity of the moral system, that is, of the institutions that repressed the expression of the rationalized instinct, such as that of the greatest moral danger: the sexual. At that time in Spain this moral danger occupied the center of social concerns, and in that sense the Spanish woman perfectly symbolized moral good through the institution of marriage and the Christian family.

The moral integrity of this latter context was threatened in dramatic fashion by the mixing of Spanish women among the forces of conquest. Thus, although we have seen examples of the attachment of such women, it is a fact that their presence in this first phase was really very infrequent.

In addition, there are reports that make us suspect the presence of Spanish women of ill repute in some frontier locales. Even a military tradition emerges in this sense throughout the years up to relatively recent times, such as when, already in the independence period in Argentina, during the rule of General Rosas, the latter ordered women engaged in prostitution in Buenos Aires to be sent out to the troops fighting the Indians where *estancias*[1] had been established, and there were not enough of them for his men (MacCann 1962, 533). This indicates that there was a scarcity of European women in the frontier areas, and their lack constituted another obstacle to the objective of securing European or Spanish settlement in periods following the fact of Spanish conquest.

It is also true that the Spanish authorities thought in very strict terms on moral matters, to the extreme of denying passage to the Indies to women who lacked good personal conduct and favorable ecclesiastical recommendations. Nevertheless, as indicated by Céspedes (1971, 394–95), already in 1526 there are reports that houses of prostitution existed in America. Still, it is obvious that, on the basis of the facility of Spanish men to accept Indian, black, and mulatto women, these houses of prostitution would offer the services of white and light-skinned mestizo women. And it is quite probable, furthermore, that the houses attracted above all those Spaniards whose social rank obliged them to maintain a public appearance and who therefore could not risk losing their exemplary positions of power through moral scandal.

→   →   →

As long as the minimal conditions of personal safety did not exist, the social integration of Spanish women did not occur in great numbers, and therefore, only a very few of them could be present in the frontier regions. From this viewpoint, only in the Antilles and soon in those regions that would become New Spain and the Viceroyalty of Peru, precisely in its Inca territory, were there opportunities to found settlements with the participation of women, who were incorporated gradually and somewhat slowly. Although we have reports of rapid settlement with Spanish women in regions such as Panama, Colombia, and Venezuela, nevertheless these also succumbed easily to Indian attacks, disease, economic failures, and the often overpowering harshness of the climate; at times, especially, the disintegration of some settlements was due to the very emotional instability of its Spanish settlers, anxious to get rich quickly and further spurred in this purpose by reports that in other areas there were ample opportunities to find abundant and accelerated pursuits.

The conquistadors dreamed of the notion of gentry, and sought to support this image with the wealth of great property. Gold and pearls were the principal incentives, to the extent that they allowed a rapid accumulation of wealth that would assure an early return to the personal enjoyment of the honors of fame and status on the Iberian Peninsula. Under such conditions the most stable settlements were those that consolidated the conquistadors in the status of a great seigniorial estate, and on it many Indians and servants capable of creating the ostentation necessary to maintain the rank that had been achieved. The encomienda was one such institution because it responded to these objectives. But when the property conferred limited the possibilities of achieving that status that fantasy had nourished, then the news that arrived about discoveries of gold, mines of every type, pearls, and more abundant lands where it was easier to achieve these aims became a factor of discontent with what one had, and soon what had been obtained was abandoned in favor of another conquest thought to be more advantageous.

Many Spaniards consumed their lives in such attempts, and in the process civil forms, especially the institutions of marriage and the family in the Spanish style, often had to be sacrificed by the Spanish themselves. The restlessness of the Spaniard of the time was prolonged on the enormous and extensive frontier of the "savage" Indians. This frontier had a greater depth and extension than the very one established by the Spanish, of both sexes. And certainly this frontier did not keep the Spanish from continuing to be attracted to the sexual freedom of the Indian women, who thus inspired the development of their own.

Before Spanish women could be placed in America it was indispensable to assure conditions of sufficient safety for them, not only in military terms but also in the way of economic stability and of social resources. And thus, even those nonmilitary personnel who exercised civil functions and who, nonetheless, barely represented security, tended to prolong the delay in admitting Spanish women because they themselves had acquired, in the process of their personal rootlessness, the emotional restlessness of the environment of the Indies. Only in those cases where Spanish society had been reproduced—Hispaniola and Cuba, especially in the early days—by means of basic political, social, and economic institutions, could one truly speak of an emotional stability capable of being transmitted to those newly arriving in an America dramatized by institutional disarray and by social disorganization. They arrived, to be sure, as conquistadors or as settlers, but in any case as transplants, or, if you will, as immigrants.

Without a situation of institutions previously established in the form of the society of origin reproduced in American territory, it was very difficult to achieve an environment sufficiently controlled to absorb Spanish women, who were considered to be an efficient factor with regard to achieving the emotional and social stability of a settlement. Without prior stability in the institutional system, the woman would become a factor of social drama, and even dissolution, because in the moral chain of the Spanish system she was a very delicate agent of equilibrium. Actually, this equilibrium could be achieved by transferring complete families from the home country, but in the case of distributing only men—which was the first historical reality of the discoveries and conquests—racial mixing was also the first great result of the absence of Spanish women.

In 1494, Columbus (Columbus 1958, 171) recognized these conditions of provisionality deriving from the absence of Spanish women in the Antilles, especially in the case of Hispaniola, when those who were employed in trades were in the same situation as the conquistadors. Columbus wrote thus in one of his letters:

> Inasmuch as some officials who came here, such as masons and other craftsmen, who are married and have their wives there (Spain) and wanted what was owed to them in salary to be given there to their wives or to the persons to whom they might send their earnings, so that they might purchase the things needed here.

That is, not even those who were not among the forces of conquest had brought their wives and families, precisely because Spanish society had not yet been reproduced in America and thus was in no condition to assure the resources necessary for social stability. Human disorder was the predominant trait of the era, and within that disorder the emotional instability of the individuals engaged in the drama of the conquests was inevitable—an instability that in sexual matters was resolved with Indian women.

In spite of the political plans of the Crown and the moral argument of the church, the Spanish woman remained outside of these first realities because, along with the church, she constituted a great part of the most strategic moral reserve of settlement. Without both of these factors, Spanish settlement would have become profoundly Indianized, not only in the biological sense of racial mixing, but in the cultural sense and in the personality structure of its subjects, precisely because Indian society had absorbed the infant members of these unions through the Indian mother, without the corresponding families and domestic customs of the Spanish. The arrival of Spanish women did not really stop biological mixing, but it did diminish cultural mixing in the context of the new societies, because it established them on a system with the same bases as those of every society: marriage and the family, and the corresponding political and economic, educational, and bureaucratic institutions, which made it possible to reinforce the Spanish way of life from cradle to grave as a model.

It is well known, thus, that the Spanish woman was destined to form part, especially, of American settlements; therefore the policy was to avoid exposing her to the rigor of the conquest itself. Everything that occurred during the latter was a matter of Spanish soldiers and Indian warriors. When America opened the door to Spanish civil life there were few places left where generations of mestizos had not been born.

Gradually, the social disarray of the conquest, the personal mobility of the conquistadors, and their emotional instability bathed in the liquid vortex of action, gave way to a civil society, organized and conventional according to the Spanish peninsular model, and in the latter the Spanish woman began the history of criollo generations.

But before that, every conquered "savage" place remained in a state more of truce than of absolute victory. Unlike the Antilles, Meso-America, and the central Andes, the rest of the continent took more than a century to become culturally Hispanic from the viewpoint of real control. The families who founded the first villas in these savage regions felt the Indian harassment constantly, to the point of being forced out of many settlements. Although many of these villas were rebuilt, others were abandoned totally because available resources were not always sufficient.

In such cases, Spanish women also constituted booty for the Indians, as the Indian women were for the Spanish. The frontier context meant precisely this: insecurity, especially for the least competitive and most dependent of its individuals: women and children. It was common, in such circumstances, after a battle, for the victors to take the women of the defeated side, and thus it was inevitable that when the Indians destroyed a Spanish settlement, Spanish women were taken as prisoners or slaves. Fernández de Oviedo (1959, 5:22), when he mentioned the events of the conquest of New Granada, said the following: "(The Indians), as soon as they had killed the Christians, went and burned the town, and took certain Spanish women, of whom, up to now, as we are at the end of the year fifteen hundred forty-five, nothing is known of their fate."

The Indians were never totally subjected to the Spanish as long as they maintained their separate political integrity, that is, with their own organization and institutions. Even when the Spanish were stably situated everywhere through the permanent colonies and were strengthening them with the formation of new villas, security was still far from complete, because these villas could scarcely defend themselves alone against the Indians when they attacked with tenacity and cut off the Spanish from the assistance that they might receive from their political centers.

The difficulty of conquering these Indian groups, who based their lives on subsistence economies and who were politically polycentric, caused many defensive disasters for the Spanish. In many cases, the Indians' facility of movement over vast and hostile territories made it practically impossible to subject and control them. Seldom could the Spanish muster as many forces as could the Indians, and although the Indian casualty rate was higher than the Spanish one, some significant losses could mean defeat for the victor in the next battle, especially when reinforcements were not available, as was often the case.

These conditions lasted a long time, particularly in the northern regions: northern Mexico, and in the Atacama [Desert] in South America, as well as in the jungle and interior regions of Central America and the interior of the Atlantic coast of South America. In this sense, there were many Spanish military expeditions that never returned to their bases of departure because their fighting forces had been decimated, or even wiped out, along with their Indian auxiliaries and servants. Take, for example, the expedition made into the territory of New Granada by Captain Francisco Becerra, in which, in 1515, his 150 Spanish troops met their death (Fr. Pedro Simón 1961, 100). And there were likewise many native groups who perished through the same process.

The numbers of Spanish military losses in these episodes of conquest were enormous, since in some instances they represented the entire expeditionary force. Such losses depended on many factors, among them, a direct clash with a vastly superior Indian force; climatic hardships; hunger, thirst, and exhaustion; tactical surprises, military unpreparedness, and calamity en route; and even internal dissension. The squandering of human lives was quite frequent among the Spanish, even when compared to that of the Indians, in terms of the percentage of military or warrior individuals engaged in combat.

Thus, as an example, Fernández de Oviedo (1959, 2:315, 316, 327) points out that of the six hundred men who embarked in 1527 with Narváez for the conquest of Florida, a total of only some one hundred fifty escaped with their lives. The author states: "and the majority of them (died) of disease and hunger."

Fernández de Oviedo would add elsewhere (ibid., 358) with reference to the lesser Antilles, that "for each one who may have returned to Castilla with money, a hundred have left their hides here, and some have even been buried at sea and offered as food to the fishes and sea animals, or left unburied as fodder for birds and wild animals, or devoured by cannibal Indians or dragons and crocodiles."

Likewise, with reference to an expedition that had ended in disaster, that of Pedro de Mendoza to the Río de la Plata, this chronicler (ibid., 2:364) writes the following about a total of two thousand individuals:

> (Of) these soldiers and civilians, after they were in Sevilla incurring expenses and going into debt waiting for the undertaking of the voyage to their destination, when Don Pedro (de Mendoza) returned with these two ships, nearly three out of every four had died, some at the hands of the Indians and most of the rest of hunger, cold, and various diseases . . . such that one thousand three hundred fifty perished in that land and province of the Río de la Plata.

On another occasion, Fernández de Oviedo (ibid., 3:135−42) has also written: "[N]ow these Spaniards (1504, in Castilla de Oro) were weak and sick from the lack of provisions and because the land did not suit them, and the waters, airs, and the region where they were, all these things were very different from those of Spain and dangerous to their health. And thus many of them died there in the space of the eighteen months that they remained there."

Reporting on an expedition made into Costa Rica, the aforementioned chronicler (ibid., 3:360) writes that "of eighty or more men, only seven Christians survived." And he adds (ibid., 3:396) that "here in these our Indies, of a thousand who arrive, not a hundred, or even fifty, return to their homelands, and sometimes, out of thirty, not one survived."

Additionally, in New Granada, of an expedition of six hundred men (ibid., 3:84) who set out from Santa María, "only a hundred seventy remained." And regarding the expedition led to the same region by Hierónimo Lebrón (ibid., 3:97), Fernández de Oviedo tells us that, "of the one hundred fifty which Hierónimo Lebrón took along, he said, eighty lost their lives." Furthermore, in commenting on a military revolt, Fernández de Oviedo (ibid., 3:202) states that "of all the mutineers, who totaled over a hundred, only eight men survived."

In the conquest of Mexico something similar probably took place, because in the words of Bernal Díaz (Diaz del Castillo 1955, 672):

> of five hundred fifty soldiers who went with Cortés from the island of Cuba, of all of them as of this year of fifteen hundred sixty eight, there are alive among us in all New Spain . . . but five, because the rest died in the wars, . . . and others died their deaths. . . . Those of Narváez numbered thirteen hundred, and only ten or eleven are alive, because all the rest died in the wars and as sacrifices. . . . And of those who set out with Garay . . . who would total some twelve hundred soldiers, the bulk of them were sacrificed to idols in the province of Pánuco. . . . Of all these I have recounted now, there are five of us followers of Cortés still alive, and we are very old and racked with illnesses.

With Pizarro, something similar happened when, in the words of Fernández de Oviedo (ibid., 5:35), in 1529, of the "possibly three hundred men which Pizarro brought from Castilla, he lost there (in Peru) in just a few days one third of his people or more." And later, then during the conquest of Peru, in 1533 (ibid., 5:115) Pizarro "lost one hundred fifty Spaniards and ten women, and almost nine hundred men and women Indian servants and slaves whom they brought in their service."

By our count, and even leaving for another occasion the analysis of the specific conditions under which each of these Spanish conquests took place, we calculate that on the average, by the victorious end of the campaign, which brought colonization and political dominance over the territory in dispute, a little more than a tenth of the members of each original expedition survived to die a natural death.

Under such circumstances, one must think that it was very difficult to risk including Spanish women in the expeditions of conquest. Where it was done it would involve expeditions where the presence of these women is not clearly explained, but which we attribute to prior ignorance of specific hardships of the enterprise, in one instance, and to the assumption of a possible positive role, in another, relating to the care and tending of a force of men on campaign.

In this ceaseless combat, Spanish women could not play an advance military and colonizing role, and thus they largely remained behind in reserve waiting to be called to do so in the cities particularly, and in the encomiendas and land grants received by their husbands as reward for their personal contribution. Apparently, however, these encomiendas were the cause of constant friction with the Indians because of the suffering that stemmed from their social position of subjugation, enslavement, and humiliation within the system. In frontier areas, the continuity of these encomiendas was in constant crisis, because the Indians were ready to return to war before they would become subject in servitude without the compensation of personal realization and status. In those areas where the natives had not been concentrated into communities by the missionaries and where they were not free to serve in encomiendas of any type, the "savage" Indians tended to flee such duties. To do so, they took refuge in places beyond the immediate reach of Spanish control, or they simply joined the forces that continued fighting the latter.

The conquest of Chile, one of the longest and most difficult due to the great number of natives there as well as to the bellicose nature of the Araucanian tribes, constitutes an example of how the encomienda in the frontier areas was unstable when it was not preceded by an intensive acculturation controlled by Spanish society itself, or as long as no solid urban center capable of attracting the natives to this socioeconomic structure was founded. Actually, the so-called "savage" Indians were neither profitable nor secure, because in the face of Spanish ambition to get rich quickly, they easily responded by fleeing and swelling the ranks of those who continued fighting.

With reference to those exceptional cases of Spanish women attached to a military force in a frontier context, a contemporary witness, Mariño de Lobera, wrote in the following manner about the general tone of behavior of the first Spanish to arrive in Chile, immediately following the achievement of one of the often precarious military victories over the Indians. Lobera says in this regard (1960, 275) that "the (Spanish) women enjoyed so many privileges that one who . . . in her own land would be a home servant, alone wanted thirty Indian women servants to do her washing and sewing, as if for a princess."

Under these conditions, if there were many Indians, few of them lived peacefully in the region (ibid.). As a consequence, the state of war continued and thus hindered the stable entry of Spanish women. The double pressure, the Spanish and the Indians at war, held back the day when these women were to establish themselves in the shifting frontier territories. Paradoxically, the harder the Spanish strove to find quick fortunes, the stronger became the Indian resistance mobilized to prevent it, particularly because the pressure to subject them to the economic customs of the conquistadors conflicted with the local or tribal traditions of the Indians' everyday social organization of labor; otherwise subjugation of the Indians meant forcing their physical efforts without having, in exchange, a corresponding prior identification with Spanish culture and with its habits of stratification.

In fact, the labor relationship that was attempted affected Indian populations of hunters and gatherers, and those with extensive agriculture and a relatively sedentary existence, with their labor disciplines and rhythms that were different and less rigid than the Spanish ways in the season of their practice. Thus, the Indians resisted these new situations because they altered the traditional order of their ecological adaptation, to the point of threatening to destroy their very integrity. At heart, this native resistance was characteristic of a population displaced from its territory by an alien one which, in addition, was attempting to employ it for its own ends by means of forced, uncontracted labor. In fact, moreover, the relationship was unequal or imbalanced not only because it held the natives in social inferiority, but also because neither politically nor ethnically did the latter recognize the Spanish presumption to decide the fate of the Indians.

In another sense, resistance could be felt as the expression of the Indian consciousness that all subjection as a labor force for the Spanish also implied their social exploitation in the form of servitude and slavery, and, in many cases, of physical abuse when the efforts demanded exceeded normal physical capacities. This combination of circumstances contributed largely to prolonging frontier conditions that inhibited or frustrated, as the case may be, civil settlements. Even some of the latter could be considered more as normalized camps, exhibiting both a military and civilian society, than as definitive settlements.

The ones who really introduced a civil character into these settlements were the merchants and farmers, more than the conquistadors. Thus, in those places where the conquest no longer was threatened with defeat by the Indian question, great numbers of traders appeared, thirsting for profit. In Panamá and Cartagena, for example, where this mercantile ideology penetrated quickly by means of men who traded cloth and acquired precious metals and pearls, or who simply sold their wares for money, this trade was impersonal and rapidly negotiated, but it involved the participation of Spanish women because a great deal of it was based on the supply of and demand for items of domestic use that were rarely the object of masculine demand.

In reality, this trade in domestic articles now indicated the presence of Spanish families living in a civilian style, and in that sense it responded to an urban reality and to a retreat of the frontier. It is also true that some regions, especially the tropics, featured difficult climates for Spanish women if there were no preexisting household comforts and ecological conditioning. From this viewpoint, many of the settlements that had been established on the basis of strategic military criteria or of mining would disappear rather easily when faced with demands of the adaptations required by the progress of conquests in the interior, or simply because the mining operations might cease. Here, Spanish women found no suitable place to settle with their husbands because, moreover, the latter kept up a constant mobility unconducive to the sedentary social role that was expected of the majority of those women. So it happened that it was the men who faced these adversities and continuous mobilizations created by the tactics of the conquest itself.

The situation with regard to the early disproportion between Spanish men and women during the first years is corroborated by other historians, among them Morales (1974, 123) when he states that on his third voyage Columbus could have sailed with thirty Spanish women for whom he had received authorization. The same thing occurred in 1509 with the arrival of other women for the purpose of contracting marriage right away with the men of the conquest living in the Antilles. From this point, in some of the expeditions made to the mainland, Spanish women began to be included, but always in very small numbers and under very uncertain security. With the news of stable settlements with attractive conditions—business and property, as well as political, administrative, and military positions on the part of their husbands—these women hastened to take their place in the social structure of the colony.

These situations seem to be confirmed by abundant documentation. The majority of them correspond to migrations that included large numbers of men attracted by word of lucrative business and news of gold and silver mines, as well as about the great possibilities of personal advancement by means of land grants being offered to them. These settlers tried to establish themselves as near as possible to urbanized areas, and there, with the appearance of merchandise, traders, manufacturers, cattle raisers, and farmers, Spanish women found their most acceptable milieu.

The Indies historian Pedro Simón reports these facts for the year 1534 (1961, 81–82). With reference to Cartagena (New Granada), describing this city's commercial importance, he mentions the immigration of great numbers of Spanish of both sexes, who in these years already felt the attraction of economic claims. This immigration was taking place at the same time that more expeditions were being prepared to reinforce the conquests already made and to expand them through the development of new ones. Elsewhere, in some areas, white women were somewhat late in making their appearance. Apparently, white women first appeared in Brazil in 1538, when some Portuguese couples arrived. Some young girls also came around 1551 and soon married other white men (Pérez de Barradas 1976, 154). It is during these periods when a society built on the principle of racial classes begins to emerge. Although this society was very soon complicated by the existence of a broad kaleidoscope of racial mixtures in various shades, the predominant tendency, once Spanish women began to arrive in large contingents, would be to make the latter into symbols of racial preference and of reproduction of a Spanish way of life. Without these women, it would have been difficult to achieve cultural continuity in the generations of the time and their descendants: the criollos.

→   →   →

Under the protection of these situations, what were opportune events arising fortuitously in the very process of the conquests were insufficient to prevent the existence or emergence of others aimed at promoting Spanish settlements, independent of the policy of political and religious attention that was being established simultaneously for the Indians. The reproduction of Spanish life was politically as important as the conversion of the Indian to Christianity.

In a large sense, there was a great initial period of difficult and prolonged conquests that led inevitably to racial mixing on a grand scale, but that, nevertheless, did not assure the implantation of Spanish culture from its own bases, that is, from the family and through homogeneous marriages between Spaniards. While the scarcity of Spanish women continued, the sexual strategies and unions of Spanish men were based on a relationship with Indian women, and gradually began to alternate with the Spanish women as the latter reached American territory and rejoined their husbands or married the Spaniards who preferred them. In any case, when these Spanish women came to America on regular voyages and in sufficient numbers, mestizo interests had already been created and legitimized, and in large measure they already represented an option recognized and, in some cases, even preferred by the Spanish. Mulatto women particularly came to signify for many of those men a greater degree of personal freedom, preferred especially by those who also lacked the economic means to provide comfort to the now very demanding Spanish women.

Accordingly, and independent of esthetic preferences, the Spanish pursued riches, and until those riches came they required a certain mobility that did not involve formal familial obligations. In this context, the woman was very demanding and had become an agent of economic pressure that not all men were in position to satisfy. In a certain way, Spanish women were expensive and demanded security. The other racial stocks were less demanding and accommodated better to the personal strategies of the Spanish men who had not triumphed or who simply remained restless and needed a leeway in their personal actions impossible for them to maintain in the context of marriage to Spanish women.

For the most part, those who had gone as young men to the conquest and had survived were united with Indian women, and their psychological and social capacity to live in marriage in the Spanish style—with its demands of conjugal fidelity and sedentary residence—was greatly weakened. Additionally, many of them were men now accustomed to their Indian women and to the freedom that the latter offered them, and in many cases it was now difficult to renounce the affection they received from the Indian women and their children.

In fact, the prestige of the Spanish woman raised her ceiling of aspiration to a higher level than could be achieved by many of the Spanish who had spent a long time in the Indies without a triumph there. Except for the case of those already married who welcomed their wives and children as part of their formal responsibilities for aid and cohabitation, there were many Spaniards in the Indies who rejected Spanish women and remained with the Indians, even when they had not contracted a legal marriage to them.

Of course, these circumstances created a large number of conflicts between individuals and with Spanish civil and ecclesiastical authorities themselves, because the objectives of the latter appeared in frequent contradiction to the freedom of action that many Spaniards had assumed for themselves. Furthermore, if [Spanish] women demanded security, and were anxious to be served by as many Indian women as possible for the purpose of grandeur and nobility, it is obvious that this option could not always be fulfilled by men who lacked a patrimony to offer them.

In such circumstances, unions with Indian women increased enormously, moreover on a polygynous scale and form, and in many cases they provoked serious conflicts with the Indians upon their seeing their women carried off by the Spanish. In this sense, on Hispaniola, present-day Santo Domingo, in 1512, not only did the Spanish marry women of their own racial stock, but, due to the scarcity of Spanish women, the Spanish had spread the use of concubinage with Indian women. This was provoking conflicts with native men, since, aside from those cases that ended in marriage, especially with female *caciques* who offered dowries, the majority of Spanish men practiced an informal polygyny that alarmed church authorities and the leading citizens of Spanish society who already formed what we call the first moral controls of the Spanish system: the families of peninsular Spaniards and bureaucratic administration. Furthermore, for the purpose of promoting the biological reproduction of Spaniards in America, and of their way of living, the authorities even allowed the importation of white Moorish slave women, who immediately married those Spaniards who still remained single (Pérez de Barradas 1976, 90).

The development of the process that led to the migration of Spanish women to America was thus governed by the prior stabilization of the conquests; through the latter, Spanish settlements extended and grew, and government officials appeared, along with their wives, both of them having come directly from Castilla. By way of textual reference to one of these functionaries, the accountant Albarnoz, according to Bernal Díaz (Diaz del Castillo 1955, 610) it was said "that the latter had recently returned from Castilla, and he came back married to a lady named Doña Catalina de Loaisa."

It is in this phase that the true Hispanicization of the American continent begins. The development of this policy of Hispanicization by means of native Spanish women began to emerge as civil functions were stabilized. In this sense Hispaniola was the jumping-off point for these household creations. Fernández de Oviedo (1959, 1:88–89) provides evidence of this when he says:

And with the viceroy's lady came some duennas and noble maidens, and all or most of them, who were young, got married in this city and on the island to leading citizens and rich men among those who were living here; because, truly there was a serious lack of such women from Castilla, and although some Christians were marrying prominent Indian women, there were many others who would never take them in marriage because of their limitations and their ugliness. And thus, with these women who came from Castilla, this city was greatly ennobled, and today from them and from those who married them, there are children and grandchildren, and they are still the greatest and noblest asset which this city possesses, because of these marriages as well as because other hidalgos[2] and leading citizens have brought their wives from Spain.

When the city of Mexico had been conquered and the Mexican Empire largely subjugated to the arms of Cortés, the immigration movement of Spanish women began. In the words of Bernal Díaz (Diaz del Castillo 1955, 450) it was noted as follows:

and so it was that when Sandoval was gathering knowledge of the population of that villa and declaring other provinces to be at peace, he received letters relating how a ship had entered the port of Ayagualulco, which is a port, though not a good one . . . and in it from the island of Cuba came Señora Doña Catalina Juárez "La Marcaida,"[3] for such was her nickname, who was the wife of Cortés, and she was brought by a brother . . . and there was another wife, her sister, along with Villegas of Mexico and his wife, "La Zambrana," and their children, and even the grandmother, and many other married women, and it even seems to me that Elvira López "La Larga," at that time the wife of Juan de Palma, came then.

It is clear that where Spanish society was constituted, the migration of women from Spain began. But in any case, the early presence of these women did not greatly alter their disproportionate numbers with respect to the men. Thus, it is said (Pérez de Barradas 1976, 156) that in Chile in 1583, that is, almost one hundred years after the Columbian discovery, there were fifty Spanish women and three hundred mestizo women among a thousand Spanish men, whereas for each native male there were five native women.

As these settlements developed and political and economic security grew in them, Spanish women arrived in increasing numbers. But in order for this to occur with a certain regularity, it was necessary to have available a rear guard of some depth in which the greater sedentariness of the women might permit the development of domestic life and, within it, the socialization of cultural and personal forms urged by the Crown and the church.

The special effort by many Spanish men to elude the moral seduction of marriage and to prefer, in their case, the freedom of their sexual unions, was hard to maintain in the face of the social pressures brought by the citizenry and those who, because of their public status as leaders responsible for the common good, appeared more subject to the political and institutional control of Catholic morality. Finally, it was common for Spanish men to succumb to the pressures of the moral environment, and many of them made their marriages at advanced ages or under conditions of combat weariness that impelled them to seek tranquillity for their reckless lives.

Thus, it was not only single women who married those Spaniards who desired to have them; there are numerous examples of Spanish widows who salvaged these restless and unstable conquistadors for marriage, to the extent that these women represented, above all, stability and cultured reproduction of their own lifestyle and personality. A mention by Fernández de Oviedo (1959, 2:435) is quite explicit in this regard when, referring to a personality of the time on the island of Hispaniola, he says:

After Governor Hierónimo Dortal was released from prison, acknowledging the insults of this world, weary of contending and laboring in vain, and desirous of better employing what remained of his life in the service of God, he determined to marry. And because his intention was good, God thus provided him good company with a widowed duenna, who was honest, virtuous, and of a compatible age, and who ate well; and her estate was worth four *cuentos de maravedíes*.[4]

Urbanization thus implied not only stability, but also a greater presence of Spanish women. In an example provided by Sanchiz Ochoa (1976, 76) we are informed that in the *Cabildo* of Guatemala,[5] when Spanish men petitioned in 1539 for a postponement of the royal stipulation that in order to obtain land grants one must be married and settled in the country, they made the argument that there were few Spanish women to marry. This provides confirmation of their scarcity. Although later, already well into the Spanish period, this lack had been remedied to the point where the women began to outnumber the men, nevertheless the numerical superiority of women did not occur until the mid-sixteenth century, and in many places still later.

Certainly, after the Greater Antilles were secured, and from the moment when they became the launching platform for expeditions to the mainland, it was easy to obtain permission to bring married women, and soon complete families, so that they might settle definitely in the stabilized regions. The historian of the Indies, Pedro Simón, tells us (1961, 52) about pacts made in 1532 for conquests and settlements to be carried out in New Granada. Included in them were combatants and some of their wives. They were headed for Cartagena de Indias, an important port at the time for the landing of stores, articles, and provisions destined for the consumption of the new settlements. In any case, the present island of Santo Domingo played an important role as an entrepot between the Iberian Peninsula and the mainland, as Cuba became for Mexico and the present southwestern United States.

The arrival of these Spanish women could even create enthusiasm among the Spanish settlers who awaited them, precisely because with them they could live in the Spanish style and because, by this fact, the stability of their triumph was confirmed. But above all, the arrival of Spanish women meant the symbolic restoration of the umbilical cord that might join them again to the mother country. In a certain sense, their arrival came to signify an act of infantile regression or of reencounter with their interrupted origins. To this degree, many Spaniards returned to their mothers through their wives, and by means of the marriage ceremony they acquired the profound shelter of another symbolic Spanish woman, that of the powerful Catholic Church, the total mother of her children. When both symbols combined in the Spanish woman, the men had their rite both profane—sexual and social domestic life—and religious—her very moral transcendence, and if the Spanish woman represented these it was because she also had the capacity to protect them by means of her power of seduction, in this case a power of prestige imbued with the strength of cultural nostalgia.

In itself this capacity was not exclusively attributable to her condition as a woman, but it also referred to the cultural fact of being, as a Spanish woman, the symbolic nucleus of longing for a faraway abandoned home. In this sense, to prefer Spanish women was tantamount to returning home, to feeling subjectively like a child, and therefore protected from the very moment of recuperating this relationship of infantile dependency achieved in childhood. The return to Spanish women, after the first and prolonged multiple experiences with Indian women, was like a symbolic return to the lost homeland, now retrieved through marriage to a Spanish woman. In fact, it came to signify an act of moral restitution to the forgotten mother.

This profound cultural identity felt through the woman is also confirmed through the proliferation of different versions of the Virgin Mary throughout the conquests and even at their conclusion. That proliferation would come to signify an expression of the need for indulgence sought by those who, in their role as conquistadors, had transgressed the moral order, a need, furthermore, recognized within the context of the total mother, likewise in transcendent symbols. In fact, the Spanish woman was symbolically reinforced in her moral position from the moment she had ceased to be a decisive material protagonist in the conquests; but of greatest thrust is the fact that what made her desirable among Spanish men was the symbolic importance of her capacity to create in them the feeling of recovering in America the lost home of Spain.

Whatever perspective we may adopt, there are numerous reports regarding the arrival of married women called by their husbands, and at that time their minor-aged children would usually accompany them, as the law required. Later on, at a time when Spanish populations descended from the conquistadors had grown, and it had become common, furthermore, that a certain percentage of that population would live in poverty and die without leaving a dowry to their daughters, it was most usual for the latter to enter convents (Sanchiz Ochoa, 1976, 76) in order to escape the lack of economic protection and paternal care.

Also symbolically, this situation of vulnerability that was attributed to the woman without father or husband in the midst of a family of weak social standing—and in a society of strongly aggressive men, such as the Spanish—would be the counterpart of what we have established as cultural nostalgia and infantile regression, in the case of those men who awaited the arrival of Spanish women in order to recover the lost home. This counterpart would consist of the expectation of the protective role of the father over the daughter. In a certain sense, this expectation would come to mean that while the man might regress toward infancy through the mother-wife, at the same time, he regained his adult personality by protecting his daughters from their social debility. That is, as long as the latter did not attain the moral retribution of marrying an adult man moralized through institutions, the father played the provisional role of protector of prohibited women until the moment that they might have legitimate possessions. At that point he sublimated his relationship to them and acquired, in the context of his society, a dimension of moral legitimacy which, on the other hand, he quickly lost outside of his group when prohibited women were not involved. In fact, here it would involve the sublimation of a guilty conscience in the memory and precedent of his own impulses and tendencies.

In this context, a moral inversion took place psychologically, consisting of the restoration, in the course of his position as a married man and father, of the moral force that he was losing, on the other hand, in his position as a single or free man. If in this latter experience he turned to the woman in order to reconcile himself with his culture, in the former he protected the woman in order to reconcile himself psychologically with his feelings of guilt about himself, that is, with his conscience.

The dynamic of these relationships would therefore consist, on the one hand, of desiring a return to the psychological security lost during the experimental course of uprooting, and on the other, a reconciliation with the culture, through a union with a Spanish woman felt as the recovery of the home, and through the moral protection provided to the woman as daughter in acts—seclusion in convents and the repression of sexual freedoms—that gave recognition, in this behavior of the father, to the predatory role of men in situations of moral uprooting.

From this perspective, the seclusion in convents of the daughter of poor Spaniards allows us to consider the relative abundance of Spaniards at the time indicated by Sanchiz, but it also serves to signify that this asset—the Spanish woman—had not only become scarce, but also was a source of anxiety and prestige for the male. In fact, his moral position appeared always sublimated, since he was a source of conflict and ethical dissolution. The Spanish woman thus had very quickly come to represent a moral value of restitution of the depleted wellsprings of culture and an instrumental mediator in the psychological recovery of lost security.

Although this is an issue that deserves more discussion, since it involves transcendent cultural categories along with other aesthetic and pragmatic ones relating to the identity and symbols of the latter, it is also true that if the problem had a political and religious aspect, so did it have an aesthetic and psychological one. The return to the lost system of security would be, in this case, part of the personal solution for many Spaniards. It is also improbable for men steeped in pure action to possess a complete consciousness of the fundamental problem of their lives, but the mediations represented by the

Spanish woman would constitute projections of the anxiousness of the conquerors and of many colonists to attempt to regain control of their own personalities in the midst of moral confusion and disorder, turning to the symbolic regression of the return to the Spanish woman.

The establishment of conditions of moral protection for Spanish women on the part of political and ecclesiastical institutions represented a metacultural component of the act of settlement. It had as its object to reinforce structural foundations of the new Hispanic society by guiding the latter to its Christian moral bases, and to those values of social integration par excellence, that is, to the family, subject at that time to a prolonged transition, specific in any case to the uprooting of populations—native and Spanish—in concrete circumstances of adaptive transformation and crisis. In essence, the model of the family that moral protection sought to restore was the Spanish peninsular one, with its strong moral control. Its reproduction implied that, at least at the outset, both sexes would be native Spaniards, so as to provide coherent cultural ingredients capable of being offered in exemplary fashion to the native and mestizo populations. This was largely achieved by instituting settlements of rural landowners and bringing in contingents of married officials and skilled workers with their immediate kin, who, because of their social adhesion, were able to form the nucleus for Spanish cultural reproduction in this initial phase of Hispanic America.

Social control collapsed easily in the course of the adaptive pragmatism that the conquistadors attempted, but from the viewpoint of the Spanish culture of origin it was morally very rigid due to the vigilance exercised by ecclesiastical institutions over sexual behavior. In its rigidity, the exercise of this extreme moral control must be attributed to the constant interference of missionaries and the clergy in the civil and military matters of Spanish behavior with regard to the Indians. On occasion, quarrels and conflicts emerged between the two groups, and the stance of moral condemnation that the missionaries often took toward the behavior of Spanish men is well known.

In this particular, missionary censures were harsh and constant, and they made an impact on even the most gregarious Spaniards, driving them to serious and worrisome feelings of hostility toward those missionaries. This hostility is easily seen in various communications sent to Crown authorities by one and another. In one of them, for example, the conquistador Melchor Bravo de Saravia, in a letter sent from Chile to the king in 1569, says (Medina 1956, 252–53) the following:

> The friars, mostly of the order of St. Francis, help us little. Not only do they say that we cannot make war on these Indians because of the bad treatment that has been given to them up to now, and that what we are doing to them is unjust, but

they neither wish to absolve the soldiers nor even hear their confessions. Your Majesty must see that if the soldier can expect no reward in this kingdom, and there is nothing in it to provide him, with what spirit and will would he act there? Thus, many of those who come prepared for war (instead) enter monasteries or flee into the forests.

The reference to the treatment given the Indians included the war against them as well as sexual conduct with regard to Indian women, while distortions of the Gospel dissolved the moral values of Christianity, in whose name the conquests of America were made. The critical attitude of the missionary fathers was of greater efficacy than was that of the regular clergy, but both in turn had become factors of social control who contributed to the pressure for the conquistadors to bring their wives from Spain as soon as possible, and with them to restore monogamy and set an example of Christian virtue, at that time impossible. The latter ended up being more a product of Indian naïveté than of pragmatic Hispanic reasoning on campaign; despite this fact, the woman was always closer than the man to the achievement of this objective because she was also more repressed, especially in matters of sexuality.

To this end, the church and, collectively, the monarchy turned to the Spanish woman as a means of moral reintegration of the man, who, involved in conquests and personal dissipation, scarcely concerned himself with reproducing the restrictive moral bases of his culture, in this sense distanced from their centers of social reference. The woman embodied a more conservative social character, and within the system she acted ideologically in alliance with the church and its clergy, because her very social capacity appeared to be linked to the realization of her person within the family in societal projection. In any case she acted in vicarious identification with the status position of the father or husband. In this sense, the Spanish woman constituted a subtle agent of control over the attempts—at times subconscious—of the conquistadors to escape the rigid legal systems that opposed the fulfillment of their impulses.

The Spanish woman was necessary in the stages following the military conquests, and her moral selection answered a concern of the Crown and of the church that was translated into the form of laws and practical measures conducive to reinforcing and implanting a system of culture. In this sense, it is clear that transgressions of the moralizing spirit did occur, but it is equally certain that the ethic of the system sought to implant a form of moral being capable of adapting to the codes of honor and respect most typical of the social character of the age, shared in ideal objectives by the conquistadors themselves. In a large sense, the woman was the repository of those ideals through the notion that in her person were symbolized the virtues of honesty and of moral control.

In moments of moral crisis and of frequent unleashing of impulses, which characterized this era of conquest, the incorporation of the woman symbolized the incorporation of a moral asset, the woman herself, which was scarce and which it was necessary to produce in the context of an anomic cohesion that broke down easily amidst the situational pragmatism of war. In this way, if control emanated from ecclesiastical vigilance, in matters of moral conservatism the woman constituted one of its most delicate balances to the extent that her absence affected the emotional stability of the male in his manifestations of personality. On this basis, the entry of Spanish women was not considered so much a just demand by their husbands and by bachelors who wished to marry them, as it was a means of constituting a master framework for the edification of a Spanish culture founded on a family model based on Christian principles and controls.

At any rate, the ones most disposed to receive their wives and children were the principal captains and conquistadors, precisely because they acted under a certain pressure to be exemplary, greater than that for their soldiers. Their links to power also obliged them to be stricter with themselves in matters of personal impulses; at the same time they assumed the obligation to share the more rigid ideals of that power. By contrast, the Spanish troops who made up the expeditions from the mother country, consisting of young, single men between the ages of twenty and thirty (Hernández Sanchez-Barba 1981, 2:185), and even the so-called mancebos of younger ages, easily escaped such obligations and surrendered to spontaneity, precisely because their personal advantages consisted in breaking with repressive traditional codes, and it was outside these where the stimuli were the most attractive. Furthermore, the greater proportion of contribution to racial mixing in genetic terms corresponded to these soldiers, particularly because they were the least committed to the moral status of power. A great part of their personal realization resided in the moral break with the symbols of power. And of course, this majority group was the one that elicited the greatest moral preoccupation among the authorities, especially the clergy, because, while [the soldiers] did serve a shared cause of Spanish political expansion, their uprooted condition and heightened gregariousness made them difficult subjects for the exercise of social disciplines that were not strictly military.

The fact that ecclesiastical control had perceived a dangerous deterioration in the moral life of many Spaniards—as the latter abandoned themselves to disordered social communication with Indian women—contributed decisively to legislation by the Crown and the Council of the Indies directed at facilitating the entry of Spanish women capable of reclaiming their husbands for family life. In reality, it is obvious that those who began as youths or bachelors in the campaigns of conquest—the majority—had no prospects for marriage and acted sexually in an unbridled manner. At the same time, many of these single men lacked a personal fortune and put off commitment that might bind them matrimonially, because they could offer no guarantee of stability nor did they even have a profitable agricultural property. Under these circumstances, the troops of many of these forces passed from one campaign to another without acquiring any patrimony, except for what they won from available booty after battle and which they were often forced to abandon on the occasion of rapid retreats.

In the frontier areas, this situation greatly prolonged the lack of control over the moral behavior of these groups of soldiers. Additionally, the lack of a reliable patrimony and the uncertainty regarding their own physical integrity caused the fundamental trait of their sexual behavior to assume the nature of a permanent adventure.

It is also doubtless that a portion of the conquistadors obtained landed estates and fixed patrimonies, and while these created the condition that enabled them to marry, nevertheless it was married men more than single ones who usually claimed their Spanish women. Even under these conditions of legal obligation, however, there were frequent cases of men who were still considered too poorly endowed economically to receive their own wives on a matrimonial basis, and because of that they delayed their claim.

Many of these personal stances following settlement and the receipt of territorial patrimony were the result of the long period of effective alienation caused by the prolonged separation that had distanced them from their wives, but in other cases the hesitation was due to the meager patrimony that they could offer at the outset to their Spanish families. Because Spanish women were more demanding in this sense than were the Indian women, the men tended to wait for more favorable opportunities to approach them. In fact, additionally, the adventurers' psychology and the very instability of the men's circumstances combined to contribute to this hesitancy.

The answer to these situations had to come from the Spanish authorities, to the extent that the latter, while they promoted colonization, also organized the political strategies of Hispanicization. As we have said, this featured two fundamental aspects: one, the Hispanicization of the Indian, and the other, the social spread of Spanish persons themselves throughout America as an indispensable political condition to assure their continuity. If in the first stage the royal political will consisted of conquering American lands, in the second stage the fundamental objective pursued the consolidation of those conquests by means of totally Spanish establishments. At the same time, through this means and through the missionary efforts, the native populations were Hispanicized.

This latter policy was assured by associating the Indians with the Spanish through the encomiendas and through their social connection with urban life or as domestic servants to Spanish families. This association was achieved by means of the so-called Reducciones de Indios, the decisive source of acculturation for the success of the aforesaid objective. In fact, in the *Recopilaciones*[6] of the Laws of the Indies the royal desire to bring spouses and their children together is clearly confirmed. This conjoining did not have a moral purpose alone; it also pursued the goal of settling Spanish populations capable of confirming by their presence the political sovereignty of the Spanish monarchy. The objective extended even to the idea of making that population militarily and politically self-sufficient, in the sense of providing them with a minimum demographic strength so that they might defend themselves against their various strategic enemies, that is, the English, French, Dutch, and Portuguese during a certain period.

These Spanish establishments or settlements, which brought conquistadors and peninsular civilians together in the same place in social activity, included a sizable native and black population employed in domestic service and as carriers and proletarian laborers. Although data and relative quantities in this regard are often lacking, they nevertheless surpassed the Spanish population itself in numbers. From a local point of view, they were also populations which, through their young women, contributed to racial mixing, because at that time there were abundant reports about more or less clandestine unions of Spanish men with women of other races—Indians, mulattoes, and mestizos—despite the scandals that they aroused in terms of public opinion.

In this context, many men attempted to evade the aforementioned laws because they had found other emotional and social ties in their life with the native women. This is seen in the provisions of Section 9 of the Law [of the Indies], where it acknowledges in certain Spaniards the desire to avoid their conjugal obligations to their first—Spanish—wives by declaring that the latter had died, in order to make it possible by this means to achieve recognition of their new unions in America, or simply to justify their current concubinage and irregular unions, especially with Indian women, but also with blacks and women of mixed blood.

Indian Women: Contexts and Situations

We have already indicated that one of the principal causes of the rapid process of racial mixing that took place in America was the slight numerical proportion of women who participated in the voyages, explorations, and conquests in relation to that of men. But this was not the sole cause. Another particularly dynamic one was the favorable attitude of the Spanish male toward Indian women, an attitude that the Spanish held in general toward other races, and of the Indian women toward the conquistadors.

In reality, the long-standing previous shared life of the Spanish with other races on peninsular soil had meant that they had a familiar knowledge of them, and of the habit of racial exchange. In this sense, the Islamic influence existent in Spain and the multiracial character of the populations that accompanied the Muslims on the Iberian Peninsula had produced a society that considered racial mixing to be normal.

At the time of the discovery of America, although politically Spain, and with it Europe, exhibited hostility toward Islam, its populations, especially those geographically closest to one another, included groups racially derived from mixing who lived amongst one another without aversion, except for religious reasons. But in any case, the long presence on the Iberian Peninsula of Islam had greatly mixed those populations where its political dominion was most stable.

If the Germanic groups that had arrived centuries before the Muslims had represented an important contribution to the racial composition of peninsular populations, and if during several centuries the Iberian Peninsula had been racially and culturally Germanized, the Arabs de-Germanized it in both senses, giving to it a syncretism both genetic and cultural.

At the moment of the conquest of America, the Spanish constituted European energy in expansion, integrated as well into the general discourse of the great Mediterranean civilizations. Racially, Spain combined in its constituent types the genetic infusion carried out there successively by other groups—Celts, Phoenicians, Carthaginians, Greeks, Romans, Visigoths, and Arabs—each of which represented in its historical moment a qualitative energy that entered selectively into the renewed Iberian populations. When the Spanish expanded into America, they were thus a mixture of Caucasian varieties with small admixtures of Negro—and even Mongoloid—genes, absorbed and even dissolved by the great Caucasian mass throughout the process of racial exchanges.

At this point, the Spain of the discovery of America represented an energy in constant expansion, reflected in the combative ambitions of its individuals and in their aspirations to status through their own personal restlessness and mobility. Spain then lived in a state of tension with itself and against a structure that constricted it. It contained an excess of action that it finally spread beyond its political boundaries by means of conquest and settlements. America was the historical receptacle that took in this social energy, an energy that did not achieve a universal expression until it emerged from itself and faced its possibilities in the very framework of action and the adaptive selection of its peoples in a historical framework which, being such and in the same fashion as its formative cycle, would have an initial tension, a vital peak, and a final distension coming from the discharge of its dialectical energies.

In fact, Spanish expansionism in America occurred at a historical moment when the racial base of the Iberian Peninsula was practically homogenized after its European generations had absorbed the different waves of Arabicized African individuals who had entered into its genetic structure throughout seven centuries of interaction. The very fact of Spain's own mestizo experience determined that its wide internal variety of racial contents and exchanges would become a decisive factor—with regard to women of other races—in the Spanish male's failure to turn to sexual scruples or to raise fundamental aesthetic considerations with respect to joining or living with women who were not of his own racial origin.

Indian Women

Indian women were no exception to this decidedly open attitude toward sexual exchange. From the moment of their landing in the Antilles, the Spanish felt attracted to Indian women; all the reports of the period lapse into recognizing the great sexual satisfaction that the Spanish enjoyed with Indian women. These women appeared naked before the eyes of men accustomed to a strong moral repression of sex, and eager, in this case, to take advantage of the opportunities that they found to receive women, Indian women, who did not resist them and who offered themselves freely and with pleasure to their demands.

Those qualities in women generally preferred by Spanish men and found in this case among the Indians seem to have referred to the whiteness of skin, to beauty, to ages between fifteen and twenty years, and to the amorous sensuality of their ways. Although in their preferences the Spanish chose light-skinned Indian women (López de Gómara 1946, 178) over other, dark-skinned ones, nevertheless, the sexual attraction that these women exercised made the question of color irrelevant. In this respect, aware of this preference, López de Gómara (ibid.), admiring the whiteness of skin of the women of the Lucayan Islands [Bahamas], commented: "The people of these islands are whiter and more attractive than those of Cuba and Haiti, especially the women, for whose beauty many men from the mainland, such as Florida, Chicora, and Yucatán, went there to live. . . . And from there I believe came the story that in that part there were Amazons and a fountain that restored youth to old men."

Some experiences on campaign seemed to corroborate the presence of white women in the Indies, at least with regard to the various reports given by informants who, in their commentaries on the qualities of the Indian women, insisted on the point that some of them were comparatively whiter of skin than others. According to this, the consideration made by the Spanish that some Indian women were to them as white as Spanish women has been recorded by the chroniclers. One of them, Fray Pedro de Aguado (1963, 1: 540) noted in his narrative on Venezuela that:

> When this village was sacked . . . among other items taken there were four Indian females of tender age and startling whiteness, because did their dress and speech not give them away, they would be taken for Spanish. When asked whether those white women were of some other stock near to this village they said no, but that they had been brought up so white because they were kept indoors, and that since their birth, they had never been in the sun, and thus, like nocturnal animals, when they were taken out into the bright sunlight, they covered their eyes because they could not see.

Actually, there are abundant descriptions on this point in the sense of considering many of the Indian women to be beautiful, ardent, and amorous in general (cf. López de Gómara 1946, and Cieza de Leon 1962, 70, 145, 157, 217), qualities that were recognized in Indian women by most Spaniards of this first epoch and that, of course, constituted an indirect factor of political approach with the Indian, to the point of softening even the initial severity of their wartime relations through alliance. In this sense, with regard to

Andean women, Cieza de Leon (ibid., 144–45) said: "Some of the women are lovely and quite ardent in their sensuality and friendly to the Spanish. . . . And when some army of Spaniards passes through their province (Cañaris), they being obligated at that time to provide Indians to shoulder the loads of baggage of the Spanish, many of them gave their daughters and wives, while they remained in their homes." And with regard to the women of Cajamarca (Peru) Cieza de Leon adds (ibid., 217): "The women are amorous and some of them beautiful."

The attraction that the Spanish felt toward the Indian women caused a great deal of the hostility among Indian males toward them. Because of the informal and unrestricted polygyny practiced by the Spanish, Indian males saw their women carried off, and in such circumstances they felt deeply humiliated by such behavior. In the Antilles the situation became very critical, and thus did a bishop of Cuba describe it when he stated in a letter to the king (Pérez de Barradas 1976, 94) that the Spanish had taken over the Indian women, and that rare was the Indian who could have one for himself, even an old one. In his correspondence the bishop declared that "The Indians are dying out because the Spaniards, lacking (their) women, marry the Indian women. An Indian man who can get one eighty years old considers himself fortunate."

If under these circumstances large-scale racial mixing was inevitable, it is also clear that the removal of women from the Indians decreased their opportunities for genetic input with their own women; furthermore it also contributed to diminishing the population of their racial group. In the Antilles the removal of women was a further cause—and a decisive one as it pertains to the dialectic of racial reproduction—that contributed to diminishing the native group, on the one hand, and to absorbing it, on the other, into the mestizo products that resulted from the union of Indian women, first with the Spanish and later with the Africans, and even in a few cases with both.

In fact, in these circumstances racial mixing appears to us as a competitive phenomenon between Spanish and Indian men to possess Indian women. The competition was more unilateral with regard to the lone sexual object, the Indian woman, because the absent Spanish woman could not take part in this dialectical process. The initial form of the process of reproduction of the Spanish and of the Indians was racial mixing, and in that process the predominant sexual object was the Indian woman, who played the same role for African men in the early stages, especially because they did not have available women of their own racial group.

Precisely, a racial disproportion of this sort in which a woman, the Indian, became an object of sexual competition among men of different races had as its consequence an intensive racial mixing dominated genetically by the victorious group, in this case the Spanish. In this way, the mestizo solution was more preponderant the less was the participation of Spanish women and of Indian males in the context of these sexual relations. Although one of the constant concerns of the Spanish political and religious authorities was to populate America quickly with peninsular families, or at least to marry Spanish men into legal and therefore monogamous unions, certainly the dialectic of the conquest, and with it of sudden individual wealth, in fact dissolved the stability of the early settlements with Spanish families and promoted the individual solution on the land. That is, the dialectic incited the provisionality of settlements by prolonging the period of conquest and by making a frontier area of most of the American continent, with the exception of the Greater Antilles, Central America, and the central Andean region.

In this particular, the provisionality of the conquests in the regions of "savage" Indians prolonged the period of personal independence of Spanish men and made them accustomed to doing without their Spanish women, at the same time that it prolonged their dependence with respect to Indian women. Until they formed themselves into citizens' councils, and in them reestablished the moral controls of their society and culture of origin, the Spanish were individuals who acted as bachelors, who indulged in decidedly polygynous behavior with regard to Indian women. And thus, their competition with Indian men for possession of Indian women was resolved historically in the form of mixtures scarcely controlled by the factor of traditional morality.

In practice, and until the cabildos appeared as a political expression of Spanish community culture, multiple unions with Indian women—some sporadic and others relatively stable in their simultaneity—were the distinctive trait of the sexual behavior of the Spanish, first in the Antilles, then on the mainland.

On the basis of the selective nature of military recruitment and the need therein to rely on soldiers biologically capable of facing the difficulties of war, it is obvious that the Spanish men were at an age (between twenty and thirty years for most) that was the most appropriate for reproduction and at which men act most impulsively with regard to satisfaction of the sexual instinct. It is also clear that under these circumstances of selective age and vigor, the instinct was less demanding in matters of aesthetics than was the biological tendency itself. Nevertheless, aesthetic preference, if it was selective, still showed no reluctance towards unions with Indian women, as has been pointed out previously through the opinions of informants when they describe the women as beautiful and amorous, and even white in some regions.

This initial attraction to Indian women was reciprocated, as we are told that they frequently favored the Spanish. In the course of the conquests these relations increased, independent of the initially violent nature that they assumed as many Indian women were carried off by the Spanish. Nevertheless, it should be noted that this was also a general practice among American Indians, which meant that any group would steal the women traveling or living with another when they would surprise them on a raid, or, as victors, they would loot the enemy camp and with it their women.

Whatever the means of obtaining them, it is clear that Indian women pleased the Spanish, and not only did they join sexually with the latter in a more or less sporadic fashion, but lived with them in a context of spontaneous reproduction according to the native conjugal model. That model was a polygynous one to which the soldiers' tendencies adapted while in a wartime situation that also promoted the dissolution of their traditional model of monogamous marriage.

Fundamentally, if combat situations unleash sexual and moral instincts of a different type usually repressed by civilian society, it is also true that in the case of America this unleashing was morally justified in individual combatants (Spanish soldiers and Indian warriors) because it was carried out between different cultures; these individuals, therefore, did not owe one another the same degree of moral responsibility that, by contrast, they must maintain in the heart of those obligations recognized with respect to individuals of their own cultures.

It is obvious that the same social context creates more moral obligations within than outside itself. In its daily reality, the exercise of a culture is more rigid in its moral components within the society that contains it. Individually, the members of a culture feel more of a moral obligation among themselves than they do with respect to those of another culture. This stance of the relative responsibility of the individual ego as a function of culture must be applied to the context of the conditions of a frontier and of moral fluidity that characterize it, as was the case in America. There, moral disciplines were more concentrated on competitive strategies of war, and in war, more on military victory than on the maintenance of moral principles that might contradict or hinder the achievement of those objectives. In fact, and this is most important, the direction of impulses in this context corresponded more to adaptive strategies in a vital competition for survival than to strategies of a moral competition. The latter was reserved for the church and for the later reproduction of civil society through its early establishments in the form of cabildos. As long as that society was not reconstituted, sexual relations were governed virtually more by vital spontaneity and opportunism than by moral disciplines.

In this way, and according to Spanish legal customs, polygyny was rejected, yet this plural solution of an informal nature turned out to be a common experience of transition which, because of its very social weakness, was considered morally innocuous by the Spanish located in a frontier situation. The frontier had not only a military character but also a moral one. In this sense, if the military frontier was fluid and adaptive, the same was true of the moral frontier. In fact, an individual situated outside his sociocultural surroundings is disciplined only by means of the repressive violence of the moral codes of the other culture. Therefore, only a stable society can exercise these moral controls and prevent itself, through the loss of authority over its members, from accepting the predominance or independence of instincts with respect to culture.

In any case, when concubinage began to be persecuted by the law, it had long been tolerated. This toleration was happening while Spanish society was still seeking to impose the authority of its moral culture upon its members and associated peoples. As long as it failed to do so, the Spanish—placed in the context of the predominance of their individuality and of their distinctive ways of acting upon an open social terrain, culturally adaptive and free of moral commitments in the sexual realm—behaved in a polygynous manner.

In terms of a process, these unions between Indian women and Spanish men became normal, so that the question was not so much how many women individual Spanish men had simultaneously, but how many women established a union with them throughout their campaigns and journeys through different regions. If the camps were the haven of multiple unions of Spaniards with Indian women in their company, the raids and incursions that were practiced against enemy villages also inspired relations of this character, as did the periods of rest that were customary among allied nations. In each case the exchanges took place such that mestizos constituted the most frequent biological product in the context of the frontier. At the same time, political exchanges between the two groups, Spanish and Indian, were occasions for acculturation and of religious and political influence. In addition, the gifts that both sides gave for the sake of friendship constituted part of their political-military strategies, and in that, the gift of women was a symbol of alliance. In its situational breadth, the context of the frontier thus satisfied the pursuit of sexual freedom and promoted the taking of multiple women partners.

Thus understood, the daily struggle for survival led the Spanish to produce a situational morality; in it, the values of priority were basically military: they included the recompense of booty in the course of seeking the ultimate objective of victory, and with it the colonies, the stable settlement, and the reestablishment of the morality of the civil society that necessarily followed the implantation of Spanish culture and institutions in America.

Before stable domestic unions emerged with the Indian women, the sexual relations of the Spanish with them were of an opportunistic nature: the men responded to a spontaneous attraction, sometimes forcibly, if we keep in mind the violence of the context, but other times also felt by the women, and in each case responding to a biological impulse more than to a social function organized within moral commitments. Perhaps the Spanish could select one from among several women when they captured women in large numbers, or when they simply included them in their military companies as porters, servants, and concubines. In this last situation, they chose the youngest and those who answered the code of tastes expressed by the soldier according to the quality of affection that might be derived from those relations. Furthermore, there were the Indian women received from the native chiefs in the interest of alliance and the desire for kinship. In this case the women could receive special treatment, that is, they were afforded a certain deference, and they constituted part of the political obligations implicit in the commitment of military strategies.

In the historical period of their first contacts, these sexual unions between Spanish men and Indian women must be considered in the context of very diverse situations: (1) as the result of direct captures of Indian women by Spaniards on military campaigns; (2) as the result of gifts made by Indian caciques as a gesture of alliance with the Spanish; (3) as the result of attractions and direct consent between Spaniards and Indian women; and then, in a second stage of peace; (4) as the result of civilian life itself or of living together in marriage or in concubinage.

✦ ✦ ✦

Certainly, then, in military clashes the strategy did not consist solely of defeating the enemy, but also of assuring a permanent tenure of the conquered territories. The capture of Indian women and the collection of booty fulfilled part of those pragmatic objectives. Bernal Díaz (Diaz del Castillo 1955, 360) states that in 1521, in Tepoztlán, Mexico, "there were very good Indian women and plunder."

Furthermore, this soldier-chronicler also points out earlier (ibid., 125) how, in a march toward Tenochtitlán certain caciques delivered women to the service of the Spanish. And thus he says: "they brought four Indian women who were good at grinding bread . . . Cortés received them with a joyous disposition."

Fundamentally, the seizure of women constituted part of a triple strategy of conquest: (a) weaken enemy morale through disorganization and panic; (b) have manual labor available for service and portage on expeditions; and (c) satisfy the sexual demands of officers and soldiers.

The constant upsetting of native communities, the harassment implied by an expedition of conquest, and the relative frequency with which many tribes abandoned their lands and hid in the forests or jungles signified a great ecological mobility. In fact, the mobilizations of war against the conquistadors lost strength when the tribes dispersed and when their chiefs lost control over their subjects. Furthermore, in the strategy of capturing Indians an observer could discern a social disorganization of the adversary through the loss of demographic forces of young and highly reproductive ages, as well as a reinforcement, through transfer, of the military capacity of the conquistador forces.

In any case, this strategy not only appeared as part of the practical rationale for the conquest, but also proved to be inherent in the very adaptive conditions that characterized these wars.

Thus, from the discovery of each political territory, the tactics of war were becoming a function of the forces deployed and of the relative resistance that the latter offered to the enemy everywhere prisoners were taken; in many places villages were destroyed, and in others alliances were simply created between the combatants. Whatever the outcome, prior behavior was flexible, because if the objective was to occupy the land and establish Spanish dominion, the policy of war depended on the attitudes and responses of the adversary. In this sense, the above alternatives held a certain correspondence with the same real possibilities of conquest that were available on the terrain itself, and they further depended on the specific personalities of the conquistadors and Indian leaders.

The variables or alternatives were different, but in each case the military progress of a force of conquest assumed the incorporation of great numbers of porters and domestic servants. For example, the so-called Molina el Almagrista (1968, 62) said that during the war against Atahualpa, "there was a Spaniard who had two hundred Indian men and women in his service, . . . (and) no woman of attractive appearance was safe with her husband, because it was a miracle if she eluded the Spanish or their *yanaconas.*"[1]

The number of these porters and domestic servants depended on the importance of the booty to be transported and on the distance and difficulties that existed between the battle sites and military depots in the rear. In fact the number of porters engaged in the transport of booty corresponded more or less to the volume and weight of the resources collected from the conquered populations. The number was also a function of the physiological endurance that the Indian porters exhibited, because many of the expeditions were made under conditions that were hazardous to the physical integrity of their participants, both for the nature of the climates and relative altitudes and for the topography, since the expeditions endured very rapid changes as they went abruptly from a tropical coastal region to another one of harsh cold. Under such conditions, there were many human losses among the Spanish as well as the Indians, and often the casualties from disease, epidemics, accidents, hunger and extreme fatigue outnumbered those caused by battle.

On this basis, porters played a decisive role from the outset of the conquests, and if young men were needed, so were young women. In any case, an expedition of conquest represented a highly biological event that, of course, admitted no one of declining ages. For this reason, the bulk of the Indian men and women added to such an expedition were young people who often had to be replaced as they succumbed to the rigors of the march, or who simply fled, or who in other cases merely fell into the hands of the enemy according to the vicissitudes and outcome of each campaign.

This need to rely on permanent Indian service took on a great strategic importance to the Spanish, as it already had in fact among the Indians themselves. In this particular, the great pre-Columbian civilizations and the tribes in general also made their wars using great numbers of porters, or *tamemes,* and it was customary to consider them as part of the auxiliary formations. The fact that the Spanish made use of porters and domestic service by women did not therefore constitute a departure in this context, nor was it one in the context of strictly civilian life.

These porters and domestic servants were provided by Indian chiefs to the Spanish in acts of peace and alliance, as they also furnished them women in the same sense. In situations of war, some Spanish obtained this service by force, and thus we have abundant reports of the demand for these human resources. In some cases they were obtained by means of collaborative agreements; in others, merely by adding them forcibly to the expeditions. Throughout the length and breadth of the American continent, and from the Columbian discovery itself, this resource was a common necessity and its satisfaction became a habitual process within the very strategy of war. Let us look at some examples that confirm this tendency.

As we have stated, this was a practice common not only to the Spanish, but had almost a general character in the context of these wars. Referring to the conquest of Mexico, Fernández de Oviedo (1959, 2:123–24) relates the encounter with an Indian woman from Jamaica who had been captured by the Indians of Yucatán and was fleeing toward the Spanish. This woman said that the Indians "had taken her to make use of her, and since she had met the Christians, she had come after the caravels (of Captain Grijalva) because the people of that land treated her badly and she did not wish to be with them."

Truly, it is valid to state that the low status of the Indian woman meant that she became both a sexual object and an object of social trade available to both racial groups, Indian and Spanish, especially in this period of military campaigns. It is totally certain, furthermore, that Indian women could be captured as well as offered as a gift. On the mainland this practice was more common than in the Antilles, because since the political organization of these islands was founded on *cacicazgos* passed down to women, the women caciques made their own personal choices. The situation on the mainland, however, was different. As Bernal Díaz (Diaz del Castillo, 351) points out in the conquest of Mexico, "what (the soldier) most engaged in was seeking a good Indian woman and finding some spoils, and what they usually did was to accuse their allies (the Tlaxcalans) of being very cruel, in order to take Indian men and women from them to prevent them from being killed. . . . Sandoval returned with his whole army to Tezcuco [Texcoco] and with good spoils, generally with very good Indian women specimens."

In 1521, near the end of the campaign against Tenochtitlán, the Spanish had captured many Mexican women, who formed part of their social world to the extent that a new context had been created. Bernal Díaz (ibid., 427–28) expresses it in the following way:

And there were many (Mexican) chiefs in search of them (of women captured by the Spanish) from house to house, and they were so thorough that they found them, and there were many women who did not wish to go with their fathers, or mothers, or even husbands, but rather to stay with the soldiers with whom they lived, and others hid themselves, and others said they did not want to return to idolatry, and some of them were even pregnant (by the Spanish) and in this way they took away only three, who Cortés ordered expressly to be given back.

These situations were recreated all over America. Thus, in Venezuela, in New Granada, and in the campaigns of the Andean region, part of the booty consisted of Indian women. According to Fernández de Oviedo (1959, 5 : 43), for example, Pizarro took from Atahualpa "six hundred women and six hundred children to distribute among his military forces."

Everywhere, Indian women and youths capable of carrying provisions were captured by these expeditions, whereas in other cases and under a kind of alliance, it was the Indian caciques themselves who offered these servants. Thus a chieftain from Caxas (ibid., 5 : 40) delivered to Pizarro "two hundred women." Thus did soldiers everywhere repeat this process. In so doing, they not only satisfied their unbridled sexual desires but also replaced the losses suffered among their complement of servants.

The attachment of these women to the forces on campaign was done without regard to their origin, that is, by alliance or by capture, because their incorporation into these military forces became a custom. Thus was created a social category of women on campaign who, in a certain sense, would represent the antecedents of the modern *soldaderas*[2] who have accompanied the soldiers of many Spanish American armies.

The chronicler Santillán (1968, 137) made it clear that there were no exceptions to such behavior when, in referring to the native custom of offering women to their authorities as a sign of respect and obedience to them, or simply as exchange in a political relationship, he said:

> Thus did they offer women to the *inga* [Inca] and to the Sun; but they have given them in greater numbers to the Christians, or they have been taken by the latter, encomenderos as well as the other Spanish who live in the land; bachelors, in order to have them as concubines, and if they are married, as maidservants to their wives and sometimes as mistresses to themselves and to others. Negroes and mestizos and *anaconas*[3] are all ingas with regard to taking women . . . such that for each woman of the inga there are a thousand. Also some encomenderos had, and some still have today, their cloistered houses for women like those of the inga, under the best guard or security they could obtain, for satisfying their sensuality, of which they have taken great advantage. That custom is now disappearing as the encomenderos are ordered to marry.

The data on captured Indian women are certainly innumerable, and involve all the expeditions of conquest. In this sense, it happened that Indian women were kept as domestic servants to the Spanish especially to prepare meals, carry baggage, and attend to their washing and personal attentions; finally, they were bedmates or simply had become sexual objects at the discretion of the soldiers.

The capture of women by the soldiers and by the officers themselves not only served these ends but also became the means for negotiating peace with Indian adversaries, while the youngest were otherwise used as interpreters because of their facility for learning languages. In the Antilles, from the outset of the discovery, Columbus captured women for this purpose, and wrote (Columbus 1958, 60) "thus, if (the Spanish) have their women, (the Indians) will be willing to negotiate what I want from them, and also these women will teach our people much about their language."

The Indians tended to make peace more easily with the Spanish when their women were captured and held than when they were not. Bernal Díaz (Diaz del Castillo 1955, 551), in referring to one of the expeditions of the conquistador Hernán Cortés, says in this regard: "and once (the Indians) saw the struggle going badly and their women captured (a total of fifteen), they sent four old men, two of them priests of idol worship, who came very meekly to beseech Cortés to give them the captives."

Likewise in Florida, during the expedition of Hernando de Soto in 1539, the chronicler Fernández de Oviedo (1959, 2:159) says that one of its captains, Baltasar de Gallegos "took seventeen persons, among them an Indian woman, the daughter of the cacique, and this logically had to be the reason that her father agreed to peace."

Besides the importance of women's domestic work in the service of the conquistadors, it seems that the giving of women to the Spanish by the Indian caciques was an important means of pacification and a habitual practice in the context of the campaigns. In all the expeditions and conquests, both sides customarily took the women of their adversaries, but obviously the vast majority of the women captured were Indians.

In some Indian villages of Tabasco in 1519, the Cortés expedition received gifts from the caciques (Bernal Díaz del Castillo 1959, 75), and among other offerings there were women: "And all of this present was nothing in comparison with twenty women, among them a most excellent woman who was called Doña Marina, as she was named after becoming a Christian. . . . Cortés received that gift with joy."

In the year 1523, after the conquest of the city of Tenochtitlán, the reports on this point are also quite frequent. The same Bernal Díaz (ibid., 539) tells how on the campaigns in the south of Mexico, "(the Indians) gave to us what they had, and we brought back . . . ten Indian women whom they had as slaves."

But, at the same time that the need for women was solved through these exchanges with Indian caciques, there was also recourse to capture when exchanges were deemed insufficient. Again, Bernal Díaz (ibid., 462–63) tells us that in the same year of 1523 the soldiers of one of Cortés's captains, who was leading an expedition, "gathered into groups of fifteen and twenty and went about looting the villages and taking their women by force."

The forces of Alvarado also did the same in Quetzaltenango (ibid., 472) when it is said: "he always carried Indian men and women captives."

This predatory excess in the course of the war became a constant, especially when the soldiers acted on their own impulses and, under the often unfounded pretext of Indian aggressions, indulged in private raids. In fact, the more intelligent Spanish military commands preferred treaties and alliances, and occasionally, they punished the excesses of their men. With respect to some campaigns in southern Mexico, after the conquest of Tenochtitlán, Bernal Díaz (ibid., 466) states that " Sandoval sent word that from then on they were to capture only those involved in the death of Spaniards, and not women or children."

The example of Mexico can be generalized for the rest of the continent, because the same raiding was done in Panama, as Fernández de Oviedo testifies (1959, 2:219) when he says: "from some (Indians) they took their wives, from others, their daughters."

In the Florida campaign of Hernando de Soto in 1539 the same procedures were followed. Wherever de Soto created alliances with Indian groups, also included in the pact was the provision of women for his service. Fernández de Oviedo (1959, 2:170–73) mentions it as follows:

> and they gave (the Spanish) porters and twenty Indian women, and they were given in peace . . . and they went on to Tuasi, where they were given porters and . . . thirty-two Indian women . . . and there in Itaba they retrieved some women who were given (to the Spanish) in exchange for mirrors and knives. . . . On another day, the governor asked (the cacique of Tascaluza) for porters and a hundred women, and the cacique there gave him four hundred porters, and said that he would provide the rest, along with the women, in Mabila, the province of one of his chief subjects.

The double condition of the Indian women in this period, as servant and as sexual object, was given testimony by Fernández de Oviedo (ibid., 172) when he referred to the conquest of Florida. He points out in this respect that the harshness of the campaigns included not only the continual replacement of Indian porters—because of death or escape from service—but also of women. In the words of the chronicler, the situation was certainly a dramatic one, and he explains it as part of the vicissitudes that these expeditions faced, and through the direct testimony of witnesses he says:

> they took those Indian porters, or *tamemes,* in order to have more slaves or servants and so that they might carry the loads of their provisions and what they stole and what was given to them. Some of them died, and others fled or became exhausted, and thus it became necessary to replenish and take more. And they also wanted the women for their own use and for their unclean practices and sensuality, and had them baptized more out of lustfulness than to teach them the faith. And if they arrested the caciques and leaders it was better that way, so that their subjects might keep quiet and not interfere with their looting.

On this point, it is obvious that the strategy of capture or of gift through alliance was generalized and corresponded to a practice common throughout the continent. That practice alternated with tactical whim, because, while it was evident that the baggage trains of the Spanish armies consisted of Indians, the presence of women created a sexual attraction greater in intensity and multiplicity than under normal civilian circumstances. This involved very young soldiers the majority of whom, as the conquests were prolonged and the number of mature professional soldiers diminished, became ever more impetuous, youthful, and undisciplined. The reports about these soldiers reveal how easily they gave in to sexual excesses with Indian women. This multiplicity of women that the so-called mancebos received represented, from a biological point of view, the rapid racial mixing of the continent.

Of course, the giving of Indian women through agreements and alliances with Indian caciques and chiefs was a general practice from the very moment of the Columbian discovery, and it was confirmed and extended throughout the continent. In the Antilles and on the mainland, the daughters of Indian leaders were given to the Spanish commanders and captains, while those of lesser lineage were offered to the troops. The objective of the Indians was to tie their lineages to those of the Spanish, who had become the object of their admiration. Clearly, under such conditions racial mixing was not just a matter of capture, but also of alliance, of policy, and of the strategy of power.

In the group of the present-day Greater Antilles, while some men took mistresses or had casual unions or stable ones with the Indian women, others married them. Some did it just for sexual satisfaction, others out of love, and still others out of interest in acquiring the property of female caciques. In the city of Santo Domingo, for example, Fernández de Oviedo (ibid., 1:50) says: "A youth from Aragón, named Miguel Díaz . . . this Miguel Díaz became friends with a woman cacique, who was later called Catalina, and she had two children as time went by."

In an equally voluntary manner, from the outset of the Columbian discovery there were also free unions between Spaniards and Indian women. Again, Fernández de Oviedo (ibid., 20) tells us that on Hispaniola, "she (the woman cacique Anacaona) and the other women of this island, although they were good to the Indians and not so openly licentious, gave in to the Christians easily and did not deny them their persons. . . . I have said before that the women of this island were continent with the native men, but they gave in to Christians of quality."

These reports indicate that in the early phases the Indian women were very affectionate with the Spanish, and Columbus confirms this (Columbus 1958, 120) when he makes it clear that "in other places all the men had their women hidden from the Christians out of jealousy."

The formulas of Indo-Hispanic alliance, symbolized in the gift of Indian women to the conquistadors, were proclaimed to serve the political strategies of both groups. In Cempoala, Mexico, the so-called Cacique Gordo (Díaz del Castillo 1955, 105–6) had given the daughters of leaders to the Spanish captains of Cortés in 1519. The chronicler says the following:

They said to Cortés that since we were their friends, and they wanted to have us as brothers, it would be good for us to take their daughters to make children; and so as to further solidify our friendship they brought eight women, all daughters of caciques, and they gave one of the *cacicas* to Cortés, and she was the niece of the *cacique gordo,* and another to Alonso Hernández Puerto Carrero. . . . And when the *cacique gordo* presented them, he said to Cortés: Tecle (which in their language means señor), these seven women are for your captains, and this one, who is my niece, is for you, and she is mistress of villages and subjects. Cortés received her with a smiling face and told them he was in their debt.

Later, the same thing occurred in Tlaxcala, on the occasion of the treaty of alliance that Cortés made with the Tlaxcalans. As a result of this friendship, the Tlaxcalans offered Cortés (Fernández de Oviedo 1959, 4:215) women of position. "[T]o preserve the peace, they gave them many of their daughters, and because they wanted them as friends, they wanted the kinship and caste of such brave men in their land, because in addition to that, these Indians of Tascaltecle and others of Guajocinco were heavily at war with Montezuma."

Thus the transactions of Indian women did serve the military and political strategies of both groups, and in the specific case of Mexico they swelled the forces of conquest, because they added warriors who were enemies of the Mexicas to the army of the conquistadors. In addition, Montezuma himself presented women of his Tenochca nobility to the Spanish. Fernández de Oviedo (ibid., 4:219) writes: "And (Montezuma) told his interpreter to ask the captain (Cortés) if those Christians with him were his subjects or his slaves, because to each one he wished to make a present according to the rank or nature of each, and that (Cortés) tell him the truth, because such was the custom in that land when a foreign captain arrived . . . and he saw what the Spanish needed and soon supplied them with women for their service and for their beds."

And Bernal Díaz (Diaz del Castillo 1955, 217) describes that situation in his own terms, when he says that "we managed to find out that the many women who (Montezuma) had as friends, he would marry to his captains or leaders who were close to him, and he even gave them to our soldiers, and the one he gave to me was a mistress over the women, and it seemed well with her, whose name was Doña Francisca."

Later on, the system of alliance between conquistadors and the Mexican nobility was cemented when, in the words of the same Bernal Díaz (ibid., 647–48), "there came a certain Alonso de Grado; he married a daughter of Montezuma called doña Isabel. . . . And there came a Juan de Cuéllar, a good horseman; he first married a daughter of the lord of Tezcuco."

In other parts of America the same process was occurring: the Spanish were marrying Indian women to become part of noble lineages, linked with ancestries of native power. Some of the women were direct female caciques of villages, others were the daughters of native ruling groups. The examples abound, and some illustrate these penchants for alliance. Thus it is said (Fernández de Oviedo 1959, 1:223) that a "sister of the inga Amaro, a brother of the great prince Atabalipa . . . married a young Spaniard, skilled in both saddles . . . the son of Baptista Armero, and well known in the court of our lord, the emperor." And Molina el Almagrista relates (1968, 83) how a sister of the Inca Huayna Cápac "in the time of Licenciado Vaca de Castro was married to a Spanish resident." Other women married other conquistadors, and everywhere similar events occurred, such that very soon America became racially mixed by Spanish men and Indian women in different situations of encounter and confrontation.

The situations were quite diverse, and one cannot merely contemplate a single example because the context of the conquest offers us the restless and dramatic, the happy and tragic, the calculating along with the spontaneous, and in any case the extremely varied in its individual notes. Within these givens, the chroniclers gather widely diverse elements that make the process complex in its components. For this reason, the process of racial mixing must be seen as the experience of a great conflict and of a dynamic symbiosis in which cultural, political, social, and economic elements are mixed, along with attractions and rejections that have an apparent common basis in the easy sexual relationship of Spanish men with Indian women. In fact, from the beginning, the problem of the processes of racial mixing was not configured as a racial confrontation, but rather appears as a confrontation between customs and between ethnic, political, and social forces vying for the control of power. The competition for power constitutes the essential dynamic of the conquest and of the different resistance efforts made by the natives, since, fundamentally, individual achievement by means of domination was always the main incentive both of the conquest and of the resistance efforts made against it.

In fact, the initial cultural barriers were overcome rather quickly by means of the establishment of Spanish policies of Christianization and of social and economic organization. For this reason, and because of Spanish technological and strategic superiority, and because of the very variety of relations of the Spanish with Indian women and of the procedures adopted in the land, the trajectory followed by the process of racial mixing was also diverse in its situations. It included violence and force, mutual attraction and love, and marriages of convenience when the aim was to reap the advantages of uniting with women connected to indigenous political power; it included states of slavery and obligatory service, servitude, concubinage, freedom of choice, multiple unions, deep emotional dependencies, and feelings of solidarity and of attraction that led many Spaniards to renounce their Spanish wives at home and that, therefore, favored the creation of a new type of mestizo society in the Spanish style, that is, having as its guiding principle the cultural and structural master framework of the Spanish society being implanted.

The process of racial mixing was, therefore, extremely complex. At first, it corresponded to a period of social disorganization, with cultural transitions, and in any case with personal circumstances suffused with feelings of insecurity mixed with conditions of the camp and of mobility that embraced Spaniards and Indians of all classes. The predominant symbol was one of instability. Thus, the character of this early racial mixing must necessarily reflect the fact of social instability and the need for constant adaptation. Collectively, this features a context of transition that affects all the individuals involved in its discourse.

This process of racial mixing thus represents the history of an enormous cultural plurality constantly confused and challenged. Its axis of reorganization was basically social, in the sense that the plurality had the possibility of acquiring historical force only through the strategic components of social commitment and of mutual necessity converted into systems of dependency between Indians and Spaniards. This conversion resulted from the fact that many of the unions of Indian women with Spaniards also signified elements of social organization of the new societies, specifically through the Hispanic-Indian family in its various facets of matrimonial unions and concubinages. Since that time even these latter have constituted an institution into which relatively large numbers of men and women from those countries have entered.

Nevertheless, before a stable structural framework was established the process of conquest represented a social variable of great importance in the above-mentioned sense of the role played by Indian women in the American conversion of the Spanish forces of expansion. In this context we see not only wars, violence, and insults; we also see the experience of a process of historical resolution that includes problems of military competition between Indians and Spanish engaged, as well, in struggles for survival and for power. But it also includes situations of alliance and other specific cases where competition was replaced by mutual adaptation, in some instances, or by the simple domination by categories of social power, in others.

In each case, the racial mixing was intensive and the actual number of biological mestizos was far greater than that which could be recognized in the ethnic or racial identity attributed socially to the products of sporadic unions between Indian women and Spaniards. In fact, the social mestizos, or those recognized by Spanish societies, were always far less numerous than actual biological mestizos. In this sense, the contexts and situations favored the process of intensive racial mixing, precisely because the weakest element of the indigenous societies—the woman—was the most flexible and adaptive, that is, she was the more seductive and desirable part of those societies for the Spanish.

Under these conditions, there could be no doubt that, independent of the moral nature of those relations, racial mixing was favored by the labile situational nature of Spaniards and Indian women. In this regard, we must provide examples that strengthen our familiarity with those variable circumstances of the individual conquistadors and of their forces, as well as of the status conditions in which the Indian women appeared in relation to the Spanish during the long and intensive phase of racial mixing. The historical elements significant to this area of interpretation of the conquest period are abundant. We shall limit ourselves to the few elements we consider most expressive.

✦ ✦ ✦

In what we call a fortuitous or spontaneous relation, we find the cases of sexual unions occurring in the field or during opportune situations. Thus these unions include the women taken from the enemy on the battlefield as booty and distributed among the troops, if not among the officers themselves. To this effect, for example, in 1535 an *alguacil mayor*[4] of Cartagena de Indias was interrogated in Madrid by the Council of the Indies (Document 766, Friede 1955, Vol. 3) regarding reports received at court about mistreatment of the Indians, which had greatly displeased the Spanish queen. Regarding this particular of the accusations aimed at certain personages involved in the conquest of New Granada, the witness, Alfonso de Torres, stated:

> 3. Questioned on this third point, he said that he has seen Indians brought from the aforesaid province when the Christians were returning from war, and that they divided them among themselves, that the governor, the captains, and the people took their shares and sold them to merchants and to other persons who took them out of the territory, and that he had seen this happen many times.

Góngora Marmolejo (1960, 215) also tells how in Chile this distribution was made by the troops selling to one another the women captured in battle. His testimony is the following: "they sold the women and the children they had taken, and the soldiers gambled among each other."

Many of these soldiers adopted the habit of capturing women, and they did so during the periods of rest on campaign as well as on the very site of battle. López de Gómara (1946, 196) writes that in the Antilles a cacique with several wives had his jewels and his women stolen. The version he gives is the following: "they took from (the cacique), according to some accounts, a great quantity of gold and women by force and came to Comagre."

In its formidable harshness, the conquest of Chile had resulted in both sides treating their adversary's women as booty at their disposal. This freedom to capture the enemy's women for one's self made the Spanish camps into places where great numbers of captive women were concentrated, and the same took place in the enemy camp. In this sense, Mariño de Lobera (1960, 520) states that in one of the Spanish camps, specifically the one where the camp commander and soldiers newly arrived from Spain were camped, there were weeks in which sixty births took place among the Indian women companions. He reports this fact as follows: "just in the place where the soldiers recently arrived from Spain were lodged, along with the others under the camp commander, there were weeks when sixty of the women who were in their service, though not in the service of God, gave birth, as the facts show, and thus were the Indians justifiably irritated."

These were sexually avid soldiers who, aside from the battles in which they fought with courage, swept the field of enemy formations; they seized everything they could when they made their surprise attacks in search of Indian boys and women, taking some of the latter for their personal service, whereas the youngest were given to wives who wished to make them into house servants, acculturating and Christianizing them in some cases. Mariño de Lobera (ibid., 527) refers to these events in the following manner:

> they captured them as slaves for the soldiers and for other worse things that they do when they have some women in their tents. And in this, to this day, there are great abuses, with gangs of soldiers going out to sweep the land, straying from Heaven with the crimes they commit, seizing handfuls of Indians to sell the boys and present the girls to many housewives of their acquaintance; and thus everything is in turmoil, each one living as he pleases.

After the battles, in their customs of victory, these soldiers showed a first preference for the most charming women who were closest to the white color of their own Spanish women, and they would select those with the lightest skin. Nevertheless, after their first impression of the Spaniards' sexual frenzy, some of the women who featured precisely this type of coloring seem to have tried to hide their light appearance by blackening themselves with paints and making themselves up to look unattractive to their Spanish captors (Morales 1974, 81). Thus, we cannot always assume that the Indian women felt universally gratified at the prospect of being treated as prisoners of war. The attraction did not come from the violence of their fate as captives but appeared linked to situations arising later; that is, it emerged in the context of the relations of alliance, or also in situations of interpersonal relations based on the inherent prestige of the victors, or of hospitality, or finally, of mutual desire and voluntary union. Thus, the situations were as diverse as were the contexts involved in a dialectic of conquest.

These were realities not only arising from war in its most brutal, tumultuous aspect, but on the basis of the resentment that had accumulated between the two sides, each participant reserved for himself a special license by which he acquired the persons and property of his adversary at his discretion when he made their capture. As for what this practice meant in military terms, the prevailing morality was relativist with regard to the treatment given to the enemy; that is, there was a lack of rigid moral commitments, except those that arose as the consequence of pacts and of political alliances.

On this point, we must make a certain digression with regard to how the informal as well as simultaneous polygyny of the Spanish with the Indian women—which gave rise to intensive racial mixing—responded to a situational morality that not only satisfied instinctual desires, but also took form as part of a profound and more or less conscious objective of reproduction of one's own self and of the same collective group present in the systems of alliance and in the need to give origin to a way of living in the Spanish style and culture.

From the viewpoint of transcendent political culture, it is obvious that after military victory a stable settlement of Spaniards was intended, as well as the most rapid conversion possible of the Indians to the Catholic religion. It is also obvious that the circumstances of war imposed certain restrictions on these objectives such that, rather than promoting Caucasian racial reproduction, they really favored the process of racial mixing.

Racial mixture was no longer just an incidental product resulting from the lack or insufficient presence of Spanish women; it responded as well to another element: to a truly dramatic situation in which sexual desire formed part of an instinctive yearning for genetic investment and for reproduction of the man through the woman. Furthermore, the vicarious symbolic power of the predominant status was assumed by the male in the union of the Spaniard with the Indian woman. Also vicariously, the latter made the descendants that she had with Spanish men more Spanish than Indian, especially to the degree that they remained with their parents, even though the context was in the transitory and unstable behavior of the camps or of posts that were certainly provisional because of the onslaught of the Indians against them.

The moral requisite as a prior condition of individual behavior remained a secondary concern in light of these circumstances. The predominant mode was, as we have said, characteristic of situational morality, on the one hand, and of a morality of ethnic, biological, and cultural reproduction, on the other, independent of the formal characteristics that civil social control might have adopted.

If every transitional situation in the historical sense includes certain processes and experiences, among them a crisis of values in individual behavior, it is obvious that the American transition of Spanish and Indian ways made relative the moral centers of each side in their sexual behavior, especially at the point where it became an anxiety to reproduce the self, and through the latter, one's own culture and ethnic identity.

Couched in the perspective of Spanish consciousness of the historic reproduction of their own ways, sharpened by the dramatic unfolding of an existence besieged every day by uncertainty, certain reports of the period, in this instance from the late sixteenth century (1589), prove illustrative. One witness, Ordóñez de Ceballos (1947, 131–32), instructs us about these anxieties and about the decisive nature that the possession of women could have in the actual context of the physical continuity of the group. Here is one version of the theme:

> Pedro de Lomelín went ashore and brought back a mulatto who, upon arriving aboard the ship, knelt and kissed my hands and feet more than a hundred times and told me the following story in a few words, as they had it by tradition through their parents, and it was that years ago a Spanish ship landed at that island and broke apart; they settled there and, since they had no women, they went out and took them from the people of the country. . . . They probably had more than three hundred Indian women of the country, because, as they multiplied, they had all the women they could obtain.

This text, in its extreme simplicity, reflects on the Spanish side a profound vital philosophy created by the desperation imposed upon the person in the most dramatic extremes through the experience of survival in the strictest sense of reproduction. This arises in a group, in this case the Spanish, that not only fought to survive, but also struggled to give to its life a more complete configuration by attempting to prolong it in its descendants.

In the report of Ordóñez de Ceballos, the attempt to obtain women to satisfy mere sexual appetites was important, but in the context of a profound historical manifestation of their existence, these Spanish had reproduced themselves not only in their descendants, but also in their social culture, since, as our testimony from the period relates: "one of the Spanish was a viceroy and two were perpetual *alcaldes ordinarios*[5] and captains." That is, in the isolation to which they were subject they had reestablished the nature of their society of origin—its social structure—to the degree in which the latter was affirmed by certain principles of stratification, which, on the other hand, appeared as a reality possible only through the fact that "it had been forty years since one hundred sixty persons had arrived there, and just one woman one hundred years old was still alive; and the descendants of all must have amounted to three hundred fifty, almost all of them males."

It is evident that present in this report are all the previously mentioned components of a historical as well as a biological consciousness in individual reproduction by means of genetic investment in descendants and also in the reproduction of cultural forms through the reappearance of the same principles of stratification and authority of the social system of origin.

In these solutions, and in the nature of the sensual tendencies of the Spanish toward Indian women, not only is there expression of an impulse to gratify a certain unsuppressed sexual appetite, but also, appearing latent in them, there is an urgent anxiety for self reproduction that, in order to manifest itself totally, had to break with civil morality and adopt situational morality; in this instance, that morality served—in addition to the particular individual—the very objectives of reproduction of his own group in its most dynamic expression, that is, in the biological and cultural dimensions. The fact that Spanish women were minimally represented in this process thus implies the development of a period of transitory dissolution—especially on the part of the Spanish—of the bonds of moral responsibility in sex, in order thus to give priority to the impulses of their pure biological reproduction. This would be independent of the moral appeals that might be raised in opposition—and that in fact appear in the condemnations of ecclesiastics and missionaries—to the expression of their most instinctive tendencies.

We cannot doubt the existence of a powerful historical consciousness among the Spanish who lived the American experience in its most dramatic expressions. Adapting to the varied ecological, cultural, and ethnic milieu of America was a test often rewarded with the violent death of its protagonists, Indian and Spanish, and less often of the Africans who accompanied the latter's expeditions. The context was necessarily a violent one in the dialectical process that followed the discovery, because the military solution was imposed as the instrument for European, and specifically Spanish, settlement.

As the conquests were extended in effort and in time, the struggle for space also became a struggle for survival and for reproduction of the group as the means of guaranteeing it. In one of its most eloquent points, and in the inevitable sequel of its dialectical violence expressing the nature of transcendent urgency attributed to the possession of women as the means of giving continuity to their own lineages, the dialogue held during the conquest of Chile between the Spanish Captain Bernal and one of the principal Indian chiefs, Colo Colo, transmitted by Mariño de Lobera (1960, 435), proves characteristic and achieves a dramatic air of epic grandeur. In their totality, language and text contain an extraordinarily clear meaning with regard to confirming the urgent sense of reproduction and continuity to which we refer at this moment. Mariño de Lobera writes as follows:

Then Captain Bernal, betraying no altered expression at such disastrous news (defeat by the Indians), replied to the Indian (Colo Colo) that he already knew about the death of all the Spanish in the realm, but those that were there were sufficient to preserve Spanish ancestry throughout it, conserving and spreading it with greater increase and restoring to advantage what was lost. The Indian then said: But what women do you have to carry forward your generation, because in the fort there are none? To this the Spanish captain replied: It does not matter, because if we lack Spanish women, we have yours, with whom we will have children who may be your masters! So great was the Indian's shame upon hearing this word that, hurling the lance and the head that was on its tip against the wall, he hung his own head and went away perplexed at such a reply.

The profoundly dramatic background to this dialogue places us in an ideological dimension where the protagonists seem to burst with ethnic pride. But here the context we wish to emphasize is that one which makes explicit reference to the open desire to reproduce one's own lineage. Thus, this desire appears to us as a definite form of historical consciousness that, in order not to be dissolved in the innocuousness of the absolute present, claims for the protagonist—the Spanish captain and his troops—the right of disposition that allows him to include Indian women as means of reproduction of generations of Spanish combatants.

Here there is a clear willingness to affiliate genealogically with the Spanish the mestizos from Indian women and Spanish men because in the latters' mentality the affiliation of their children and the recognition of their status appeared linked to the express will of their paternal ancestry, especially in this case, when the woman, being an Indian, was of a different ethnic condition from that of the Spaniard.

In the insolent arrogance shown by the Spanish captain and by the Indian chief, characteristic of soldiers and warriors determined to establish their complete dominion over the foe, a deep passion for one's own lineage is declared, and within it the unmistakable desire to prolong it through descendants by way of paternal recognition. Within this framework of personal strategies, the moral system of the Spanish captain maintains the aggressiveness of one who struggles to survive and reiterates in his announcement to Colo Colo the intent to make Indian women the mothers of the future Spanish of America. Racial mixing thus would be a form of reproduction of the Spanish way, and the morality inherent in these multiple experiences with Indians had a great deal to do with this genealogical ideology when the Spanish kept the Indian women who had their children, as well as incorporating the latter—identified with their objectives—at an early age into their militias of conquest.

In this way, the sexual morality imposed in multiple unions had a double nature: on the one hand, a fortuitous one, with no more transcendence than the mere satisfaction of the instinctive desire, and on the other, a genealogical foundation in its expression of historical consciousness of self-extension through reproduction, just as the Spanish captain said. Thus, here we may consider the genealogical ideology as an anxiety for reproduction in individuals who, as in the example of this captain, transcend the self in their descendants, imparting to them their mystical ideals of immortality.

In the total context we are considering, certain qualities of proof predominate, and the genealogical aspect appears as one of the principal attitudes among the Spanish. And in this respect, the outstanding requisites of worthiness in the validation of the individual are the deed and with it the supreme qualities of honor and reputation achieved within one's own group, independent of those demonstrated by his adversaries. As to the adversaries, there is interest in their material strengths and weaknesses and in their strategies of combat because in matters of values the balance of judgment is ethnocentric.

→   →   →

The nature of dramatic survival implicit in the struggles for conquest and in the stubborn resistance of many native tribes made value systems relative and made individual behavior dependent on specific situations. Thus, the energy of each resistance was answered with a corresponding energy of survival. And in each case, the moral system of the civil society was vulnerable because in the reality of each campaign personal virtues were understood as qualities that should relate solely to victory over the enemy.

The personal privilege that emanated from a victory constituted a sort of universal right to dispose of the property of the vanquished, and even of his person. This is a general experience in the practice of war that we can see in every era, and America was no exception. Thus, women came into this context in a special way; that is, to the degree that they were not combatants—and many of them were—they were treated as the spoils of the victors, whether the latter were Spanish or Indian. Because of the scarcity of Spanish women at this time, Indian women obviously became a significant part of the enemy's property.

Apart from the Indian men and adolescents who formed a part of the different expeditions, the transporting of Indian women had a rapid effect with reference to racial mixing and to the growth of the mestizo as a population incorporated among the Spanish and, to a lesser degree, among the Indians. If the capture of women was a habitual practice in wars among the Indians, and if from these came interethnic mixtures, nevertheless, in a strictly racial sense, and on an intensive and simultaneous continental scale, these mestizo products appear in relation to the Spanish expeditions; furthermore, the racially mixed offspring soon became tri-racial, with the incorporation of the Africans, there being few or no women from this group during the first stage of conquest and pacification.

Logically, in these conditions of struggle for survival, the extension of moral values was limited in its application to one's own group, by which its limits of control became very flexible when dealing with the adversary, and also when the very uncertainty and precariousness of his life caused the individual at risk to become fatalistic and paradoxically urgent in his appetites. In this sense, we have clear and constant references to disastrous expeditions in which all or most of the participants died, and we are familiar with the suffering and hardships that were experienced in the form of starvation, disease, and unhealed wounds.

This context seems to us imbued with early enthusiasm for conquest and with status anxiety. It is also full of aggressive individuals psychologically equipped and driven by the urge for quick riches. But in fact, these goals were barely achieved by a very few out of the many who ran the risk to attain them. Along the way, some adopted the pragmatism of situational morality and adapted their early zeal and personal toughness to a sort of compromise, that of remaining soldiers even after their victories. This made them relativists in moral matters dealing with sexual behavior based on situations of survival; and whereas they reserved for themselves a final mystical will, in the meantime they also infused with sexual sensuality what was denied to them in pleasure by their total existential environment.

This relativism occurred not so much because the ethical principles of each culture—the Spanish and the Indian—might be different, but because the military confrontation between both contenders imposed upon individual existence the pragmatism of survival values. In their unfolding and in the limitless expansion of their adaptive resources, these values dissolved the respective centers of individual self-control as applied to the most instinctive yet most contradictory concerns: the reproduction of life through sex and the destruction of life because of the threat of losing it. Furthermore, the immediate objective of military victory itself relegated to lower levels any other consideration of a civil nature that might impede it. In this sense, it is clear that the decrease of the adversary's property implied the increase of one's own and, according to the amount of booty seized, reinforced awareness of the value of greater personal achievement in one's aggressive struggle.

The dialectic of this process centers on the fact that seizing goods from an enemy diminishes his competitive capacity and at the same time weakens by repetition his confidence in his own strengths. In this context, seizing women from the enemy meant not only enjoying them sexually but also denying them to the adversary and thus preventing his own reproduction, as is pointed out in the dialogue of the Spaniard with the Indian. In another sense, the fact that the woman is a physical asset of a moral character, transcendent in the genealogical context of a strong historical consciousness on the part of the man, led also to another result: her physical loss by the adversary affected his combat morale, because it humiliated him by subjecting him in existential reflection as well as in genealogical virtuality to the awareness of his inability to protect his own.

In a certain way, hostility toward the enemy, in this case toward the Spanish, reached its greatest convulsion in these losses of women, precisely because the greatest proof of manhood lay in one's relative capacity to protect the asset—the woman—who prolonged and confirmed it in his descendants. If humiliation is the cause of resentment, it is obvious that in the present case it became a factor in alienation, precisely because the seizure of women prevented the reproduction of the self and, in so doing, drained the personality of its sensual wellsprings of confirmation. What would be a psychological problem was also an existential problem for the ethnic group and, within the latter, one involving feelings of identity.

From that point, the dramatic sensitivity that all warfare sets off in individuals grew to its greatest intensity of transcendence when the self, threatened with dissolution, also faced more or less conscious anxieties about reproduction. The woman and children were an existential part of that anxiety about reproduction and played a critical role throughout these frontier confrontations, especially when, in the arena of competitive disputes over the assets of the locale, those assets also appeared in the form of persons considered as part of the totality of the self. The capture of women not only disorganized the social life of the subjects who lost them, but also forced them to reorganize their most profound orientations, in the sense that if every loss implies a loss of quantity, to take away from the self part of the emotional reality means to diminish it in part as a measurable psychological quantity.

The products of racial mixture were thus the first products of a frontier military morality that was always denounced but never repressed, because in their reality these sexual experiences embodied a release of tension and made up somewhat for the lack of mundane pleasures that the soldiers had given up. This is a historical phase in which the physical orientation prevails over the spiritual. Each has different esthetics and ethics and, in a certain way, they constitute the moral dichotomy of every historical expansion that seeks to reproduce itself beyond its borders. In this sense, while the conquistadors governed themselves by the strategy of temporal survival, the clergy and missionaries identified themselves with the ethic of salvation through renunciation.

Fundamentally, this divergence involved a strategically geopolitical division of labor. The conquistadors opened the continent to Spanish life and culture, relieved the peninsula of its aggressions and internal tensions, and imbued the most restless and subversive individuals, ready for the most combative and critical generations of the interior, eager for status, and brimming with revolutionary energy, as shown by the frequent cases of rebellion against the Crown in America, with a profound ideal of escape and fulfillment. The missionaries and clergy, meanwhile, with their methods of Christianizing and personal sacrifice, developed on this continent conditions for the domestication of the most difficult Indians through their so-called Reducciones de Indios, as well as contributed a spiritual foundation of transcendent morality and social control to the Spanish settlements themselves.

Certainly, the church was the moral control through the rectitude of its ethical strivings, and although there are many cases of charges against clergy involved in concubinage with Indian women, it is true that even these unions could have been assimilated as conjugal relations of a civil nature were it not for the complication of their personal vows of chastity.

In any case, the relative ease of union between Spaniards and Indian women, not to mention African women and various mixtures, must be understood as a factor of a decidedly intensive racial mixing. The inverse, that is, the mixture derived from unions of Indian men and Spanish women was a much rarer experience in frontier situations, although data for the period in Chile inform us that some five hundred Spanish women were eventually captured in war by the Indians, and with them the latter also procreated mestizo children.

Many of the raids and bloody battles that took place between Spaniards and Indians were caused precisely by the irritation produced by these captures of women. Nevertheless, the ones most damaged by these acts in terms of demographic losses were the Indians, since from the outset their women were the only sexual object of the Spanish. Not only that, but from the standpoint of individual freedom and independence, the Indian women offered the Spanish the greatest personal advantages, because unions with them were devoid of matrimonial commitments and meanwhile allowed the Spanish to wait for a formal arrangement with Spanish women. The latter, however, did not always become a reality, because in numerous instances men ended up acknowledging their unions with Indian women and legitimizing the legal status of their mestizo offspring. Up to this point, the course of conjugal formalization was long in the majority of cases and went through vicissitudes of great upheaval, alternating with times of strong emotional attachment to the Indian women, and with them to the children that were born. Here, then, we must turn back history to the point where those vicissitudes reflect the dramatic episodes of racial mixing in its different frontier circumstances.

The process that concerns us tells us that in the initial stage, the Indians, already enslaved since the first campaigns in the Antilles, lived at the disposal of the Spanish who obtained them in war through either trade or gift. In this case, many of the Indians were sold and assigned to expeditions as porters or as servants to individual soldiers, as their property or as that of military commanders who appropriated them according to their needs for service in warfare or in the homes of well established settlers. At other times, these Indians were acquired by the villages of Indian allies of the Spanish who either gave up their own prisoners or simply provided men and women to the Spanish by virtue of specific commitments of alliance. Regarding the sale of these Indians, an auction document (Friede 1955, 1:51–52) dated 1514 in Santa María la Antigua in Darién [Panama] serves as an example of such acquisitions, because it states the following:

I, Antonio Villas, scribe of Our Lady the Queen . . . certify that . . . the Indians of Santa Marta were sold in auction, . . .

First, an Indian called Juanico was auctioned to Becerra at seven pesos in gold. On the tenth of said month, an Indian women with a knife scar on her head and with her nursing daughter was auctioned to Diego de Arenas for fourteen pesos in gold.

An Indian girl who said she was called María was auctioned to Jerónimo Ramírez de Antequera for twenty pesos in gold.

Another Indian woman with a nursing child was auctioned to the aforementioned Jerónimo Ramírez de Antequera for fourteen pesos in gold.

An old Indian woman was auctioned to Ledesma for five pesos in gold.

An Indian woman who was captured at Isla Fuerte, with a child, was auctioned to Juan Gaitán for seven pesos in gold.

The woman companion of the cacique's wife, who was ill in a hut, was auctioned to Fernán Sánchez at his risk as she was, for six pesos in gold.

A girl as much as four years old was auctioned to Juan Arana for four pesos in gold.

A young Indian girl was auctioned to the auditor Diego Martínez for five pesos in gold; she was placed in custody.

An Indian woman with a child was auctioned to Fernán Valiente for eighteen pesos in gold.

An Indian woman called Isabel was auctioned to Master Barrera for eight pesos in gold.

The movement of Indians, Spanish, and blacks was general throughout the continent because of the expeditions to which they were attached, though with different social statuses. The Indians, in particular, eluded the watch of their guards and escaped into the forests. In this respect, the Spanish preferred young women and boys under the age of fourteen because neither of them escaped as easily as did the older Indians. In reference to this particular, a governor and captain (Document number 997, Friede, 4:231–36), who in 1537 was serving in the city of Santa Marta, asked the king that the Spanish be permitted to make slaves of Indians and of their women and children, especially since, in view of the difficulties presented by the conquest of New Granada, women and children were preferred because they were not "for running away," as happened, by contrast, with the men. In addition, any wartime occasion was good for capturing Indian women and children, especially since neither of them much resisted the Spanish and they had fewer resources and experience to escape Spanish control. Fray Pedro de Aguado (1963, 1:508) confirms this opportunism in this short narrative: "They found that the people of this village had recently left it. The captain, wishing to have some Indians in order to learn from them what he needed to do, took with him as many as eighty men and five horses, and setting out in search of them, after two days he came upon a site with twelve or thirteen houses. In them were the women and children of the owners, who had gone to fish. All these people were ordered rounded up by the captain, along with what food was in the village."

In any case, from the earliest expeditions on the mainland, the Spanish were already accompanied by servants, on some occasions by more than fifty individuals per mounted soldier who, with the status of domestics, were given the name of *naborías*[6] in the early period, because they came from the Antilles. As the Spanish penetrated the continent and arrived further south, to the aforesaid naborías were added the yanaconas, who had a similar function but were natives of the Andes.

Both naborías and yanaconas would escape on some occasions, while on others they would remain faithful to the Spanish. Everything depended on the treatment they had received from the latter and on their prospects of being well or badly received by the different tribes that they encountered during military expeditions. There are many reports regarding the particulars of these campaigns with Indian servants and of their escapes that confirm the reality of these different circumstances. For example, in a document of 1520 (in Friede 1955, 1: document 7), written in Santa María la Antigua del Darién (Castilla del Oro, in present-day Panama) it was stated:

> Inasmuch as Blas de Bastos had been in charge of Their Highnesses' Indians who had been brought back from the expeditions that had been made to that land, to keep and heal them until they were sold, and many of the aforesaid Indian men and women during said time that he had them in his custody had run away and never been seen again, either had died, and still others were given to certain persons by order of the señor governor, Pedrarias Dávila, and of the lord officials of Their Highnesses.

In this sense, the Indian women who accompanied the Spanish, along with naborías and yanaconas, shared the hardships of these campaigns, since as women on the side of the conquistadors they were treated as enemies, especially when they did not come from the same tribes as the Indians they were fighting. But the difficulties of these expeditions also included starvation and sickness, and the chroniclers abound in reports of this nature. The following examples will suffice. In 1520, in evidence given in Santa María la Antigua del Darién, it was stated (in Friede, 1955, 1:63–64):

> to the aforesaid treasurer Alonso de la Puente fourteen male Indians and one woman were delivered by the auditor Diego Márquez from among those brought from the island of Hispaniola and who belonged to His Highness, and it is also known that said treasurer received an Indian called Gasparico who belonged to Vasco Núñez de Balboa, and said treasurer having all these Indians in his custody and healing and feeding them as expected, some of the men and the aforementioned woman died because of the strangeness of the land, as did many others from this city as well as the native born.

Fray Pedro de Aguado (1963, 2:81) tells us the following in regard to Venezuela in the mid sixteenth century, reporting on an expedition made against Indian villages: "and he found the people who had become very weak with hunger were there, so much so that from this cause and some slight illness, he found three Spaniards dead and many of their servants."

Equally disastrous were the diseases that they contracted, as Cieza de León affirms (1962, 89) in relating the environmental changes that the conquistadors experienced due to the movements occasioned by the expeditions that they undertook and that involved passing from cold regions to other hot or temperate ones, according to the circumstances; these demanded a strong adaptive constitution, diversified more than specialized, and adequate diets. In this regard, Cieza de León says: "and the Indian women servants of the Spanish died (of pestilence), few or none of them remaining."

It is obvious that because of changes in environment and diet, and depending on the treatment given to their persons, the Indians were more or less physically vulnerable. In general, it was soon recognized that they needed protection from the treatment of some conquistadors. In 1525 (Friede 1955, 1:88ff.) an anonymous Franciscan wrote to the king about the need for better treatment of the Indians, and to achieve this he recommended taking them away from the "soldier boys who are no good," because the naborías, seeing themselves transferred from one master to another and from region to region, preferred to escape, or as the priest puts it, "in sorrow they go to the forests and misfortunes occur."

The Indian caciques contributed their own Indians from among their own personal servants, so that they might act as domestic servants to the Spanish (Friede, 1955, 1: document 17). In such cases, this contribution was understood as a gesture of goodwill by the caciques toward the Spanish, and thus the caciques reinforced the commitment to alliance between them. Actually, it was part of native custom for its leaders to have slave servants or members of their own tribe attached as domestics. Although this personal use of the Indian in domestic service was not criticized, there was great resentment, nevertheless, against the change of environment that separated one from his family and exposed him to physiological and adaptive hazards that, in many cases, he could not endure.

These were factors that directly affected the physical normality of the Indians, since, being more vulnerable than the Spanish to these movements, they fell ill and were the easy victims of epidemics. In these circumstances, escape from the expeditions, taking advantage of carelessness by the soldiers, was a frequent solution.

In these environmental situations, the transfer of Indians presented a constant threat to their persons. In fact, and in the specifics of his way of life, the American Indian constitutes an example of ecological adaptation, in balance with nature, in the sense that rarely did the tropical Indian move suddenly to live in a cold region, or from the coast to the highlands. At most, such changes took place under conditions of specialized daily travel, such as those of Indian messengers, whom we can think of, really, as young athletes or runners trained to cover long distances; and those of porters who, with certain exceptions, were accustomed to carrying burdens for short distances, generally within ecologies of localized experience and in accord with their traditional endurance and physical energies, that is, the demands of their social services were balanced. Incidentally, Indian diets were light in fats and proteins, since the vegetable prevailed enormously over meats in the more densely populated regions of the continent.

Certainly an exception to the above would be the southern Indians, with diets based on meats in the interior and on shellfish and marine animals on the coast. But, as a condition of their hunter cultures, they were also groups accustomed to a permanent nomadism within an ecologically specialized zone that required them to carry light burdens on skins in an economic flow achieved on the terrain. But, in any case, these Indians consumed greater quantities of proteins and fat, which resulted in greater combative energy and endurance than that shown by those who, being basically gatherers and cultivators of small clearings, were attached to the expeditions of the Spanish conquistadors.

For the rest, the native dietary regimen was physiologically valid within the traditional ecological localities and in keeping with their cultural conditioning, especially because the latter provided the technological limits for obtaining energy and was adapted functionally to the possibilities of consumption demanded by the respective types of labor of the natives. But in cargo labor involving long, dangerous, and physically demanding travel, such as that imposed by the demands of the Spanish expeditionaries, the situation was different.

The consumption of a traditional diet under these conditions of constant movement and the environmental changes which it occasioned did greater harm to the health of the Indian than could be attributed to the ill treatment he received from the "soldier boys," in the words of the Franciscan. Actually, that movement should be considered as a selective filter that put the physical faculties of those undertaking these experiences to the test. The most specialized of these Indians succumbed in them, and in a small sample, we can see that the greatest vulnerability of the Spanish occurred precisely in the tropical regions of Venezuela and of the Amazon basin. In those areas, many of the Spanish succumbed to environmental "pestilences" and disastrous epidemics that, if they did not lead to death, caused irreversible damage to their organisms. By contrast, these Spaniards easily endured the highlands of Meso-America and the Andes, where they proved their quick adaptation. The tropics were their main enemy, but in any case they endured them better than did the Indians from elsewhere who accompanied them, precisely to the degree that they were better prepared physically for these expeditions and in addition constituted, in themselves and with regard to military necessities, a biologically selective group by age, hardness, and zeal in the fulfillment of their objectives.

It is obvious that the nature of the conquests was not only violent in battle itself, but was extremely grueling in its total process. Only a physical constitution diversified in its adaptive capacities could overcome the physiological hardships to which it was exposed during changes of environment. Such was the case of the Spanish who took part in those conquests. Their health and adaptive hardiness, as well as the force of their characters, were decisive elements throughout their survival experience.

In considering this process of racial mixing as a result of the lack of Spanish women during these early stages, we must not overlook the fact that the period of conquest was a long one in its experience with the so-called savage groups. In this sense so was the period of cohabitation of these Spaniards with the Indian women in their service, if not with those who lived stably in the villages en route who were offered to them in acts of alliance, of pure attraction, or of simple capture. Examples abound regarding these experiences of massive racial mixing in the areas of campaign. Additionally, violence was not always a part of those relations.

In fact, because of the demands of campaign, the Indian women servants who accompanied these expeditions were rather young women, most of them—in the words of the reports—girls, and the most attractive ones in their selection when it came to preferences for these sexual relations. As a result, their mestizo descendants were individuals more hardy in adaptive capabilities than they would have been had they had biologically specialized parents as their progenitors. Fundamentally, however, and independent of what happened to the health of the participants in these expeditions, it is clear that Indian women and Spaniards maintained a close relationship that was emphasized as the care of their descendants demanded their commitment, especially when the association was extended over time and thus created dependencies and conditions of solidarity.

In practice, this demand led to situations of mutual affection, notable for the fact that it was not always necessary to guard against Indians escaping, because in their strategies of conquest the Spanish took advantage of existing rivalries between Indian tribes in order to establish alliances with one of them to fight together against the common enemy. This exploitation of rivalries was a universal experience, and it brought the frequent result of weakening the effort that should have been applied toward the immediate military objective of winning territory. These alliances included mutual aid, and at times merely Spanish protection and a friendship consisting of respect for Indian allies, though in exchange for the latter's obedience to the authority of the king and their agreement to convert to Christianity. The villages and territories of these Indians were made rear zones to which the Spanish repaired to rest, reorganize their forces, and supply themselves with food and even reinforcements. These were occasions to heal wounds and enjoy the Indian women.

Captain García de Lerma (Document 201, in Friede 1955, 2:112–13) tells how in New Granada in 1520, after a battle with the Indians from which the Spanish barely escaped, his entire war camp rested in a village of friendly Indians, and in this regard he reports, "After (the battle) I arrived here (a friendly village) with all my badly (wounded), and made sure that everyone had beds and shelter and medicines, barbers and women, and everything they might need."

This was acceptable conduct as part of the campaign system and provided an opportunity to prove the worth and fulfillment of the commitments that the Indians had made to the Spanish. This would be one aspect of the particular circumstance of the relations between the Spanish commanders of military expeditions that operated in the name of the king and that therefore established alliances with native groups. Another aspect of a different stripe was the one resulting from the wartime right to enslave the defeated enemy, which, in this context, was expressed in the form of particular relations between master and slave. In this system, those relations were specific to the particular nature of each circumstance and of each person. There were some who treated their slaves and domestics with benevolence, while others behaved badly or even cruelly toward them. But in each case, all shared together the problem of environmental adaptation.

Thus, for example, it was common for the Spanish conquistadors approaching their death to make wills of protection for Indian women and their common offspring, even when they had contracted formal marriages to Spanish women. Pedro de Valdillo, on the island of Hispaniola in 1531, declared in his will and testament, among other desires, the following:

> Item. I order that the Indian woman Juanica, a slave of Francisco Núñez, a citizen of the villa of San Juan de la Maguana, be purchased and ransomed, and that in addition to the ransom she be given thirty pesos in gold for her marriage.
>
> Item. I order that the bastard son of my brother Martín Fernández Marmolejo and of Ana de Morales be provided with food, clothing, books, and classes for ten years so that he may become learned, and so that he might graduate, and for whatever he might need, I grant him a hundred thousand maravedíes, which hundred thousand maravedíes should be given to him from my assets before my heirs possess them.
>
> Item. I give to Elena, sister-in-law of Sebastián Moreno, sister of Isabel Fernández, a mestizo woman, one hundred pesos in gold to contribute to her marriage.
>
> Item. I order that Estalina, an Indian woman of Yucatán, and Leonor, my slaves, be set free and each given thirty pesos in gold for her marriage. . . .
>
> Item. I give to María, former daughter of the cacique Luis, fifty pesos in gold for her marriage.
>
> Item. I order that if Teresa, daughter of Teresa, my naboría, and of Diego de Jaén, be left in this villa in order to marry here, she be given the hundred pesos that I have committed to her, and if not, and she is taken from this villa, that she be given twenty-five pesos in gold and not the hundred that I have given her. (Document 202, in Friede 1955, 2:118–26)

This particular will, under the circumstances suggested by its context, allows us to infer the presence in the penitent memory of many Spaniards of the experiences of companionship and affection that they had shared with Indian women and, especially, the respect of responsibility that emerged with regard to their descendants, particularly when it involved unions that, independent of the social status of either party, had lasted a long time and had settled into a process of solidarity.

Insofar as it was extended in time and massive in its intensity, this racial mixing produced a certain number of results: many of the troops used on the continent were already mestizos, the product of unions between these Spaniards and the Indian women of the Antilles. Those mestizos, and those who would follow, would be those soldiers whom Fray Aguado (1963, 1:336) later would call "Indianized," bold and arrogant, and usually the enemies of the Indians during this period. But in each case they were considered needful of forceful command and prestige in order to mobilize and control them in their excesses, since, as Captain García de Lerma said (Document 201, in Friede 1955, vol. 2) in his report during his expedition to New Granada, with reference to mestizo troops: "the people of this land are not as well led in my absence as would be necessary."

What is certain is that in this first period, and in the struggles against the "savage Indians," the latter were taken as slaves and sold for profit to defray the costs of the expedition, in addition to their being used in the service of Spanish conquistadors, and later for a certain time of Spanish settlers and encomenderos. As long as they were not distributed among the conquerors, the Indians and their women remained in the war camps or in the provisional custody of the soldiers. When there were not enough Indians to carry the baggage of an expedition, then its captain would send a force into the native villages to obtain them. Fray Pedro de Aguado (1963, 1:230) confirms this assumption when, with reference to the campaign of Federman in Venezuela, he reports that when his expedition was short of porters: "in order to remedy this need Federman sent three of his captains with some men to various places to find Indians for the aforesaid purpose, and within two days two of them returned well supplied with natives."

Under these conditions, the soldiers who undertook these raids were mostly the so-called *chapetones,* [literally, "rosy-cheeked ones"] so described because the bright pink of their cheeks had barely faded from their white faces. Collaborating with them were the "Indianized" mestizos, who, in the words of Ordóñez de Ceballos (1947, 75), were "boastful . . . spirited, and bold" people. As the number of Spanish soldiers waned, with the increase of these mestizos raised amid the confusion and disorganization implicit in the upheavals, the sexual aggressiveness of the generations was sharpened; under such circumstances, the confused social milieu favored civil indiscipline.

The chapetones were the soldiers of "youthful impulse" to whom Fernández de Oviedo had referred; they constituted the boldest group and the one most prone to sensual liberties, and along with the "Indianized" mestizos they were the cause of disciplinary concern for their commanders.

In any case, this movement of populations of both sexes of Indian and Spanish, and to a lesser degree, Africans, gave origin to these generations of mestizos. Of course, as we have pointed out, the profusion of sexual exchanges between Spanish men, Indian women, and then between mestizos, was high and justified by the state of the interracial relationships. The soldiers were at their most sexually vigorous ages, and so were many Indian women, since the latter, with their numbers in captivity, were selected according to their youth and physical vigor, that is, for their qualities of endurance on campaign.

Thus, it is no surprise that such a great number of mestizos was produced from the beginning in the Antilles themselves. If in an initial relationship with Indian women unions were preceded by the violence of war, soon afterward the reports we receive from Spanish sources already differ, because the behavior of both racial groups was noted for a mutual attraction that already included courtship in many instances, especially when "lustrous" women were involved, as in the case of those who belonged to Indian families of prestige, such as Incas, for example. On such occasions, as Castellanos reports (Pérez de Barradas 1987, 140), there were even pastries given. This took place in times of peace, and also, in another context, to show gratitude for the good treatment received by a Spaniard from an Indian woman while he was a prisoner of the Indians. In Chile we have an example of this, brought to us through the narrative of Mariño de Lobera (1960, 284), who writes the following on this particular subject:

> Then (the general) commanded them on his part to go to Doña María, who was the Indian woman who had treated him kindly during his captivity, to ask her to come there and see him; she was carried on a very ornate litter on the shoulders of Indians with a large retinue. General Alonso de Monroy came out to meet her on the road with many Spanish people, and embraced her and took her by the hand to a dais that he had prepared with a carpet and cushion that he had brought for her from Peru for this purpose. . . . It being the hour to dine, he invited her with great love . . . and he seated her at the head of the table, and with her, Captain Cateo, giving them a sumptuous banquet.

By contrast, when they involved relations on campaign, unions had a less conventional cast and reacted to the laws of whimsy and to decisions made by the soldiers in the field. These were decisions based especially on the fact that each soldier could have many women in his service, as many as he obtained or were provided to him by the captains themselves.

In this tenor, it is obvious that once certain alliances that served Spanish strategies were set up with Indian tribes, the provision of Indian women by native caciques was habitual and carried a dual purpose: on the one hand, to contain the Spanish and dissuade them from violence against these native populations, seeking in advance to keep them satisfied with the gift of women; on the other, to pursue a more elevated political end in the linking of native lineages with those of conquistador captains. This was the case in Meso-America with the Tlaxcalans, Nahuas (Aztecs), and Mayas in general, and in the Andean region with the Incas. And in campaigns against less civilized populations than these, it was common for the collective alliances with the caciques to include the gift of women to the Spanish. The chronicler Fray Pedro Simón (1961, 43) in discussing the conquests of Pedro de Heredia, states: "The Spanish learned what happened to Don Pedro de Heredia and his soldiers in the town of Cipacú, where, while they were lodged at a certain farm not far from the town, after the cacique had sent them four hundred (women) carrying different foods, he sent the captain more than a hundred young women, all of them so attractive, charming, lovely, and smiling that they caused our people to name the town Las Hermosas."

In a similar context, it appears that the relations with these allied caciques were important because their towns became areas of rest, provisions, and security, and because they also served as an example of the will to protect that the Spanish were capable of extending to the tribes that served them faithfully. In this sense, we also have reports of numerous Indian populations who resorted to alliance with the Spanish in order to fight against their traditional enemies, or simply to assure themselves of protection against the latter. The Arawaks would be a good example of seeking the safety that the Spanish provided against the Caribs, and in Mexico we would find the classic example of the Tlaxcalans seeking safety against the Mexicas. In any case, the etiquette and ritual of these alliances included the giving of young Indian women at ages of easy reproduction who, at least on the part of the native caciques, were considered as honorable proof that said alliances were being strengthened through the guarantee of friendships and of kinship derived from the exchanges between both sides. Any rejection of these women was taken as an affront to the ethnic pride and good will of the tribe who offered them. This is clearly seen in the narrative of Fray Pedro de Aguado (1963, 2: 17), who says the following:

> The lords of those provinces (Venezuela) were accustomed to giving the Spanish captains presents of gold and slaves that they had from the wars they fought with others in their region; and if the Spanish, or their captains, did not wish to receive the presents being given to them, the Indians became truly angry with them and said they should be declared as enemies; but I know for a fact that there were few who did not wish to receive the gifts of the Indians.

If these gifts of women corresponded to desires for alliance with the Spanish, for the latter they represented the fulfillment of needs for functional service toward the success or failure of the expeditions themselves. Without the prior assurance of this service by Indians of both sexes and of vigorous age, the expeditions could not be very long ones because they had to return frequently to their bases, especially when we recall that the Indians carried, in addition to the provisions, the booty taken in campaign; additionally, and as a service, the Indian women attended to the soldiers in their rest and in the preparation of their meals. There is no doubt that without these numerous Indian servants many expeditions would have failed or at least would have taken more time, unless a greater number of Spaniards had enlisted in them. In some instances the system of alliance replaced the need to resort to capturing Indians. In addition, on occasion, the Indians who were received from cacique allies as servants for the Spaniards were also enslaved prisoners of these caciques taken in war, and in this sense, the exchange or provision of Indians to the Spanish corresponded to a custom already established among the Indians. It is said (Fray P. de Aguado 1963, 2:17) that it was most common to offer captives to the Spanish for these purposes. To this we must add that when they lacked Indians for transport and service, the Spanish were accustomed to raiding the latters' villages in order to obtain them.

Nevertheless, insofar as they constituted both a tactical and strategic need for the Spanish, the women were distributed to them in a selective sense, since the soldiers received common women while the captains were favored with the daughters or female relatives of the caciques. In these circumstances, Fray Pedro Simón (1961, 136), referring to what was then New Granada, wrote: "they decided to tighten their friendships through kinship. Uraba (Indian cacique) thus gave to Gutiérrez in marriage one of his sisters of very pleasing appearance who became a Christian and who was given the baptismal name of her godmother, which was Isabel, to which was added the surname of Corral."

Meanwhile, in the various campaigns of South America the notions of alliance with the Spanish were repeated. In Paraguay, a soldier of German origin, Schmidel (1962, 291–92) reported that

> they came, these aforesaid Carios,[7] and asked for pardon from our captain, general Juan Ayolas, that he receive them in forgiveness, and that they would do everything we might want. They also brought and presented to our captain, Juan Ayolas, six women, the oldest being eighteen years of age . . . and gave to each soldier or man two women to take care of us, cook, wash, and attend to other matters that one had need of at that time. . . . With this, peace was made with the Carios.

Political ties were thus tightened by means of these gifts, especially when the tribes could offer no other assets that, as soldiers of fortune, many men were pursuing as their principal booty in this instance: gold. Nevertheless, there were the major geopolitical counterforces of the Crown and the church, who imposed legal and sometimes severe limits on individual license.

Yet, they paid special attention to the fact that these alliances were considered important to achieving the rapid Spanish population of the Indies and also an early religious indoctrination of its native populations.

At certain moments in these campaigns, the captains with a surplus of individuals in their service could be generous with their troops, and indeed this took place when they distributed among them the women given to them by the Indians, even in the case of friendships and as proof of alliance. Thus, military policy was rigid in the maintenance of discipline among its forces, and we have numerous examples of punishments meted out to soldiers who had committed excesses in their behavior with Indians who either were friends or were apparently neutral and best kept away from all hostilities. In the course of military operations against natives having a poor economic structure, that is, with subsistence economies, it was a general pragmatic policy to accept their gifts of women, although they might incur moral resistance on the part of the priests who usually managed the conduct of the soldiers. Despite the fact that there was always a conflict between the military and religious sectors, what is certain is that racial mixing was more a product of the military's permissive policy than of ecclesiastical policy. The latter inclined more toward the separation of the Indians than toward their mixture with the Spanish, particularly due to the fears that the soldiers created in the sense of their seeking personal benefit more than the ultimate goal of the Indians' conversion, as well as their political identification as subjects of the Spanish Crown. If in some instances the clergy favored the unions of Indian women with Spaniards, the latter nonetheless favored the fluid status of unstable relations in the hopes of marrying Spanish women. By contrast, the condition of marriage within the church implied a minimal racial mixture in comparison with what resulted from informal polygyny, either successive or simultaneous, according to the circumstances. But in any case, it is obvious that military strategies had to prevail over the religious ones because, in reality, they led more quickly to achieving the political goal of incorporating the Indian under the Spanish Crown, and because only military victory could make missionary activity possible on a large scale for the church.

Based on these conditions, it was important to reconcile geopolitics with religious morality, but in any case the latter held a secondary place among what were truly the pragmatic necessities by means of which it was possible to achieve dominion over the native populations. Everywhere, thus, the strategy led to this practice of the ritual offering of women on the part of the Indians. In fact, accepting these women was also a form of committing them as hostages and as a guarantee of friendly behavior on the part of the Indians who gave them. Thus, it seems unquestionable that these gifts became a very important asset of negotiation, since apart from the conquest itself of a land still unproductive in the immediate expectations of the Spanish captains, there was little of which to take advantage other than receiving these women. The gift of women by the Indians was sometimes the greatest asset that the caciques could offer. And it is obvious that war with these tribes was awkward and difficult, not only because it prolonged the conflict, but also because the conflict made it impossible for the Spaniard to exploit the Indian. In Paraguay, Alvar Núñez Cabeza de Vaca (1962, 43) said, regarding the Aperúes,[8] that

> as a sign of the peace and friendship that they wished to have and keep with the Christians, they brought certain of their daughters, and begged the governor to receive them, and so that they might feel more certain and sure that they were friends, they were giving them as hostages. . . . The governor received the women and children that they gave to him, and also so that they might not be angered, believing that because he did not take them he did not accept them, the governor gave those women and children to the missionaries and clergy so that they might indoctrinate them and teach them Christian doctrine and show them good manners and customs.

The meaning of these gifts of women was always the same: to please the Spanish, be at peace with them and produce descendant kinship, in this case, mestizos. These unions, as we have seen, were abundant and occurred everywhere. It should be noted that the very Indian women serving as concubines to the Spanish, upon being Christianized, sometimes took the Spaniards' surnames automatically for the simple fact of living with them. This could cause us confusion when we think that lists where women with Spanish surnames appear were listing Spanish women, when in fact they were Indians. In this regard, Irala (1962, 116) tells us the following about this concubinage and the adoption of Spanish surnames by the Indians of Paraguay: "During this time of Mendoza,[9] Juan de Salazar Cuparatí, Francisco Ruiz Mairarú, Lorenzo Maquerati, and Gonzalo Mairarú, all of them mongoloid Indians, lived in Asunción, and their daughters were mistresses of the Spanish, whose names they had taken."

Additionally, once the Spanish were in possession of Paraguay during a period of relative peace, Irala concludes that those Spaniards were living in an Islamic fashion in what can be called matrimonial polygyny with the Indian women. The scarcity of Spanish women, combined with the abundant availability of Indian women, and the predisposition of the conquistadors to undertake such unions, resulted in what Irala (ibid., 457) considered a behavior much in keeping with the teachings of Mohammed and his Koran. This situation so scandalized Padre Francisco González Paniagua that he wrote: "The Christian is content with four Indian women because he cannot have sixteen, and thus here (one has) two or three or more, otherwise it is someone very poor. No one has less than five or six, the majority (have) fifteen, twenty, thirty, and forty" (Azara 1962, 437).

Referring to these relations in Paraguay, with regard to the different sexual morality of Indian women compared with that governing Spanish women, Azara (1962, 416) pointed out that the former showed no cultural restrictions in the expression of this impulse, and in noting it, declared: "Perhaps there is no example where an Indian woman ten years or older has said no to any solicitor, be he old or young, free or slave, white or black."

Alvar Núñez Cabeza de Vaca also recognizes the existence of a special attraction of the Indian woman toward the Spanish in that time, and he writes (1962, 79) that they were given to sensuality; in this sense the commentary in his report is quite conclusive when he states that "by custom they do not withhold their persons, and they consider it a great insult to deny (sex) to anyone who asks them for it, and they ask why it was given to them if not for that."

In reality, this phenomenon of intensive relations between Spaniards and Indian women began to assume a general character as the contending parties were pacified, regardless of the cultural position of the native group. A note from López de Gómara (1946, 233) clearly describes this favorable disposition of Indian women toward the Spanish when he relates an incident that occurred in Peru with the women of the Inca Ramiñahui. It involves a typical reaction of injured male pride at the apparent satisfaction he noted in his women at the inevitable arrival of the Spanish. The information is marked with drama and reads as follows: "Said Ramiñahui to his women: Rejoice, because the Christians are coming, with whom you can enjoy yourselves. Some of them laughed, as women do, perhaps none of them with ill intention. Then he cut the throats of the laughing ones."

In other cases, and turning to the relations of the black with the Indian woman, Humboldt (1973, 63) also affirms the preference that the native women of New Spain showed for blacks, because in the latter they recognized lively impulses that did not appear in what he termed the "outer calm of the Indian." In any case, Humboldt said of the Africans: "This contrast causes the Indian women to prefer the blacks not only over the men of their own caste, but even over the Europeans."

In a context relative to Brazil and the Portuguese and to the conduct of Indian women toward them, Padre Anchieta (Pérez de Barradas 1976, 154) made similar comments when he stated: "The women go about naked and can refuse no one, rather they impose themselves and pursue the men, because they hold it a great honor to sleep with the Christians."

The type of report that we have received on the particulars of these unions expresses in the clearest terms that, once peace was achieved with the Indian tribes, the bulk of the Spanish soldiers who had carried out the conquests remained united with the Indian women in a system of concubinage. Their number depended as much on their economic possibilities as on their sexual energy. In fact, ecclesiastical policies could scarcely intervene effectively to prevent this, because in many cases Spanish civil society had not been transplanted, that is, had not been established with Spanish women, but largely with Indian women.

In Paraguay this was more common and intensive than elsewhere, with the consequence that this civil society, founded on cabildos and families of peninsular Spanish origin, was replaced by a society with a culture and institutions of a Spanish stamp, but with strong and even superior human contingents of native origin. It is evident that Spanish women came in small numbers to these areas as much because the instability of the settlements extended over a long time as because the initial economic conditions did not favor the establishment of those women. The fact is that under these circumstances, they could not compete with the Indian women, since the latter neither resented their social status as concubines nor felt any economic estrangement with regard to the paucity of their means.

Thus, it was the Indian women who assumed most of the social role of sexual companions to the Spanish in these areas, and gradually many of them—through selection and emotional ties with their Spanish companions—became true and even legitimate wives. For these reasons, if the instability of war hindered the bringing of Spanish families and prolonged the interim nature of illegitimate polygynous unions, nevertheless, the reality of this cohabitation and of its social structure lent to the fact that their mestizo products were limited in quantity only by the number of Indian women available to the Spanish and by their relative fertility. Thus, on the basis of the unbridled polygynous tendency of the Spanish and the attraction that they held for the Indian women, it is obvious that mestizos were created in great numbers and that they soon constituted the majority populations in some regions of America, especially in the Antilles, Venezuela, and Paraguay.

This informally polygynous social structure had one clear effect: it favored biological mixing in greater numbers than would have resulted were the principle of monogamy strictly respected. In a certain way, although Spanish civil society was not reproduced, part of the culture employed by both groups was also mestizo in the sense that foods and materials especially were taken from the land, and thus the majority of them were indigenous. By contrast, those cultural elements introduced from the Iberian Peninsula were Spanish, such as domestic animals, plants, methods of cultivation and cattle raising; ideology and political, administrative, religious, military, and economic institutions in general; and a language in expansion as an idiom that facilitated communications at universal levels. So, too, was the family model when it became legalized through canonical and civil means.

In this sense, we must recognize the existence of (1) a provisional society consisting of soldiers and Indian women who lived in camps with the other Indians and Africans and who developed polygynous social structures, frail at best in their stability, and (2) another solid social structure that, while it was reproducing the Spanish model of the monogamous family, was establishing a different society, one strict in its moral demands, which would gradually become the predominant one throughout the entire process to follow.

Meanwhile, with regard to racial mixing, the greater numbers would arise from the first, or transitional, model among those young soldiers who, free of discipline but now settled, were not awarded encomiendas and thus found it difficult to establish themselves with sufficient economic guarantees to support wives of Spanish origin. Many of these soldiers ended up forming households with their Indian mistresses that, if at first provisional, soon became permanent forms of association. Conversely, those who would soon become encomenderos through the distribution of Indians created the rural model of the seigniorial and patriarchal Spanish family. They were dominant with regard to social power and in the majority of cases were the origin of the criollo caste, along with those other settlers who had come directly from Spain and who also gave rise to these racial products.

Nevertheless, based on their relative economic success, many of the latter's descendants would unite with Indian and mestizo women, especially when they lacked the means to do so with criollo women with dowries for their marriages.

With this digression, we can return to the scene of the first events insofar as these define the conditions in which the racial mixture of transition was appearing, to the degree that no other type of mixtures emerged. The latter would include those resulting from urban development in particular and from the more or less surreptitious sexual behavior that continued to give rise to intensive interracial unions, despite the establishment of a colonial society based on racial classes and on internal differences, founded on strong aristocratic tendencies, within each class.

This society was being created to such a degree that the period under discussion was one of great openness and was developing on the basis of the frontier character adopted by civil reality. Thus, this frontier was in fact profuse in mestizo products, but to the extent that Spanish soldiers could choose according to their own preferences, as they established obligations of alliance with Indian caciques, it is obvious that biological as well as social selectivity was produced. On the one hand there was a biological selection that derived from the youth and vigor of the individuals who constituted the majority of these unions, whereas on the other, a social selection was gradually produced consisting of the preference for establishing unions with Indian women of the highest possible status, that is, the daughters of caciques who would contribute economic patrimony or territorial assets to what were already marriages. This selectivity appears to correspond to what we could describe as unions dominated by interest in *social blood,* unions in which both parties preferred one another to have personal patrimony and social status. In this sense, it is obvious that not every Spanish soldier enjoyed this combination of advantages, but it was achieved by those who in each circumstance had the opportunity to establish themselves with a fortune and servants in native lands. This happened particularly with military commanders, who really were the ones preferred by the Indian caciques for the purpose of establishing kinship with the Spanish.

The metaphorical concept of social blood that we have used to refer to some of these unions—more stable ones in this case, resulting from the events of the campaign itself—must be understood in a double sense: biological and social. In the biological sense those individuals tied to Indian power, in this case the daughters of the caciques, represented, besides a social selection, a biological selection due to the fact that they belonged to competitively victorious ancestries within their own social structure. In a social sense the daughters of caciques contributed status and patrimony that were denied to common Indians. On the Spanish side, the soldier was already a guarantee of youthful health and as regards his social position, his very nature—certainly admired by the Indian—lent him the prestige that he needed to achieve such a union. In fact, the soldier had as his sole patrimony those virtues that brought prestige and were the object of admiration on the part of the Indian. The social blood would consist of the competitive superiority demonstrated by the protagonists involved in these relations.

It is quite clear, then, that in referring to social blood, we recognize the existence of a certain relationship between social functions and specific personal aptitudes in periods that call for selected biological qualities to carry out certain functions, in this case, those demanded of soldiers and warriors in a struggle for survival. Social blood thus does not refer so much to the class in power as to the fact of the competitive superiority recognized in those individuals who are carrying out some action and in so doing distinguish themselves from the rest. This superiority does not refer, therefore, to a status ascribed at birth or independent of the competitive merits of the individual—an aristocrat concept—but rather to the status that an individual attains in competition with others and that he uses in establishing kinship with another, of the opposite sex in the case under discussion, who also represents a status at least vicariously competitive.

Under such conditions, social blood was that which was specific to the victors in conditions of direct struggle for survival, and in this sense they established kinship with daughters who, if in one sense were not necessarily the most vigorous women in their group, were nonetheless genetically related to the men of higher status achieved in competitive situations. In many instances, the native women who united with conquistadors were the most vigorous in their behavior, as shown by the female caciques who exercised tribal power in many parts and who demonstrated capacities for command and struggle superior to those common to other women in their group. The Indian Isabel, cacique of the island of Margarita, who had married Captain Fajardo, would be a clear example of social blood in her character of competitive preeminence. So would other cases in the Antilles and on the mainland where the custom of the exercise of a competitive power, tested constantly through intertribal warfare and thus ratified in the process of that exercise, made it possible for local chieftaincies to constitute a status whose enjoyment required the permanent consensus of the local group, based on these abilities to defend it.

If intertribal warfare provided the opportunities for status among the Indians, especially among the so-called savages, and if the maximum competitive tests were understood within the context of struggles for survival, then social blood resulted from the emergence of functional capabilities that were proved during the very process of competitive selection. Under similar circumstances, those who achieved preeminence also played this metaphorical role of social blood. It is in periods of transition, such as that of the conquest, when this social blood really plays its most decisive role, because within the constant breakdowns to which customary institutional forms are subject, and within the frequent disarray resulting from the clash of cultures and their mixing, those who appear leading the competition and who strategically reorganize their own status in terms of achieving greater personal advantages turn out to be our group of individuals characterized by what we term social blood. In any case, in the context of our discussion, that social blood would be characteristically specific to periods of transition, where the tasks of survival include the capacity to ascend in status; also specific to those periods are those deeds of power that result from the competition between similar individuals within a social class, for whose leadership are selected those who triumph over the rest thanks to the better use of strategies of domination and status.

Independent of these qualities, it is clear that during the processes of conquest that we are discussing, notable for their moral disarray resulting from strategies of survival, the permanent risk that was incurred during the campaigns greatly loosened those disciplines related to the moral discourse of the soldier; among other results, risk dissipated many of the disciplines ascribed to his behavior in his culture of origin, subjecting the latter to the mere satisfaction of impulses. The immersion of their expectations in the uncertain hazards of war made these soldiers into players with death, but their good health also made them capricious and active sexual individuals who dealt with their female captives at will. In this respect there appear to be no great exceptions with reference to commanders and troops. For example, an alguacil mayor of Cartagena de Indias, interrogated in Madrid by the Council of the Indies, declared the following (Document 766, in Friede 1955, vol. 3) regarding sexual behavior with Indian women:

> it is publicly said and held to be true that the Christians take some Indian women forcibly from the villages that resist and set upon them carnally, some of (the women) not being Christians, and that they have others baptized, and that in this way many Indian women have been seen in the possession of Christians. . . . (I)t is no cause for surprise or alarm that the Christians do with the Indian women what has been reported, because the governor does it.

Control of the sexual impulse was largely unchecked in the context of the permissiveness arising out of what could be considered as the spoils of war. Yet, this sexual license was the object of open censure by ecclesiastical authorities and those others exercising civil functions who did not partake directly in the struggle against the Indians. From this standpoint, Fray Pedro de Aguado (1963, 1:336), in his scandalized commentary regarding the behavior of the "Indianized," or mestizo, individuals accompanying the Spanish conquistadors in Venezuela in the mid-sixteenth century, said that this soldiery dared to "fornicate with the (Indian women) so shamelessly that I know not how to say it, because in front of the Indians themselves, husbands and fathers, they perpetrated this evil." In fact, this dissolute proclivity toward these Indian women was possible only when considered from the purely biological perspective of the physiological resources of these individuals, based on the squandering of prodigious amounts of energy and health. As Varallanos states (1962, 40), confirming what has been said of the Spanish conquest of America, this was the "epic of good health."

The chronicler Fray P. Simón reports, for example (1961, 133), that in Zenú, New Granada, the Spanish at war with the Indians captured "all their women"; and in Puno, López de Gómara (1946, 222) says that the soldiers of Pizarro took sexual advantage of the women of that place, an action that the Inca governor so greatly resented that he ordered his people to confront the Spanish. Likewise in Túmbez (Peru) in 1544, Vasco Núñez de Balboa had to free the Indian women held by Spanish soldiers because they constituted a scandalous example (ibid., 250), especially with regard to the maintenance of military and social discipline. And in Venezuela in 1541, Pedro de

Limpias, after entering the area of Maracaibo, had brought back five hundred natives of both sexes who, it is understood, were taken in battle and were sold as slaves (Oviedo y Baños, 1965, 60–61).

In its amplest pragmatism, this sexual dissolution was now a common adventure among the soldiers of the conquest, and it was accentuated whenever they operated beyond the direct discipline of their commanders or with the latters' passive consent to their soldiers' sexual appetites at times of leisure. The majority of these adventures, and the captures that resulted from them, were carried out by commando groups driven by the idea of booty. Oviedo y Baños describes them (ibid., 96) as young men who let themselves be carried away by their "youthful inclination." This clearly was a product of expeditionary periods, because in times of peace an attempt was made to restore the moral discipline made precarious by the idleness of the troops by means of severe legal provisions as well as through the very installation of Spanish civil society, which in its ways and customs became a social control that watched over the acts of its members.

Nevertheless, what was discipline and control with regard to one's own countrymen was different for outsiders, the Indians. The mestizo chronicler Guamán Poma, writing at a time of peace in Peru in the late sixteenth century, says that the Indian women had been corrupted by Spaniards, mestizos, blacks, and mulattoes, who went about in their villages forcing themselves upon them, according to the author, although the report does not appear thus when we look at its context (see Varallanos 1962, 85). The text reads as follows: "and (the Indian women) wear short skirts, cloaks, shoes, and blouses, and all carry a half dozen mestizos and mulattoes, *cholos, zambahigos.* . . . They no longer wish to marry their Indian equals. . . . The main cacique comes to marry his daughters and sisters to mestizos and mulattoes. Since they see the chief and the other women, they no longer want to marry Indians, and the kingdom is lost."

In the initial context, the period of conquest, the capture of Indian women was most frequent. In Chile, Francisco Aguirre, a member of Valdivia's forces, made these raids in the nighttime (Góngora Marmolejo 1960, 86). Otherwise, the soldiery entered the villages where there were no men left and coupled with the women they found there, in many instances without violence or force. Thus commented Diego Alvéniz de la Cerda (Pérez de Barradas 1976, 111–12), who, on the occasion of the campaign for Paraguay in 1520—with reference to the conduct of the soldiers of Lope de la Puebla, who had just arrived at the first Achagua[10] village—said:

> the entire regiment poured into the unexpected village. But the nakedness of its inhabitants excited them enormously. Those women were young and beautiful girls, though with extremely dark skin, with their breasts exposed and likewise

their intimate parts, without the slightest trace of pubic hair. The soldiers felt an intense attraction and began to enter all the dwellings. . . . The soldiery satisfied its appetites, its hungers, and its passions, and the following morning native women and Spaniards mixed and writhed in the most pleasurable and tumultuous orgy.

The context of the Spanish conquest among warrior societies politically oriented toward war, as occurred with the so-called savage nations, appears to us within cultural characteristics that are quite specific to them, such as the fact that social prestige was inclined to favor the status of those men who performed deeds or who distinguished themselves in battle. From this perspective, such individuals claimed for themselves the social rewards deriving from the recognition given to victors. On this basis, and to the degree that the Spanish conquistadors arose victorious over the Indians, they were the objects of admiration of Indian women, as well as of the men of these societies.

In reality, if the Indian women were accustomed to admire the men from their own culture who triumphed in battle; if as a consequence they became the sexual objects of the victorious warriors; and if the latter often were granted the privilege of choosing whichever single woman they might desire for a sexual partner, it is obvious by extension that the Spanish entered into the context of these values and were preferred on the vicarious basis of status by the Indian women who identified with this system of prestige. At heart, it was a question of acts of admiration incorporated into the social ego of the Indian societies themselves. Both sides used similar models of behavior.

In this way, with the ease of sexual relations, it was not surprising that in many cases—and this is one of them—the Indian women preferred those who triumphed in these battles and with whom, on the basis of a vicarious identification, they also obtained, aside from purely sexual satisfaction, the symbolic reward of joining with a victor. This led to scandals of polygyny that were considered unjustifiable under the ecclesiastical morality of the time and were denounced as immoral conduct. This disapproval is affirmed in the words of Góngora Marmolejo (1960, 174) in reference to one of the conquistadors of Chile, Pedro de Villagra, of whom he says: "He was . . . merry of heart, given to talk, and a lover of women, for which reason he was held in disregard."

This description would be a concise report of the tendencies and personality structure of many of the conquistadors of this period; it would also be the example of the man denounced by the clergy concerned with questions of public morality. Thus, the pursuit of women, a common trait among the Spanish, was set forth as a tendency that must be repressed with regard to its polygynous content and because it created social dissolution by threatening the very stability of the political order whose establishment was being attempted in America. Fernández de Oviedo was one of those who condemned the dissolute morality implicit in the aforesaid sexual tendencies of the Spanish, when he stated (Hernández Sánchez-Barba 1981, 2:54): "I ordered it preached that no man should have a public mistress."

Nevertheless, the reality of the process was otherwise: Indian women appeared in long-standing relationships with the Spanish, and even with blacks, as we are told at a somewhat later period with a tone of indignation by Solórzano de Pereyra:

> From this abuse (concubinage) it follows that many Indian women leave their Indian husbands, or detest and abandon the children they have by them, seeing them subject to tribute and personal service, and they desire, love, and give to those Spaniards, and even blacks, whom they have outside of marriage, because they see them totally free and exempt; this clearly must not be permitted in any properly governed Republic.

These situations were repeated elsewhere, as is revealed to us by the chronicler Agustín de Zárate (Varallanos 1962, 44), who says in reference to the battles of the conquest of Peru: "With Atabalipa taken prisoner, the next morning they went to inspect the field, and it was amazing to see so many silver jars . . . and more than five thousand women came willingly to the Spanish from among those who were in the camp." And it was López de Gómara (1946, 19) who added in this regard: "although sad and abandoned (the Indian women) enjoyed themselves with the Christians."

The same attitude of mutual pleasure arises on another equally dramatic occasion of war, in Peru, when Cieza writes: "And there were in the camps many women *pallas* [var. of *payas,* peasant, country women], natives of Cuzco, who, having seen the final day of the war, being much loved by the Spanish and feeling that same love for them, were pleased to be in the service of such strong men."

In any case, the practice of capture alternated with that of good nature and mutual will that both the Indian women and the Spanish men could demonstrate. In the former case, the capture of women had become established as normal practice in wars of this type, and here between Indians and Spaniards. A German soldier, Schmidel, a participant in the conquest of Paraguay, said (1962, 301) that in the war against the Guarocoquis,[11] they had taken as prisoners some twelve thousand individuals of both sexes and different ages, and that he personally had appropriated fifty of them for his different needs and services.

African Women, Zambos, and Mulattoes

General Thesis

Although the African populations are located basically in the tropical regions of America, nevertheless, through gradual adaptation and expansion they are now situated in every region. The Spanish brought with them a very small number of blacks directly from the Iberian Peninsula as servants, but in their expeditions of discovery and conquest there were no women of this race. Black women began to arrive on American soil when the Spanish had already established their civil settlements and when their economic exploitation began to need African labor, especially in the mines and sugar mills.

As these African populations were being utilized economically, black women were also imported, and they served to keep the black men in their settlements. On this basis, rather than a massive "mulattoization" or racial mixing between Spanish men and African women, one should speak at the outset about "zamboization," or racial mixing between black men and Indian women. Nevertheless, as soon as the first black women were sent to the Antilles, and gradually to the mainland, their Spanish masters began racial mixing with them. This also rapidly produced a mulatto population, although, given the small number of women introduced into America, this mixture of Spaniards and black women could never be as intensive as that which was occurring between Spaniards and Indian women.

By contrast, as black women slaves began to appear, unions between them and the Spanish began to occur, surreptitiously but with results similar to what was happening with the Indian women. These unions did not have the same historical nature, however, because the black women were situated with the Spanish in the condition of slaves acquired through their purchase, and in some way they formed part of an asset of sexual disposition on the part of the Spanish.

From this perspective, the mixtures resulting from the union of Spaniards with black women were later than those that occurred between Spaniards and Indian women. Nevertheless, as soon as African women appeared in the expeditions as slaves, and once they were sent to the places where the Spanish had set up stable settlements with economies that basically employed African labor, these women also became sexual objects for the Spanish on a regular basis, though not ones institutionalized by the moral controls of society at that time.

In fact, black women were available to the Spanish as long as they were slaves and the Spanish their masters. Logically, under these circumstances, and to the degree to which the Spanish could have easy disposition of these women, mulattoization was also a rapid process, such that in a very short time there were many mulatto offspring mentioned in our sources.

Despite that fact, the reports that we have regarding the relations of the Spanish with these women are quite scarce in comparison with those we have about Indian women. It seems as if these reports lacked the emotional and descriptive, almost heroic, quality with which relations with Indian women are sometimes mentioned. The fact that the slavery of the African women appears institutionalized, without prior struggle or through simple commercial acquisition, has greatly diminished the historical value of these relations in the chronicles and narratives of those who wrote on the themes of the expeditions and conquests, because their historical interest turns out to be less than that of relations to Indian women.

This would be one of the reasons for the scarcity of reports on the Africans' way of living and on the relations between Spanish men and black women throughout the formative periods of American societies. Moreover, in the same way that on the Iberian Peninsula there were already blacks and mulattoes, and if we keep in mind their economic importance more than their political importance, it is obvious that the relations of the Spanish with these populations were absent from their reports, to the extent that the mentions of these women are anecdotal in nature rather than well ordered as was done, by contrast, with the Indian women, because the latter held a permanent interest.

The fact that in 1538 (Domínguez Company 1978, 127) the viceroy of New Spain, Antonio de Mendoza, prohibited the keeping of black slaves of either sex without declaring them to the authorities indicates that already in this period black women had been brought into Mexico, and therefore this makes clear that it must already have occurred previously in the Antilles. That is, once the military conquests became stabilized, the economic enterprises that were regularly set up also entailed the importation of African women so that their numbers might be in proportion to those of the men of their race.

This was necessary not only for the economic objective, but also for the express purpose of maintaining the social balance of the new societies, because if there were no women of their own race, the blacks would become a threat to the Indian populations when they turned to Indian women in their search for sexual solutions. In general, such solutions led to conflicts between blacks and Indians, and Spanish authorities were forced to import numbers of black women in order to avoid the moral and material harm that resulted from the entry of African men into the midst of native populations.

Additionally, the fact that these African women were directly situated under the social and economic control of their Spanish masters implied that the latter would often choose them to satisfy their sexual needs; however, many of the black women preferred these unions with the Spanish, even though they were considered illicit, because having children with their masters gave them a certain guarantee of better treatment, although that did not necessarily imply a juridical recognition sufficient to obtain their freedom. Nevertheless, in some cases these unions multiplied more precisely because, as slaves, the African women were at the permanent disposition of their masters or of the latters' sons and relatives, and even of the mestizos themselves who coexisted in the same social context.

As a consequence of their permanent location in stable homes, these black women were the medium for unions that, though casual, led nonetheless to a dependent relationship with the Spanish. Thus, whereas the zambo populations were the early results of the relation between blacks and Indian women during the expeditions of conquest, the mulattoes were the result of colonies and of the economic activities that kept Africans of both sexes in a productive domestic relationship with their Spanish masters.

In any case, whereas black males arrived with the first military expeditions, the women of this racial group arrived generally in relation to economic activities, that is, separated from the context of military conquests and therefore already within the context of a truly Spanish society. It is under these conditions that zambo and mulatto populations developed, and furthermore, that the mulatto populations appeared institutionalized in social status more easily than did the zambos, precisely because the parents of prestige, being those who bestowed social worth on their descendants, were the Spanish. It was they, finally and definitively, who gave or withheld juridical recognitions that permitted the development of the system of castes that was gradually implanted in viceregal society, as the conditions of Spanish social and political superiority over other racial groups were established. Above all, to the degree that blacks were held in the status of slaves, it was easier for the natives to obtain a better position than the blacks within the social structure.

Nevertheless, it is also true that because of the greater situational solidarity against the Indian that often emerged between Spaniards and their African servants, the latter frequently attained privileges as artisans and even soldiers, in the case of being incorporated early on into units of conquest and of defense. This resulted in their social legitimization as free men through the companies of *pardos* [brown or otherwise dark in color; in the Caribbean, a synonym for mulatto], and also, obviously, through mulatto descendants frequently legitimized by their own Spanish fathers, as happened with the mestizos as well under similar conditions.

Contexts and Situations

With these first general considerations in mind, there exist certain doubts as to whether blacks took part in the first Columbian expeditions. It does seem true that on his fourth voyage, Columbus brought with him a black cabin boy called Diego (Fernández de Navarrete 1954, 1:230). Nevertheless, it is also probable that some African might have been involved in one of the earlier voyages, especially since it was common in Spain at that time to use them in domestic service. At any rate, and even though blacks might have sailed on these Columbian expeditions, it is unlikely that black women would have been aboard. Basically, black women were incorporated into American settlement with the beginning of civil colonies and the stable development of economic activities and their social organization. Of course, the fact that blacks lacked any significant status at the time of the Columbian expeditions could have caused their names to be omitted from ships' lists. The latter would be a still unverifiable hypothesis.

The reports that are available regarding the entry of blacks in the first Spanish penetrations of America, including those made by Columbus, are very spare, but in general one can see that there were a few accompanying [blacks] who are difficult to recognize, not only because in some cases they were not specifically declared as such in the ship's lists, but also because, by having become part of these expeditions, they were culturally assimilated and carried Spanish-style names and surnames. This means that they could be confused with the whites of this Iberian class. Nevertheless, because of the chronological progression of the discoveries and conquests, the Antilles and particularly Hispaniola were the first to receive blacks, first individually, then in groups.

In this regard, Fernández de Oviedo (1959, 2:97) mentions how a Spaniard being attacked by the Caribs "leapt to his horse, and took with him two or three of his blacks and a Christian laborer, and went in pursuit of the Carib Indians."

In fact, thus, the first blacks were brought to America from Spain itself, not through the slave trade, but by taking advantage of those populations already assimilated. In reality, the slave trade would be a later phenomenon of traffic run initially by the Portuguese.

It is well known, additionally, that already in the early years of the founding of Hispaniola, around 1505, according to Las Casas (Casas 1965, 3:276), "there were at that time on this Island 10 or 12 blacks who belonged to the king who had been brought to build the fortress that is above the mouth of the river."

Nevertheless, according to Céspedes (1971, 396), trade in blacks had already begun in 1501, when the king authorized such traffic in order to utilize this labor force for the purpose of housing and the economic activities of the settlers. Additionally, in 1513, the citizens of Hispaniola were authorized by the king to import women, probably black,[1] who would be destined for domestic service for Spanish families. As Fernández de Navarrete points out (1954, 1:520), the king granted "permission that each citizen of said island who might wish can take from these (Spanish realms) a female slave to serve his house, because of the need that they have there for servants."

Given the conditions of domestic service, these women were "Christians, raised more than three years in Castilla" (ibid.).

Thus, there is no doubt that they were not sent for the direct purpose of marrying other black slaves, precisely because they were linguistically acculturated. For this reason, they communicated more easily with the Spanish than with the blacks who were unsophisticated or who spoke only African languages. Sexual access to these women was surreptitious and opportunistic in nature, but at any rate single Spaniards wove sexual schemes with them as much as they did with Indian women, or perhaps more so, by virtue of the advantage of being able to communicate in the same language, one which thus allowed for emotional intimacy and, in a certain way, continuity when these Spaniards remained for some time in the same place. Additionally, experience with black women was easier, because of their status as domestic slaves, than that which could be had with Indian women, often fraught with conflict because the friars became the moral scourge of the conquistadors.

According to this policy, and later in Costa Rica in 1540, the service of black women in the houses of the Spanish became commonplace, and this presence occasioned disputes among the Spanish over their ownership. In one of these suits (Fernández Guardia 1907, 129), it is stated in this regard: "Salvador de Medina, His Majesty's scribe who accompanies Your Mercy, and Alonso de Orozco spoke some words to a black woman of mine, and was told that where they were spoken there were some of Your Mercy's people, and I told him to give me testimony regarding what kind of treatment the aforesaid people were giving to my aforesaid black woman."

In this sense, as well, a black woman slave destined for domestic service could bring prices even higher or at least equal to those of a male slave. Zavala (1938, 38) mentions that in 1580 a citizen of Seville paid 130 ducats for a black woman slave, whereas a few years earlier (1571) a black male slave had cost 125 *ducados*.[2] Later than in the Antilles, therefore, those married Spaniards on the mainland with the economic means to obtain women for their service used to acquire black women. In 1580, expeditions of families to the mainland customarily carried these women with them. Ordóñez de Ceballos (1947, 47–49) says, with regard to the mishap that befell a ship which ran aground, that "only the wife of an auditor and one of her black women were endangered."

In the context of this same accident, upon having to abandon the ship, he lists (ibid.): "a son of the auditor, who had two sons and four daughters and two black women and one black girl. Another man, a married passenger, [with] a wife and two small daughters and another black woman, and a pious woman and her black woman."

In general, from the moment that Spanish families first appeared, constituting a civil society, one has the impression that in all of them it was common practice to take black women with them for domestic service. Some of these women were quite young but in each case susceptible to being desired by Spanish men and, based on social control, accessible more to single men than to married men.

Of course, we must recall that, just as there were no Spanish women on the expeditions of conquest, neither were there black women. In this sense, although there were some exceptions on the conquests of the mainland, insofar as the islands are concerned there seem to have been no expeditions involving black women, because what did occur was the participation of black males as the servants of some few Spanish commanders. These servants were assimilated, that is, they spoke Spanish and had adopted the Spanish lifestyle of the era. The majority of them went to the Indies as the slaves of those who had acquired them in Spain. It is even true as well that, other than blacks, some of these servants were mulattoes from both Spain and Portugal. In the Canary Islands a certain process of mulattoization, and therefore of assimilation, had already taken place. The Canaries were also the later point of embarkation for many of those traveling as the servants of Spaniards, be they conquistadors or officials and civilians who were heading for the Indies with a desire to establish themselves in those Spanish possessions.

The question of sending black slaves to America soon became a problem in the sense that mulattoes also were sent, who, because of the condition of being racially mixed, do not seem to have had such a clear juridical status as slaves as did the blacks. In 1543 Carlos V was obliged to issue prohibitions (*Recopilación de Leyes* . . . , Law XXI) where it is stated: "Under general permits mulattoes may not be sent."

Therefore: "By virtue of our general permits to send black slaves to the Indies, some mulattoes and others who are not blacks are taken and sent, from which problems ensue. . . . Let no slave who is not a black be allowed to go, even though he is a Mulatto, without our special permission."

Fundamentally, this seems to indicate that the concept of the slave was applied more to blacks than to mulattoes; furthermore we are given to understand that while the former were the direct products of the slave trade, the latter assumed a different nature, or at least it was pretended that they were not directly absorbed into the business of the trade. Nevertheless, the first blacks introduced into America must have been assimilated ones who could therefore communicate in the Spanish language. It is obvious, in addition, that at the beginning of the conquests, black women had no specific social function among the military forces, not even a sexual one, because in this case the Spanish and their accompanying forces were cared for by the Indian women.

To the degree that the conquests of the Antilles were being consummated and Spain's political dominion over them was affirmed, civil power developed its colonies and settlements with an eye to producing its own society and economy. In those beginnings, black women began to occupy positions in the new societies, as the men of their race had done previously.

On the basis of the call by Las Casas to import blacks to the Antilles (1519–20) because of the decline of the Indian population in the islands, slaves began to arrive on a large scale. Las Casas's idea consisted not only of freeing the Indians from the slavery to which they were subjected, but also of achieving progress in Spanish agriculture and cattle raising, as well as building a population within the Catholic spirit of having all Christians married, whatever their race.

Nevertheless, being the equals of the Spanish in their early sexual dependencies with regard to Indian women, the blacks showed as great an unbridled interest in them as did the conquistadors themselves, to the extreme that in Guatemala in 1533, blacks had to be denied access to the springs and streams where the Indian women washed clothes; likewise, in 1537, local laws prohibited them from entering native markets, and the same was done to mestizos and even to some Spaniards (Remesal 1964, 1:109–10); the conduct of blacks with the Indian women created disorders and conflicts with the latter's husbands and relatives. In any case, zambos, or the products of blacks and Indians, quickly proliferated in America, although on a lesser scale than the mestizos, if we keep in mind the greater number of Spaniards and their greater freedom of access to Indian women when compared to those of the blacks.

Whatever may have been the first numbers of blacks imported, demand for them certainly responded to the notion of their greater economic productivity, since, as Herrera stated (1936, 116): "a black works more than four (Indians), for which reason there was a great demand for them."

Likewise, though with reference to much later dates (1667), but within the comparative context of labor productivity, Alonso de Solórzano wrote of the Indians in the region of Buenos Aires that "the work of thirty Indians does not match that of one black slave."

Thus, it is obvious that the main reason for the demand for blacks was economic, as much because they were more productive as because politically they entailed less conflict. The effort to bring them to the Indies had begun from the very moment that the natives turned out to be extremely fragile to be employed in the harsh labors that the Spanish imposed upon them. It should be mentioned that in Puerto Rico in 1510, a certain Gerónimo de Bruselas, a foundryman by trade, was authorized by the king to bring in two slaves (Díaz Soler 1970, 23).

This authorization shows that very early the residents of the islands, especially those of Hispaniola, began to solicit the king in order to import black slaves. Padre B. de Manzanedo, in a letter to the monarch dated in 1518, requested authorization in the name of citizens and public employees to bring in unskilled blacks, that is, those brought straight from Africa, because those from Castilla would scarcely obey and were a source of rebelliousness that made it difficult to handle and control their movements. Manzanedo's letter (1918, 62–63) says, among other things: "those padres and I, along with Your Highness' officials, Judges and some *regidores*[3] of Santo Domingo, spoke about this item, and given the need of this island, we all agreed that it would be good to bring them so long as there were as many, or more, females as males, and they are unsophisticated and not raised in Castilla or anywhere else, because those are real scoundrels."

The enticement to bring them consisted in mentioning the economic possibilities that were opening up on the islands with this labor force, the lure of the extraction of gold, and the conviction that by setting it up in activities useful to the Crown, black labor would imply the establishment of the Spanish. Las Casas (Casas 1965, 3:276), motivated by the first successful results of the sugar harvest on Hispaniola (1505) and the beginning of the sugar mills, also requested the king to authorize the importation of black slaves, arguing in the same terms as had Manzanedo. Aside from acknowledging the existence of "10 or 12 blacks who were royal property and had been brought in to build the fortress" he pushed for the authorization that every Spanish citizen might bring "two, three, or more slaves, half of them male and half of them female, so that they might multiply" (ibid., 129).

In fact, these slaves were recognized to have a greater economic capacity than the Indians, but for our purposes what is significant is that after that time [1505], authorization to import them began on a grand scale. Thus, Las Casas (ibid., 177) states on that same occasion that "a royal letter was dispatched to the officials of the [Casa de] Contratación in Seville,[4] to meet and discuss the number that they thought appropriate; they replied that for these four islands, Hispaniola, San Juan, Cuba and Jamaica, it was their opinion that for the present 4,000 black slaves would suffice."

This royal letter was the beginning of the mass importation of blacks of both sexes because, fundamentally, black women constituted factors of stability in the social establishment of the black men. At this time the Portuguese were already taking blacks from Africa to the islands, as Fernández de Oviedo (1959, 5:404) acknowledged when in 1543 he wrote:

Seven ships and caravels embarked from the city of Santo Domingo on the Island of Hispaniola on July 20 of the year fifteen hundred forty-three bound for Spain. Among those vessels was a Portuguese ship, which had come to this city loaded with blacks to sell, because they are valuable here and are necessary for our estates and the service of the citizens and country farms and mines, to extract the gold, and for the sugar mills (there now being such a number of the black slaves that many of them have run away from their masters . . .

The Portuguese also had no problem in introducing great numbers of mulatto slaves from their own territories (Díaz Soler 1970, 63), such that mulattoization often arrived in concrete form from Spain or Portugal. Nevertheless, traffic in black women had already begun in the second decade of the sixteenth century, and the first were specifically destined for the service of Spanish families in the islands. Within this context of the large-scale trade, these women were considered appropriate for men of their race, although their masters, by virtue of their powers of disposition, also assumed sexual rights over them.

Around 1537, the black slave trade constituted a regular activity run by the Portuguese, and Alvar Núñez Cabeza de Vaca (1957, 106) mentions the case of a French ship which, under armed attack by the Portuguese in the Azores, had to abandon one of the latter's caravels that it had captured and that "was loaded with blacks."

Incidentally, these black women were preyed upon by the Carib Indians, and the Spanish frequently undertook punitive expeditions in order to rescue them, such as on Dominica, for example, where around 1528 Fray Pedro

Aguado (1963, chap. 27) points out that after capturing Carib Indians at war against the Spanish, "they took the black women, from whom they learned at great length everything mentioned above," that is, news about the hostilities to which the Spaniards and blacks were subject. According to this, and with the exploitation of sugar and mining, the blacks became the most highly prized labor force in the islands, such that, as Fernández de Oviedo indicated (ibid., 1:107), "it is necessary to have constantly at least eighty or . . . a hundred blacks, and even a hundred twenty, and some more."

Of course, the blacks entered the continent early with the first conquistadors, as they had done previously in the Antilles, working in the service of Spanish citizens. For example, at his death Pedro de Alvarado, the conqueror of Guatemala, left blacks as an inheritance (Remesal 1964, 1:286). These were employed in various jobs in the service of the Spanish, in their homes, in the mines, in the sugar mills, in pearl fishing, and on military expeditions.

There is also the case of a black woman, the rich widow of a Spaniard named Solano in Puerto Rico, who freed two hundred Indian slaves at the same time that she fervently supported missionary work by providing the priests with copious alms in food (Remesal 1964, 1:343−44). At this time (1544−45) one could speak of mulattoes (ibid., 456) in the service of the encomenderos.

Black women appeared linked above all to domestic service and to secondary tasks on the haciendas and were also assigned as wives to the African men clustered in the slave quarters or in the very interior of the sugar mills where they worked.

There is no doubt, by contrast, that mulattoes soon achieved a status comparatively higher than that of their mothers, precisely because the white Spanish patriarchy indulged in the formation of emotional sentiments toward the children born of black mothers, especially when they were born nearby and lived in constant relation with their natural fathers. The frequency of this physical relation with some black women more than with others created relatively stable relations with the master or with his white employees, particularly with the single men; thus, many of these mulatto offspring were favored and even freed, with preference given to those born of uncontrolled casual relations and those in which only maternity was certain. In the Antilles this was a common experience after the moment—the first quarter of the sixteenth century—in which Indian women became scarce and were replaced by black women as more or less stable sexual companions.

In fact, these black women soon abounded in the homes of the Spanish, particularly if we keep in mind that by 1517 in Puerto Rico haciendas needed for their development between eight and ten servants to tend just to domestic duties (Díaz Soler 1970, 150). These servants came to depend in general on the master and doubtless on the wives of the latter, whom we know were exceedingly jealous of the black women because they were usually available especially to white men who occupied trusted positions on the haciendas. They were equally available, as we know, to the soldiers—most of them bachelors—who formed part of the garrisons manning the fortresses.

It is also evident that from very early on, many black and mulatto slaves attained freedom and worked their own lands as subjects of the king. Between 1574 and 1592, Title Five of the *Recopilación de Leyes de Indias* says the following in this regard: "Many male and female slaves, black men and women, Mulatto men and women, who have gone to the Indies, and others who were born there, have gained their freedom and they have farms and haciendas."

In addition, by the middle seventeenth century Puerto Rico had become the place of refuge for blacks fleeing the dominion of non-Spanish nations. When they reached the island, these slaves gained their freedom as long as they converted to Catholicism and swore obedience to the king (Díaz Soler 1970, 83). This means that conditions were quite favorable for interracial sexual interests and exchanges, particularly because of the mobility and circulation of both Spanish and black groups which, as a result, could never find sufficient sources for familial stability. This personal instability doubtlessly contributed as much to intensive mulattoization as did the very sexual availability of black women to the Spanish.

In some way it is also true that Spanish laws were more favorable to black slaves than those applied to them by other European nations. This would be confirmed not only by the above-mentioned law that recognizes the existence of a large number of freedmen working their own lands toward the middle of the sixteenth century, but also by the fact that the slaves themselves appreciated this situation, as expressed by Motolonía (1971, 370–71), who wrote the following:

> that black who wrote from this New Spain to another friend of his, also a black slave, and had been in Santo Domingo or in Spain, said in his letter: "Friend So-and-so, this is a good land for slaves: here the black man eats well; here the black has a slave to serve him, and the black's slave has a *naboría*, which means attendant or servant. Therefore, work so that your master will sell you and you can come to this country, which is the best in the world for blacks.

The island Spanish, especially the poorest ones, soon began to think about emigrating to the mainland, because the success of the expeditions of conquest also confirmed the great possibilities for enrichment that in the Antilles, by contrast, were beginning to wane. Also, certainly, the situation of the black slaves employed in domestic service, that is, in the very bosom of the

Spanish family, over time appears to have had effects similar to those that result from a long coexistence. As Díaz Soler remarks (1970, 151), manumission was frequent in masters' final wills, to the extreme that many of these slaves having been treated well, preferred to "continue working on the haciendas" upon regaining their freedom. Under these conditions we could not generalize about the treatment given to slaves because that depended largely upon the interpersonal relations between them and their masters. Basically, nonetheless, those employed in domestic service or as servants were always the most favored.

And in another sense, many of those who came with the Spanish acted in social identification with the latter's culture. In this respect, it is interesting to note that in Puerto Rico, on the occasion of the census count on 11 November 1530, a black named Francisco declared that he was married to a woman of his race and that he also owned slaves, of whom eleven were blacks and three were Indians (ibid., 251). In general, the Puerto Rico census some years earlier included a total of 1,523 blacks, among whom 355, or 23 percent, were women (Alvarez Nazario 1974, 72–73).

It seems important here that by the third decade of the sixteenth century, the blacks had become well established on the islands and furthermore were beginning to be an economic and social factor in the growing demographic process. In this sense, it is especially significant that some blacks had obtained the social position of slave owners, where control was exercised according to the predominant model or in the style of the Spanish themselves. Additionally, while this was going on, the island Spaniards were beginning to feel the pressure of the scarcity of land and the hope of achieving their personal fortune by emigrating to the mainland. All of this was taking place at the moment when some slaves were being freed and were becoming, furthermore, masters of their own fellow blacks and Indians. At the same time, black women were already playing an important role in the processes of miscegenation that would give rise to mulatto populations, while mestizos and zambos, along with other genetic combinations, already constituted numerically significant populations that were biologically more important than was declared in the censuses. From this perspective, when the Spanish went to the exploration and conquest of territories on the mainland, a great number of these products of mixture were already part of their culture, although socially they might occupy a subordinate position of status. In this way, the blacks and mixed bloods who had remained with the Spanish were preferred by the latter as servants on their campaigns, precisely because, as we have indicated, they fit into the conceptual category of assimilation and were more prone than other groups to identify themselves with the interests of the Crown.

If blacks and mixed bloods had participated from the beginning of the explorations as servants and attendants to the Spanish, and if they actually appeared among them, they did so as assimilated slaves. One of them, Jesús Garrido, a black born in Angola and raised in Seville, was already a free man when he accompanied Juan Ponce de León in 1508 to begin the colonization of Puerto Rico. A mulatto, Francisco Mejía, arrived at Hispaniola as a servant of Ovando and married an Indian woman cacique in Puerto Rico. Alvarez Nazario (1974, 30) also points out that another assimilated free black, Francisco Piñón (mentioned before in another context), who had come to Puerto Rico married to a black woman, came also with another black, Diego Hernández. Together in 1530, these were citizens of San Juan and owned African and Indian slaves, that is, they followed the social method of the Spanish and thought like them.

That early period shows that some blacks of this type, assimilated and free, were establishing themselves in the islands as Spaniards. Those who arrived in that category were people who, at the same time that they served as servants to some Spaniards, shared with them the vicissitudes of war. They were, thus, "Spanish" blacks who aided the soldiers and who shared in the ideology of conquest, that is, they captured Indian women and made them concubines and slaves. This was the origin of the first zambos.

In Mexico, the situation was oriented more towards zamboization than toward mulattoization, especially in those places where the blacks remained close to Indian women. In the case of Spaniards who had black women at their disposition, the opposite occurred. Aguirre Beltrán (1972, 257) quotes a letter from the viceroy of New Spain to Felipe II in which he tells him:

> and the Indian women are very weak persons and much given to the blacks, and thus they indulge more with them in their houses than they do with Indians, and the blacks, no more, no less, marry them rather than other black women in order to have free children. For such a large number of blacks came each year, and the mulattoes are multiplying so rapidly . . . and the latter are the masters of Indians, having been born and raised among them, and they are men as unafraid of death as any Spaniards in the world.

According to Aguirre Beltrán (ibid.), mixture with Indian women was very frequent among African men, and since the products of mixture remained in the midst of the indigenous communities, the latter were the ones that inherited their descendants as a cultural form. In any case, it is obvious to us that this acculturation was occurring simultaneously with that being experienced by the Spanish. In addition, in those places where black women were attractive to their Spanish masters and for the white retinues under their control, they represented sexual objects and thus became vehicles of mulattoization more than of zamboization.

With the rapid demographic saturation of the Antilles, due to the technology and means of the period, and the massive transfer of Spaniards to the mainland, the successive expeditions to the different territories of America included blacks in greater numbers than before. These blacks are mentioned in every one of the expeditions. For example, the black Estebanico appears in the conquest of Florida, and with Hernando de Soto in 1539 an assimilated black named Juan Vizcaino is recognized as a servant to Juan Ruiz Lobillo. This servant ran away (Fernández de Oviedo 1959, 2:171–72) during the course of events. And in another part of Florida (ibid.), "it was learned that they had killed Don Teodoro and a black who had come from the boats of Pánfilo de Narváez."

The conquest of Mexico had a similar cast. Hernán Cortés took blacks with him as personal servants who also took part in military operations. Bernal Díaz (Diaz del Castillo 1955, 50) mentions "Joan Sedeño, a citizen of Havana (who brought) his own ship, a mare, and a black." And Las Casas (1965, 3:227) adds that in the Cortés expedition that left Cuba for Mexico in February of 1519, "there were in it . . . certain blacks whom they had as slaves."

Additionally, Bernal Díaz (ibid., 482), referring to encounters with the Indians in Chiapas, speaks of "our black artilleryman we had with us, who could be called very black, paralyzed with fear and trembling, could not even shoot or put flame to the fuse, and finally, driven by our shouts at him, he fired and wounded three of our soldiers, which gained us nothing."

In 1568, blacks already were established in Mexico and thus were in the service of the Spanish. In San Juan de Ulúa (Vera Cruz) Chilton (1963, 34) said that there "the King keeps some 50 soldiers and officers who guard the forts, plus another hundred blacks who are employed year round in bringing stones for buildings and other uses and in helping to tie up ships which put in there."

Before that, with the conquest of Mexico assured (1521), we read (Fernández de Oviedo 1959, 4:258) of "the wife of Francisco López, their black maidservant (and) a black man very tall in stature."

With regard to expeditions, the Spanish of social lineage in command, such as the Marqués de Cañete in Peru, carried black women with them for their domestic service, as did Spanish women, married and mistresses of households, who also preferred them. In one case (Lizárraga 1968, 130) we are told:

(The Marqués) would rise very early in the morning, and with just a page for a guard he would go upriver . . . following his trail, he heard sobs like a woman's from one who was grieving because the only black woman he had—who prepared bread and sold it in the plaza, thus barely providing him with a living—had died that morning. . . . Then the father of the poor, the good Marqués, turned back and, with the page who accompanied him, he sent the man a silver bar assayed at 250 pesos (at the time unskilled blacks were not yet worth very much), telling him to worry no longer and to use that bar to buy another black woman to serve his needs.

Regarding this point in the establishment of blacks in America, one could say that the black men were treated very patriarchally and the women were treated as companions for white women, particularly in the bosom of the families who had them as domestics. Padre Motolinía had already recognized this kind of treatment in the citation above, but it is equally correct to add that many black women had become the confidantes of their mistresses, and the same thing was taking place between the masters and the slaves in their service.

Brazil was no exception. At the beginning of Portuguese penetration into that territory, union with black women was similar in nature to what we are describing for the Spanish areas. The Portuguese, most of them single males, united with black women as they had done and continued to do with the Indians. With the women of both races they established a sort of polygyny, at once simultaneous and successive, which lasted until very recent times, especially in those regions where white women were scarce and where black women served on sugar plantations and in domestic work. In those places the whites had little hesitation in uniting with the "black women brought from Africa to work in the sugar mills, the mines, and rural and domestic labor" (Barreto 1959, 81).

According to Barreto (ibid.) this meant that even by the beginning of the twentieth century it was common for the big landowners to have many illegitimate children. One of them, in 1907, "recognized 157 children, of whom 12 were legitimate" (ibid.).

Gilberto Freyre (1943) throughout his works has stressed the patriarchal nature of rural Brazilian society since the sixteenth century, based on the holding of plantations where the black played a decisive economic role, situated at the social base of the *fazendas*,[5] colonizing institutions par excellence. Meanwhile, other Portuguese, driven by individual adventurism, moved throughout the vastness of Brazil and, as on the fazendas, miscegenated the country, soon giving it the aspect of a mestizo and mulatto region, besides those Indians, Europeans, and Africans who managed to remain more or less pure. But, fundamentally, it was black women in the service of white men who initiated the mulattoization of Brazil, and, along with Indian women in different periods of intensity, they were, as Freyre points out (ibid., 2:137), the ones who provided the young colonizers the sexual outlets they were seeking. Later, when rural and mining life based on black slavery had been established as the predominant type of society, it was (ibid.) "the mulatto woman . . . who initiated us into physical love and transmitted to us the first complete feeling of being a man."

Mulatto women held a great fascination for Europeans, who in many cases preferred them to their own women (ibid.). Thus, once the first generation of mulattoes was established, the children of whites, and even their own fathers who exercised positions of dominant patriarchality—along with the other social levels of single white men seeking a position in that society— had mulatto women as mistresses or as preferred sexual initiators, not only because with them there was less of a social commitment, but also because of sexual satisfaction. In fact, Barreto (1959, 116–17) writes that "concubinage and the licentiousness of custom conferred upon lordly despotism the most complete polygamy."

Commonly, it would be necessary to distinguish between domestic blacks and those employed in the mines and in the mills because, while the former joined familiarly with the whites, the latter were isolated. The former would be the most favored in social treatment. In addition, black males were the companions of the Spanish in their expeditions, explorations, and conquests. For example, Vasco Núñez took with him thirty blacks, who in turn, as Las Casas writes (Casas 1965, 3:79), "were served by the Indians, whom they called dogs, wretched and abused."

In this sense, the blacks not only shared in many aspects of the fortune of the Spanish conquests, but along with the expeditionary soldiers they easily became the adversaries of the Indians; blacks ended up taking advantage of them and exploited them socially and economically, making them their servants, while they used the Indian women as concubines. In the islands and on the continent both Spaniards and Africans, respectively, formed the frequent unions with the Indian women that led to the creation of mestizo and zambo populations.

Furthermore, the blacks certainly behaved as did the Spanish with Indian women, that is, they took them as mistresses in a polygynous system, from which resulted large numbers of zambos. Around 1540, the baptismal register of the Lima cathedral showed seventy-six zambos in ten years (Hart-Terré 1973, 139–41), while the total for mulattoes was seventeen. Here, we are not seeking to recognize these forces as statistics of actual zambo and mestizo formation. The fact that the *provisor,*[6] Luis de Morales, recognized in 1541 (ibid.) that "the black slaves in the provinces of Peru who belong to the Spanish have many Indian men and women native to that land for their own despicable ends, to the great prejudice of the latter, who number more than fifteen or twenty and whose labors and duties for the Spanish are not enough, but rather they are compelled to serve Slaves," allows us to establish clearly that both products—zambos and mulattoes—numbered many more than those legally registered by the church because the circumstantial nature of many of those unions suggests the lack of legal recognition for such mixtures.

A moral factor—the notion of sin—and another one of institutional organization applied to social control, as well as those factors of personal prestige ascribed to the principle of status and self-esteem, also hindered the bestowal of paternal recognition on these zambos and mulattoes (especially the latter), all of which came to mean that miscegenation was very intensive at all racial levels, including the fact that (ibid.) the "aforesaid black slaves who are in the said province and belong to the Spanish, have several Indian women native to the aforesaid province at their will."

Elsewhere, in 1560, as an example of a sexually adventurous attitude, the blacks took over (Aguado 1963, 2:611–12) an Indian village, Caricua, in Colombia, "taking away their daughters and wives and mixing and engaging with them, which engendered another different mixture of people . . . who, although called mulattoes—and by their mixture they are—have very little similarity to the offspring of black women and white men."

Thus, during these periods of conquest black women played little or no part in the context of total miscegenation. By contrast, it was black men who played an increasing role in the development of mixtures, and along with the Spanish—though to a lesser degree than the latter due to their difference in numbers—they participated largely in the genesis of different types of racial mixtures.

In Panama, as had occurred in the islands, many blacks had banded together outside the political and economic control of the Spanish. These were the so-called *cimarrones*[7] who in those early times (mid sixteenth century), according to Ortiguera (1948, 219–20), "did enormous damage to those two cities (Nombre de Dios and Panama), taking black men and women captives from the service of their Spanish masters, to whom they belonged, . . . and such was their force that they already had an army and squadron of over 1200 men and women . . . because in that land there are no other servants than black slaves."

Ordóñez de Ceballos (1947, 63), citing the case of the cimarrones who went about attacking those who traveled along the roads of Cartagena de Indias, pointed out that "I set out with fifty men, thirty-six freed blacks, and six of mine and eight belonging to different soldiers."

This reference implies clearly that not only were there runaway blacks who even formed organized republics and fought against the Spanish, but also that at the time it was a common practice for every Spanish soldier to have at least one black soldier at his service. Among commanders there would be more black servants, because Ordóñez was a *veedor*[8] and states that he had provided six blacks of his own to the punitive expedition against the cimarrones. But in addition—and this is important—at this time (1580–90) among the group of cimarrones who faced this punitive expedition there were 150 black women (ibid., 64–67), one of whom bravely rushed against Ordóñez, for which he turned to her, reporting that "I said to the woman: Let me fight for your life against that black (the leader Martín) . . . and you will see whether I am your countryman, and I say again that I respect you and will make you free and have the Crown give you an hacienda. She said: Go and slay him; thus shall I be without a husband and can serve you."

Meanwhile, the woman tried to fight against Ordóñez without success, until they all surrendered to him, and the battle's end showed (ibid.) that "among the dead were over fifty black women and thirty men on their side, and on ours, not counting the three aforesaid men, two blacks and three Indians and almost everyone was wounded."

In light of other considerations of a political, military, or other nature, what is important is the fact that a great number of black women had already become established on the continent since the mid sixteenth century, and in this sense it is obvious that, in addition to the fact that they were intended to marry the men of their race, they also entered into sexual combination with the Spanish themselves.

During this period there are abundant accounts of cimarrones and of events in which many of these black slaves obtained their freedom from the Spanish, but in any case the most important point is that the establishment of Spanish civilian settlements constituted the main condition for the process of mulattoization, precisely because it was the moment when the great expeditions of black slaves of both sexes were begun. As we see, there were considerable numbers of black women in the Antilles and on the continent. Furthermore, there is no doubt that the conditions already existed for an intensive mulattoization.

Generally, sexual unions with black women on the part of the Spanish rarely resulted in marriage. The major obstacle was the difference in status and the very origin of that status, especially slavery. In addition, mulattoes were born in greater numbers between young soldiers and black women than between married masters and their black servants. Furthermore, since the mulatto was held to be inferior to the mestizo, the tendencies of social prestige sought to confine relations with the black women to fortuitous and circumstantial exchanges, that is, outside of strict social controls. In another sense, in colonial times the mestizo color enjoyed greater social advantages than did the mulatto and those derived from zamboization. Actually, the lighter the individual's complexion, the better might be his initial possibilities for social advancement. Even for marriage, with the lack of Spanish and criollo women, the conquistadors and settlers preferred mestizo women.

This preference, first for Indian women over black and for mestizo women over mulatto, was created under the aegis of a certain social simplification with reference to status: that is, many Spaniards married Indian women who contributed native nobility and territorial property, when not significant dowries. In addition, Indian women were free persons like them, whom the Crown promoted because they were simultaneously allied with the conquistadors and with the Indian leaders who had submitted to them. Other Spaniards quickly grew accustomed to Indian and mestizo women, and their legal status as free persons made them socially more legitimate than black women. In addition, there were other primary factors: the Spanish began to establish themselves in America after an initial uprooting, and in this case while the personality of the Spanish soldiers, and among them that of the single men in particular, was sexually dependent on the Indian women, their establishment in America had its beginnings through their relations with them.

Of course, a mere sexual relation would not itself have led to the development of this psychological need to feel one's self in the midst of a familiar setting and thus reinforce one's sense of security. There was something denser in the environmental context: Indian and mestizo women also offered the Spanish a home and, with their love, mitigated their longings for family life. Thus, as long as the Indian and mestizo women lived in their lands, with them the Spanish managed to regain their confidence as productive social beings. Psychologically, the mechanism of the need for settlement consisted in making a life with the Indian and mestizo women, more so than with black and mulatto women, because the latter were also as strange to America as the Spanish and criollo might have been in the early days.

Here, it is evident that the first feelings of establishment began with the Indian women and the creation of more or less stable homes with them. But in any case, psychologically, the resolution of the outsider complex that the Spanish might feel occurred especially through social union with Indian women.

Beyond that, black women did not come in as free persons, and under those circumstances the Spanish limited themselves to using them as sexual objects outside of any social commitment. Possibly—and the same had occurred with mestizo women—it was mulatto women who could also offer to the Spanish this idea of an emotional foundation that was so necessary as part of the resolution of their feelings of foreignness, especially among single men. When black and mulatto women began to establish themselves in

America, in many areas they played a role similar to the one that Indian and mestizo women had acquired before; not only were they the sexual objects of a more or less urgent relation, but in many aspects they represented emotional solutions because they offered the Spanish a certain familial life, one that was sometimes ambiguous and provisional because it emerged devoid of formal obligations but that ended up with the settlement of many Spaniards.

This process took more time to occur than it did with the Indian women. In fact, it was necessary for another generation to appear. But this presumed need for affection, as well as a strictly sexual solution, was very soon satisfied by the Spanish with black and mulatto women as well. There were places, such as the Antilles, where early on these women replaced Indian and mestizo women in sexual unions. It was the garrison soldiers above all who showed a preference for uniting with blacks and mulattoes. Alvarez Nazario (1974, 76) says that in 1701 Padre Labat acknowledged that the mulattoization of Puerto Rico was a general phenomenon. And in 1744, Juan Colomo, as governor of that island, pointed out (ibid.) that "two thirds of the battalion (defending the island) were married to mulatto women, for which reason there is no need at present for barracks."

Thus, the soldiers lived in the houses of these women and had new descendants by them. Additionally, in 1761, Marshal O'Reilly, in a letter to the Spanish governor (ibid., 76) would say something similar in this regard: "The two companies and two squads that were sent to Puerto Rico at the beginning of the last war to reinforce the garrison soon followed the established example of these undertakings. These latest troops remained in the barracks, but each soldier set up house with a black or mulatto woman whom they called their housekeeper."

An initial process of mulattoization was gradually becoming a process of whitening due to the fact that each generation of Spanish soldiers was repeating this experience. This meant that after several generations the Spanish authorities could scarcely discern the differences that might exist between a white and a mulatto woman, and the extreme of this confusion was accepted officially when Governor Benavides said in Puerto Rico (ibid.) that dances held by mulatto women were practically dances that could be thought given by white women, in order to justify the attendance of white men.

This dynamic had begun in the sixteenth century, based on the great percentage of Spaniards in Puerto Rico who were single. In most cases, white men cohabited with black and mulatto women, and in this respect a governor of the island was accused in 1569 of permitting it as a practice (ibid., 74). One must consider this situation as a stabilized custom in the Indies, and it was one of the factors in the multiplication of the mixed populations; cohabitation did not cease as long as there were unmarried Spanish civilians and soldiers, even though there were attempts to establish rigid social controls designed to prevent it.

Something similar was taking place everywhere. In Colombia, Spaniards and blacks were, from the outset, also comrades on expedition, and with the establishment and foundation of cities, villas, and towns, Africans were incorporated as a labor force into the Spanish economy. In a short time Africans of both sexes began to become numerically equal, since, apart from the fact that royal policy called for sending proportional numbers of both sexes to the same places (Document 377, in Friede 1955, 2:281), the greater exposure and physical risk for black men also decreased their numbers. This led to their numerical leveling with black women, if we keep in mind that the latter were less exposed than the men to harsh labor and to the vicissitudes that they endured in the wars of conquest and pacification. In any case, in 1530 (ibid.) the queen was giving "permission to send a hundred black slaves, half of them men and half of them women."

Fundamentally, to the degree that the Indians were neither sufficiently acculturated nor subject to the juridical and social discipline of the Spanish, the blacks were even considered indispensable. Fernández de Oviedo (1959, 3:168) acknowledges this situation when he says, with reference to New Granada: "And that night a gang of blacks escaped (from the Spanish), and the master went after them, and on the following day he overtook them and returned to the camp with them, because without them the Christians could scarcely be served."

Certainly, then, the campaigns in what would become New Granada were already being undertaken with blacks, and thus the same Fernández de Oviedo (ibid., 5:19) pointed out the following: "Lieutenant Peña sent blacks and Christians to open the route to Cali." And in the civil wars that confronted Pizarro and Almagro in 1537, blacks took an active part (ibid., 184), and in other theaters of war they died alongside the Spanish in clashes with the Indians. The author (ibid., 203) also tells us: "And they killed Villadiego and thirteen or fourteen others, as well as many blacks, and Indians from Nicaragua, and yanaconas."

With the completion of certain conquests in Colombia in the late sixteenth century, blacks were present in large numbers, employed principally, as Ordóñez de Ceballos writes (1947, 303), in the extraction of gold, and thus, "more than fourteen thousand of them are mining gold." Since gold production promised to be greater in Popayán, the king was advised of the need to have blacks for this work. Ordóñez himself (ibid.) says that in Popayán "there are no blacks at all, for if there were, ten times as much (gold) would be extracted. And His Majesty should be requested to send to that district and to Antioquia . . . six or eight thousand blacks, and they were entrusted to each citizen."

Almagro (Molina [El Almagrista] 1968, 90) in 1536 had in his service a "mulatto boy" whom he used as a messenger to the Inca. We do not know in this case if this was a young man born in America, but certainly by that time there were already generations of mulattoes born on the islands, who, as occurred with large numbers of mestizos, were assuming Spanish culture and social identity. These mulattoes appear with a certain frequency in the Peruvian campaign of the latter half of the sixteenth century. For example, Lizárraga (1968, 148) mentions that in one clash with the Inca Condorillo, the latter wounded a mulatto, and in a fight against the Chiriguanos,[9] the latter (ibid., 152) "killed a Spaniard and one or two mulattoes, and I don't know how many Indians." Basically, blacks and mulattoes were thus operating as members of the forces that undertook these campaigns, and if black women remained in the rear, as did the Spanish women, and if—as the facts of mulattoization would demonstrate—they were the sexual objects of the Spanish, it is obvious that the process of mulattoization was beginning to intensify. In any case, there were always two categories of black women: the domestics, who were assigned directly to the service of Spanish households, and those who lived with black males in work areas under the supervision of their masters or of various kinds of authorities.

In Venezuela in the seventeenth century, the blacks who extracted gold were concentrated at the mouth of the Zulia River (Arellano Moreno 1964, 290), while other mulattoes extracted gold in the province of Nirgua. And in Costa Rica in the mid seventeenth century, in 1635 to be specific, in the city of Cartago, blacks lived in a separate neighborhood from the whites (Olien 1980, 17). In the eighteenth century in Puerto Rico, with the flood of blacks fleeing to this island from non-Spanish European colonies, it was necessary to set up a town expressly for free blacks (Díaz Soler 1970, 236), who achieved that status precisely because they took refuge among the Spanish.

In the cities the blacks were now acting as a social force, especially in the service of Spanish masters, and some of them were employed in trades. For Peru, in 1553, Garcilaso (1965, 4:69) mentions them in the following way: "I passed by the doorway of Tomás Vásquez and saw on the street two saddled horses and three or four blacks with them."

Similarly, two years later Garcilaso de la Vega again (ibid., 74) tells us that "after the battle of Sacsahuana, a black slave of my father, a beautiful master tailor, made a cordovan jacket for Don Pedro de Cabrera."

In these years, therefore, the Spanish already formed military units with blacks. Francisco Hernández, in revolt against the king in 1555, formed

> a company of over one hundred fifty blacks from the slaves they captured and inheritances that they looted. Later on, continuing his tyranny, Francisco Hernández had more than three hundred Ethiopian soldiers, and so as to honor them and give them spirit and courage, he formed an army with them. He gave them a captain general, whom I met, known as Master Juan; he was a skilled master of carpentry, and was a slave of Antonio Altamirano. . . . Without higher officers, he appointed captains and instructed them to appoint an *alférez*, [10] sergeants, squad corporals, fifers and drummers, and to prepare flags. The blacks accomplished all this with great diligence, and many on the king's side of the battlefield crossed over to the tyrant when they saw their kinsmen so well honored by Francisco Hernández, and they fought against their masters throughout the war. (ibid., 91)

Such reports show that the role of blacks had grown considerably and that, especially in these campaigns in Peru and even farther south, they were employed as trusted personnel by the Spanish as were those who, as slaves, performed skilled work in controlled activities. The facts from this period establish, additionally, that it was much easier to count on the fidelity of a black than of a mulatto. While the black acknowledged in his master the law of power and prestige, another contributing factor to his loyalty to the Spaniard was the fact that in that commitment he had become an adversary of the Indian, not so much because the Indians were, by themselves, his enemy, but because he was more familiar with Spanish interests and became identified with them during the very dialectic of the conquests. In any case, Spaniards and blacks were alien to the Indian and thus created an inevitable solidarity that united them against Indian warriors.

Many mulattoes, by contrast, like mestizos, were in different circumstances with relation both to the Spanish and to the Indians. A certain percentage of mulattoes lived in resentment at feeling themselves disdained because of the illegitimacy of the unions of their mothers with the Spanish; in some cases they felt detached from moral responsibility toward the latter. Furthermore, given that much of their socialization had taken place in Hispanicized settings—at least linguistically and in dependent association with Spanish institutions and persons—they had acquired this culture in its most aggressive features, including those that stemmed from uprooting. War was a profound motive for personal achievement, an achievement which, given the hierarchical structure of the Spanish social system, they could not accomplish quickly. Meanwhile, their resentment, ambitions, and technical resources were the appropriate elements with which to achieve their objectives of status and the satisfaction of their hostile tendencies against the father—in this case the figure of the Spaniard.

The Indian offered such possibilities for achievement and satisfaction in certain cases, and many [mulattoes] went over to the Indian forces and among them became good commanders against the Spanish. In this way, within mulatto and mestizo groups there were always individuals who sided with the Indian cause, or simply the black cause in the manner of runaways. Nevertheless, most mulattoes, as well as blacks, identified more with the Spanish than with the Indians for the previously mentioned reason of their social familiarity with the Spanish. This was more true the greater the extent that they became assimilated.

In this sense there are abundant examples of personal valor provided by mulattoes. During the grueling campaigns in Chile in 1578, Mariño de Lobera (1960, 503) spoke of mulattoes who earned the admiration of the Spanish. One of them (was) "the mulatto Juan Beltrán, who, with another companion of his lineage and some friends who were following him, showed such courage in this and set such a good example for the republic through his life and works, that the marshal came to consider him for missions of honor and awarded him a grant in the name of His Majesty."

Around this time, with the Spanish established in the city of Valdivia, in Chile, Góngora Marmolejo (1960, 117–18) says that the black woman of one of its citizens was captured by Indians who had rebelled. This author-witness tells it as follows:

> When the Indians revolted . . . they took a black woman from a citizen named Esteban de Guevara. They carried this woman to the bank of a river and tied her hand and foot; stretching her out, they splashed buckets of water on her and scrubbed her with sand as hard as they could, in the belief that her color was not a natural one, but a compound. And when they saw that they could not rid her of that black color, they killed her and skinned her in their cruelty, and carried her skin stuffed with straw around the province. All of this took place in these cities in the aforesaid year of 1556.

This account shows that wherever the Spanish settled permanently, in city or countryside, they preferred the service of black women. In such cases, these women were found everywhere the Spanish asserted their political establishment in some way on Indian territories. In fact, given the general hostility of Indians toward blacks, that black woman's fate was also shared by men of her race. In this regard, Mariño de Lobera (1960, 316) says that

> the savages, though routed, managed to capture the black slave of a Spanish soldier named Francisco Duarte; they grabbed this one more eagerly than the others because he seemed a monstrous thing to them. Not knowing whether his color was natural or artificial, they just washed and scrubbed him to see if they could remove his blackness, as was also done to another black by the Indians of Mapuche and

the Paramocaes.[11] But when they saw there was no way to remove that color, they sent him freely back to the Spanish, not wishing to aggravate the latter against them. Rather, having been chastised, they went the next day to make peace.

Another black during this time of war against the Araucanians also suffered the same fate (ibid., 285–86), that is "they washed him with scalding water, scrubbing him with corn cobs, and making every effort to make him white. After all this, they killed him with great cruelty."

Thus, there is no doubt that in these campaigns blacks and mulattoes shared the fate of the Spanish, and it is also clear that they were employed basically in domestic service or as servants to soldiers and commanders. In addition, elsewhere, such as in Paraguay, they were made to settle near the Indian frontier, thus making them into a territorial shield for the Spanish. Azara (1962, 428) cites such a case in Paraguay, and says the following: "The governor, Don Rafael de la Moneda, extracted a number of blacks and mulattoes from the Spanish households where they were sheltered; with them he created this town that it might be a bulwark against the invasions of the Albayas."[12]

These blacks and mulattoes thus appear everywhere, and fundamentally, in critical situations with the Indians, they identified with the Spanish. In another sense, toward the mid sixteenth century, the Spanish soldiers had already taken in mulatto women as companions. Fray P. Aguado (1963, 508) confirms this for the case of Venezuela when he says: "A mulatto woman traveling in the company of a soldier was greatly harassed by the bats of this town. . . . They cured her and she regained consciousness."

What is certain is that from their island experience the Spanish soon arrived at the conclusion that blacks were economically more profitable than were the Indians. Additionally, the Indians—defended by the missionaries—began to be the object of settlement policies that sought to isolate them from Spaniards, blacks, mestizos, mulattoes, and mixtures of all kinds that now formed part of the new Spanish society. Meanwhile, in the civil areas black and mulatto women replaced the Indian woman in many cases, even when the latter held advantages over the former because of their better juridical status. Nevertheless, this did not hinder the sexual relations of black and mulatto women with the Spanish; rather, as they became more assimilated they became more attractive to the Spanish. The processes of these relations thus would relate more to the founding of the civil society than to the military expedition. By contrast, with respect to Indian women the process would be different: basically, it would be the primary process—direct and unstable— of the conquest. When the civil society replaced the military, the Spanish, especially the single men, tended to exchange sexually with women of both races, although the coastal garrisons in the Antilles and in the Caribbean areas coupled more with black and mulatto women than with Indians. Thus, simultaneously both Indian and black women historically became part of the process of miscegenation that took place with the Spanish. By the latter part of the seventeenth century, Gilli (1784, 245) was saying "there are many (in Peru) who take black women, not only as concubines, but also as legitimate wives, which should be attributed not so much to the beauty of these women as to the excessive familiarity with which they are treated."

In the eighteenth century, the companies of mulattoes, or *pardos,* constituted a sector of the Spanish army. In 1719 in Costa Rica, three of the ten companies of infantry consisted of pardos (Olien 1980, 17). In that century, confirming the significance of these (mulatto) populations, it is stated that in Costa Rica there are places, such as the valleys of Esparza, Bagaces, and Nicoya (Meléndez 1981, 35) where "all the inhabitants are mulattoes."

This has caused some authors, such as Konetzke (1972, 83), to think that by the mid seventeenth century the mulattoes already constituted 2.17 percent of the total population. Nevertheless, we believe that their number was much greater than this author sets forth. In the mid nineteenth century, for example, washerwomen in Argentina were "almost all black women" (MacCann 1962, 559), and at least in relation to the total time that had passed since the first years of the introduction of blacks into the River Plate area, their numbers were most likely greater than 2.17 percent.

In Santiago de Chile in 1759, the company of pardos was formed by two hundred mulatto and black men (Sáenz-Rico Urbina 1967, 1:110), and in Puerto Rico in 1776 there was a corps of chasseurs constituted by free blacks and mulattoes incorporated into the local militias (Díaz Soler 1970, 236). And the actual practice in this regard supported this policy when in 1623, it was recognized that: "The Company of Free Blacks of Panama hastens to every action that arises in our royal service, much to the satisfaction of the governors, digging trenches and standing the usual guard duty day and night. And they have been entrusted always with the main security guard and have received reinforcements as with the other soldiers who come from other parts in times of war."

What we could call the process of juridical liberation of the black made it possible for there to be in Spanish Santo Domingo in 1754 110,000 free persons out of a total census population of 125,000 individuals (Hernández Sánchez-Barba 1981, 3:63–64). This indicates that for some time the conditions existed that allowed for the incorporation of the descendants of Africans—and even those who were Africans themselves—into Spanish military contingents with few restrictions. This liberation was taking place, as we have seen, very early in the islands as well as on the mainland. In Lima in 1560, an ordinance pointed out that "all the free black men and women who presently live in the aforementioned royal city . . . are settled with Spanish masters, the aforesaid black women not being married to Spaniards."

What this statement confirms is the notion that black women had achieved a freedom of circulation that in some way made them accessible to all men. In addition, if the labor of blacks had been stabilized by the end of the sixteenth century (Hernández Sánchez-Barba 1981, 2:190), that also meant that mulattoization was growing as a result of the greater social accessibility of black women. In this sense, with the establishment of viceregal society, the development of mulattoization by 1740 was quite intensive, such as occurred, for example, in Cartagena de Indias. There (Juan and Ulloa 1978, 49–50) they spoke of *chapetones,* as young, recently arrived Spaniards beset by misfortunes because of poverty and disease. It was said in this regard that

> taking pity upon seeing them suffer so helplessly, the free black and mulatto women pick them up and take them home, where they tend and cure them at their own expense with great tenderness and dedication, as if they had some specific obligation to do so. If one dies, they have him buried through charity, and even have masses said for him. The usual result of such demonstrations is that the *chapetón*—having regained his health and being grateful for such kindness—either marries the black or mulatto woman or one of her daughters, and from then on he becomes established in a much less fortunate state than he could have in his homeland working at whatever might come along.
>
> . . . The selflessness of these people in this particular is such that it is impossible to believe that the hope of marriage is what motivates their charity, because often it happens that they do not wish to accept them, either for their own husbands or for their daughters, so that (the Spaniards) might not be trapped. Rather, the women seek the opportunity for them to join the service of some person, who might send them to the interior.

This reference gives recognition to the significant role in releasing tension that black and mulatto women exercised in the context of a free or integrated society, beyond the moral constraints that predominated in the context of the formal institutions of traditional Spanish society. In fact, these women easily became a refuge for these young Spaniards who, at the height of their sexual vigor, carried out an intense mulattoization of the continent.

In Paraguay, Charlevoix (1910, 1:103–4), in reference to the Spanish, says that in 1756 "some even took black women as their wives, from which has resulted the great number of mestizos and mulattoes that exist in the province."

Strictly speaking, there was no community where sexual relations with black and mulatto women were really prohibited, and furthermore, in 1571 in Law XXVIII of the Laws of the Indies (*Recopilación* . . . , vol. 2: Regarding mulattoes and blacks) it was stated: "but if the free black or mulatto woman should marry a Spaniard, she may wear some gold *garcillos* with pearl." In other words, if there was an attempt to favor Spanish women over black women in the question of social privileges, important concessions were made to the latter, nevertheless, when they achieved the condition of free women and were married to Spanish men. Such marital permission, however, was not a general practice when slave women were involved, and this fact led to the tendency to form unions based on concubinage or cohabitation (Saco 1938, 2:50).

In 1523 Fray Luis Figueroa, a Hieronymite father, advocated bringing black women to Hispaniola. As for males of this race, he preferred them to be under fifteen years of age, basing this on the suitability of this age group for their religious and linguistic instruction. But especially significant was the fact that, in principle, black women constituted no racial problem and that, sexually, Spanish men accepted them, especially in their condition as bachelors or when they had been cohabiting with them for a long time and had children by them. Accordingly, as the colonists increased the pressure to bring blacks to the Indies, certain qualities were demanded of the women. For example (Meléndez 1981, 28) in Costa Rica in 1701 and 1714, there are reports of the purchase, at public auction, of "an unskilled black girl, gotten in a public auction of other black women."

And with regard to skills, in 1809 (ibid.) "offered for sale is another slave woman who knows how to embroider, sew, and cook." Such qualities began to be in demand very early on, especially when the women were sought as domestics in Spanish homes. For this purpose it was necessary that they be Christians and speak Spanish, since under those circumstances they were considered to be assimilated, that is, trained in Spanish culture and thus of greater worth than the unskilled black women who, brought directly from Africa in the "trade," had not gone through the prior process of acculturation. In such a case, these women were destined to marry other blacks in order to gain that familiarity, that is, to live in society alongside the Spanish, especially on the haciendas. Commonly, the important qualities for unskilled black women, among others, were their age and state of health. Meléndez (ibid., 31) relates the case of one of these women, one of those sold between Spaniards, whose sale was made in the following terms:

> Doña Margarita de Morales sells to Captain Juan de Lugue, resident of this city (of Cartago) and a citizen of Granada (Nicaragua) a slave woman called Juana Josefa, of dark skin, 20 years of age, fine looks, and a round and pleasing face, neither pledged nor subject to any debt obligation on the part of the seller, and having committed no offense; free of any public or secret disease, weak heart,

gout, buboes, or watery eyes; being neither a runaway nor a thief nor drunkard nor having any other defect or flaw that might hinder her from serving well. Price 300 pesos.

The notion of marrying male and female slaves was already mentioned by 1514, in a letter from the King to the treasurer, Pasamonte, on Hispaniola (Saco 1938, 1:128). It reads thus: "Female slaves will be provided to marry the male slaves who are there, so that the latter will cause less concern about escaping; and as few males as possible . . . being males, no, because it seems there are many and this might bring problems."

Fundamentally, it was an attempt to stabilize the males in order to subject them to a social discipline that they did not observe as unmarried men, and in this moral control, black women exercised a moderating influence on the rising aggressivity of black males. Additionally, however—and this is important—the progeny that resulted from these marriages increased the number of slaves and therefore made the slave trade unnecessary. Although the black man was given (ibid., 129) "a woman companion in the name of law and religion . . . (this served) the interests of the master as well, because by being obliged indirectly to buy women, he could increase his slave holdings by means of legitimate reproduction."

Most importantly, therefore, black women were playing a domestic role that Indians had gradually lost as many of the latter were subjected to "Reducciones," in addition to being persons less prepared for the labor demanded of them by their Spanish mistresses, particularly in those cases where the black women arrived as assimilated or acculturated individuals. In addition, the sons and daughters of slaves in such circumstances could then be considered assimilated by the domestic environment of the Spanish and generally by means of the overseers themselves and through the cultural identification that resulted from the need to adapt and integrate themselves into new institutional contexts.

Geographical Variations in Racial Mixing

The difficulty in measuring the degree of racial mixing attained by each Ibero-American population is, concretely, a very large one and casts doubt on many of the results to date. In this sense, we have data only for certain localities, so that the vast majority of the population of Ibero-America is scientifically unmeasured with regard to its racial classification. Nonetheless, we do have a certain number of measurements—some morphological, others genetic—that may be used as indicators and that can largely be taken as the expression of certain tendencies. Such is the case of this work.

From the outset we can state that in certain regions the Indian contributes a greater biological input than does the Spaniard to racial mixing, whereas the latter predominates in other regions. Nevertheless, the Hispanic—or collectively, the Iberian—cultural contribution gave sociopolitical unity to Ibero-America.

As for the racial group of blacks, their most outstanding characteristic consists of their being absorbed gradually by the other two, although they continue by means of miscegenation to contribute their genes to the products of mixture. Furthermore, the cultural traditions brought by the blacks to Ibero-American life carry less functional weight and almost disappear within the structural design. They do emerge, however, in the areas of folklore and religion and in certain esthetic expressions. Therefore, while the Indians and Europeans have maintained their genetic and cultural contributions, the former through their internal reproduction on that continent, or the latter by means of constant new demographic inputs, the genetic and cultural contribution of the black groups has been weakened because of the influence of several factors, the most important of which are: (1) the gradual reduction of their demographic number in relation to the other racial and ethnic groups; (2) the interruption of their migratory contribution, through which the biocultural flow of the African black to the American continent had been growing; and (3) the decrease in their relative genetic participation to the degree that the proportions of the other racial groups were growing in the context of interracial combinations and among groups of mixture.

The greatest mixing among the three basic racial populations has occurred particularly in the Atlantic region and in the vicinity of the northwestern apex of South America. Additionally, in Brazil the white and black populations are the majority with regard to Indians, in absolute numbers as well as in terms of their qualitative cultural participation in racial mixing. The dominant hybrid population here is mulatto, the same as in the Antilles, where the native population has disappeared, absorbed especially by a hybrid type of black and white components. Both in Brazil and the Antilles, especially in the Lesser Antilles, the Caucasian and Negroid groups are in themselves minorities of great numerical importance. In Brazil, the Caucasians are now the majority and grow proportionally faster than any other racial group. In the Antilles region, the black constitutes the majority on the smaller islands. In the Greater Antilles there are many hybrids of Caucasians and Negroes, whereas the native components have been absorbed through rapid mixing with the former. There is also a great influence of whites in Cuba, the Dominican Republic, and Puerto Rico, simultaneous with that of the blacks, though the whites are fewer in number. In Haiti, the blacks constitute almost the absolute majority of the racial spectrum.

In the Lesser Antilles, particularly the British parts, racial mixture with the African group has been somewhat rare and reflects a contrary tendency to what has occurred in Ibero-America. Thus, we can observe the fact that the European ethnicity is a minority or is practically submerged into a population whose vast majority is African, or Oriental in some cases. In this sense, we can state that wherever the Hispanic ethnicity has been displaced or replaced by Anglo-Saxon ethnicity—as in the Lesser Antilles and in certain mainland territories—the process of racial mixing has slowed, and in some cases collapsed. In its place the independent development of each racial group has prevailed, with the specific growth of the Negro genetic and demographic component due to its greater volume of multiplication at the beginning of the historical formation of those societies in their contemporary political and cultural form. In this case, however, the British colonial structure has also imposed its institutional design, especially its administrative and juridical, as well as economic, models.

We can speak of a biocultural racial mixture that is well integrated nationally in those areas where the high native cultures developed, as occurred in the Central American highland plains of Mexico and other countries to the south and in the Andean region. In each of the national human landscapes of these countries we encounter regional variants deriving from the fusion of Hispanic culture with the different basic native cultures: Nahuas, Mayas, Quechuas, Aymaras, Araucanians, and other less widely extended ones. In these areas, the mestizo cultural product is distinguished by the presence of a large number of regional syncretisms that appear in their body of customs relating to religious, economic, technological, and esthetic spheres: to clothing, food, and the eidos, and to the social sphere in general. In the political sphere, the Hispanic mode has largely prevailed, although since the beginning of the present century ideological forms that are characteristically mestizo have taken shape (Esteva 1961) and describe in their components the modular mestizo geopolitical trend.

The rest of Ibero-America, the tropics of South America and the South Atlantic region, features an Iberian cultural predominance, with some significant Indian and African infiltrations. Though to a lesser degree, this formulation is equally valid for the biological sphere, since in that case, black and Indian genetic proportions are more important than their cultural ones. This relative predominance is greater in those regions of America with climates similar to those of Europe, such as Argentina, Uruguay, central and southern Chile, and southern Brazil; it is emphasized lately in the urban areas of Venezuela, as well as in the tropical areas being populated by Europeans and then absorbed by the Iberian model—traditional and modern—that constitutes the nucleus of the national cultures of those countries. This geographical aggregate, of a basically Iberian predominance, today generates certain demographic expansions—particularly Latin, European, and also Slavic and Germanic—that are characterized by their having buried the Indian and his ways numerically, in some cases, or simply by their having integrated over time with the existing Ibero-American cultural model.

Thus, according to the specific native tradition that exists in each region of America, the result of the symbiosis with the Hispanic sphere will vary, but through the final component of this combination—racial mixture—it always presents a perceptible number of common features everywhere. This is true for the fact that the majority of Ibero-American societies are united with one another by traditions and cultural institutions that presume a common heritage where the basic model is Hispanic. Nevertheless, the latter does not involve the elimination of national differences determined by the different native traditions. Thus, for example, Meso-America is defined by a Nahua tradition in the central high plains and by a Mayan tradition in the south. By contrast, the Andean region acknowledges a tradition that we will call Quechua in a broad sense, since there are different native cultural influences and contributions. Therefore, the specific combinations of each of the indigenous heritages with Hispanic cultural models have served to create a peculiar cultural composition that allows the student of these matters to speak of a Mexican national character, a Peruvian character, and so forth, with a specific national character for each of the nations that form the Ibero-American mosaic. The same can be stated for the regions constituted by the countries of the Atlantic coast, with their basic mixture of Ibero-African components and the specific results of basic personality that have derived from this interethnic interaction.

In each case, there are national characters that are mestizo in nature, not only because of a mixture between Iberians and Indians, but also because these mixtures have expanded in recent years to exchanges between European groups and between the Europeans and those long established in the countries of America. In themselves, the differences are created by the results attending a common cultural model—the Hispanic, or Ibero-American, as the case may be—which is mixed with the cultural forms of each corresponding native region. Therefore, the supranational core of racial mixing is Hispanic, and its regional variants result from the very character of the specific native cultural heritages, and to a lesser degree of African heritages. In less important respects, regional variants can be influenced by the specific regional origin of the Hispanic group.

According to this, we can indicate that the psychological content of racial mixing, considered in its emotional flow, is profoundly national, but the institutional structure that is the backbone of all the national variants in a formula that we call Ibero-American, is Hispanic or Portuguese. In this way, even in some Spanish-American countries such as Guatemala, whose population has a native cultural tradition, we find that since the cultural heritage of the dominant economic and political group is Spanish-American, the influence exerted by that heritage through the conquistadors and the founders of towns, villas, and cities of Spanish origin has penetrated deeply into the heart of native society, modifying it in Hispanic terms (Adams 1958). Therefore, it is valid to state that wherever the Spanish have exercised control over the indigenous population, or at least have maintained some form of stable contact, there has been a genetic and cultural exchange: a racial mixture (Service 1955, 421), although this exchange could have been interrupted by the implicit desire of the Spanish Crown (Barón Castro 1946, 799) to protect the Indians as a society and as an ethnicity, in its wish to prevent the outrages to which the Indians could be subject at the hands of the Spanish, blacks, and mestizos. Whatever the official Spanish policy of the era may have been, it is certain, as Steggerda (1950) points out, that the native tribes of Ibero-America can be considered today as mestizoized aggregations. Though this statement cannot be sustained totally, it is most probable that biological hybridization has also occurred where there has been acculturation. In this sense, only total isolation has managed to prevent the occurrence of some form of cultural or biological mixing. Very few such isolated population groups in Ibero-America are to be found.

We can thus affirm the postulate that the Atlantic slope, excepting parts of the Antilles, has developed in a culturally Hispanic or Portuguese mode, though, as we have said, with African influences and mestizo ingredients appearing in the form of syncretisms in the way of living. By contrast, the Pacific slope, especially in its Mexican, Central-American, and Andean high plains, has developed a basically mestizo cultural model, although certain ethnic groups, acting as marginal residues, have preferred to maintain the Iberian mode of the mestizo sphere, or more properly the Indian mode of this mestizo being, in each case through certain social classes. As a consequence, the fundamental mixtures that appear as dominant are the Hispanic-Indian in the western high plains, which correspond to the populated centers of pre-Hispanic America, and the islands of the Caribbean.

In contemplating the formative process that leads to racial mixture in Ibero-America, we can observe two different geopolitical styles: (1) the pre-Hispanic, and (2) the Hispanic. Both retain later influences on the development and characteristics assumed by the genetic or biological exchanges between the specific racial groups involved.

The pre-Hispanic style is oriented along the Pacific slope and develops, as we have mentioned, in the high plains interspersed among the mountain ranges of Mexico, Central America, and the Andes. This native development is conditioned by the longitudinal direction of the cordilleras and mountain ranges of the Americas, which favor passage from north to south, while they hinder movements attempted from east to west. In addition, east-west movements are hindered by another great obstacle: the equally impenetrable bodies of tropical jungle and their enervating climates. Here disappears the stimulating element of the inhabited temperate areas of the western high plains, at least in terms of their interior valleys, which became the outstanding centers of the high pre-Hispanic cultures. In native geopolitics immediately prior to the Columbian discovery, the high plains were the basic settings of historical or expansive action, whereas the coasts, on the contrary, provided settings for the discontinuous development of lordly domains and the lodging of secondary cultural groups seen in terms of the great imperial states. In fact, the coasts were themselves places occupied by culturally and politically secondary tribes with respect to those that inhabited the high plains of the populated centers of America; whereas those other tribes who developed urbanism, trade, and higher cultures lacked sufficient geopolitical depth in the exercise of the notion of permanent military domination. This type of development corresponded largely to the regions of the populated high plains, although the Mayas, for example, and some cities of the Andean coasts played an urbanized and cultural role historically prior to the exercise of power developed by the great imperialism of the Mexicas and the Incas. The coastal regions never managed to achieve a stable and colonialist share of imperialism such as that attained by the Nahua and Quechua groups, who were in this case more ecologically and politically aggressive and cohesive. The great cities and the most populous centers flourished on the cool highland plains of the west, while the attempts at development in the tropics faced the problems of dispersion and the enervating climate.

The Hispanic geopolitical style in America is twofold, because it appears conditioned first by the initial political-military need to dominate the native population centers in the aforementioned high plains, and second, by the need to populate those other areas that later became more attractive and ripe for a homogeneous expansion of the Spanish culture of the era. This second aspect is the Atlantic one. In their later development, we can recognize the influence of a Spanish, or Portuguese, policy and culture that is homogeneously Iberian in the Atlantic regions, and homogeneously mestizo, or Indo-Hispanic, in the regions of the Pacific. We can observe the achievement of a contemporary Ibero-America with different shades of cultural and biological regions, determined in turn by the action of the factors of racial and ethnic distribution previously mentioned, because of its relatively different historical structure.

As a result of what we have discussed, we can consider the achievement of the following phenomena of race formation in Ibero-America:

(a) The process of Hispanic-Indian mixing appears nearly consummated in five countries: Mexico, Honduras, El Salvador, Nicaragua, and Paraguay, where we can see, in general, an approximate 85 to 90 percent of miscegenation.

(b) Hispanic-Indian mestizoization is in a process of homogenization due to the social and geographical mobility of indigenous groups in Guatemala, Ecuador, Peru, and Bolivia, although its greatest development has emerged in Colombia and Peru.

(c) Trihybrid mixing, such as Ibero-black and Indian-black—the latter to a lesser degree—is greatly developed in the Antilles, Panama, Colombia, Venezuela, and Brazil.

(d) Iberoization, with later Italian and German-Slavic contributions, occurs basically in certain parts of southern Brazil, as well as in Chile. Its maximum integration has been attained in Argentina and Uruguay. In Costa Rica, the basis of the population continues to be Hispanic.

(e) Although in less significant proportions not considered here, racial strains of modern Asiatic origin also appear and tend to be absorbed by the Ibero-American mass in its different racial shadings and mixtures.

Population and Racial Mixing in the Cities of Ibero-America: The Eighteenth Century

The matter of studying racial mixing in the cities of America during the Spanish and Portuguese eras from a demographic as well as cultural point of view presents difficulties because we have censuses that are poor in data and in details, and because, additionally, the sources are insufficient in method to show clearly the particularities of ways of living. To such problems we must add others no less significant: The infrequent synchronization of regional demographies or censuses, which accentuates the problem of establishing relative racial distribution at a given moment in Ibero-American history. In each case the exactness we have employed is diverse in nature.

We have attempted to estimate the population of the late eighteenth century in various aspects because during the latter half of that century demographic statistics were produced that help to fill the gaps existing in the first population surveys undertaken by the Spanish and Portuguese authorities in the early stages of conquest and colonization, as well as later ones. Furthermore, the later eighteenth century is obviously the final phase of the process that sets the conditions for a new chapter of the American peoples in their struggle for freedom, and as such it is a stage that prepares the foundations upon which the sociocultural structure of the new nationalities will rest.

Demographically, this second half of the eighteenth century represents something of a transitional phase, not only because it is the prelude to a great historical change, but also because it appears to us as a period of crisis in every order: political, economic, and social. It is the moment when all social forms seem to be in motion, either latent or in the practice of mobility of persons and of groups. From this perspective, the process of social mobility also involves a profound potential push toward great changes in the status of persons and in the culture itself. In a certain way, in the latter half of the eighteenth century the peoples of Ibero-America were defining themselves in terms of new ways of living or of desires to forge a new reality, another structure of social relations.

What the mobility of populations represents within the framework of social reorganization is a substantial and simultaneous redistribution of ethnicities, races, and social groups moving toward an organizing consciousness of their political, social, and economic reality. The second half of the eighteenth century is for us not only a time when the Americans prepared to attempt their independence, but also a time of the redistribution of the social forces that would make it possible. This is why we are interested in defining the demographic structure of the continent and of the Antilles from the viewpoint of their racial proportions, as well as the degree of relative urbanization that can be derived from statistics.

What we are doing in this work is to consider, especially, the population numbers given by Alcedo in his *Diccionario geográfico-histórico de las Indias Occidentales o América* of 1789. We prefer to work with these figures because—being those presented by a single author—they offer a greater homogeneity than those taken from various sources, although in this case we have not had available any others that might help us to develop more conclusive statistics. In considering that we are dealing with a homogeneous source, we are conscious that even in this case Alcedo is also an incomplete source, dependent in turn on reports that he collected from other sources of the period. For example, it is obvious that the basic information referring to New Spain has its origin in the work of Joseph A. de Villaseñor y Sánchez, *Theatro americano* (1746). But it is also true that in this case the criterion used by our author, Alcedo, is homogeneous in its form of presenting the data, as can be ascertained through a critical review of his work. Thus, from this point on, Alcedo will be our principal source for statistics.

Checking these figures presents some problems. In the first place, Alcedo did not have statistics for all the locales that he mentions, because only in a certain percentage of them does he achieve the minimum precision necessary for our purposes. Second, the different castes or racial groups for each locality are not always stipulated. Except for certain cases, the figures for racially differentiated populations are mixed or confused, which means that we are forced to ponder total statistics on the basis of samples or partial figures. From this incompleteness come statistical approximations that, if local figures become available, could be corrected in the future. Also, Alcedo makes frequent reference to the existence of more numbers of population without specifying the exact figure. In so doing, he merely indicates that in such and such a place live "some" or "many" or "numerous" citizens, or Indians, or other castes. In this way, the figures with which we are working should be considered low rather than high.

Admittedly, there could be a greater number of localities, and in this sense Alcedo probably has listed a total population that would be lower than the true demographic reality. It is in light of this consideration that we have contemplated a larger population. Finally, it is also true that in the period in question, data relative to the Indians not subject to the political or institutional control of the Spanish and Portuguese are also insufficient. In most cases the existence of the ethnicity or racial group is recognized and its affiliation is noted, but its true number of components is unknown. In this way, the number of Indians counted also turns out to be lower than their actual numbers. Accordingly, any statistic that does not include the totality of the necessary data comes to have an approximative value. Such is our case. Nevertheless, the most important value that we can ascribe to the considerations that we have pointed out is that they can be taken as an indicator of tendencies, in this case referring to urbanism and to racial distribution. Here, we are inclined to emphasize that the statistical considerations that we have made in this work not only represent approaches to the demographic problem of Ibero-America in the second half of the eighteenth century, but they are also important as a population sample in a given moment in a history, by means of which the respective emphasis of each demographic form is made evident in its racial and ecological aspects.

→   →   →

If, during the period under discussion, what stands out for us is the continuity of a process of transition toward the racial homogeneity of the American continent and of the Antilles, nevertheless, it can also be pointed out that the principal tendencies of that process are configured toward cultural, more than biological, mestizo types. As we shall see, white and Indian polarities constitute the most important feature of the biological phenomenon, although the percentages of genetic mixtures indicate the direction of the progressive possibilities of mixture when social conditions are favorable for miscegenation. The mestizo form was not yet dominant statistically by the late eighteenth century. It was only a tendency beginning to manifest itself in some strength in some regions in contrast to others. What is certain is that the process of miscegenation, so intense in the early years of conquest and colonization, seems to have stagnated; it appears lethargic, though it exists as a latent tendency in every social stratum. Despite this widespread latency, the expression of the sexual exchange between different racial groups was more intensive in the Spanish middle and peasant classes than in those of superior status (Esteva 1964, 454ff.), precisely because the former were the ones who maintained a more direct contact with the natives and with the colored [*castas de color,* dark-skinned, nonwhite population, especially African, mulatto, and variants, including Indian mixtures] castes.

Such a low index of relative mixture as presented in the figures might possibly conceal an actual biological number of mestizos, if we keep in mind the unstable nature of many unions between individuals of different races. It is probable that this form of sexual relation would hinder the civil registry of the offspring as a mestizo. It is also probable that the strictness of racial classification based on the nature of sexual unions influenced the relative racial identification of the individuals, such that, according to those criteria, the number of mestizos is probably biologically greater than that acknowledged in the censuses. Clearly, in the absence of explicit acknowledgments to this effect, we are obliged to make our judgment about this reality based on statistics that in themselves are incapable of revealing to us in their formal objectivity the real problem of racial mixing. In such a case, the figures merely acknowledge what was already established convention.

Elsewhere, we have indicated that this process of mestizo formation was relatively intensive in the early periods, based on the fact that the Spanish and Portuguese came practically unattached, or without women of their own lineage, to the conquest and colonization of America. This fact and the social characteristics of the contact with native populations that favored miscegenation—by means of polygyny and ample sexual freedom—determined that the process of racial mixing would produce great numbers of population in the early years. Later, however, the very sexual self-sufficiency of each group, especially the Iberian—having attained a solid number of women of their own class and constituted a rigid social stratification—contributed to reducing the intensity of the process of racial mixing. The continuous arrival of Europeans and Africans in the New World modified racial relations, and all of that, in close association with a stratified socioeconomic system, lessened the tendencies toward miscegenation; in those cases where the latter occurred, its relative numerical importance was low. The tendency of the phenomenon we are discussing would be: the more advanced in years the colonial period to which we might refer, the less will be the tendency of racial groups to mix with one another. To the degree that the colony became a stratified social system where racial groups were transformed into castes, social separation as well as the relative sexual self-sufficiency of each class or caste were favored.

In the late eighteenth century the rigidity of each stratification was beginning to crumble as a consequence of the political and economic crises besetting the system and especially because of the geographic mobility of the populations, which made them socially and physically more aggressive. Mobile populations, acting in the form of heavy migrations, destroyed the traditional social disciplines by flooding into the cities and thus disorganizing the balances in the system of life. In this way, in the late eighteenth century not only the social barriers but also the psychological ones that might block miscegenation between the various castes began to fall. This phenomenon of intensive migration accelerated the process of racial mixing.

The results of these crises on the highly stratified systems of political, social, and economic colonial organization would be conflicting. But at the same time they would facilitate ethnic and genetic exchanges between the castes to a greater measure than was permitted up to then by the conventions adopted in social relations. The late eighteenth century is thus a period in which racial exchanges increase again, and therefore it marks a new process of racial mixing on a double scale: biological and cultural. Despite that new mixing, the conventional forms of role/status continued to emphasize the social differences between individuals belonging to different castes, and in this sense the fact that people of color and natives occupied inferior positions would also mean that their descendants would inherit the conditioning imposed by the status system, but insofar as the descendants were socially more aggressive and bolder, they also hungered more for status and therefore began to contend for it with the traditional classes.

Working especially against this conditioning was the migratory mobility and the very crisis of social consciousness of the castes in their status and confrontations. This type of crisis led all the lower social groups to a greater flexibility and aggressivity in their relations with the upper, or white, classes. The fact, recognized by some travelers, of the growing emergence of *leperismo*[1] in Mexico, for example, and the growing fear of léperos' actions shown by the so-called persons of decency, were in our opinion nothing other than the result of the gradual loss of individual social control. They were also an expression of the crisis of authority—physical and moral—of the traditional system, no longer capable of imposing itself charismatically over groups of the people, as well as a manifestation of the greater social audacity of the lower castes, who were inhibited and marginalized until then, without political decisiveness, and were now seeking to establish themselves by facing their social possibilities with the white castes, who were striving in their turn to prevent social audacity and even to become more flexible, renewing their political solutions. The organized consciousness of this crisis not only conditioned the process of stratification but led to the need for political independence. This consciousness therefore contributed to the formation of new social adaptations that were more mestizo to the degree that they implied greater social exchanges between the various racial categories, and also a greater opportunity and opening in terms of social circulation and of cultural creation. This process was manifested basically in the cities.

During the second half of the eighteenth century, the mestizo ways of living that had emerged in the early sixteenth century would have extended and cohered particularly into a cultural amalgam and a way of life; and especially in those centers where Europeans, Indians, and Africans lived, the process of miscegenation took form in terms of ideologies and syncretisms, as the mobility of the castes toward the cities became more open through migration. The phenomenon of racial mixing acquired its specific cultural modes according to each region, and therefore according to the influences and traditions contributed by each racial component to the sociocultural mix. For example, in the urban areas Spanish culture was more influential than any other, whereas in the rural areas there tended to be a greater balance between the Indian and the Spanish, and in some cases between Africans and the other two groups. There were regions where the importance of their cultural traditions reflected the specific influence, as is evident when we consider Meso-America, with its expansive Nahua and Maya cultures mixing with the Spanish, and the Quechua culture of the central Andes mixing in the same fashion with the Hispanic. In any case, the mestizo way of life took form in the cities and in the country, or wherever racial coexistence also involved the circulation and different use of different cultures. The greater or lesser degree of specific influences would be a functional matter, to be decided ultimately by political power, which created the master systems—political, administrative, economic, religious, educational, and judicial—with their radiating auras of prestige and social identification, and by the adaptive possibilities of these systems to the real conditions and traditions of each region. Thus, in the cities each master system would have a greater force than in the country, especially to the degree that in the latter, urban controls were weaker, or failed to attain the same degree of direct functionality over the groups who subscribed to pre-Hispanic traditions.

The Demographic Diagnosis

Within this structure, the development of urbanism in the period of interest to us corresponds to the most intense development of racial mixing in its various forms of racial composition. To the degree that the racial classes came into contact they mixed together and needed one another, because they became mutually dependent. Let us say that if urbanism created populations with greater genetic exchange from the various racial strains, it also made them socially more aggressive by providing them with better opportunities for social contact. In the interest of establishing the figures relative to hybrids—especially mestizos and mulattoes, aside from other combinations—our interests, as stated at the beginning of this chapter, will be to examine the data given by Alcedo.

The total number of populated centers surveyed by Alcedo for the eighteenth century for the region more or less limited on the north by the present

Mexican border with the United States, and on the south by the south-ernmost mainland, would be 8,478. Their distribution or classification—considering the urban and rural concepts as definitive of the relative ecological and cultural form—would be:

Towns 8,004
Villas 229
Cities 245
Total 8,478

If we combine the concepts of villa and city, and if we consider that this combination is equivalent to interpolarities of urban forms, we would obtain for the continental whole, including the Guianas as well as the Antilles, a total of 474 localities of urban character, or at least of a character not rural in their ecological and cultural structure. Let us say, in this sense, that these localities share a common characteristic provided by the fact that they are based principally on commerce, public and private administrative services, and industry, and let us keep in mind that the industry may not be well developed and that the difficulties of transporting merchandise—bad roads and dependence upon carts and draft animals, especially mules, and even men—would force the cities to develop their own peasantry and cattle raising nearby to supply them with food. Therefore, that peasantry would maintain an intimate contact with people of a specifically urban culture, to the point of becoming confused with them in the form of contacts that would make apparently ambiguous the sociocultural identification of many persons who lived in the cities.

We might acknowledge the existence of degrees of urbanization within the cities themselves, although the metropolises—especially Mexico City and Lima—would have greater degrees than would the other urban centers. The idea is that urbanism would be relatively little developed, in terms of comparative populations as well as of individual behavior, so that rural traditions would have great importance in the mentality of the middle and lower classes. Despite this, the practices of urbanism were not alien to the peasantry, if we keep in mind that the latter maintained intensive contacts with urban culture, and if we consider, additionally, that that culture, through its political power, determined the functioning of an economic, administrative, juridical, educational, and religious macrostructure whose action extended throughout the entire sociocultural system of the peasants. In this way, the cities featured an advanced intensity of urbanization among the so-called cultural or upper classes and even the middle sectors, but this intensity diminished as one descended to the other social classes and castes. But at the same time, we can also say that the more or less direct contact between rural regions or villages and the cities would also be a vehicle for urbanization in some aspects of its ideology, which means that there would be a certain compensation between what we might call the relative urbanization of the peasants and the relative ruralization of the cities.

According to what we are indicating, 94.4 percent of the localities counted by Alcedo would be classified as rural, or devoted basically to agriculture and cattle, and many of them to mining. However, we should consider the so-called mining towns as a direct function of city interests in their commercial and industrial aspects. If we consider the intense, though not permanent, demographic concentrations that the different mining towns attained or developed, and if we think of the great quantities of food and industrial manufactures that mining centers consumed, it should be noted that the town concept applied to the *reales de minas,* for example, would be contingent in character, inasmuch as many mining towns, because of their occupational structure, should be classified as urban, or, if preferred, as pre-urban, more than truly rural. In the Alcedo census 311 centers classified as mining towns appear, but 241 of them are recognizably more rural than urban in structure. The rest of them would consist of 24 mining villas and 46 cities, it being understood in each case that part of the population was devoted to extractive operations.

Having said this, however, if we note that of the total of 8,478 localities mentioned by Alcedo, we can recognize 474 as urban, and if to this we add— by approximation and inference—that half of their populations devoted to mining were more urban than rural because their members were occupied in extractive operations and related ones such as the washing and processing of metals, artisan skills and services, then we can add 120 more localities to those already classified as urban, such that their urbanized centers would be 7 percent.

It is true that some population centers appear as urban, yet are, as we indicated, really nothing other than villages of larger size, but by contrast, others that are categorized as towns would be objectively more urban than rural. The criteria for villa and city are interchangeable from the urban perspective, but what is called a city at a given moment does not always turn out to be one in reality, if we consider that we tend to term as cities those centers founded in order to concentrate services, but whose size and occupational structures did not develop in accord with this purpose. Nevertheless, what mainly would distinguish these urban centers, whatever their demographic volume, is that their founders or settlers came from an urban culture: they were individuals raised in the ideology of the cities, even when their economic pursuits were agriculture, cattle, or mining. In many cases they acted as persons in charge of business of this type, if indeed they did not themselves perform the manual work.

Given that volumes of population are also aspects of the assessment of urban status, let us say that some of these cities soon would disappear under the impact or pressure of certain more or less constant vexations, such as the climate, epidemics, war, economic crises, and other forces that caused their historical stability to be relatively provisional. There is what we might call a permanent state of crisis in many of these urban centers. At times, the crises were resolved by the abandonment of centers, whereas others adopted the form of latent or larval states of disappearance, or of "getting by" without development. Given these situations and the imprecision of many data, we will define a body of tendencies more than a truly particular image of each case by the estimates we make.

Some villas and cities are described as having deteriorated for various reasons, among them, decline or alternatives to mining, but also the destruction and anxieties caused by Indian attacks, as well as the diseases and epidemics that ravaged America in that period, which underline the instability of urban life in certain regions, especially on the continent. Thus, for example, Alcedo says with regard to Acla, a city of a mainland kingdom, that it was small and that the Spanish abandoned it as unhealthy. In other cases, there is mention of cities that were important but that yielded to pillage and to Indian wars until they became towns of greatly reduced population. In many examples we are told that urban centers were abandoned as the cost of their growth became greater than their potential benefits, or than that of their very maintenance.

The city of Logroño, in the province of Quijos y Macas (kingdom of Quito)—after being sacked in the mid eighteenth century by the *jíbaros* [the Jivaro Indians of Ecuador and Peru], who killed all Spanish males and carried off their women—was never rebuilt. The same happened with the city of San Luis de Loyola, capital of the *corregimiento* of Cuyo (kingdom of Chile), which was demolished in 1599 by the Araucanians, although it was later rebuilt. A similar fate befell the city of Osorno (kingdom of Chile), destroyed by the Charaucabi and Araucanian Indians during the same year of 1599. The same thing happened to the city of Altagracia (New Granada). The city of Baeza, in Quijos y Macas, is another example of decline brought on by Indian raids, since it once had a population that Alcedo formally estimated as numerous, but by the latter's day it barely contained thirty individuals. The same thing was happening to the city of Corona Real, in the Cumaná district of the province of Guayana, which finally had to be abandoned by its settlers under constant harassment from the Carib Indians. Alcedo mentions many more such cases.

The disappearance of cities founded for the purpose of controlling the Indians was a frequent phenomenon of the frontier areas. Alcedo reports on a great number of cases, and in each of them the explanation for their ruin or decadence is attributed to Indian raids and to the difficulty for their urban inhabitants to readily obtain relief supplies for the military garrisons set up to protect them. These cities were rather easily abandoned when government interests did not obey a solid intent to remain, or they were also evacuated when their extinction did not entail substantial losses of control over a territory considered strategic for communications or the basic policy of settlement. These disappearances show that the instability of some urban centers was a function of the Indian problem, it being understood that many of latter populations, especially the so-called savages,[2] showed themselves to be resistant to submitting to the system of settlements and therefore resisted being incorporated into European political dominion. These populations systematically opposed the efforts at domination by the Spanish and Portuguese, or by Europeans in general and therefore carried on constant warfare with the settlers from those ethnic groups, as well as their descendants and associates, particularly Hispanicized Indians, those from rural communities, and blacks, mestizos, and mulattoes.

Actually, if the purpose of these urban foundations was to put towns in place that might serve as frontier shields to the warlike or hostile incursions of native "infidels," such a goal was achieved only in those cases where there existed permanent presidios or garrisons capable of insuring the urban development of their settlements. But at the same time, for their continuity the protected settlements also depended on the degree of economic and military self-sufficiency that they were capable of producing on their own. When it was important to maintain an urban population that they were stabilizing, they did so by creating an adequate military force, at times aided by armed militia ready, even with cavalry, to defend, pursue, and punish Indian incursions even into the interior.

Many of the civilians recruited to settle in those frontier urban populations were individuals of bad reputation, considered to be vagrants or persons of unruly conduct. Their recruitment attempted to take political and economic advantage of their unbridled energy, in addition to seeking gradually to advance the frontiers of European penetration to the very regions of the hostile and nonsubject tribes. It was thought that the aggressivity of the European settlers was in itself a guarantee of their success against native aggression. But in the individual perspective of each case, these urban centers were unstable because recruited individuals lacked an ambitious creative ideology, because their relocation to the frontier was in the nature of an adventure and did not serve an active, stable illusion. The devastating Indian raids, the lack of ade-

quate military protection, the ultimate loss of economic interest in these regions, and the low creative morale of this type of inhabitant represented permanent conditioning factors and lent continual disintegrating influences to
the political and social system.

Elsewhere, the flooding of mines and their subsequent ruin for exploitation brought with them the abandonment of towns on a large scale, bringing
about social decline, as in the case, for example, of Laicacota de Alva (Peru),
whose community of three thousand homes would be reduced to a handful
after its famous silver mines were flooded. In many aspects, this instability is
reflected in the very fact that demographic figures relating strictly to mining
centers are frequently inaccurate or nonexistent, whereas those given for
centers classified under the concept of towns—that is, devoted to agriculture
and cattle—are comparatively abundant. The imprecision suggests, in this
sense, the difficulty of exercising census control over these types of centers,
precisely because their stability was fluctuating and indeterminate, if one
considers that many veins played out or were flooded, thus forcing at least a
dynamic portion of their inhabitants to emigrate. In this way, some towns
appeared and disappeared as a function of mining. By contrast, some of these
operations were stable ones and therefore founded permanent communities
where industries and services were developed, in addition to maintaining
nearby agriculture and cattle raising, whose activities complemented those of
the mining sector and thus formed a relatively complex socioeconomic
system.

The mines located in fertile regions where agriculture and cattle raising
prospered do not appear to have been the economic base of the area in the
majority of cases, to the degree that working on the land had always been the
principal economic activity. In this sense, the majority of the demographic
references made regarding localities where there were working mines come
combined with data about the population employed on haciendas and in
farm labor, which makes evident the stabilizing role played by agriculture
and cattle raising in the establishment of mining communities, counteracting
in this way their tendency to fluctuate between boom and ruin.

Otherwise, population shifts were quite frequent, and in this sense very
rapid demographic losses occurred in certain areas, along with migratory
floods into those localities—especially the large cities—which, in addition
to guaranteeing a certain safety, offered a more diversified labor market. In
another sense, some urban declines would be due to reorganization of the
political and administrative systems of the kingdoms and viceroyalties in their
local adaptations. Fundamentally, what seems to stand out is the fact that the
Ibero-American populations in the era of the eighteenth century were largely
affected by occupational mobility, such that the boom and bust phenomena

were as commonplace as were the insecurities in their system of life. A general remedy in this case would be migratory mobility. For this reason, a peculiar state of uncertainty or malaise seems to manifest itself in frontier cities and villas or in those close to the villages of the so-called savage Indians. But, at the same time, in those centers that owed their origin and growth to mineral deposits the phenomenon of discontinuity also emerged with greater intensity, since in the same manner that they had appeared and prospered demographically, they likewise spent themselves and ceased to have importance with the decline of mining.

Thus we have evidence that the fate of Ibero-American cities would be a function of three factors, epidemics and natural disasters, mass destruction as the result of war, and the relative boom or decline of their economic structures, each in turn influencing instability. The fate or fortune of the mines would constitute still another factor of contingency, because any playing out of the mine brought on a crisis for the dependent economic sectors in the region: commerce, transportation, public and private services, and especially the region's agriculture and cattle industry. In such cases, the continuum or network formed by the primary, secondary, and tertiary sectors behaved as a function of mining in areas where the mine represented the point of departure or of reference for the demographic form.

The instability we have indicated can be extended to the frontier communities, particularly those that formed the mission-presidio-Indian complex, where abandonment frequently occurred, leaving those areas as "no man's land," open to precarious domination by the first to occupy them. The problem of community instability was not solved with the conquest nor with colonization, and thus only the great metropolitan centers where economic and political power were concentrated—along with the other cities located in regions that created communities with interdependent economies—resisted the disintegrating tendencies arising from the various forces mentioned above and from the various divisions suffered by the social system with the continuous displacement of individuals and even of entire groups.

Migratory Mobility

This eighteenth-century instability seems to point toward a significant epiphenomenon: the depopulation of many mining centers as a consequence of the exhaustion of their deposits, as well as a shortage of labor, on the one hand, and political and social insecurity, on the other. That epiphenomenon caused emigration from the peripheral communities toward the centers of power and thus of security. There is frequent mention that many mines were not working because of the lack of labor. In such cases social insecurity would have combined with the exhaustion of mineral deposits in the traditionally accessible areas in what we might term the demographic crisis of the eighteenth century. This crisis would not necessarily involve a loss in the general population but rather a demographic reorganization or adjustment stemming from migratory oscillations and movements.

As an example in this regard, Humboldt (1973, 1:327ff.) points out that in the late eighteenth century the population of New Spain was growing, as could be seen from the great number of new houses and those under construction in the countryside, and from the various technological advances that were being produced in economic life and in the area of prevention against disease. Humboldt (ibid., 337) even estimates an increase of 150,000 individuals per year (?), as long as such calamities as famine and pestilence did not occur. This meant, largely, that epidemics and natural calamities, as well as the struggle against the Indians, would have contributed to the creation of an economic and social picture that was clearly unstable. This would be the moment in which crises of social control would emerge, with their states of social aggressivity and disorganization contributing to a greater sexual freedom and to population growth, demonstrating precisely that cultural traditions were collapsing under the impact of the same unequal demographic pressure, mixing heterogeneous populations. This instability would cause a release of enormous social energies, and these, in turn, would become a potential or latent source of class pressures, especially active in the heart of the urban centers, which were the most susceptible in this case with regard to their becoming receptacles for the demographic surpluses issuing from the areas in decline or in crisis.

Therefore, the periods of urban growth coincided with those in which there were no epidemics and in which, furthermore, surplus production was a function not only of the external market, but also of the relative functional complexity of the occupational structure and the relative biological health of the population, along with stability in the mines. Then, the demographic form of the cities attained progressive surpluses parallel to those of the economic, social, and political equilibrium. In every case, nevertheless, the experiences of the eighteenth century seemed to promote interracial conflicts to the degree in which the various castes of color established themselves as groups within a social dynamic, now uneasy in their status and conscious of their possibilities, and therefore, members of the castes pushed for their promotion and for an improved social level as individuals. They did so at the time in which population mobility nurtured their ambitions for status, as well as facilitating their escape from the social controls of those who dominated them. The crisis of authority in the political system caused gaps in social control and thus motivated the individuals of the lower castes to seek their own personal affirmation outside the channels of traditional conventions.

This dynamic took place especially in the cities, where the greater anonymity of persons implied a greater freedom of action and weaker social control on the part of systems of power. Whereas in the country the techniques of authority were maintained through direct controls over persons, in the city the prospects for control were weaker because control did not extend physically and morally to the acts and conscience of every person. Let us say that the loss of authority in the cities in the late eighteenth century would be as much a consequence of population mobility as an effect of the weakening of the individual consciousness or notion of the system of traditional norms that maintained social security.

The conflict between the new Americans and the Indians, furthermore, left unresolved the definitive integration of Ibero-American cultures, such that those cultures, in addition to being racially and ethnically diverse, were also heterogeneous to the degree that on their margin lived the so-called savage nations of Indians. The fact that those nations resisted integration into European cultural modes means that only in the cities and in those towns that constituted a political and economic function of the cities was it possible to create stable populations and move in this manner toward the institution of relatively uniform societies, ensconced in their integration within the context of a power macrostructure organized around an urban framework of political decision conditioning all other organizations: economic, administrative, religious, educational, military, and juridical. This macrostructure carried a Spanish stamp, but it took on regional peculiarities according to how important and specific were the local or native cultural traditions, aside from the purely Hispanic or African ones, or the Portuguese ones in their Brazilian territory.

The regional context for the integrations of rural culture revealed early on the influence of the Nahua, Maya, Quechua, Aymara, Araucanian, and Guaraní traditions as exponents of pre-Hispanic crystallizations flourishing, to a greater or lesser degree, at the time of the Columbian discovery. In the cities the influence of these cultures was less, yet some of their components reappeared frequently in the course of grave political crises, when the internal disorganization of the macrostructure endangered its stability, or simply altered it in some of its aspects. In such cases, a part of the population, especially the rural natives, sought to reorient themselves, turning unconsciously toward the solutions of the past in an attempt to recover the security they were losing in the transition process of the crises. This was like a defense mechanism in which the individual and ethnic groups attempted to return to the generating sources of their personality cohesion.

The emergence of latent states of forms of native culture until then buried by Hispanic political power and by the charismatic prestige of its symbols of domination—such as those of the status implicit in the Spanish economic, educational, religious, military, and political authorities who constituted the system of control par excellence in urban and rural societies—occurred in the late eighteenth century, and in some earlier attempts at nativist affirmation. When this system of control wavered or entered into crisis, and when its credibility or prestige diminished in the social consciousness, then the political attempts at a resurgence of native culture reappeared. But when that case arose, other forms of European cultures—French, English, or German—played their role as a form of domination through new ideological currents recognizable in the new institutions that emerged from the political turmoils. In this way, the cities were not only centers of political power, but also cultural organizations impregnated with European elements and with the various syntheses of that culture with indigenous or African elements or small cultural complexes. And to the extent that peasants were a function of these forces, the reappearance of indigenous forms of culture had a decidedly ephemeral effect because, even in their momentary victories, their instruments and ideology of action had ceased to be indigenous or pre-Columbian. At the most, they were mestizo.

Nonpeasant Indian Cultures

The savage Indian was not integrated, nor is he in modern times, 150 years after American independence. This meager integration cannot be considered a Hispanic legacy because these thousands of villages were not integrated in the times of the Incas and the Mexicas either, since they resisted the imperialist policies of absorption employed by the latter with the violent methods characteristic of all military conquests. The problem of the frontiers during the eighteenth century was similar to that of the preceding centuries: the frontiers advanced or receded according to the force with which urban societies attacked or imposed their control.

In Alcedo's dictionary there are more than five hundred Indian communities designated, without distinction, as savage and infidel, whose salient characteristics would be hostility and aggressiveness against non-Indian (in the cultural sense) and white communities, a hostility felt equally toward those Indians by the non-Indian and white communities. This statistic would reveal that the urban phenomenon in Luso-Spanish and European America developed in general under the mark of turmoil in the areas bordering on the jungle regions—the Amazon and Orinoco basins, in Darien and Central America—and in the arid zones of northern Mexico, as well as in the Gran Chaco, Araucanian Chile, and the *llanos* of Argentina, precisely because the Indians constituted marginal cultures that were not adaptable to urban and rural systems, at least in the initial phase of interdependence.

Outside of these regions, which actually represented the most extended surface of the American continent, the high native civilizations would have evolved, and it was in the areas inhabited by the latter that Hispanic culture largely developed. The fact that these civilizations had created a strong demographic base concentrated in cities and a technically efficient or trained labor force in agriculture and in the industrial arts, and the fact that their populations constituted an urbanized, sociocultural complex lent to the rapid accommodation of their peoples to the new Hispanic power.

This rapid accommodation was true particularly to the extent that Hispanic urbanization represented a technological advance for the new societies and to the degree that the installation of a new Spanish political and military power was implanted in the form of a replacement of the dominant native castes—especially the Inca and Mexica—by another, that of the Spanish conquistadors, which was to perform this accommodation of native peoples while it was establishing itself in its role of domination by means of a rigid social stratification.

What stands out here is that the episode of the Spanish conquest in these circumstances is, besides a violent geopolitical struggle for domination of the space and its peoples, a triumph of the greater technological possibilities of European civilization at that time. Therefore, to the degree that cities were its principal social expression, Hispanic urbanism left its stamp on a macrostructure whose influence reached over all the populations that the Mexica and Inca empires had managed previously to accumulate, in addition to the new ones who were being subjugated as expansion progressed.

The creation of cities on the coasts—the case of Lima, or of Brazilian cities, for example—obeyed a geopolitical scheme, despite which the cities could rely on nearby populations of farmers who carried out their activities in accord with the demands of the urban market. In any case, the new cities were not the result of improvisation; rather, in general terms, they were organized on the basis of their utility and of the possibility of rapidly integrating the pre-Hispanic populations whose agricultural and urban traditions assured a stable work force. Without the existence of the new coastal cities, urbanism and the integration of a strong Ibero-American society would have proved costly, and in many cases it would have been economically unprofitable.

The "taming" of native populations of forest dwellers and hunters—from northern Mexico to the extreme south—was a slow process, more parallel to that of the expansion of settlements than to that of military conquest, because in the latter case the result was the extinction of the rebel Indian. Thus, today there still exist native communities who live their lives according to pre-European canons or models. We can have no doubt, then, that the forms of urban culture were relatively stable and rapid in their development or maintenance, at least where there was a previous pre-Columbian urban tradition. Where this tradition did not exist, the process was slow and was constantly threatened by the instability of economic exploitation related especially to mining, by Indian raids, and by the process of absorption by the Indians of the Spanish and Portuguese cultures. The expansion of the market economy would produce over time an expansion of the urban frontiers, and therefore of racial mixing. Native mission settlements were not only the work of evangelization, but were also an effect of the needs of urban civilization and of the transformation of the Indian into a labor force at the service of a new economic ideology. The ecological retrenchments of the Indians and the resistance to being incorporated into Hispanic models would not be the consequences of an a priori rejection of such models, but rather the formation of a critical consciousness consisting of the fact that the preservation of political freedom and of their independence as a group was also the condition for their survival as a culture.

Demographic Proportions

In the rural sector, the native represented 75 percent of the estimated continental population, a figure resulting from the numbers of families surveyed and those classified by Alcedo as Indian families devoted to agriculture and cattle raising, compared to the families classified as belonging to other ancestries. These proportions show that the natives maintained their numerical preponderance more in the country than in the urban areas. In the population survey sample to which we have referred, the comparative proportions of lineages in the country and in the urban centers are different, because the Indian maintains a ratio of approximately 75 percent in the villages and 4 percent in the cities and urban centers. These proportions also indicate differences not only in the numbers of individuals according to their racial ancestry, but also in the influences of each culture with regard to the demographic mass relative to each racial lineage.

Although the ratio of culture to demographic volume must be considered relatively valid, because the cultural importance we assign to it tends to be more qualitative than quantitative, nevertheless, the demographic weight of one group with respect to another is culturally decisive when the political power exercised by the minority over the majority is not very strong. In the American case, Spanish political power was exercised very forcefully and systematically over the native and colored populations in the cities as well as in the rural areas. This assumes, as we have indicated, the predominance of Spanish culture over the native and other cultures, particularly in what we call the sociocultural macrostructure.

Specifically indigenous cultural complexes appeared more as a functional value of a tribal, local, or regional nature than as an urban one. The certain fact is that the native peasant cultures of the eighteenth century appeared mixed with the Spanish in the form of local syncretisms whose specificity tended, nonetheless, to be a function of the Spanish urban political system and of its economic or religious interests, carried out through a juridical organization that embraced all the populations to be found under its political or administrative control. This control was exercised, directly or indirectly, either through authorities designated by an official institution or through the very persons of the Spanish, who through superiority of status assumed a certain de facto juridical personality on site, in the absence of an official delegation. And in other cases, the system of control acted through native authorities themselves, recognized as such by the Spanish political system.

Given their nature, the native cultures did not prevail, despite the fact that they were always superior in numbers to the other races. The relative importance or capacity for survival of native culture is manifested more through racial mixing than through its own autonomous expression. All of what has remained of indigenous culture is present in mestizo ways of life. Apart from these, as more or less pure cultures the Indian way appears only among the so-called savage nations, that is, among those which remained, and still remain, relatively autonomous from all urban culture, whatever may be its character: Spanish, African, or European as an extension of the Spanish.

With this consideration in mind, the demographic phenomenon or relative size of population and of racial proportions in the countryside and cities of Ibero-America, is not necessarily equivalent to a relation between size and cultural importance, because, as we can see, this importance is relative to the specific qualities of political power and to the capacity of the latter to organize the members of each native group according to its own bases and interests. Hence, there is no doubt that Spanish culture prevailed among the indigenous cultures based on the macrostructural systems that we have mentioned. The differences that might arise with regard to the relative influence of the native or of the Spanish model in one area or another would be an issue that we need to explore in the very forms of racial mixing in its specific regional syncretisms. They would appear in the form of the customs and vocabulary that are the definitive indicators of these cultural influences on a regional level, with different intensities when urban or rural societies are involved. In any case, the Spanish mode was a constant in the social life and the culture of peasant communities, in proportions that differed according to area and depended upon the direct interest that individuals or official institutions might have in such a presence. From this perspective let us see what results from the demographic estimate that we are discussing.

From an examination made of a total of 199 haciendas cited in Alcedo, whose populations break down, respectively, into Spanish, Indians, mestizos and mulattoes, and sometimes blacks, the majority of whom pertain to New Spain, we have obtained the following proportions:

Ethnicities or castes	Number of families	Proportion
Spanish	484	15.81%
Indians	1,929	65.74%
Mestizos	214	7.29%
Mulattoes	327	11.14%
Totals	2,934	99.98%

These proportions would give us a peasant demographic form racially distributed in the proportions that we have just indicated, if we keep in mind that the participation of mulattoes and blacks in this type of economic extraction would be greater than in the towns, with regard to the Indians, in that as a labor force they were more adaptable than the Indians because of their easier social availability as well as their performance in the hard labor—especially in the mills, mines, freighting, and cattle raising—where they were employed. When we turn from the haciendas to the towns, the proportions of Indians increase, precisely because the Indians constituted more closed and ethnocentric societies, and because blacks and mulattoes operated closer to the Spanish than to the Indians. In addition, the low numbers of mestizos that appear are often more the result of the fact that they were assimilated into the category of Spaniards than of the fact that there might necessarily have been more Spanish than mestizos. In such a case, the number of mestizos would continue to be low in the census compared to what would be accepted at a later time, in the independence period and after reformulation of the bases of the political, juridical, and social system of the societies of America.

As we see, the population of each hacienda would average 14.74 families. Given that there would be structural differences with regard to the size of the families, considered from the viewpoint of the conditions in which the castes lived and in terms of their respective social adaptations, we must recognize that no universal model for family size existed. Although similar tendencies can be observed among the native peasants, variations would exist, nonetheless, that would be a function of the specific adjustment of each group to the various structural forms of each locale: political, economic, juridical, and ecological.

Thus, for example, in Chinchero (Cuzco), a Quechua community that in the latter half of the eighteenth century (1772) had a total of 1,545 inhabitants, it is shown that the size of households varied ostensibly (Esteva 1972, 321ff.) from 1 to 11 individuals, but the most common were those of 2 to 4 persons. The relatively small size of native households in Chinchero suggests that they consisted of nuclear families whose houses were clustered together according to the principle of the extended family—that is, parents, children, and siblings resided in neighborhoods where their respective dwellings were together, except in those cases where, through marriage, some male offspring lived in a more or less permanent matrilocal residence. In general, nevertheless, the tendency was to live in separate but nearby houses in order to assure activities of cooperation and mutual assistance in work and on different ceremonial occasions—communions, weddings, baptisms, godparent rites, fiestas and parties—or those that called for the exchange of favors and the gathering of the group, as well as crucial episodes: birth, the rites of passage, serious illness, and the death of some family member.

The average family per household in Chinchero at that time was 3.3 persons. In this sense, the census criterion of the period was of the type that took into account only the nuclear family or the head of the family who figured at that moment as the one responsible for the house for the purposes of their payment of tribute or for their civic responsibilities. Nevertheless, considered functionally with regard to familial structure, this family was a wider social unit, because it included the children of a principal father, his respective wives, and the unmarried descendants of each nuclear family, in each case living clustered in nearby houses. In this way, family size in the census would not imply an independent or self-sufficient economic unit, given that in the majority of cases the basic social unit was formed by larger family groups.

Cook and Borah (1971, 161ff.) give similar averages for Mexico in the second half of the eighteenth century, insofar as the averages for native households can be computed as being similar to those for Chinchero for the same period. Let us say, in this sense, that the average would be somewhat greater for mulattoes, mestizos, and Spaniards if we consider that—unlike that of the Indians—their socioeconomic systems relied more on the individualistic organization of each domestic unit than on the interdependence on the local level of several domestic units constituting something like an extended family for the purposes of cooperation and mutual assistance.

According to that system, the domestic population "surpluses" would go to the cities.

In Chinchero, the homes with more than four individuals pertain to heads of family registered as local nobility. This gives an average total of five persons per household. Thus, this statistic would mean that the usual indigenous household would have a smaller population than a noble one precisely because both the house was smaller and the extension of farmland under cultivation was also of a limited area, and because the formation of labor units was based on marriage, it being understood that there were few unmarried children included of marriageable ages who might continue to form part of their parents' dwelling. Given this productive system and its cooperative orientation, the households of Spaniards, mestizos, and mulattoes differed from the native through the fact that, while the latter preserved a more collectivist orientation, the former were distinguished by their greater economic autonomy, and in most cases by the use of nonfamily labor employed on a full-time basis.

Our estimates are 5 persons per household/family for Spaniards, mestizos, and mulattoes, and 3.5 per native household/family. As we pass from the scattered rural populations, as in the case of farms and haciendas, to larger and more concentrated populations, such as towns, villas, and cities, the size of the households grows larger. In the cities the scarcity of dwellings among persons of the lower class would give rise to their clustering their houses. This problem would affect the Indians and the colored castes especially, as it habitually affects working groups in urban societies of great migrant influx, particularly when the supply of labor is greater than the capacity for its economic absorption. The fact that the second half of the eighteenth century was a time of great migratory mobility toward the cities—especially because of the weakening of the traditional social structure, and due, additionally, to gradual decline of mining and the colonial system—caused the uprooted populations to flock to the cities, resulting in a promiscuity of habitation in the case of the native and colored populations.

Although we have no detailed census evidence regarding the urban demography of this period, it is also true that certain distinctions can be made with reference to the characteristics of these types of populations, if we keep in mind the role played in them by their prior histories. Thus, those cities not founded by the Spanish maintained a great proportion of native population. For example, Cholola, in New Spain, had 53.9 percent; Pátzcuaro, also in New Spain, had 80 percent. And other cities, such as La Paz, in present-day Bolivia, whose climatic conditions and altitude made it difficult for Europeans and Africans to adapt, had a very strong native presence, in this case 84 percent, while the Spanish totaled 5.8 percent and mestizos and people of color, 9.4 percent. The same situation occurred in Cuernavaca, New Spain, where the proportion of native population was 66.45 percent and that of the Spanish was 26.7 percent, while the mestizos and mulattoes shared in 6.8 percent. By contrast, the cities founded by the Spanish show higher percentages of the latter and of the colored castes, as occurred, for example in Lerma, New Spain, where the natives represented 33.3 percent, mestizos and mulattoes, 46.6 percent, and Spaniards, 20 percent.

In one case, that of Sonsonate, a capital of Guatemala, when 1,900 of the citizenry were counted, 400 of them were Spanish, which indicates a proportion of 21 percent of the latter. This figure reinforces the notion that because of the variety of antecedents or factors that caused the concentration or scattering of numbers of the population according to their racial group, these proportions would also be variable in the cities and in the rural areas. For these reasons, we are obliged to formulate considered averages derived from quantitatively representative figures whose general amounts serve to indicate the direction of the relative proportion of social and racial distributions.

Accordingly, and mindful of that perspective, if we apply such different criteria and distinguish the different racial proportions as they involve cities of pre-Hispanic or European origin,[3] we would then find that the emphasis of distribution of the racial populations varies significantly. In the present case, we apply, respectively, the proportions of Indians (33.3 percent), Spanish (20 percent), and mestizos and mulattoes together (44.6 percent),[4] which were compiled for the city of Lerma, in New Spain, in the case of those cities we consider Hispanic, and those given for Cholula, a city of pre-Hispanic origin, whose proportions would be, successively 54 percent Indians, 4.4 percent Spanish, and 41.6 percent mestizos and mulattoes.[5]

We must also remember that the pre-Hispanic mining cities maintained higher proportions of nonindigenous populations than other cities. Such would be the case of Pachuca, New Spain, where the proportions would be 10 percent for natives versus a remaining proportion that we could distribute, taking into account the population of the mining and farming town of Taximarca, in Maravatío (Michoacán, New Spain), which contained, respectively, 460 families of Spanish (72.3 percent), 110 families of mestizos and mulattoes (17.3 percent), and 66 families of Indians (10.4 percent).

In this way, we are presented with a wide variety of racial proportions whose specific flux or decline was relative, furthermore, at the time they were surveyed. There are even cases such as the one of Coquimbo (kingdom of Chile) where no native population appears, precisely because the latter kept away from the others, such that only whites, mestizos, and blacks appear. In this sense, we will apply to those populations the known proportions for León, New Spain, although recognizing the ecological distances separating the two. Despite that distance, we understand that the principal sociocultural form was not too different, if we exclude the specific indigenous influence in each case.

What seems certain is that the proportions of whites and Indians vary according to whether rural centers or cities are involved. In the cities the relative proportion of Spaniards is higher, whereas that of the Indians is higher in the country. Nevertheless, in each case the proportion of mestizos and mulattoes usually remains balanced, although with a tendency to rise where mining centers are involved, due to the fact that those groups constituted a labor force especially sought for this type of activities. According to the above patterns, Spanish-Indian racial mixtures would appear more frequently in farming communities than in mining communities, so that in the latter, Spanish-black mixtures would predominate. At the same time, the racial mixtures of both basic combinations—Spanish-Indian and Spanish-black—would appear in greater balance in the cities than in the country.

With reference to the average size of urban families, we lack specific data, but we are inclined to adopt the average proposed by Cook and Borah (1971, 161) for "persons of intelligence" in Mexico of four individuals per family, though retaining the fact that in some[6] urban populations, on average, there was one servant for every four persons. In addition, because of their lower infant mortality, it is very likely that Spanish and mestizo households were larger than those of the natives and of the colored population, except in the cases where the native and colored households lived clustered in promiscuous quarters.[7] But in any case, with reference to family size we are inclined to adopt the criterion of five persons per family for whites and mestizos, and five for Indians, mulattoes, and blacks. According to these formulations and the estimates that we applied to the partial figures of Alcedo, we would obtain the following population tables for Ibero-America in the late eighteenth century, whose extraction we have carried out on the basis of an adaptation to the possibilities of these statistics. Thus, in order to establish the urban population we have started with a sample of 95 cities and 38 villas for which census data were available, which produced the result shown in table 9.1.

If we keep in mind that this total gives an average of 10,930 inhabitants per city, and since another 150 cities remain to be surveyed in order to complete the total of 245 that are registered in the Alcedo census, and if we apply this coefficient of 10,930 persons and multiply it by the 150 cities remaining, we get a total for the latter of 1,539,500 more individuals, which we would add to the 1,038,318 from the sample of 95 cities surveyed. Thus, the total number of individuals living in cities at that time would be 2,577,818.

Table 9.1 Sample of 95 Cities

Ethnicity or Caste	Number of Inhabitants	%
Indians	581,406	58.50
Spanish	301,340	26.80
Mestizos	81,630	7.26
Mulattoes	69,967	7.04
Blacks	3,975	0.40
TOTAL	1,038,318	100.00

In the following table (table 9.2)—in which there is a survey of thirty-eight localities that, as we have said, we can consider urban for the purposes of their ideological orientation—we have compiled the population figures given for this type of grouping. In this case, we respect the distinction made by the census between cities and villas, although later, with regard to urbanism, we treat them within a single, general urban typology.

If we consider that the resulting calculated average of inhabitants per villa is 5,851, and keep in mind that another 191 villas remain to be surveyed, the multiplication of the aforesaid coefficient of 5,851 by the remaining 191 villas gives a total of 1,117,541 individuals. Added to those in the sample, they make a total population of 1,339,880 inhabitants living in villas in this period.

The respective totals of urban populations, according to the characteristics of their division into cities and villas, would thus be:

Population in Cities	2,577,818
Population in villas	1,339,880
Total	3,917,698

With regard to racial or *ethnic* distribution, there is a notable decline in native proportions in urban populations related to the other races, which emphasizes the fact that the more urbanized the cultural form of the population, the less was the percentage of Indians living in it.

With respect to mining communities, the censuses taken give us the proportions shown in table 9.3.

The calculated average of families for mining locales is 373, and that of inhabitants turns out to be 1,388. If we add to these localities another 82 to total the 120 that we have considered as urbanized, and if we apply to them

Table 9.2 Sample of 38 Villas

Ethnicity or Caste	Number of Inhabitants	%
Indians	22,234	10.0
Spanish	100,497	45.2
Mestizos	77,596	34.9
Mulattoes	20,900	9.4
Blacks	1,112	0.5
TOTAL	222,339	100.0

Table 9.3 Sample of 38 Mining Communities

Ethnicity or Caste	Families	%	Individuals
Indians[8]	7,354	51.9	25,739
Spanish[9]	4,253	29.9	17,012
Mestizos[9]	839	5.9	3,356
Mulattoes[9]	1,173	8.3	4,692
Blacks[8]	560	4.0	1,960
TOTAL	14,179	100.0	52,759

the coefficient of 1,388 individuals each, we would have another 113,816 inhabitants, which, added to the original 52,759, give a total of 166,575 persons. Thus, the urbanized population according to communities surveyed would be:

In cities 2,577,818
In villas 1,399,880
In mining centers 166,575
  Total 4,084,273

On the mainland the racial or *ethnic* distribution in urban areas shows that the figures for total population increase as we go from the mining centers, where the contingency of employment was certainly notorious, to the villas, which were more stable locales preferred by the Spanish, and probably were

Table 9.4 Racial or Ethnic Distribution on the Urban Mainland

Ethnicity or Caste	Cities	Villas	Mining Centers	Totals	%
Indians	1,508,024	133,988	86,452	1,728,464	42.3
Spanish	690,855	605,626	49,806	1,346,287	33.0
Mestizos	187,150	467,618	9,828	664,596	16.3
Mulattoes	181,478	125,949	13,826	321,253	7.8
Blacks	10,311	6,699	23,673	40,683	1.0
TOTAL	2,577,818	1,339,880	166,575	4,084,273	100.4

centers of culture and of society configured in terms of Hispanic models. The cities of the continent were cosmopolitan racial and ethnic conglomerates, but in any case they offer us the notion that the Indian and the Spaniard, or white, represented the basic strains of the social system (table 9.4).

Thus, it is clear that the native figures in the continental total integrated into the Hispanic system of culture are basic to understanding the dynamic of the political, economic, and social process in general for this region. Just as in the process following the stabilization of the Spanish conquests and colonization in the Antilles and in its Portuguese counterpart in Brazil, it would be the black and the mulatto who would set the pattern for interracial conflicts, so in mainland Spanish America it would be the Indian. It was enough for him to reaffirm his social personality for conflicts to occur, that is, it was enough for him to establish himself as the heir to an important cultural patrimony. Nevertheless, for the purposes of his cultural possibilities, this reaffirmation would come too late.

By the nineteenth century, the criollo, and by the twentieth century the mestizo, would have used the Indian for their own ends, and in a certain sense would have restored him as part of the Ibero-American cultural form. Yet, when this restoration took place it would be already somewhat late to attempt to make of his traditional culture the basis for the modern culture of the continental nations of Ibero-America, excepting, in a certain sense, Mexico and the Andean high plains; but even there, Western culture, through its urban models, permeates the behavior of the modern Indian and makes him want to emulate those models. In a certain way, nonetheless, in the late eighteenth century the preceding table defines some racial proportions that serve to demonstrate the nature of the native situation and its relative importance as a problem with relation to the other racial groups.

Table 9.5 Sample of 2,252 Rural Communities

Ethnicity or Caste	Families	%	Individuals
Indians[10]	336,900	75.00	1,249,150
Spanish[11]	68,537	16.40	274,148
Mestizos[11]	18,871	4.50	75,484
Mulattoes[11]	15,658	3.80	62,632
Blacks[10]	1,341	0.30	4,694
Chinese[11]	220	0.05	880
TOTAL	461,527	100.05	1,666,988

Table 9.6 Total for 7,884 Towns Surveyed

Ethnicity	Inhabitants	%
Indians	4,376,001	75.0
Spanish	956,886	16.4
Mestizos	262,560	4.5
Mulattoes	221,717	3.8
Blacks	17,504	0.3
TOTAL[12]	5,834,668	100.0

Peasant Population

Continuing with the formula of calculating these population figures for the rural areas, we would get the results to be seen in the following tables, results which, furthermore, are statistical indicators that refer indirectly to the type of society that was developing on the continent (table 9.5).

When we consider the fact that the average number of inhabitants per town would be 740 individuals, and multiply this coefficient by the remaining 5,632 rural communities, we would have an added total of 4,167,680 inhabitants. Thus, the total population living in towns would be 5,834,668 individuals. These would be distributed as indicated in table 9.6.

Alcedo makes frequent references to *ranchos* and *rancherías* and to other types of small rural localities. In each case the latter were not recognized statistically, and therefore we lack data in this respect for them. There must have been a large number of these locales, and they suggest a considerable quantity to be added to those we have calculated for rural communities. In every sense, they represent little-connected or isolated communities that in a nomenclature would represent an amount probably five or six times greater than that for those population entities compiled in the *Diccionario* of Alcedo. In the case of Mexico, for example, in 1950 (Durán Ochoa 1955, 14) the number of localities of from 1 to 99 inhabitants amounted to 65,090, and they represented 65.73 percent of the total towns surveyed. But also, those of from 100 to 499 inhabitants numbered 24,979, and their portion of the total census was 25.22 percent; thus, both classes of community together totaled 90.95 percent. With regard to population, they represented a total of 7,525, 251 individuals, or 29.2 percent.

If we keep in mind, additionally, that the number of localities of between 500 and 999 inhabitants in Mexico in 1950 represented 4.99 percent of the total and that their total population (ibid., 13) was 3,406,603 individuals, and if we start with an average of 740 inhabitants per town, as we indicated for the census of Alcedo, then we should increase somewhat the percentage of localities (500 – 999) compared to total localities, up to at least 32 percent. In the case of the late eighteenth century, considering its greater rural character in comparison to that of the present, this percentage of communities of less than 750 inhabitants not compiled statistically by Alcedo should be increased to give us an approximate overall proportion of 40 percent more of rural population.

This is more or less what needs to be added to the census picture of rural Ibero-America in the late eighteenth century, as given to us by Alcedo. That is, a large number of such communities was not acknowledged in his data. In general, we could accept that around 40 percent of the rural or peasant population of Ibero-America was not registered in the Alcedo census, such that to the totals we have given, we would need to add an amount equivalent to the 40 percent that we have established.

According to this conclusion, to the 5,834,668 inhabitants in the census of 7,884 towns, we would add 2,333,867, so that the total rural population for continental Ibero-America would be 8,165,535 persons. In these terms, and according to the ethnic distribution we have made for rural populations, the specific proportions of this continental population (table 9.7) would be as shown in table 9.7.

Having established the racial and ethnic proportions for continental Ibero-America within the specific framework of their rural and urban distributions, and having represented their different magnitudes, we have unquestionably indicated that the statistical weight of the native population in the

Table 9.7 Continental Rural Population
of Ibero-America

Ethnicity or Caste	Number of Inhabitants	%
Indians	6,126,401	75.0
Spanish	1,339,640	16.4
Mestizos	367,584	4.5
Mulattoes	310,404	3.8
Blacks	24,506	0.3
TOTAL	8,168,535	100.0

Table 9.8 Racial Proportions on the Mainland[a]

Ethnicity or Caste	Rural Dwellers	Urbanites	Totals	%
Indians	6,126,401	1,728,464	7,854,865	64.1
Spanish	1,339,640	1,346,287	2,685,927	21.9
Mestizos	367,584	664,596	1,032,180	8.4
Mulattoes	310,404	321,253	631,657	5.2
Blacks	24,506	23,673	48,179	0.4
TOTAL	8,168,535	4,084,273	12,252,808	100.0

NOTE [a]Excluding the population of "savage" Indians

general proportions approaches two-thirds of the total. Nevertheless, since the specification of physical differences between races was adjusted more to follow a social criterion—that of status—and a cultural criterion, the way of life, most likely these respective coefficients would be subject to change in cases where census methods of rigorously anthropometric classification were employed. The fact that among the native populations there was a certain number of mestizo and even white individuals born and socialized in their midst and therefore classified as Indians on the basis of their being members of Indian peasant communities would indicate a greater likelihood (table 9.8) that a certain number of mestizos and whites were registered as natives than the reverse: natives entered as mestizos or whites. What really mattered at the moment of classification was, more than race, the ethnicity or cultural group that constituted one's own way of life. What was important was whether one behaved or did not behave as an Indian, as a mestizo, or as a white, with the understanding that this difference included the status group more than the racial one, since classification followed the principles of ascription to a given caste.

Estimates for the Antilles

Since Alcedo provides no information on the entire Antilles, we have made our estimates in this regard, keeping in mind the present-day proportions that exist between the Antilles and the Ibero-American continent. In this sense, the demographic proportions of the Antilles around the middle of the century are equivalent to some 11 percent of those of mainland Ibero-America. Nevertheless, given that in the colonial period the Antilles were areas of greater geopolitical importance than today and played a comparatively more significant economic role than their current one, we should raise this percentage. In this case we would place it at 15 percent, such that the Antilles would have a total population of 1,837,921, in addition to the 12,252,808 which we allotted to the mainland south of the Rio Grande.

We can understand the urban-rural distribution of this Antillean population as being similar to that of the continent, although in some cases the urban form would include strong military and maritime concentrations as well as floating populations that are qualitatively and quantitatively difficult to define now. Despite the fact that we think the continent was less urbanized—even with the inclusion of pre-Columbian civilizations—we believe that if we maintain the proportions given for the latter we shall not be far from reality, keeping in mind the uniform nature of the socioeconomic program imposed upon all of their possessions by the Europeans, even where we admit adaptations or variants of a regional stamp.

According to this demographic distribution, in the Antilles we would have a rural population of 1,225,342 individuals (66.67 percent), and an urban population consisting of 612,579 inhabitants (33.33 percent). Given these facts, we think the mainland and Antilles population of Ibero-America that was not Indian—in the sense of savage nations—and therefore rural and urban, would total 14,090,729 inhabitants.

As for its racial or ethnic proportions, this Antilles population differs from that of the continent, since its native inhabitants were comparatively scarce. By contrast, the African predominance would be evident. One reason for this would be that in the Antilles the majority of racial mixing was between blacks and whites, and what little mixing that occurred between Indians and whites, or between blacks and Indians was disseminated or assimilated by the great current of the first type, especially by white men mixing with black women. Thus, the proportions of white-Indian-black mixtures can be considered as absorbed into the greater mulatto component. The Indians, who soon disappeared in the violent impact of the Spanish conquest and were decimated by diseases and epidemics alien to the New World—against which they lacked organic defenses—ceased to have demographic importance shortly after the beginning of the Spanish, or European, period. Especially in the Greater Antilles, geopolitically the more important, Indians were quickly replaced by the Africans employed in plantation labor and in domestic service. Since the plantations were of great economic importance from the beginning, their need for a labor force was also great, and in this sense the importance of black slaves was incessant, until they outnumbered the white population.

The structure of slavery, as defined by the dominant role played by the whites, made of the black woman a sexual object at the disposal of European males, and soon a mulatto population of great demographic and social importance was created, although while the slave system remained in force the black population seems to have been larger, precisely because of its regular demographic renewal and because the social stratification imposed by class barriers and the greater sexual self-sufficiency of the European group allowed a large·portion of white men to do without black women.

In Alcedo's sample of Antilles populations, with which we are working for the purpose of establishing the relative racial distribution of its totals, there appear no breakdowns for mulattoes or for mestizos, and thus we are forced to turn to historical sources of a demographic nature. In a certain way, these approximate the actual proportions among blacks and mulattoes especially, since the proportions between these latter and the whites would be reflected in Alcedo's own distributions. Of course, in places such as Cuba and Santo Domingo (sic) the proportions of whites[13] would be higher than in the rest of the Antilles in general. Despite that, however, the demographic weight of the black on the other islands would result in the creation of a joint population greatly superior in their favor in corresponding racial proportions (table 9.9). The very nature of slavery and of the plantation system favored this demographic superiority.

In this regard, we have in mind the proportions we have gotten from the Alcedo census itself, in some cases. Analyzing those figures in terms of their proportions, in regard to population—which we calculated previously—the resulting estimate would be as shown in table 9.10.

Table 9.9 Sample of Antilles Populations

Race or Ethnicity[14]	Inhabitants	%
Blacks	388,270	47.9
Mulattoes	200,019	24.7
Whites	220,299	27.1
Indians	2,019	0.3
TOTAL	810,607	100.0

Table 9.10 Estimated Total Racial Population
in the Antilles

Race or Ethnicity	Inhabitants	%
Blacks	880,364	47.9
Mulattoes	453,966	24.7
Whites	498,077	27.1
Indians	5,514	0.3
TOTAL	1,837,921	100.0

If we apply the proportions given by Humboldt (1960, 168) for Cuba in 1791, corresponding to the city of Havana and the cities and villas in its jurisdiction—consisting of 52.9 percent of whites and the rest of colored persons—and if we analyze them in terms of the urban proportions that we acknowledge for all the Antilles, as well as the estimates that we have made for blacks and mulattoes, we would have the situation shown in table 9.11.

In the country, the proportions would incline ostensibly toward the colored populations, with the understanding that the latter would form the basis of the labor force. In this sense, considering that Humboldt (1960, 185) points out that in the sugarcane and farm areas of Cuba the proportion of whites with respect to persons of color barely came to one-third, and in the sense that Cuba was one of the most urbanized of the islands, we can accept a different racial proportion for the aggregate of the rural areas of the Antilles. We establish these proportions respectively, and according to the remaining proportions, as they appear in table 9.12.

Table 9.11 Urban Racial Distribution
           in the Antilles

Race	Inhabitants	%
Blacks	190,512	31.1
Mulattoes	98,013	16.0
Whites	324,054	52.9
TOTAL	612,579	100.0

Table 9.12 Racial Distribution of Rural Dwellers
           in the Antilles

Race	Inhabitants	%
Blacks	633,801	54.17
Mulattoes	342,924	27.98
Whites	213,103	17.39
Indians	5,514	0.45
TOTAL	1,225,342	99.99

The Indian Nations

If we consider the figures given by Alcedo with respect to the populations of Indians called *savages,* or *infidels,* whose total number is 175,910 individuals, and if this figure purports to be the total sum for a very small number of tribes or nations about which Alcedo had statistical information, then it must be recognized that the native population not controlled by the Spanish and Portuguese was much larger when we see that the number of nations entered as savage or heathen in his dictionary is 619. The majority of these nations are characteristically inhabitants of forests or semiarid regions, and are distinguished by the fact that only a few of them practiced subsistence or grub agriculture, so that, in general, they were collectors, hunters, and fishers.

If we give special consideration to the fact that this number would involve cultures adjusted to specific ecological conditions, that is, showing a direct relation between habitat, technology, and demography, then the problem to consider is to what degree we can calculate this correlation. We think that once the basic samples are established as the model, we could conclude that the so-called savage nations represented a numerically calculable and significant population.

The basis on which we seek to determine the number of Indians is that of the kind of possibilities afforded by the physical environments in which they lived. First, we must point out that such environments were relatively marginal to the interests of the Europeans of the time, and given that the latter exercised no pressure at all on the Indians for the purpose of occupying their territories, and that the cost in lives and efforts necessary for their control brought little return, the European acted upon the Indians through frontier geopolitical policy more than for effective penetration; thus, the Indians remained relatively secure in their lands and could live, furthermore, according to their own cultural traditions. Nevertheless, their wars and raids against the whites were devastating, because bit by bit, the latter were conquering their space and thus were gradually pushing the Indians toward the more inhospitable regions.

To these wars and raids between whites and Indians must be added the internal warfare of tribe versus tribe, such that by the late eighteenth century the process of ecological retreat for the Indian had reached its relative maximum: the free Indian occupied only the marginal areas. The rest of the native population formed part of the Indian "reducciones" run by the clergy or constituted peasant communities. Therefore, in each case of coexistence with the whites, the processes of acculturation were swift. They consisted of becoming peasants or servants of urban and colonial societies, part of whose economies were oriented toward satisfying the demands of their European metropolises.

Thus, the Indian whom we acknowledge as such was the one who lived in jungle or semiarid regions that were inhospitable, or at any rate not occupied by the European. Populations of this type lived in the way of their traditional culture, and although in many cases they were directly or indirectly acculturated in aspects of their material belongings, nonetheless, their political structure remained independent and retained its tribal nature, even though the number of their individuals was gradually diminishing.

The regions that entered largely into this marginal character were a big portion of northern Mexico, the basins of the Orinoco—including the Guianas—and the Amazon, the Gran Chaco, the Pampas, Patagonia, and Tierra del Fuego. Together, these regions would have a total extension of some 10 million square kilometers [3.9 million square miles]. In this sense, calculating for the culturally Indian part of northern Mexico, an area of approximately 1 million square kilometers [390,000 square miles], we shall apply to this the calculation estimated by Kroeber (Forde 1966, 49) for the population density of California, which would be 1 inhabitant per square mile. This would give the northern region of Mexico a total Indian population of some 600,000 individuals, that is, 0.6 inhabitants per square kilometer [.23 per square mile]. As regards the area including the Orinoco, the Guianas, and the Amazon, covering some 7.5 million square kilometers [2.9 million square miles], we will assign it an average population density of 0.25 inhabitants per square kilometer [.1, or .097 per square mile]. In this way we get a population of approximately 1,800,000 individuals. For some of the tribes inhabiting the Gran Chaco, occupying an area of some 300,000 square kilometers [115,800 square miles] not under European control, the population would be somewhat greater: 0.4 individuals per square kilometer [.15 per square mile], which would give some 120,000 savage Indians. For the aggregate of the Pampas, Patagonia, and Tierra del Fuego, with an area of some 800,000 square kilometers [308,800 square miles], and mindful of Wagner (1964, 164), who, for the Ona of the large island of Tierra del Fuego, gives a density of 1 inhabitant for every 3 square miles, the population density would be some 0.2 inhabitants per square kilometer [.077 per square mile]. Thus, there would be some 160,000 in this region in that period. From this viewpoint, the politically independent Indian inhabitants would be those who appear in table 9.13.

These Indian populations appear to us in this period as demographically diminished above all by the mortality of the wars of extermination, since the normal ecological adjustments of a technology that found it hard to control and prevent diseases and epidemics include these low densities. That is, they are assumed, and in this sense the ecology plays the role of natural selector,

Table 9.13 Population of Independent Indians
            in Ibero-America

Geographical Region	Inhabitants	%
Northern Mexico	600,000	22.4
Orinoco-Guianas-Amazon	1,800,000	67.2
Gran Chaco	120,000	4.4
Pampas, Patagonia, Tierra del Fuego	160,000	6.0
TOTAL	2,680,000	100.0

where the resources appropriated are related to the specific capacity of the technology to produce them. That is, in the case of predatory or subsistence economies—of captures of food—the population base or density would correlate to the relative capacity of their group to produce their food.

The differences in density per square kilometer that we noted between semiarid regions and the forests and grasslands would be those that exist between peoples who live close by agrarian and urban cultures or those superior in technological evolution, and peoples who live far from them, as occurred in the Amazon Basin. The case of the Gran Chaco would be an intermediate one, because the diversification of its flora and fauna and the influences of the Andean region would have stimulated the cultural development of many groups, especially the cultivators and hunters. Therefore, their possibilities of feeding themselves would be somewhat better, because they would also enjoy a more efficient technology of capture and production of foodstuffs.

Thus, the truly Indian populations would be the so-called savage nations, so that the Indian problem would be the one resulting from the contact between urban colonial society and these nations. The other nations, called simply Indian, were not truly a problem in the same sense. Rather, they constituted the problem of peasant communities "confined" to their sphere by the rigid system of social stratification and therefore without political self-determination, and whose sociocultural opening was a function of the will of the urban society and of its political power. Symbolically, this involves communities confined to their own system of authorities and bounded by the colonial macrosystem of castes, but as politically autonomous societies they would have lost control over their old tribal or national unity. Now they were but corporations with restricted rights, placed within a system over which they had no opportunities for decision making. But their culture, as we have already indicated, was no longer purely Indian. In general, it would be a mestizo culture with alternately Indian or Spanish modes or emphases, but with ways of life integrated into a single system: the Hispanic. Thus, the racial mixture hidden behind the mask of the data would be culturally greater than the biological mixture itself, although the latter would also be more abundant than is acknowledged by the census figures or population tables for the period.

Ibero-American Population: Cultural and Racial Proportions

We see that the population of Ibero-America in the late eighteenth century would barely total 17 million individuals, distributed in the manner that we can observe in table 9.14. This figure is far from the 23 million postulated

Table 9.14 Ibero-American Population:
Mainland and Antilles

Cultural Category	Inhabitants	%
Urban	4,696,852	28
Rural	9,393,877	56
Savage Indians of the Mainland	2,680,000	16
TOTAL	16,770,729	100

by Wilcox (Thompson 1956, 972) for the whole of Ibero-America in 1800. Of course, it approaches the estimate of Carr Saunders, who gives a total of 19 million for this same date (ibid.). Thus, we are certain that the populations of this period were formed according to a farming, cattle, and mining economy where major trade was a function of the demands of European countries, such that industrial development would be very poor, and urbanism would be more a function of the administrative apparatus and of viceregal power in charge of societies of the period through juridical, military, educational, and religious organizations—in addition to the complex of services that emerged in response to the demands of the internal and external markets—than of the economy.

Urban life thus would be related to the worlds of commerce, of public administration, of university education, and of the arts, to which would be added the world of industry, some of whose establishments would be associated with mining. In accord with this nature of urbanism, the ideological differences between urban and rural society would be revealed in terms of the upper and middle classes of the groups that were directly related to their social and economic life. In this way, the groups directly related to the upper classes would be, by association, urban in nature, but the upper classes would exhibit the maximum degree of urbanism. In this sense, the urbanization of the lower social classes living in the cities was in degree, and in a certain way many of their individuals resembled peasants more than urbanites. In fact, urban ideology would be less prevalent than we would be given to understand by the figures or percentages of urban population (28 percent) that we have obtained as a statistical estimate.

On the basis of these facts, urban populations expanded relatively less than

Table 9.15 Total Distribution for Ibero-America[a]

Cultural Categories	%	
Urban population	33.3	28.0
Rural population	66.7	56.0
Population of savage Indians		16.0
TOTAL	100.0	100.0

NOTE [a]The first column refers to the percentage derived from considering only the societies or cultural classes that were controlled by the European political system. The second also includes the populations of savage Indians, who were independent of this system.

did the rural, and represented, as we shall see in the next table, percentages characteristic more of a mercantile and administrative system than of an industrial one.

Having considered the distribution of the population totals in the Antilles, according to its racial aspects, we must add that the urban and rural proportions on the mainland and in the Antilles follow somewhat different models, since it appears that urbanization was more developed on the mainland than among the savage Indians, a group that, in contrast, was practically nonexistent in the Antilles. In any case, the corresponding table (table 9.15) gives an idea of these racial proportions, but with the exclusion of the savage Indians.

It follows, then, that the rural populations appeared to be not only the most important numerically, but that they also were based more upon the Indians than upon any other group. In contrast, in the urban areas the Indians ceased to have this overwhelming demographic weight and distributed their population among other races. Additionally, after the Indians, the white population was the most important, so that their social and cultural race of prestige—aside from the purely political one—not only appeared as decisive from the point of view of their role as dominator, but, in addition to their social role as rulers, their significant demographic numbers provided them support, thanks to which they were in a position to maintain a political, military, and social strength sufficient to assure their position as the dominant group.

This position, by vicarious association with other ethnicities, especially involved internal groups that exercised control—rural and urban leaders in

Table 9.16 Ibero-America: Total Urban Population, Mainland and Antilles

Race	Mining Centers	Villas	Cities	Antilles	Totals	%
Indians[a]	86,452	133,988	1,508,024		1,728,464	36.80
Whites[b]	49,806	605,626	690,855	324,054	1,670,341	35.56
Mestizos	9,828	467,618	187,150		664,596	14.15
Mulattoes	13,826	125,949	181,478	98,013	419,266	8.92
Blacks	6,663	6,699	10,311	190,512	214,185	4.56
TOTAL	166,575	1,339,880	2,577,818	612,579	4,696,852	99.99

NOTES [a]Though we can recognize Indian individuals in the Antilles, the percentage of their presence would be minimal. The same could be said of mestizos.

[b]In the majority of cases this refers to the Spanish, but the inclusion of the Guianas and the non-Spanish Antilles makes it necessary to modify the concept.

the service of the Spanish or of the whites—who occupied positions of command in the social scale considered in terms of class differences and according to the caste to which they belonged. The white group held power at the summit, but in addition, through its own internal stratification it spread its decision-making capacity throughout all groups, acculturating them and integrating them into the Hispanic social and political system.

In this sense, the high number of Spanish who appear in the statistics (see table 9.16) suggest that not only were they in a position to exercise an enormous political and military control, which would have been impossible to maintain without the indispensable support of active numbers of servants, but also that this number, by propagating themselves throughout every latitude of America, carried out their mission of spreading their culture and their way of life. As this Hispanic way of life was becoming socialized through its powerful means of domination and control, to that degree the culture of this Hispanic population was becoming established as the most developed one with respect to the other racial populations. Thus, the important number of whites or Spaniards who appear in the demographic proportions constituted an essential factor in maintaining Hispanic power, especially in maintaining this culture.

Unquestionably, it was in the cities where this culture flourished intellectually, but it was in the rural communities where it was consolidated in a profound way. In the early stage, the mestizos became the agents of this culture, but with the growth of Spanish settlement into the remotest areas, the agents of its spread in many cases ended up being the Spanish themselves, who settled among the Indian peasants or who in the cities and villas carried on commerce, crafts, public administration, or education of every type.

The mestizos soon became associated with this group, and with it they developed the cultural identifications necessary for Ibero-American society to be essentially Hispanic in character. The continuity of the migratory flow from the Iberian Peninsula was also a condition that from the outset prevented *criollismo* from succeeding in its separatist efforts. When this criollismo sufficiently increased population and therefore expanded its influence, it was also then in a position to impose its political standards, although its culture continued, at heart, to be that of its progenitors.

The urban nature of Spanish culture exported to America is the main element to be recognized in the complex of what we have called the macrostructure or total system of the various societies of Ibero-America. That macrostructure acted as a kind of pressure and control on the whole system, including the rural parts, and it was its administrative form that wove the network uniting the entire system. Wherever it reached other groups with its political controls, this culture also extended there. Thus, the Western urban way of life was served by the Spanish and the Portuguese even when, in specific cases, their economic role was one of farming or cattle. Except for those who were peasants by birth and by family tradition, isolated for generations from contacts with the urban world, the political quality of the Spanish extended beyond their own ruling class. The Spaniard, wherever he was, became an achiever of Spanish policy on the local level, insofar as, given his predominant economic role in most cases, he took an active part in the development and control of the social life of the rural communities, influencing them and conditioning them through his role as cacique or local personality (see table 9.17).

Having delineated the characteristics of these Ibero-American populations, we must still determine the overall distribution of their racial proportions, with the understanding that, for biological purposes, the mixtures of Spanish or whites with Indians and blacks should be considered as mestizos, whereas for cultural purposes, mixture must have reached all populations in the form of syncretisms, wherein the populations influenced one another to different degrees, but were mutually acculturated and, to some degree, each used the culture of the others. In this way Ibero-America was syncretizing the cultures, and in this respect the process was more rapid than that of miscegenation, as can be seen in table 9.18, where the mestizo is still a minority statistically little developed. This shows clearly that the system of castes had become an obstacle to biological mixing, though not necessarily to cultural mixing.

Table 9.17 Ibero-America: Total Rural Population, Mainland and Antilles

Race or Ethnicity	Mainland	Antilles	Total	%
Indians	6,126,401	5,514	6,131,915	65.27
Whites[a]	1,339,640	213,103	1,552,743	16.52
Mestizos	367,584		367,584	3.91
Mulattoes	310,404	342,924	653,328	6.95
Blacks	24,506	663,801	688,307	7.32
TOTAL	8,168,535	1,225,342	9,393,877	99.97

NOTE [a] As with the total urban population, here we have replaced the category of "Spaniard" with that of "white."

Table 9.18 Ibero-America: Racial Proportions, Mainland and Antilles

Race or Ethnicity	Rural Dwellers	Urbanites	Totals	%
Indians	6,393,877	1,728,464	7,860,379	46.87
Whites	1,552,743	1,670,341	3,223,084	19.22
Mestizos	367,584	664,596	1,032,180	6.15
Mulattoes	653,328	419,266	1,072,594	6.39
Blacks	688,307	214,185	902,492	5.38
TOTAL	9,393,877	4,696,852	14,090,729	84.01
Indian hunters/ gatherers			2,680,000	15.98
TOTAL			16,770,729	99.99

Here it appears very clear that at the time, the nonmixed racial groups still maintained strong numbers, the most dynamic cause of which was the system of stratification that distanced one group from another. This relatively lessened the opportunities for sexual exchange outside one's own group, and furthermore, engendered distinctive attitudes between racial groups; of course, the system relating to racial superiority or inferiority developed as a function of class interests as crystallized in their status, and also of classes who were likewise crystallized in terms of an exclusive identity of race or caste. The principles that justified the nonmixture of those who occupied the highest level of the social pyramid were a function of that group's stratification.

And just as racial mixing was intensive at the beginning of the conquest with regard to the number of individuals who took part in the exchange— for reasons that I have already indicated and discussed elsewhere—to the degree that the system of status was being consolidated and opportunities for social mobility were closed off, to that same degree the high incidence of racial mixtures was also cut. By the end of the eighteenth century, the process of racial mixing was very slow, and only the revolutions and interregional mobility actively reopened the process. Let us say that Independence did not produce substantial changes in individual attitudes toward miscegenation— though it did in the laws—because in fact the victorious classes continued to be the white groups, in this case, the criollos. It is only during the twentieth century that in some countries the emergence of mestizos into political power (Esteva 1961a, 56ff.) has made it possible to give vigorous renewal to this process of miscegenation. That process began through the politically based revival of native culture, that is, with the promotion of a mestizo mystique of indigenism. Nevertheless, the upper classes would continue to show reluctance toward miscegenation, especially in those cases in which differences of status, prestige, and wealth coincided with racial or ethnic differences, according to the circumstances.[15] Not until the mestizos achieved political power did the racial barrier, based on the internal reproduction of the upper classes of colonial origin, begin to crumble.

These Ibero-American populations of the late eighteenth century were basically rural ones, and, in accord with the incidences of racial mixture, the proportions of mestizos were quite low because the social mobility of the different rural strata was also low. The margin of social mobility in the cities was greater, precisely because, as we have said, social controls were weaker and more indirect: persons in particular acted within a more flexible and more anonymous social boundary. In this social context, the different racial groups crossed or exchanged their relative cultures with greater ease, and so increased the opportunities for miscegenation.

Among the rural groups, mestizos, or hybrids of Spanish and Indians, represented 367,584 individuals, or 3.91 percent,[16] whereas among the urban groups the proportion was greater, amounting to 14.15 percent. If, as we have said, racial mixing must include all the mixtures produced in the New World and particularly those created between the three basic trunks— Indian, white, and black—then the proportions of mestizos will include the

Table 9.19   Ibero-America: Mestizos and Mulattoes,
                     Mainland and Antilles

Region or Area	Mestizos	Mulattoes	Total	%
Mainland	1,032,180	631,657	1,663,837	13.57
Antilles		440,937	440,937	23.00
TOTAL	1,032,180	1,072,594	2,104,774	14.93[a]

NOTES If we take into consideration the urban and rural distribution of mulattoes in the
Antilles, with populations of 98,013 and 342,924 respectively, we obtain a total of
440,937 individuals. If we add this Antilles total to those for the mainland—321,253
and 310,404 respectively—we register a total of 631,657. According to that, the total
estimate would be 1,072,594 mulattoes for all of Ibero-America in this period. Thus,
the total of rural mulattoes, or of those devoted to agricultural production, for both
regions would be 653,328 individuals, and for urban dwellers, 419,266.

In addition, it seems certain that the Spanish census registers based racial classifications more on the status position of the individuals and on their culture than on their
strict anthropometrical and biological characteristics. Thus, the number of biological
mestizos was much greater than the one given in these tables. In fact, the social stratification in the form of castes had become an impediment to mass racial mixing, so that
each racial population had less opportunity to mix with the others.

[a]If we include the "savage" Indians, the total percentage drops to 12.5.

mulattoes, which results in higher figures: 6.95 percent for mulattoes among
rural dwellers, and 8.92 percent among urban dwellers.

Thus, it appears that the total of mestizos on the mainland—since we are
excluding those of the Antilles because they do not appear significant enough
insofar as they are not entered as such (see table 9.19), and since the main
racial mixing in the Antilles was carried out early between whites and
blacks—was 1,032,180 (6.15 percent), whereas that of mulattoes, considering the mainland and the Antilles, was 1,072,594 (6.39 percent). Thus, both
groups of hybrids together totaled 2,104,774 individuals, that is, 14.93
percent.

As can be seen from these results, up to this period miscegenation had not
developed on a large scale, especially because of the obstacles of social stratification that stood in the way of interethnic or interracial sexual exchange
wherever attitudes relating to social distance had not been weakened. To this
degree, the spirit of social stratification included the exclusivism of caste and
led to the closing of each group with respect to one another. It is in relation
to this obstacle of social stratification that interracial sexual exchanges were

hindered institutionally, since the reports from this period abound in recognition that there were many clandestine interracial unions which, in any case, were socially condemned by the stratifying spirit of the time. Nonetheless, we must acknowledge that much individual behavior did not conform to the formal model and frequently violated the values implicit in the attitudes of all stratification.

Spanish men, single and married, did not hold attitudes of sexual repugnance toward Indian or black women. What they really maintained were class distances. And these distances were what hindered a stable sexual exchange between various racial lineages converted into relatively open castes, if we keep in mind the flexibility of individual behavior, as well as the fact that the mobility of the populations also involved the relaxation of moral adaptations and attempts to pass from one status to another.

The path between the prior situation and the new one would be equivalent to a period of relative freedom from controls that would include a greater variety of social alternatives and therefore of sexual alternatives. With reference to the lower classes of Indians and blacks, this possibility of access to white women remained consciously repressed, and it was largely the mestizos and mulattoes who, by their racial proximity, served as intermediaries or had more probabilities of access to the aforesaid group of women. Nevertheless, due to their superior social position, white men were normally the individuals who could take sexual initiatives, and they were the ones who definitely produced the greatest frequency of racial mixture. To the extent that the status of the man was of greater prestige than that of the woman, the latter also played a more passive social role, and in this sense it was the white man who assumed the advantages of his status over his own women as well as over those of other racial origins.

Miscegenation in the cities had a more dynamic character because direct social controls were weaker, but in any case the greatest frequency of interracial sexual exchanges occurred between white men and women of other groups. Given the nature of the woman's inferior position in the system of status, she remained far from all initiative in this sense. The white man's position of prestige over the other racial groups also reinforced his ability to inhibit any tendency of the white women to have sexual relations with men of every race, precisely because the social ideology of the period assumed that the direct capacity for reprisal was a decisive function of the man more than of the woman.

The attitude of rejection that a white woman would adopt toward a black, Indian, or mulatto man was more violent in its consciousness than that shown by the white man toward women of other races, precisely because the white man could act with greater personal freedom of choice and, as a man, was the objective and vicarious cause of the prestige of the woman. Thus, racial mixing was more fluid in the cities than in the country. In the latter, the structure of the system was less varied and complex and therefore created less alternatives for sexual activity. The fact that men had more possibilities for evading formal ethical norms in the cities than in small towns meant a greater expansion of casual or spontaneous unions between white men and black, mulatto, or Indian women. It must be acknowledged that such unions occurred in the country through relations between masters and the female slaves or servants, or simply by means of an identification of prestige between a white man and a woman of another group. But these relations did not represent such a wide range of possibilities as that in the cities. By the late eighteenth century social stratification limited, but did not prevent, concubinage by married men in rural communities to a greater degree than in the urban centers.

It is with regard to the nature of social relations that we must understand the problem of the low miscegenation that we see in the figures for racial mixing in its two aspects of mestizos and mulattoes. But there is more. We acknowledge that in the urban centers, miscegenation was a more accelerated process than in the country, not only as the result of a more rigid social control, but because the protection of Indian peasant communities over time became a genetic barrier as well. This is something that did not occur in the cities or in urbanized localities where the social mix was more fluid and the barriers imposed by the double system of class and caste were insufficient to close off the exchange systematically.

In many cases sexual exchange became easier with black or mulatto women than with the Indians, because the latter were also more protected by law, and also because sexual access to the Indian woman raised more formal difficulties—control of their members' behavior by the Indian peasant communities—than did access to black women by the white man. He acted more openly in the status of master with the black woman than with the Indian. The greater amount of miscegenation in the cities thus would be attributable to the greater sexual accessibility of its objects, as well as to the fact that with these women, the mestizos more easily avoided the stigma of illegitimacy and therefore were in a better position to establish themselves individually. Hence, the cities constituted the psychological and social formula for more tolerant and more anonymous activities, and this formula would explain the greater frequency of those activities when compared with that of rural localities.

10

The Biological Question

There are several points to resolve when we refer to the question of understanding the biological problems that have arisen from the study of the hybridization resulting from racial crossing; but there are two that seem extremely significant: (1) what are the characteristics that distinguish or clearly define one race from another when we consider their definitions empirically, that is, as observable in terms of a product of mixture; and (2) to what degree are the adaptive capabilities provided by the genetic apparatus of a mestizo initially different when compared to those exhibited by the parents.

Both are points to be clarified, because advances in physical anthropology and in human genetics are still insufficient to determine the adaptive potentials that differentiate and distinguish one race from another when both develop in the same environment. Nevertheless, it is also true that racial taxonomy operates on the recognition of the existence of distinctive traits that are superficial or observable, and certainly measurable or, if you will, quantifiable, such as skeletal proportions, pigmentation, hair texture, and especially, facial features. In general, we are dealing with specific anatomical differences, particularly when we compare populations of morphological characteristics whose indices or frequencies are homogeneous in their formal expression.

Yet, we still have not established whether these morphological differences have to do with environmental capabilities of adaptive superiority or refer instead to evolutionary indicators that are not transcendent from the biological viewpoint. We do not even know to what degree we can consider Negro characteristics, or body hair, or any other racial characteristic as evolutionary primitivism, or whether these involve an adaptive provision that might confer biological advantage in concrete environmental contexts to the Caucasian, Negro, or Mongoloid person.

At most, we know certain relative scales of racial distribution but know nothing of their evolutionary significance. And in intellectual matters, the progress of knowledge is seen as a phenomenon of great historical mobility, which is interchangeable and of wide ethnic and racial circulation when political conditions are favorable to social exchange. Initially, scientific knowledge about racial mixing is still a mystery capable of manipulation on an experimental level. For now, scientific knowledge deals basically with field observations and historical reports that register, in each case, pragmatic value judgments from which we can define concrete attitudes toward the producers of mixture and references to ways of defining racial differences. Additionally, there is no doubt that today we can rely on two worthy sources of scientific information: physical anthropology and genetics; the latter is gradually gaining command of the scientific use of the questions that affect the subject of races and mixtures. We rely on both sources as supporting disciplines, but genetics will serve our purpose more than physical anthropology.

The main field that has conducted racial studies up to the present has been taxonomy, and within that field, intraspecific comparison. The latter has constituted almost an end in itself. Confusing results have also been produced by the attempts to establish correlations between racial groups and intelligence, and of course, evolutionarily considered, the anatomical differences among healthy individuals of different human races do not cease to have great significance when one attempts to carry them to the field of causal explanation in terms of civilization and culture. Perhaps anatomical differences make significant the fact that certain adaptive tendencies exist for given environments, but in empirical observation it also turns out that the adaptive capabilities of human beings are highly plastic and in similar conditions tend to appear as relatively localized elements in time.

Under these conditions, in the current state of knowledge of morphological anthropology, we have scarcely moved beyond the stage of comparative taxonomy. In this sense, we would emphasize the contributions in the area of human paleontology and of classification in general, without morphological anthropology's having arrived at the development of a body of theory that might make it possible to advance sufficiently in experimental hypotheses and in correlations of morphology, culture, and ecology. For example, a sizable lacuna exists in the demonstration of possible correlations between inherited racial dispositions toward cultural production. We know more about environmental influences and conditioning than about human behavior, and even more about animals in general—whatever their species—than about strictly racial dispositions acting upon specific environments.

From this initial standpoint, progress in human genetics, with reference to the demonstration of adaptive qualities, is promising. From the viewpoint of taxonomy, serology has contributed in recent years to the classification

of human populations to a degree that greatly complements the contributions of human morphology. In certain aspects, the results of genetics
seem more dynamic than do those of traditional physical anthropology. In
any case, the different behaviors and potencies of the products of mixture
constitute a truly complex experimental dimension. Historically, we can see
that studying them begins with morphological anthropology's establishing
that mestizo groups represent metrically intermediate populations (Salzano
1965, 137), and it continues with genetics' establishing the genealogically
transmitted components of heredity and the probable adaptations of the latter
to the elements in the environment that exert pressure on the organism. At
present, these disciplines have provided few answers to the fundamental
problems of human hybridism, especially those that involve the study of the
inheritance of specific characteristics from racially differentiated parents. This
lack of answers to problems is also true of the adaptive qualities demonstrated
by the products of mixture in relation to specific environments, and of the
capabilities characteristic to them, but, above all, of the evolutionary formation of human hybrids in terms of selective values. In general, scientific research into such questions is working in still inconclusive territory. Though
important progress has been made in these fields, we continue to operate
more in the sphere of qualitative observation than in that of empirical
experimentation.

The most valuable contribution to our purpose achieved to date by this
research is to be found in serology. Within the particular accents of this discipline, and with regard to the keys of racial mixing as a biological phenomenon, we consider the data of serology to be the most directly applicable to
our needs, especially when we consider that the geographical distributions of
human hybrids and of other racial populations in America obtain a more
precise quantitative representation when we use concepts about certain genetic frequencies than when we use only data of comparative morphology.

Nonetheless, for this case it is also important to recognize that the prime
bases of racial classification refer essentially to anatomical features—skin
color, types of hair, form of the head, face, and longer bones, and of other
features—without which there would be no taxonomic point of departure
on which to base genetic classifications. Finally, it is obvious that, while morphological anthropology has provided us a certain number of racial typologies, at the same time, in situations of multiracial populations—such as the
American ones, in general—that are socially mixed into a single national
political structure, it becomes difficult to classify those racial typologies by
relying on the traditional measurements of physical anthropology. This is a
good reason why here, for the purposes of quantitative consideration of racial

distribution, we prefer the data of serology, and particularly those that refer to the geographical distribution of the blood groups of the ABO system.

→   →   →

From the biological viewpoint, we think the basic phenomenon of human hybridization consists of the fact that mestizos possess a more diversified heterozygotic genetic apparatus than do their progenitors. According to that fact, their capacity to adapt to different environments is greater initially than that shown by their parents. In addition, the progenitors of products of mixture vary not only because they are of a different race, but also because they can come from different environments, such as the case of the union of an African and a European in the Americas, or of one of the two with a native of this region. Also, in their origin the individuals of each of these races can come from very diverse ecologies and from equally different cultures. Furthermore, unions between individuals of different races on American soil can involve individuals adapted to that setting by length of residence, or simply by being tied genealogically to assimilated cohorts in specific American environments. For these reasons, the genetic apparatus of the mestizo varies with respect to that shown by his progenitors, based on the combinations of the different variables that act to create a given individual and organic environmental adaptation.

In each case, the genetic apparatus of the mestizo varies according to race and environmental adaptations of the parents, as well as to the relative susceptibilities to health and disease contributed by the latter. In any case, the effects of adaptation are different when we think, for example, of the qualities of the environment—relative altitude, climate, fauna, flora, topography—in terms of an ecosystem, on the one hand, and in terms of the qualities inherited by the mestizo from generations of progenitors, on the other. Most dynamic is the type of culture—based on conditioning—the environment exerts, in the form of specific adaptive results, on its users. Thus, it is in terms of the relative satisfaction of organic and social necessities, and of goals more or less achieved, that the context of racial mixing takes instrumental form.

Within this scope of variables the possible correlations are certainly diverse, and thus it is only necessary to generalize about principles and assumptions, whereas the situations and the adaptive precedents of those variables are specific experiences. With regard to variability, one can even state, with Salzano (1965, 136), that the differences between hybrids and their racially different progenitors are not very great; nevertheless, the qualities of hybrids are more variable than those of their parents (ibid.). We must add, at the same time, that Caucasians are less varied than hybrids, but are more varied than the other races (ibid.).

Given this point of departure, we should state that the effects of racial mixture are not in themselves good or bad, because they depend on the quality of characteristics transmitted by the progenitors to their offspring. The effects depend as well on the way in which the mestizo is treated during the course of his relations with the social milieu in which he lives (Klineberg 1951, 32). According to these conditions, the only valid rule for producing good descendants is for the progenitors to have biologically healthy characteristics: a good physical constitution and a no-less-sound mental disposition (Benedict 1941, 69). In any case, the more vigorous the genetic characteristics of the parents, the more vigorous the characteristics that can be expected from their children.

Therefore, in principle, racial mixture is not unfavorable for the individual who forms its product; hence, any specific inferiority of the latter with regard to his parents will be due more to the transmission of defective qualities or of defects of the external milieu than to the deficiencies deriving from genetic combinations that might be unavoidably adverse to the mestizo.

Hence, it is important to acknowledge from the outset that if America, beginning with the Columbian discovery, has been the setting for interactions between different races, then its genetic variability is implicitly great, and this great variability can be extended to adaptive situations based on environments, societies, and cultures.

We cannot generalize about the specific physiological behaviors of mixed offspring, except at the local level; and when this occurs one must have genealogical controls available, not only in the order of successive social generations, but also in the order of the generations considered biologically in their relations with the environment. Under these conditions, we cannot generalize about the idiosyncratic characteristics attributed to hybrids, except when they are considered within the localized adaptive order. Without this requisite, it is difficult to arrive at an adequate generalization, except in other senses, such as those of attitudes toward sex, racial and ethnic differentiation, and the values that accompany the social behavior of one generation or another considered in the context of interracial relations. In this sense, hybrid products as such are genotypically determined by means of visible forms, but their genetic potential still constitutes a biological resource in qualities and quantities that are scientifically localized or verified in the form of sufficient study with regard to identifying in them a process of universal validity.

In any case, racial mixing has both a biological and a cultural connotation and therefore has a historical importance related more to its diagnosis than to its prognosis. In a large manner, biological mixing in the human species is a question of cultural and of social form, both with an external milieu representative of the total result of the relation of a group to an environment.

From this perspective, racial mixing as a biological process constitutes a complex phenomenon to understand, not only because its network of adaptive genetic relationships is complex, but also because its superorganic mechanism—culture and society—is complicated, especially when it is considered in terms of its influence on the organism of each progenitor and the organisms of the products of mixture. In this sense, we know more about specific adaptation than about the universal structure of mestizos. Nevertheless, in spite of the current uncertainty regarding knowledge of the genetic qualities of human hybrids, there are objective resources of localization when we base our studies on their environmental adaptations, the sociocultural history of their groups, and the comparative contrasts in the nature of the activity and structure exhibited in general by hybrid generations.

It is thus that certain principles are derived; these are: the recognition of the existence of a dynamic variability founded on genetic structure; heterosis based on the relative healthiness of the progenitors; and adaptation with regard to culture, society, and environment. These variables are generally applicable when we seek to explain realities that are universal and specific at the same time. In the present context, these variables seem the most relevant.

Therefore, every selection appears to be what Sahlins (1976, 76) has called "a local principle of directional change." That is, as long as the environment or the conditions that make selection possible are maintained, so is the nature of what is characteristically an adaptation. The significance of this local character in selection is that it endows evolution with the principle of opportunity, which presupposes the creation of an environmental time for the adaptive form of the offspring. Under these circumstances, mestizos do not become natural selections until they have established an environmental time.

The meaning of this environmental time is equivalent to the fact that their stability is relative to the time that the factors and conditions that gave their origin to the mestizos remain present. In the Ibero-American case this means, additionally, that when the mestizos achieved variability they did not necessarily assure it to their descendants, unless the latter continued in turn to receive factors of variability in terms of both environment and heredity. Specialized localization can produce specialized descendants, but their variability will diminish over time unless the factorial structure grows with that of its populations in terms of structural heterogeneity. Here, in racial mixing the perspective consists of determining to what degree this condition of variability is permanent or purely fortuitous.

If it is permanent, its initial condition consists of maintaining factorial heterogeneity; if it is purely fortuitous, its condition consists of dissolving the hybridization and restoring—through homogeneous environmental time and equally homogeneous factors—the local qualities of adaptation, that is, the so-called geographical race.

Thus stated, the biological problem of racial mixture must be studied with consideration of the fact that each race is the transmitter of a certain percentage of characteristics in the products of mixture—at the same time positive and negative with relation to a given adaptive function—that are transmitted to their descendants. It is also true that, due to the mechanism of genetic dominance, if the racial mixture is maintained at a constant, the presence of that dominance will improve the descendants, such that, in general, with racial mixing the more favored biological traits increase their possibilities of being transmitted in greater proportions than the more defective ones. In addition, as Hrdlicka has pointed out (1946, 197), another fact arises that is no less significant: at no time can we expect the process resulting from the fusion or mixture of two races to give us a type that repeats the characteristics of both, since not even the individuals of a single race repeat one another. It is hindered by the very historical process of transformation—a slow or rapid one as the case may be, but a process nonetheless—that results from the evolution of the environment, and in that environment, of the equally evolutionary adaptations of the individuals who live within it.

In that sense, the phenomenon of hybridization implies individual possession of one inherited genetic apparatus that, when compared with another hybrid, will be at least partially distinct. This means that the products of mixture are not necessarily the same from one individual to another, much less from one generation to the next. Therefore, the probability of two individuals having the same genotype is remote, even in the case of twins, and despite the influence of the adaptive factor (Harrison 1960, 33).

The specific biological phenomenon that we wish to emphasize in racial mixing deals here with the fact that the latter is disadvantageous to the individual only when one or both progenitors, belonging to two different races, are also unhealthy individuals. This can be affirmed to the utmost, since, while it is undeniable that the available scientific data regarding racial mixture are scarce, there is also no doubt that racial mixtures generally produce healthy individuals (Montagu 1960, 400). In this sense, we must point out that a certain agreement exists among most anthropologists when they assert the principle that we have no demonstrative proof that hybridization between individuals of two different human races creates adverse biological results for its mixed offspring. Thus, for example, when Montagu (1972, 10) states that human history should be considered as a permanent process of hybridization by means of which races are created and disappear, he also points out that there is insufficient evidence that racial mixing itself might be biologically prejudicial. Thus, we adopt the perspective that the variability that derives from racial mixing includes an increase in the adaptive possibilities inherent in greater degrees of genetic combination, all of which contributes to the increase of the evolutionary possibilities of the human species (Garn 1971, 133).

Some researchers, such as Davenport and Steggerda (1929) have expressed their disfavor toward racial mixing, specifically toward the kind resulting from the mixture of white and black. In this sense, they drew unfavorable conclusions regarding the mulattoes of Jamaica when they considered that the hybridization resulting from unions between Caucasian and Negro types produces morphological disharmonies caused—according to these writers— by the combination of incompatible racial characteristics. Nevertheless, the method followed by these writers was considered deficient, especially for their failure to analyze favorable evidence and because of the relativism of their data (Shapiro 1954, 46ff.). Furthermore, scientific criticism has been opposed to such conclusions, based on the fact that mestizos do not inherit separately the characteristics of their progenitors (Klineberg 1951, 31), nor do they even give predominant creation to the unfavorable genes of their parents, but rather tend to develop genetic norms better able to adapt to environments.

On this basis, and in light of recent studies, Garn (1971) establishes unequivocally that hybrids are as fertile and long-lived as their progenitors might be, but especially, therefore, they are not biologically inferior to them. In this regard, the adverse factor par excellence involving biological fertility is geographical isolation (Jacobs 1971, 152–53), insofar as it diminishes selective capability while it increases specific environmental adaptation. In itself, the latter offers a more limited capacity for evolutionary variability than that created in the process of exchange and of the circulation of genes of different populations. In reality, reproductive isolation caused by geographical isolation comes to create effects that consist of localized genetic fixings. Thus, such would be the fate of geographically isolated races. On this point will develop what Montagu (1972, 23) would designate by the name "geographical race."

Most contemporary anthropologists describe the mestizo as an individual endowed with better adaptive capabilities than those of their parent races considered separately. Looking at concrete examples, Hooton (1946, 654) adds that when the mixture is created between kindred races, for instance between Alpine and Mediterranean stocks, the heterozygotic combination tends to increase the possibilities of creating brilliant individuals, or at least those of superior mental capacity. This is true on an individual level, but from the standpoint of decisive results for human history it is even more so, when we consider that the mother civilizations of our culture, for example, Egypt, Greece, and Rome, were products of biological as well as cultural fusions. This means that racial mixing does not imply degeneration, but rather the development of positive combinations that are certainly favorable in specific cases. Racial mixing means the enrichment of factorial combinations.

This conclusion is also shared by Schwidetzky (1955, 168) when he alludes to the fact that the flourishing of the great civilizations appears linked to the fusion of different, though racially proximate, peoples, as in the mixture of Germanic and Mediterranean types that led to classical Greece and to the Renaissance. In this sense, those civilizations would not constitute an immediate product of mixture, but would be the brew that would make them possible. Racial mixing in itself, adds Schwidetzky, does not necessarily imply cultural talent and creation, but when it occurs there is a greater probability of those qualities appearing as the product of such combinations between eager and competitive peoples—favored by evolution for their physical and cultural energy—than could derive from individuals of isolated groups spending themselves in their environmental and racial specialization.

Comas (1944, 22) also concurred in this theme when he pointed out that the high cultures have emerged in regions with strong lines of interethnic conflict. This case, we add, would involve a conflict that should be related not only to strictly territorial disputes, but to groups that have departed from the simple principle of territorial occupation and plunder to embody the principles of cultural confrontation and biological crossbreeding that result from surmounting ethnoterritorial barriers. Along with this crossbreeding they have adopted principles of exchange, breaking with those systems of specialization implicit in the inbred way of geographical races.

In this sense, it is worth noting that localized races are usually in greater danger of static, specialized reduction than are those characterized by differences or expansive receptivity. In these terms, we must say that the groups biologically more prone to physical and cultural evolution are those that most employ receptivity and exchange in a space with others. In any case, racial mixing assumes the genetic and adaptive growth of the homozygotic parents in the following generation.

Additionally, if racial crossbreeding includes cultural growth, the greatest probabilities for the development of an advanced future civilization will likely have been provided, though not necessarily in the first generations. The importance resides in the combination of a strong, expansive energy with an intelligent cultural expression. What had occurred in the classical antiquity of the Old World was reproduced in the pre-Hispanic era in the exchange between Mayas, Toltecs, and Nahuas in Mexico, and between coastal dwellers and Incas in the Andean region.

In such cases, their civilizational developments combined, in their fusion, the expansive energies of some groups with the scientific and technical intelligences accumulated by others. The emergence of these civilizational forces in pre-Hispanic America was not the result of a chance of restricted selection, but constituted the effect of a prolonged period of biological and cultural sifting gradually converted into the power to act over a great human space. Hybridization and its corresponding civilizational strength assume, therefore, a combination of biological energy from the progenitors with another combination of cultural evolution capable of promoting an articulated and expansive cultural synthesis (science, technology, and philosophy, especially) beyond the spatial limits of their beginning stages.

Nevertheless, what is really most meaningful to us is the fact that civilizational energy can be of three different types: (1) that which results when an advanced culture is transplanted from one space to another, suppressing all native influences, as were the Anglo-European and Luso-Hispanic cases in the present-day United States, Argentina, and Brazil; (2) that which results when a native population receives groups that are culturally inferior but of greater demographic and competitive energy, such as the cases of the Germanic peoples in Greece and the Nahuas in Mexico; and (3) that which results when a high culture, such as the Hispanic one, is transplanted and is then confronted by other equally advanced cultures, as in the case of Meso-America and the Andean region.

This third type includes not only different races in contention for political dominance, but also different cultures in competitive interaction. Nevertheless, the most important thing here resides in the fact that the Spanish demographic transplantation was insufficient in terms of genetic predominance. Although the predominant cultural system would be the Hispanic one, the lack of racial demographic strength with respect to that of other racial groups makes biological mixing the historical product most reflective of the principle of selective filtering of biological groups. Therefore, while great populations remained to be Hispanicized, and while this required a long process of induction and seduction, simultaneously with this long process the Hispanic effort was fading, and gradually, through the expenditure of its physical energy, the effort dissolved into racial mixture as a new form of civilization.

Although most of these different racial populations are not yet mestizo, the emergence of a great civilization as a result of their abundance and adaptive variability must wait for dissolution to occur in just one social and cultural body of the respective parent formations. What is mestizo in the biological sense apparently does not turn out to be an advantage in the cultural sense because to be one it is necessary, in addition, to expel the colonial sense from the first long period of the biocultural transplantation. That expulsion took place with the independence movements of America, and it is at that moment that the conditions began to emerge that would make possible the emergence of a great mestizo civilization in America.

Such is the case of Mexico in the future, although in order to achieve that civilization it still needs to finish its process of integrating its great ethnic variety into a great national formation, consolidated into a single cultural model, and endowed with great social and political strengths and intellectual surpluses, as well as with a demographic energy capable of sustaining and replacing the great losses inherent to every process of mobilization and circulation, as would be the case for present-day Mexico. Its internal political, economic, and social pressures constitute, in our view, the concrete syndrome of this expansive energy that has yet to achieve hypostasis. When that occurs, the long process of localized selection will have the advantage of an environmental time with internal variability, an indispensable condition for civilizational birth.

In light of these preliminary explorations of the historical course of civilizations with regard to racial mixing, we must enlarge more on the biological question in terms of its demographic results. This is an issue of unquestionable importance in human evolution and in the survival of any species.

In addition to the several reasons noted about the genetic variability that hybrids produced by healthy progenitors carry with them, it is also proper to emphasize another fact: that there are many anthropologists who acknowledge that the mestizo has an advantageous genetic makeup for the formation of phenotypes resistant to the various confrontations that are part of natural environments. Anthropologists such as La Barre (1961, 144) even go so far as to consider racial mixing to be the salvation of the human species, particularly when judged with regard to its future evolution. This claim rests, above all, on the argument that hybrid offspring—because of their greater genetic variability—are more adaptable to changes in the total environment. Therefore, within the circumstances of variability introduced by the crossbreeding of different races, it is foreseeable that the very heterozygosis of hybrid offspring in societies that are genetically pluralistic could represent a favorable factor in the sense that the products of mixture might increase demographically based on those individuals and groups who cease to practice racial endogamy. With this increase, diversified adaptive reactions develop in the midst of social heterogeneity, giving rise to a multiplicity of combinations. When one arrives at the conclusion that the first mestizo generation is heterozygotic and representative of adaptive variability, it is also important to recognize that not all mestizos are alike, because their progenitors are also unalike, and the environments in which the latter live are usually different. Thus, it is very important to point out that, if, on the one hand, hybrid vigor leads to that variability, and if the latter takes part in generating the resources necessary to biological evolution, it is nonetheless patent, on the other hand, that in plants and animals hybrid vigor diminishes when mixed generations unite with one another. That diminution implies that for the continuity of heterosis, it is necessary to maintain crossbreeding between first racial generations (*Encyclopedia Britannica,* 1974 ed., s.v. "heterosis").

What is certain is that the phenomenon of the greater adaptive capacity exhibited by the heterozygotes can be explained by the fact that through racial mixing attributes of plasticity increase, and therefore, there is a growth in those attributes that deal with their specific and general adaptation, since they allow the individual to be more flexible toward climatic challenges and environmental circumstances. J. Huxley (Montagu 1960, 405) points in the same direction when he states that racial mixture and migrations are the factors that lead to the increase in human variability and, therefore, are those that make possible a greater capacity for survival in a given space. That variability is favorable not only in terms of evolution in general, but also because it is accompanied by an apparatus more favorable to the development of a human group confronted with a process of natural selection (Roberts 1960, 50). These tendencies can extend into the cultural sphere, especially when we consider that an expansion of the cultural system in terms of structure involves providing one social group rather than another with greater instrumental capacities of domination over their surroundings and with resources of knowledge that favor their specific development in a given setting.

With regard to the biological sphere, there are two qualities that contribute basically to the complexion of better adaptive capacities: (1) heterozygosis is itself adaptive, and (2) the so-called hybrid vigor resulting from the mixture between healthy individuals is a consequence of the balanced genotypical integration that derives from the fusion of characteristics (Harrison 1960, 42–43). For this reason, a continuing racial mixture that is the result of the sexual exchange between healthy individuals of different races serves to counteract the operation of recessive genes of a negative character that might be in the progenitors. In this way, heterosis constitutes a stable phenomenon when there is a constant genetic exchange between two or more races by means of crossbreeding of their individuals (ibid., 43).

An immediate consequence emerges from these facts: with the formation of a cultural environment and of a mixed biological structure, phenotypical variations increase; thus, there is an increase in the potentials for adaptability. For this reason, that specific capacity for adaptation of the mestizo with relation to the environment also implies the formation of a more balanced polymorphism. In this sense, Harrison (ibid., 42) confirms that heterozygotes are more capable than homozygotes with regard to the achievement of homeostatic functions, as well as being more fertile. If, by contrast, exchange is limited to mestizo individuals themselves, then there is a tendency toward homogenization, but hybrid strength or vigor also diminishes in the product of mixture.

It is thus that a highly significant phenomenon results: the exchange between the races increases fertility during the first mestizo generations, whereas constant sexual interaction between hybrids decreases it, so that the maintenance of that fertility seems to be conditioned by the frequency with which the genetic apparatus of a population is renewed. Definitely, in this case, the condition for heterosis turns out to be entailed in the relative health of the parents and in the crossbreeding of racially differentiated individuals.

The hybrid vigor exhibited by generation F usually diminishes in the following generations if descendancy is restricted to the exchange between mestizos. This understanding has been emphasized by Shapiro (1954, 45) with reference to the natives of Pitcairn, an island located in the South Pacific, in Oceania. On that island, inhabited since 1789 by the descendants of nine English sailors who survived the mutiny on the *Bounty* and of nine Tahitian women, a totally mestizo biological type was created because of the group's isolation. As for fertility, it began to diminish as sexual exchange took place between individuals descended from the first mixture. According to this pattern, on Pitcairn the first generation of women had an average birth rate of 7.44 children; for the second generation it was 9.10, and the third reached 5.39 (ibid.). According to Shapiro, the average birth rates continued to fall in succeeding generations.

The importance of these results for the progress of the theory of racial mixing is that Pitcairn seems to be one of the few cases over which we have had documentary control regarding the various mestizo generations based on two different racial groups—here, English and Tahitian—of men and women, respectively, that are numerically quite balanced.

The information obtained from Pitcairn is confirmed by experimental observation of rats. For example, among the latter the first hybrid lives longer than its progenitors (*Encyclopedia Britannica,* 1974 ed., s. v. "aging"). The same occurs with plants (ibid., s. v. "heterosis"). Additionally, we know that mestizo populations have less stillbirths than their progenitor populations (Salzano 1965, 137). On the basis of this statistic we assume, as we understand it, a selective linkage to the environment and to the culture. That is, here already the phenomenon of environmental filtering has become significant.

Additionally, in the same way that hybrids are not necessarily disharmonious because of the fact that they are products of mixture, neither are they inevitably vigorous, especially because the genetic differences between the races are not entirely clear-cut. The only thing we know about the phenomenon of heterosis involves a few variables, while it is certainly clear that—independent of race, ethnicity, class, and culture—if the progenitors have genetic defects there is also a great probability that these will be inherited by the descendants (Montagu 1972, 24 and 113). In any case, some generalizations can be formulated with the notion that here we are not assuming that every heterozygotic combination will lead always to a greater adaptive capacity. What we see are tendencies. Singularly, one's surroundings are an important factor with regard to favoring adaptability or not, and adaptability is also a function of the relative internal balance achieved by the organism (Salzano 1965, 136). When that balance is attained in the progenitors, not only is heterosis produced in the descendants, but the individual is also endowed with greater aptitudes to triumph over whatever pressure the environment might bring (*Encyclopedia Britannica,* 1974 ed., s. v. "breeding").

Actually, if man is one of the most genetically mixed animals in comparison with other mammalian species (Montagu 1972, 117), it becomes evident that hybridization has made him more evolutionarily apt than the rest, until he has become the species with the greatest internal variability and with the greatest propensity to experience a more ideal and frequent evolution in intelligence. Most important, for the purpose of producing a biologically dominant group, there must exist previously the highest possible number of individuals participating in interracial interaction because, in order for there to be a selection and reproduction of dominant qualities, the mass or number of participants is an important factor (Schwidetzky 1955, 169). In this sense, heterosis will mean genetic circulation expressed within a great mass of characteristics being selected in the course of interaction with the environment, on the one hand, and of the elimination, through competition, of those characteristics least resistant to the social pressures and adaptations created by the culture, on the other hand.

Among racially pluralistic social groups, one can observe a high degree of aggressivity, including attempts at domination and subordination that are alternately repressed, suppressed, or achieved, according to the case. In the context of this process toward dominance, and as an effect of the latter, subordination consists of the socially weaker group managing to survive when it continues to outnumber the stronger group. On this basis, the weaker group tends to reproduce itself when it demonstrates that it has a certain capacity for endurance by successfully facing the selection that the total environment exercises over its individual members. By contrast, when this weakness coincides with a scant demographic strength in competitive relations, and if the weaker group does not have the protection of a certain isolation, then it is most probable that as a group it will be assimilated by the other in a position of dominance or will be truly destroyed by it.

In the case of the Americas, populations of mixture have become aggressive to the degree that the social structure has been open to individual competition. This aggressivity would not have been possible without the existence of biological qualities adequate for survival, especially when we note the experience of environmental difficulties—in terms of structure—that have characterized the social filtering of American populations. Consequently, permanent Spanish and general European emigration to America constitutes an unbroken exponent of mestizo formation, and from a demographic standpoint, the fertility of their populations appears as a demonstration that the aforesaid hybrid vigor has never been halted. Thus, variability has been accompanied by social energy and internal aggressiveness, and with these the products of mixture have accentuated their competitive pressure.

The phenomenon of the increase in mestizos in America coincides with their gradually more dominant sociohistorical role during the process of formation of the Ibero-American reality in those lands where great differential racial masses emerged, masses that also were led to widespread interaction as the social structure opened up. Only the constant influx of Caucasians, through immigration, has caused mestizos in some countries, especially Argentina, to constitute populations genetically absorbed by the former. Nevertheless, the enormous internal circulation characteristic of American societies is as much a phenomenon for social selection as for biological selection. Heterosis has contributed largely to the fact that, in certain Ibero-American nations, mestizo variability plays the role of biological dominance.

In another context, results of this type are confirmed by the different regions of America about which controlled data are available. Thus, the census statistics of 1910 regarding the Indians of the United States show that those among them who possessed mestizo characteristics were more fertile and were distinguished by greater vitality than those who were relatively pure-blooded (Hooton 1946, 657). Boas (1940, 138ff.) reinforced these conclusions when he established the greater fertility of mestizo Indian women in comparison with Indian women who were not mestizos. In this way, while the median of fertility among the former was 7.9 children, among the latter it amounted to only 5.9. The same distinction occurred with relative sterility, because the mestizo group had a rate of 3.5 percent and the others, of 10 percent. Therefore, given healthy components of racially different progenitors, it seems to be shown that the infusion of characteristics of one race into another implies a reinforcement of vigor, and commonly, an increase in its size and adaptive efficacy (Hooton 1946, 654).

In these phenomena, what is significant is the fact that hybrid vigor diminishes to the degree that racial mixture is suppressed, that is, when mestizos exchange genetically only with themselves. This factor determines that subsequent generations will lose much of that capacity for adaptation that they acquired with the racial mixture of their parents (Harrison 1960, 447). At any rate, racial crossing produced in circumstances of good health on the part of the two parent races is shown to be beneficial to its offspring. In this regard, Krogman (1935) points out that the mixture of Seminole Indians with whites and with black slaves has created a biological type that is certainly slender, vigorous, well-proportioned, and with no observable symptoms of genetic degeneration. The same is true of the mestizos born of Spaniards and Mayas. In this particular, Williams (1931) emphasizes that fifteen generations after hybridization occurred, the biological types produced from mixture are vigorous and anthropologically homogeneous.

In the case of hot climates, the mestizo is considered more apt for creating a tropical civilization. Thus, in Brazil the miscegenation that took place in São Paulo, for example, between white men and black or Indian women during the sixteenth and seventeenth centuries provided a sample of extraordinary vitality, which is maintained even in the later mestizoized generation. Additionally, Arthur Ramos (1952, 49), when he establishes the somatic qualities required for the population of the Brazilian tropics, points out that their settlement was possible thanks to the fact that it was accomplished by hybrids—in this case, by the descendants of whites and Indians, and by mulattoes. This means that the dramatic adaptation of racial groups to a natural environment different from the one of their own origin was more likely to be successful through racial mixture (Schwidetzky 1955, 113) or its equivalent: the intervention by at least one progenitor from that environment.

These examples lead us to recognize that the characteristics of physical superiority or inferiority of one racial group compared to another, in a given setting, is conditioned by the specific capacity for adaptation to that setting. In this sense, it seems clear that mestizos are individuals who contribute genetic and cultural combinations more powerful than those of their parents—at least with regard to one of them—with reference to the specific endurance they offer against certain environmental challenges, among them diseases, endemics, and harmful tendencies. Thus, although hybrid vigor is less measurable in humans than in plants and in other animals (Montagu 1960, 192), its appearance is confirmed, for example, in the resistance that mestizos offer to diseases that are mortal to one of their progenitors. In Tierra del Fuego, for example, while the natives were succumbing to the measles, the mestizos were able to resist it well (ibid.). According to this example, whereas Linton (1942, 53) warns that one cannot state absolutely that hybrids are superior to pure-blooded stock, they certainly are superior for certain adaptive functions such as those we have mentioned.

If we continue with this question, in the Andean regions the mestizo has achieved the capacity to resist bronchio-pulmonary diseases better than does the Indian, while he also possesses a better phenotypical capacity than does the European type for adapting to high elevations (Vellard 1956, 89). On the basis of such examples, there exists in the Andes what Monge (1949, 271ff.) has called "climatic hostility," a phenomenon that affects those individuals who lack a systematic adaptation to the environment in which they live. *Soroche,* a severe headache, is one of its syndromes, as is hypoxia, which affects the functioning of the heart. As for the mestizo, his specific adaptation is best understood when we turn to the observation of certain contrasts. In this sense, there is great significance in the biological phenomenon of the relative incapacity of the Spanish women to adapt to the tropics and to the Andean highlands during the early years of the conquest and colonization of America. This phenomenon, along with other socioeconomic and military factors, greatly limited their participation in the first Spanish settlements, at least with regard to participating in equal numbers with Spanish men.

Climatic hostility, when applied to the physiology of reproduction in the Andes, consisted of—as Montagu (ibid.) has pointed out—the fact that not until fifty-three years after its conquest was a criollo born in Potosí, a city located at an altitude of 4,300 meters [over 14,000 ft.] . While survival was difficult for the first criollos, the mestizos reproduced easily. Visual observations also agree in acknowledging the existence of great difficulties with climatic hostility in different circumstances. Some writers of the early period of the Spanish conquest in America point to a significant fact, doubtless the result of their specific experience in situ: the excellent qualities of the mestizo in shouldering the difficulties of those military campaigns, this being a tacit recognition of good mestizo biological characteristics. In addition, in the Andean case the endowment of qualities resistant to climatic hostility in that region with regard to the criollos constitutes a process that, according to Monge (1949), took more than a generation to produce; that is, they had to wait for the effects of climatic heredity to disappear among the individuals not originally from that area. Once this adaptive process was concluded, biologically speaking, according to Monge (ibid., 278), in the Andean high plains we can speak only of one Andean race. This is because the ancestral type has absorbed the Spanish type genetically, and in the same sense it absorbed any population that is not native to the region and that, therefore, does not possess the biological resources that characterize the adaptive responses to inherent hostilities of altitude.

In any case, to paraphrase Genovés and Passy (1976, 25), the problem involves what the authors term "differential fertility," which means that, independent of the interracial mixing that may have occurred in an initial sexual exchange between Spaniards and Indian women—and between both groups and Africans—the most important influence in racial mixing involves the number of genetic characteristics that each racial stock contributes to the succeeding generation. As stated by Genovés and Passy (ibid.), this is a matter of genes, which assumes that if the Spanish did not reproduce in numbers at least equal to those of the natives and the Africans, their presence in racial mixing was less in those areas where the demographic numbers of other racial stocks predominated. On this point, it is difficult to speak of heterosis, except for the strict biological vigor that each stock might possess on its own. Perhaps the hybrid vigor will have diminished or increased according to the relative continuity of racial stocks in the context of sexual interaction, but fundamentally, the most important relationship will be provided by the number of individuals who have preserved their characteristics through their genetic transmissions to their partners.

11

Heterosis In Social Dominance

It is said (Ginsburg 1968, 117) that, historically, the instinct for domination—especially among the vertebrates—appears in concrete form in the products of mixture. When one considers the products of mixture within their specific social contexts and compared with their different racial progenitors—and considers one of these, particularly the Spanish or European group in Ibero-America, as the group of the dominant tradition and therefore the one exercising the culture of power—one can see in the course of the dominance of the Spanish or Europeans a gradual surrender of their political, social and economic control to their mestizo descendants as they, in turn, identify with Spanish culture.

This is a historical fact that has emerged slowly, and it has appeared particularly in countries with the heaviest mestizo populations. In those countries where mestizos were a minority, the group of European origin has retained its dominance as a race identified with power in comparison with the weaker influence exercised by the rest in their different identities. By contrast, where mestizo populations have reached numbers superior to those of European stock—in the most open and progressive sociopolitical centers of America, such as Mexico—elites have emerged as well from among mestizo groups.

Of particular importance is the fact that the formation of mestizo elites has been a function of the existence of an initial organization of colonial society into stratified castes. As the latter have been destroyed as a form of identity, however, they have remained in the form of interpersonal attitudes of rejection or social distancing on the part of European groups. Certainly, one can perceive the continuity of a certain tradition of psychological colonialism as part of the distinctive character of these societies, even within the framework of their contemporary history. This continuity occurs even after the dismantling of the formal structure of public institutions that once maintained social differences in racial terms. Thus, at times one notes in the tone of interpersonal relations a certain surreptitious feeling of racial competition concealed by an apparent competition based on class.

Yet, the products of mixture appeared early in the scenario of social competition and have exerted a strong pressure precisely because, in the course of their historical selection, individuals have appeared who are better adapted to conflict and to environmental hostility than are others of differentiated racial stocks. The greater competitiveness of mestizos coincides largely in Ibero-America with the pressure created by a historical consequence: the social and often biological depletion of the first dominant elite in the context of its dialectical confrontation with the initially weaker racial group. Actually, the biological depletion of a now sedentarized competitive population—as would be the case of the Spanish in their military expeditions, and of their native allies and African servants—would be in line with the notion of a nervous exhaustion caused by constant mobilization and, along with that, an overload of tension on the endocrine hormonal system, as has been indicated by Battegay (1981, 17) in experiments made with rats. Prolonged tension on the latter diminished their reproductive capacity.

If, as Pribram states (1976, 65), war implies competition, the destiny of the first Hispanic-American mestizos would be marked by their development of strength and strategic intelligence for the domination of their space and the control of their assets and resources. The mestizos of the second, or peaceful, phase would constitute the product of social cooperation, and in this case, of love. That is, the relationship between second-phase mestizos and the larger society would be relatively competitive in the context of the established society—in which social choice and perhaps confrontation of the couple would be involved—whereas the interaction between the man and woman would assume another character: that of a selection based on love, interest or affinity, or attraction. Under these conditions, the corresponding heteroses should be understood as characteristic of historically differentiated situations, not only because the protagonists are selected in a different way by their surroundings and by confrontation, but because the social structure that provides their context is also different. The mold of those of the first period carries the stamp of physical effort and muscular strength, whereas that form of those of the second period pertains to stable relations that mean social cooperation, or at least structural interdependence.

The mestizo was, first, a product of the same social instability and circumstantial encounter of his progenitors. It was an initial situation marked by turbulence. The Spanish progenitors acted as territorially uprooted fathers and thus were relatively free of moral controls with regard to their sexual behavior. In a certain way, their biological impulses came from necessity and were scarcely repressed by the moral codes of their origin.

The fact of the spontaneous impulse of sex was genetically a positive one. In the case of the Spanish conquest and colonization of American territories it involved energetic and vigorous individuals who were also selected for the physical effort and the intelligent employment of strategies of social domination. In reality, the products of mixture associated with these Spanish bloodlines inhabited an unstable world that contributed to the development of their aggressive tendencies. At the same time, given the selective energy of their progenitors, the products of mixture possessed the hybrid vigor inherent in the mixed offspring of the individuals who were energetic in their very mobility and permanent confrontation with the environment.

Therefore, the foundations of the first Hispanic-American societies were constituted by these environments of adaptive difficulty, which require not only effort but also the energy capable of carrying out the intelligent foundation of a society new in style and racial combinations. Without that energy, there barely would have existed one new culture: the Ibero-American, and within it, specifically, the Spanish culture. This prior recognition of the necessity of extreme energy in the effort to conquer foreign nations and to prevail in the challenge of adverse spaces is also valid in the consideration that these first mestizos were also products endowed with the best heterosis because they were also engendered by bloodlines physically selected in the course of environmental adversity and migratory adaptation. Precisely because the mestizo was above all a biological phenomenon derived from the union between vigorous, fertile, and healthy lines on the basis of the very demands imposed upon the objectives of conquest and settlement, mestizos were genetically more healthy than those offspring who might have resulted had the exchanges taken place between races who were isolated and in decline. The fact of organization for the struggle of conquest, as expressed by the Spanish, appeared in practice in the form of a strong sexual tendency, while fundamentally, sexual activity was not just an act of love and cooperation, but also appears identified with a principle of aggression.

Given the characteristics of the initial relationship between Spaniards and natives and the selective character of power and the dominant position of the former over the latter; and considering the sexual unions between both racial groups, we can recognize the first mestizos as endowed with a greater degree of heterosis than were those conceived within the framework of stable relations of cooperation inherent in being from the same social structure. This characteristic of the Spanish-Indian relationship lends a more favorable probability to heterosis. I am referring in this sense to the fact that the politics of alliance pursued between Spaniards and Indians included the distribution to the Spanish of young women of the Indian ruling classes. These women therefore represented not only a social selection, but also a biological selection based on the fact that dominance—in the circumstances of discipline and physical training characteristic of warrior groups—includes supremacy in biological qualities and intelligence tested in the environment, qualities that are the result of selections of anatomical and physiological attributes that are comparatively superior to those contributed, in general, by the subject classes. In terms of biological selection in relation to racial mixing, it seems doubtless that the women received by the Spanish conquistadors from American tribal leaders for the purpose of alliance, were selected biological products. In the case of the Spanish, who did not partake in these distributions the other kinds of sexual union was itself a factor of heterosis.

In this sense, if the position of social dominance in historical situations of mobility is recognized by means of political and military victory, as occurred in the early experiences in America, it is certain that throughout the most competitive of the Spanish centuries—the sixteenth and seventeenth—the Spanish exercised the power of decision only after prevailing in the competition of intelligence. The power and dominion that resulted from that competition not only were reproduced through descendants and by means of social heredity, but also had to be ratified on a continual basis in order that they might be prolonged throughout a more complex and economic competition. This ratification was something that required varying the principle of the competitive struggle for status into all situations of the tensional contest.

Under such conditions, the struggle for power was never decided in a definitive manner in each generation, since each of them had to face its own historical circumstances, such that biological selection within the American settings and landscapes was incessant. From the selective viewpoint, racial bloodlines were continually renewed in selection by means of the constant migration of Spaniards—and Europeans in general—and of Africans through the slave trade. Meanwhile, the natives suffered the consequences of this turbulent mobility, either through continual territorial relocation, or through war itself, or simply by their character as populations whose members formed part of the Hispanicized labor force.

In the final analysis, the Hispanicization of America was a constant test of environmental selection in which decisive roles were played by the relative energy of each bloodline in terms of its specific resistance to the difficulties of the environment, to disease, to spatial mobility, and to the struggles of war. This permanent selection played an effective role in giving heterosis to the different individuals who were produced by interracial cooperation. But it is also important that this selection included the sexual couple, whose individuals were attracted by induction or by seduction, which means that the degrees of social power that they attained also contributed to the fact that the relative position of dominance was the one most favored in biological selection. In this case, all such individuals were favored, whatever might be their racial background.

Nevertheless, in their dominant condition, the Spanish contributed higher degrees of heterosis to their descendants in the early phases because the latter were also the offspring most selected to triumph competitively. That is, as long as they continued to live in war and mobility, the Europeans generally exercised dominance, and their mixed offspring benefited from their energy. Immediately thereafter appeared the leaders of the natives and the populations of this stock who excelled in social movement within the Spanish or Portuguese institutional structure. Meanwhile, African cimarrones and those others who were beginning to achieve importance for their aggressive competitiveness contributed to the common gene pool those qualities inherent to their competitive energy. There were possibilities to exercise that energy based on the foundation of a common—Hispanic—social structure that was always competitive during the sixteenth and seventeenth centuries, although in this case the competition was selective in spatial mobility and in the environmental confrontation, while in the social sphere the competition was limited basically to the Spanish—peninsular and criollo—and to those mestizos who opportunely assimilated into Spanish culture and its ways of social living. Here, in the social sphere, the selective relationship in terms of sexual cooperation was similar to the ones created by the upper classes in advanced societies, where the men, particularly, as part of their exercise of power, also exercise the ability to choose from among those women who symbolize the model of beauty and physical attributes that correspond to the aesthetic ideal of superiority or of excellence that is attributed to them. In such cases, if beauty is a factor in the social promotion of the woman in our societies, a similar value of social advancement appeared in relations of sexual cooperation between power and women in America. The selective character that can be attributed to this cooperation also had a biological basis.

Heterosis was a constituent ingredient of the first products of mixture created in the context of these selective conditions. What is less certain is what happened with the casual unions that emerged in the course of the sporadic sexual relations that took place at random in the midst of a common social structure. In such cases, the certain fact of the ancestral adaptation of the native woman to her environment, and the attraction exerted by the Spaniard—mostly in cases of alliance and cooperation—always represented a positive element for heterosis, since at least one of the parents, by playing a social role of dominance in selective risk, also conferred those qualities that contributed to the social role upon his or her descendants.

Heterosis also occurred among those mixed offspring born of unions between Spanish and Africans, and of unions between the latter and natives. This was especially so when we keep in mind that in the harshness of their environmental conditions the most energetic and intelligent survived, such that hybrid vigor was a common component in these first generations of mestizos and mulattoes. Less certain, by contrast, is what happened to some lower-class generations of blacks, Indians, mestizos and mulattoes who—in conditions of social adversity, hunger, and economic instability—constituted selective denial with regard to the exercise of the dominant role. Under such circumstances, heterosis in the mestizo generations resulting from the genetic combinations between parents stabilized in social degradation and under conditions of subordination within stratified caste societies would be selectively less probable.

According to this concept, heterosis reached its maximum in the first generations of mixed offspring, or under those conditions where each group contributed its best genetic qualities to individuals of mixed blood. This was the case of Spaniards, Indians, and Africans who lived in specific adaptation within the same social structures, or in relations of interdependence. In each case, the respective adaptations carried the stamp of their social possibilities, but they also represented the concrete results of environmental selection, that is, of the tropics, of the mountains, or of the city and of the country, on the one hand, and of biological selection itself, on the other. And in every sense, the relationship to the surroundings included especially the pressure of the different cultural processes at work within each social structure as dynamic factors of social filtering.

This means that if adaptive limits are not determined exclusively by biological constitution—rather, we will find them obstructed by climatic systems (Schwidetzky 1955, 115) and by contrasting cultural efficacies—the action of these elements becomes more negative in the absence of mixed offspring who make it possible to compensate for the initial disadvantage of one of the progenitors in his or her descendants. These are disadvantages that might arise from the first environmental uprooting, and from interracial adaptive confrontations, and even from the need for functional improvisation created in those individuals transplanted from one setting to another, some of whom are thus subjected to the pressures of environmental hostility and others to sociocultural hostility.

Perhaps this need to improvise without any significant biological failing is one of the qualities we can most emphasize in the Spanish type who was coming to America and who, once there, developed some outstanding adaptive abilities that have scarcely been established by the historiography of Spanish colonization. The climatic and environmental variability could be overcome only by individuals who, while engaged in adaptive struggle, were obliged at the same time to improve functional responses of every degree.

If, in general, migrations are usually undertaken by the most restless and potentially the most expansive individuals in the society of origin, it is also true that in the course of those migrations, the aforesaid expansion is exemplified biologically by means of a certain optimization of adaptive flexibility to different environmental changes. That flexibility also includes a greater resistance to the pressures that, in many cases, constitute the germ of dissolution of the will to dominate.

The migrant is, additionally, an ambitious individual not only biologically and socially, but also—because of the demands of age and health necessary to his migratory impulse—in terms of fertility; he embodies average conditions that are superior to those characteristic of sexual conditions in very stabilized populations that reproduce themselves culturally. If stabilized populations feature the superiority of localized adaptation, migrants possess the superiority of expansive aptitudes. In any case, changes in surroundings require a greater selection on the part of migrants than on that of native receptors, and under these circumstances the Spanish and Africans who survived represented highly significant combinations and designs of biological selection from the viewpoint of heterosis.

Actually, the fact of the displacement of Spaniards and Africans from their original environments involved capacities for diversified ecological adaptations, but it also called for dietary changes in which plants, animals, and climates played an extraordinary selective role that, under competitive conditions such as those of the encounter and confrontation in America, could be overcome only through the possession of biological qualities specifically endowed for self-preservation within changing contexts and processes.

The overcoming of all kinds of climates and adversity by conquistadors, founders, and settlers constitutes a fact of the greatest importance concerning their contributions to the physical vigor of their mixed offspring. This same phenomenon should be pointed out among the Africans because if, at the outset of Spanish colonization, they were considered especially capable of adapting to the temporal regions, it is also clear that they survived the challenges of cold and high altitude. In any case, the survivors of these difficult environmental tests formed a base of biological vigor for their reproduction in the form of mixed offspring, those born to Spaniards or Europeans as well as those born to natives.

In practice, given their subordinate and enslaved status, the Africans were more prone to physical deterioration than were the Spanish; because, while the latter played the dominant role and determined their lives relatively more on the basis of privileges inherent in the power they had assumed, the Africans could not do so. These are reasons to consider that the mixed offspring with the greatest adaptive breadth were the ones who had a Spaniard as one of their progenitors. Despite the existence of two barriers—the tropics and the high altitudes—and secondarily the areas near the colder extremes because of their scant economic and geopolitical interest that impeded Spanish expansion throughout the American continent, these barriers were overcome precisely by the impulse for dominance and by accompanying technologies that were more effective than those of the natives and Africans and that drove the Spanish to excel within a spirit of expansion.

Additionally, once the obstacles of the experience of war and its corresponding environmental adaptations were overcome, there is no doubt that this role of social dominance contributed more to the biological protection of the Spanish than to that of the other racial populations. In such a case, the heterosis that might result from the product of mixture between Spaniards and other groups was more probable than in the offspring of Africans with natives, especially when the primary conditions of social status and health did not favor them.

When Aguirre Beltrán (1972, 83) refers to hybrid vigor he mentions observations carried out by the Spanish authorities in New Spain regarding the physical superiority of the mulatto over the mestizo, by which it is understood that under normalized conditions of health heterosis occurred more frequently among the mulattoes than among mestizos.

In contrast to the Africans, the Spanish had the advantage of being able to choose their surroundings, and at the same time they made the social decisions with regard to culture. These were the important factors in their development of an advantageous capacity for contributing to hybrid vigor. Nonetheless, the Africans singularly were the population whose elements of contribution to the heterosis of their mixed offspring faced major environmental and physical problems, after the Spanish had already faced the same challenges. In this context Aguirre Beltrán (1972, 180) also states that the blacks worked more than Indians or Spaniards not because they were biologically superior to them, but because they had been chosen for the specific function of producing more than others in certain labors based on youthful vigor and proven capacities of physical endurance.

In addition, the natives began their adaptive difficulties from the moment when their ways of living were interrupted and even wiped out in the context of the new Spanish institutions, especially when they became part of the labor force in the nascent Hispanic-American societies. The normalized biological reality of the natives deteriorated with relative ease when they had to face a change in their economic and social context, which often led to their downfall when their usual forms of social organization and of cognitive behavior broke down.

From the moment in which the native cultures became alternative institutions subordinate to Spanish dominance and hegemonic organization, they lost their discursive center and henceforth drifted in the waves of the great European tide that was becoming predominant. In reality, this drift consisted of breaking the rhythm of the native cultures, especially their social adaptations; after that, the native cultures could never recover their independent position. For the natives, the rigor of Spanish culture and society was harder than the rigor of their own ecologies.

Furthermore, the fact of cultural alteration itself would not have represented a fundamental biological problem were it not accompanied by an adaptive effort that was greater than the resources of their biological rhythm and of their capacity to sustain themselves independently, especially because the very process of interracial conflict included forced changes in environment and location, as well as forms of labor that demanded adaptations superior to the customary ones. The natives were thus driven to frustrations of personality that carried with them the mark of confused identity, the loss of control over their reality, and the awareness that their existential style had been stripped of its cultural coherence.

Under these circumstances, as the Hispanic cultural style tended to reproduce itself and expand on American soil within the framework of political, religious, economic, social, and technological institutions, and as it achieved dominance in the heart of interracial relations, the natives found refuge in the "Reducciones" run by the missionaries, settlements whose isolation shielded them from the total breakdown of their traditional milieu. Thus, in the same way that Spaniards and Africans changed environments when they came into contact and established themselves in American space, the natives also changed settings when some of their populations were transferred. They also changed their sociocultural context when they joined, in some cases, or, in others, were added to Hispanic societies and were subjected to Spanish dominance.

In these first stages of incorporation of the natives into Hispanic societies in America, there was no competitiveness for status between the two groups. What emerged were relationships of dominance and subordination that included processes and situations of conflict and uprooting on the part of both natives and Spanish as well as of Africans. Under such circumstances this stage constitutes a typical one of transition in which the most vulnerable are those individuals who do not exercise dominance; that is, they are more vulnerable in the sense of being the least favored socially and also the one most prone to social degradation as well as to impoverishment of the ego and to physical deterioration, while they are likewise prey to losses of organic health, along with periods of sickness and susceptibilities to epidemics without the counterweight of psychological compensations. In these conditions, though he was adapted by ancestral generations to the American setting, the native did not evade the principle of selection through competition, and therefore, with the Spanish and the Africans, he participated in the awful trauma that the change of milieu wrought among each group. For all of them the changes were of context and represented a confrontation with new conditions and situations. And if one group—the Spanish—did found a sociocultural hegemony over natives and Africans, they were also vulnerable to epidemics and adverse ecologies that in many cases not only shrank their demographic forces, as had occurred with the other racial groups, but made evident the rigorously selective nature of biological and cultural competition in American time and space.

Under these conditions, those who survived in each racial group and reproduced through racial mixtures also had to submit to the filtering effect of environmental influence in its different constituent facets: ecological, cultural, and structural, or economic and social. In this sense, if the ecology was an initial advantage for the natives, the culture of dominance soon became a dynamic countervailing disadvantage. As a consequence, what in principle might appear as a mere biological dialectic emerged as a dialectic deriving from the political culture of the Spanish and from their technological and cognitive predominance. The result was that political dominance was extended to biological dominance, precisely because the latter carried out selection by means of migratory selections themselves and by means of the selective consequences inherent in the promotion into power on the part of those—the Spanish, in this case—who formed the dominant group. The effects of that selection were not only political, social, and economic, but also psychological and biological, such that the probabilities for hybrid vigor arose on the basis of combinations in which the Spanish, along with members of the native upper classes who had established marital relations with them, played the most important biological role.

In this aspect, the function of dominance through the upper native classes and the Spanish groups who had achieved power through military victories was decisive with regard to providing the most favorable qualities of heterosis to their mixed descendants. Later, as the health of the individuals within each subordinate caste continued to improve, the latter exercised a stable reproductive capacity, such that in these conditions the mixed offspring defined their heterosis on the basis of the relative health of their progenitors.

The Africans achieved this capacity very soon with the native women, just as the Spanish and Portuguese had done with both groups up to that time. In addition, while the migratory flow of the Spanish was maintained through young individuals in search of status, by this measure of being young and expansive they assured the continuity of physical vigor in their mixed descendants. Thus, these are good reasons to consider that the initial selective factors were not only biological, but also cultural and social to the extent that power, in open periods of competition, is a relative function of adaptive capacities, intelligence, and vigor in the course of tests that are combinations of environments and strategies of manipulation of reality with the objective of transforming the latter; all this relative function of power presupposes qualities of endurance along with technological tools adequate for each specific situation. On this point the Spanish contributed such qualities, and they combined them with greater strength than did the other racial and ethnic groups.

From another viewpoint, it should be pointed out that in their first experiences on American soil, the Spanish had to assert their dominance in conditions of active struggle by means of wars and alliances, whereas the Africans were struggling to stabilize their survival, not through direct war against anyone—except for a few individuals and groups of runaways—but by active adaptation to conditions of slavery and environmental adversity, even in the tropical regions. The gradations of hybrid vigor thus came to be a function of the way in which each of the three different racial populations overcame for themselves the different barriers and difficulties that, according to each case, either hindered or facilitated their mutual historical relationship.

Thus, we can affirm that the qualities present in the form of hybrid vigor were differentiated not only by the genetic contributions of each race to specific immunities—such as to malaria on the part of the Africans, to influenza by the Spanish, and favorable adaptation to altitude on the part of the Indians—but also by the muscular strength of the mixed offspring; in this last perspective the African contributions were highly positive ones.

In a certain way, it is of course true that the products of mixture resulting from sexual relations with individuals belonging to native groups lacked the muscular strength achieved by those born of the union between Spaniards and Africans. Nevertheless, the social superiority of the Spanish always constituted a selective factor of health and physical vigor that contributed to the fact that their descendants—in northern Mexico, for example—today represent types of great muscular strength. A great contributing factor to this would be the abundant diets of milk and meat on the cattle haciendas, which was also true of the southern regions of South America. It should also be established that the short Mediterranean statures of many Spaniards were offset by the effect of their improved diets in America, while the same physical selection to act in expeditions of conquest demanded more vigorous muscular endowments than were common in agriculture, for example.

As Schwidetzky notes (1955, 77), if the degree of biological selection is more intensive among those groups who undertake expansive movements—the case of the Spanish in the stages of conquest and settlement—it is also true that the process of establishment and spatial stabilization for these groups led gradually to a reduction in their birth rate, which is an indicator not only of their lesser degree of restlessness or enterprising ambition, but also of the increased pressure brought against the expansive group, the Spanish, by the receiving group. In this case, that group would include the natives and mestizo offspring, as well as runaway or free Africans, who, because of their greater numbers, inundated, or rather weakened by wearing down, the foundational dream of the Spanish, who, because of their stability and rootedness in American soil, caused their culture to triumph more than their biology because the latter had become socially specialized. This social specialization took place through the stratified social structure of a society organized into castes, in which each Spaniard at the same time that he sought to marry a white woman or one closest to his race, was losing his formerly active ambition for settlement and conquest. This loss was occurring while he was transmitting these capabilities in a revolutionary form to his descendants, criollos as well as mestizos and mulattoes.

In reality, since the mid eighteenth century, these three groups had already constituted political forces that were conscious of their capacity to lead, and in their identification through socialization and daily social life, they fully practiced Spanish culture and the various European ideologies, while they dissolved the ideological beliefs of the groups of hegemony and also displaced them from their secular power by means of the constant and irresistible political pressure against the Spanish sitting atop the social pyramid.

On this point, it seems evident that the population growth of mestizos and mulattoes, on the one hand, and of criollos in better defined positions—but all of American sentiments—on the other, represents the progress of biological functionality. The natives were gradually incorporated into this process as the development of the political independence of the Americas coincided with the appearance of new processes of dissolution or weakening of native ethnicities, if we recall that many of those ethnicities, or at least certain percentages of their populations, were incorporating with the different national ethnic identities that were being adopted and that represented a new adaptive option for the Indians.

Certainly, this option meant the development of new interracial relations, along with which appeared a new phase of mestizo formation. At the time of the political independence of the various countries of America, the native populations had recovered their rhythms of prolific reproduction, although frequently, the demographic description would hide this reality when it recognized as natives only those who remained politically separated colonial entities, in one case, and independent ones, in others.

At the same time this recovery was taking place, the dominant colonial elite had declined in terms of governing energy, and in this circumstance the more biologically expansive groups manifested themselves on the basis of emergent selections and on the basis of the criollo groups of European origin who replaced the traditional upper strata of the colonial period in power. The criollos and the several varieties of mixed offspring who were socially and politically victorious became stocks with more expansive demographic energy than that of the dominant colonial strata at that time. This was also a period of opportunity for the Spaniards and Europeans who identified themselves with the course of independence, since by taking over political power from monarchist groups or Crown loyalists, they added to the economic power that they had established within the traditional colonial society the very political power abandoned by the losers. The new, independent, political situation opened a new, wider channel of social circulation, and in its flow was created a new period of mestizo formation.

Although governed by the reigning formula of power, biological selection in the human situation rests on control of the cultural means of domination employed by an individual or ethnic or social group on the basis of the demonstration of a given political and material superiority erected especially through technological strategies. Since these strategies represent forms of specific practical control over nature, the context of possibilities for heterosis in Ibero-American history appears largely conditioned by a cultural selection that either develops or diminishes according to the relative social access of the races, in this case to available material assets. In addition, if assets were distributed unequally in the social structure, and if some racial groups had easier access than others to those assets, then the effects of these differences also involved consequences in terms of health and illness, and therefore in terms of heterosis. The role of social structures consisted primarily of distributing power and dominance, and as it selected socially, it also selected biologically.

Thus, when we refer to hybrid vigor in Ibero-America we think basically of products of mixture who resulted from tendencies or from frequencies that arose according to several situations. We think:

(1) Of conquistadors who crossbred, in some cases through political alliance, with the daughters of native chiefs, or who simply did so in a contingent way with native women strictly for satisfaction of a chance sexual impulse.

(2) Of Spanish individuals who chose native women according to their aesthetic attraction as defined by cultural tastes, or according to social convenience.

(3) Of Spaniards who, having achieved social power, practiced the sexual selection of racially different women in a discreet fashion, that is, in accord with their selective preferences and, though surreptitiously, often in limited numbers with regard to the desirability of their sexual objects.

(4) Of Spaniards who, according to their status, had to limit their selection of women of other races in obedience to norms of formal monogamy with women chosen for their status and cultural adaptation to these men.

(5) Of Spaniards who, as slave owners, freely chose black or mulatto women and made them concubines.

(6) Of Spaniards who cohabited with Indian or with freedwomen and who formed plural unions based on their relative capacity to sustain them economically and sexually.

(7) Of Africans and mulattoes who united with native women under diverse conditions, that is, either as slaves, freedmen, or runaways.

(8) Of natives who united in rare cases with Spanish women and more frequently with mestizo, black, and mulatto women, or with other women of mixture.

(9) Of products of mixture who exchanged sexually among themselves and who disseminated their relative hybrid vigor in a random fashion.

Within the varied spectrum of these possible situations, individual diversity becomes obvious with regard to biological capacities, which arise in turn as a function of age and sex, of racial characteristics, of environmental adaptions, of specific sexual attraction in each personal situation, of the social status of each individual, of nutrition, of his or her concrete health and vigor at the time of mating, and even the psychological fatigue of each individual in the context of psychic tensions and their effects on his or her organism.

The number of options existing in the different historical stages through which Ibero-America passed, and continues to pass, is very large, and the combinations of mixture vary according to each personal situation with particular reference to hybrid vigor. On this point it is impossible to achieve a quantitative control over each one of them. Nevertheless, it seems clear that some combinations were more probable than others, on the basis of certain generalizable circumstances. For example, conquest in open warfare called for young men or those of vigorous reproductive ages; migrations also were undertaken mainly by young persons ambitious to win themselves a place in each new society; African slaves were individuals selected for their strong, muscular makeup, since the object of their use was to get the best labor production from them; the desired native women generally were young and fertile. And above all, the sexual instinct appeared largely unleashed during a long period of transition, and although a rigid moral system governed its expression, the reports of the period do not reflect a praxis of imposition of a heavy zeal with regard to the strict observance of ideal sexual values, especially as regarded monogamy as the lone sexual solution and fulfillment of marital fidelity.

In general, sexual selection was subject culturally to the social strategies and possibilities of each individual, and especially to the relative opportunities of maximization of his or her personality in the context of each specific situation. In this way, biological potential was governed by cultural rationalizations and by the options given socially to each individual.

In these terms, the range of situational combinations favored hybrid vigor, but this was created on disproportionate scales, although the particular nature of this history tells us that heterosis consisted of a phenomenon that coincided with a strong development in social adventure. This heterosis was, therefore, a development in which the free forces of sexual instinct were reinforced by the physical attraction exerted between individuals who were bearers of biological potentials based on the best ages for reproduction, on selection resulting from individual triumph over climatic adversity, and on testing that stemmed from experiences with illness, epidemics, and vexations that agitated the nervous system. Incidentally, the greatest obstacle threatening hybrid vigor turned out to be the aging of the reproductive stock, as well as the decline of some groups of the latter due to laxity, in some cases, or to the deterioration of the personality because of endemic, or, if you please, phenotypical, nutritional deficiencies, in others. Therefore, hybrid vigor had much to do with selection, and within that, with the triumph of the individuals of one culture—the Hispanic—over others that were also organized in the form of historical tradition and ecological rootedness, as were those of the natives.

According to these historical options, the frequencies of racial mixture and hybrid vigor had to do with the junctures and happenstance experienced along with the relative penetration of Hispanic culture into the continent and its success and specific reproduction on the basis of social strategies. This contingency implies that if there was a scale of social dominance, and if the latter appeared as racially defined, the products of mixture were also a function of the individual opportunities and of the adaptations of racial groups to one another. In this way, the historical nature of the racial configurations and the conditions that made sexual unions possible between individuals of these stocks varied greatly, especially according to social structure, from the moment that it was stably constituted. Or what is equivalent: when the Spanish institutionalized their culture and their different formal political, military, religious, economic, educational, and social organizations, a regime of unified culture was created within a social structure common to all the races that converged interdependently within the Spanish legal system.

This convergence signaled the end of individual adventure and of collective exploration, at least with regard to the domination of decisive geopolitics, which in this case was concentrated in the populated centers of America—New Spain and the Viceroyalty of Peru—and their neighboring spheres of influence in the middle and southern Atlantic. It is at this moment that formal limitations were placed on circulation, and that racial mixing entered into a historical context more controlled by social discipline and by moral laws and interests. When military operations faded, then there was a flood of social strategies of a Hispanic culture whose members practiced racial crossing within lines of behavior that consisted of social and economic possibilities, on the one hand, and personal circumstances that often opposed racial mixing for reasons of political security, on the other.

Although this ambivalence might have existed, it is certain that the moral system and aesthetic preferences did not reject racial mixing, and therefore, in the absence of this ethical scruple, the obstacle that could have hindered stable miscegenation disappeared. Although it still must be admitted that periods of mixing fluctuated in their relative intensity, fundamentally, pragmatic and individual selections of partners constituted a philosophy of opportunism imposed over purely political solutions. For this reason, racial mixing represented a permanent fact, and in this, heterosis appears as a chance phenomenon, but a frequent one when we recognize that the populations involved were really representative of rather young groups or of generations endowed with an ecologically selected adult vigor. In reality, hybrid vigor allowed a demographically constant development, despite the endemic catastrophes suffered by the different populations and the epidemics that occasionally decimated localized populations or that caused great losses in numbers in the original racial stocks.

This being so, the survivors of the original stocks, acting as progenitors of mestizos, should be considered representative of these environmental selections, particularly when we refer to biological filtering through climatic hostility or of an ecological nature. Here, organic selection consisted of protecting the victors more than the vanquished, because victory in a competitive confrontation such as the one that took place in America acted upon the milieu in one sense: in the imposition of the form of decision-making power and its benefits in favor of the victors. This meant the filtering of racial populations on the basis of their different degrees of domination over the environment and over people.

Beginning with the second half of the eighteenth century, the Spanish peninsular contribution to hybridization diminished in comparison to the early periods of Spanish conquest, colonization, and settlement. Actually, the next phase of hybridization emerged with intensity with the new European immigrations during the nineteenth century, but these increased the interaction between groups of whites, due to their sexual and social self-sufficiency being greater than that which the Spanish had achieved during the sixteenth century, and even in much of the seventeenth.

With their great migrations to America, renewed in the second half of the nineteenth century, what really increased were the European demographic numbers and the tendency of the various European ethnic groups to mix with one another more than with the other races. After that tendency developed, racial mixing would be less intensive and would create products of greater racial proximity, for one thing, where the lesser degree of anatomical difference would increase the probability of mixtures between different groups, such that the gradations of racial mixture would show as dynamic features with regard to the relative continuity of mixed offspring. In these conditions, the mating between a white person and another, slightly darker individual appears more frequently—and so forth on a progressively darker scale—than does the mixture resulting from the union between racially opposite individuals. Incidentally, racial mixing resulting from the crossing of individuals observable phenotypically as being from different races would be conditioned more by the relative frequency of common interests of class than by caste interests.

Once the national societies of America were unified culturally with their political independence, their racial values continued to exist as criteria of subjective social discrimination; nevertheless, this factor of class and relative economic strength also had a great influence in the selection of mates, as did the historical legacy of sexual attraction exercised by mulatto women and some black and Indian women in the continuity of miscegenation. Still, with regard to the tendencies of stable unions, white prestige continued to be a preferable value in the choice of a conjugal mate. Among different races unions had a more unstable character, at times surreptitious and socially rejected, especially in the midst of white groups.

Otherwise, as a colonial legacy, the white groups assumed economic, social, and generally, political power as well, such that only those who were racially close to them—that is, mestizos and light-skinned mulattoes—enjoyed great probabilities of being accepted among white groups. In this way, new immigrations from Europe were distinguished especially by their scant contribution to racial mixing, since the whites had sufficient numbers of men and women to accommodate the tastes and marital interests of their race. For this reason, interracial relations had a more casual than formal character; they were expressed more as furtive, though frequent, tendencies than as stable, institutionalized ones.

The gathering and participation in the same culture by those who, through the caste system, occupied socially separate positions assume the addition of the factor of selective superiority in quantity to that of demographic superiority. From this perspective, during the colonial period the pressure against the Spanish was no longer just social. Rather, it was possible to make that pressure triumphant because it was employed using the same cultural options as did the Spanish without the latter, in turn, having the same drive and energy that had led to their original dominance.

As their dominant institutions became stabilized, the neo-Hispanic societies lost the impulse of mobility and, therefore, also exhibited a decline in biological energy; that is, they exhibited the depletion of their own social organization. In a certain sense, there had been a great initial biosocial energy whose result had consisted of the foundation and expansion of a Hispanic culture in America. This phase of expansive capacity lasted for two centuries and a half, because in the second half of the eighteenth century it seems to begin its decline due to its demographic depletion. During the two and a half centuries to which I refer there occurred what, in the terminology of Schwidetzky (1955, 19), can be considered a period of "sexual filtering," it being understood that this represents a kind of drifting selection of social specialization, which includes the tendency for men of success—through their intelligence or competitive worth—to pair with women whose beauty makes them sexually preferable individuals whose selection also appears as an aspect of the privileges of power. Applying these selection processes to the case of America, the consequence of such behavior is that the relation between groups of dominance leads to the selection of superior individuals in terms that may embrace different qualities, and this includes the strategy by which mixed offspring that are also selected are produced.

When one considers historical and social stratification in heterosis, it is seen that heterosis is selectively more probable in situations of mobility than in situations of stability, precisely because when the latter constitute the institutionalized social form, the selective values that lead to heterosis have also been weakened. That is, in conditions of stability, group endogamy is a social phenomenon that creates biological products characterized by the reduction of combinational components precisely because, in heterozygotic conditions, deleterious genetic elements are less harmful (*Encyclopedia Britannica,* 1974 ed., s. v. "heredity"). In other words, the genetic components of individuals in biological proximity are poorer in adaptability and more prone to sickness when they are located in settings that are different from those of their environmental specialization than those components that result from values derived from individuals distantly related to one another.

In the case of the Spanish in America, the fact that their dominance over the other groups had become stabilized also entailed a decrease in unions between the former and the latter. The significance of this fact is that the incidence of heterosis decreased, especially when we understand that heterosis no longer was occurring through biological selection among different racial groups involved in a competition for dominance, but that it was taking place among generations that, because they lived in a state of stabilized stratification, no longer possessed the same impetus of biological struggle for space. Rather, they had acquired other qualities of historically defensive character: those corresponding to the reinforcement of self-sufficient power—and with it the diminishing of the selective nature that accompanies every stage of competition for dominance—and that quality relating to the growth of preference for the aesthetic life. Both of these types of qualities are conservative characteristics reinforced by the constant pressure of bureaucratic regulations, which tend generally to restrict cultural creation and therefore to diminish the social energy of the groups most directly capable of producing it.

In any case, if heterosis occurs mainly in situations of natural selection and of competition, and if, in the period of Spanish conquest and colonization, selection was mainly part of a process of domination that was carried out militarily and concluded in the form of victors and vanquished, it is also true that the role of racial exogamy was more pronounced in this phase than it was in periods of institutionalized stability represented by the gradual system of a society formed into castes. The selective role of competition for space was replaced by the selective role of bureaucratized competition for power, such that the social controls exercised by means of rigorous laws and through caste and social class interests restricted the opportunities for mobility and led to greater instances of racial endogamy. On the basis of the latter, heterosis appears related to the fact of a power of surreptitious selection of sexual mates as far as the Spanish are concerned, because in this context it appears that while moral codes acted as strict social controls over illicit unions, at the same time the Spaniards and Africans united with native women at the risk of social condemnation. This sense of risk is an extension of the instinct for domination, manifested in this case in the form of social filtering, and often manifested as the unconscious function of producers of heterosis.

If there occurs among vertebrates what Ginsburg (1968, 119) calls "psychological castration" among those individuals excluded from competition for sexual access to the females chosen by the dominant males, in the symbolic castration that we are assuming here, it is important to recognize that in the midst of every group—the dominant and the dominated—a similar qualitative selection takes place by means of which, through depletion or lack of competitive exercise, some of its members decline and lose social strength, that is, energy to rule. Thus, their place is taken by others who prevail on the basis of the pressure, at once horizontal and vertical, that they exert toward dominance.

This concept of psychological castration appears as a reality among the socially weakest, and, in contrast with the strongest, it appears related to the ability of the latter to select women according to an ideal of beauty that generally also includes a selective plan, one in which the triumphant layers of society go through a somewhat lengthy period of reproduction of their selected biological types. In this way, in contrast to biological castration, the individuals most endowed for power within each racial strain are stimulated to biological selection by means of their choice of a sexual partner. It is generally the males who tend to exercise this privilege, such that, in a certain sense, the victors tend to be the beneficiaries of this capacity for domination, at the same time that they leave the vanquished psychologically castrated.

One might wonder what degree of relation between psychological castration and racial mixing we will admit for the context of heterosis when we speak of psychological castration applied to the situation of racial mixing. Actually, what we are stressing here is the fact that if each competitive group has within it its own guiding selection, and if each one of its subordinate social selections is itself a historical result of its internal competition, it is a fact that one result of winning this competition would include the right to castrate the losers symbolically.

In situations of competitive interracial struggle, the stimulus offered by women as a prize for the victors is extended in descending order to all those who are aware that triumph also includes the right to selection of their social environment and therefore to the denial of certain assets to the dominated sectors of society. In forms of racial crossing, through the polygynous exercise of the victors, this selection comparatively limits sexual access by the losers to the women of the victors, and while the vanquished are consigned to monogamy and the relative reduction—comparatively speaking—of their demographic numbers, those who practice polygyny alter the quality of their progeny in superiority of vigor. From this perspective, the biological selection of the losers becomes very localized, while that of the victors, because of their greater mobility and social desire, chooses its descendants according to greater degrees of adaptive variability than before the competition.

Thus, when we refer to psychological castration, we are translating this symbol into the idea that in the case of America, the closer its inhabitants were to power the more probable was heterosis as a result of racial mixtures. In the sense opposite to the symbolism of psychological castration, the radically dominant groups represent the extension of the image of a male mammal eliminating his competition and assuming for himself the selective consciousness of his own descendancy. This consciousness would be part of the awareness of a psychological castration that would fade as the place on the social scale of the subject rose. Furthermore, this scale would also be a parameter of relative biological dominance in the racial comparison that would be involved in the adaptive qualities inherent in hybrid vigor. The stratification implicit in so-called psychological castration must be explained as a symbolism ascribed to the social condition of the vanquished.

In this sense, the symbolic nature of the concept of psychological castration consists in indicating to us that within a given social group certain individuals—in this case, and generally, the most desired women during competition—are excluded as the sexual objects of men of the subordinate social class or race. Therefore, the role of dominance consists of dominant men's extending their competitive ability to indicative acts of decision making of a community, acts that also include the fact that dominance represents an individual energy exercised at the expense of those who seek to challenge it, or who simply seek to exercise it from a less energetic position.

From this perspective, in the case of Ibero-America we can integrate social dominance in competitive periods into the complex of relatively greater physical energy displayed by the individuals of one group over others in the context of their competition within a given space. This energy refers both to the muscular strength of the progenitors and to the intelligence that they express in the course of their political and adaptive strategies. In this sense, the Spanish in this history represented a combination of dominant culture and physical and social energy that, in the material aspect of their action, are an example of adaptation for power and for a racial mixing that was optional or certainly favorable for heterosis. In this case, power and heterosis derive from the strategies of an action that, without this energy set in tension, would have been less probable.

We must distinguish, therefore, between the fact of dominance as a factor of heterosis in descendancy and the fact that, if there was a period of racial confrontation, and if the latter was notably selective for all racial strains, it is also true that this confrontation mobilized the energy of all the populations living on American soil. This mobilization was obviously selective, even when considered beyond the explorations for conquest and new territories, the military struggles between Spaniards and natives, and the colonization and settlements that followed territorial occupation.

This extension beyond is understood in the sense that the biological energy expressed in the form of social selection broke down the traditional structures in which the different racial groups had lived initially. This break consisted of the promotion of Spaniards with no lands or dominions in their places of origin, at the same time that it served to dissolve the native aristocracies and caused the appearance of local leadership based on identification with the Spanish. This combination acted with militant behavior over the territory.

The appearance of this process of social selection was manifested in the form of a great individual and collective energy. We must keep in mind that the reflection of a traditional structure as powerful as the native one and the individual promotion of the Spanish to the status of *señores*—as well as the integration of socially, ethnically, and culturally broken and uprooted African populations—was done on the basis of employing an energy greater than was common in any of the societies of origin. Therefore, for decades, while the process of mobilization of the social energies of the different races continued, heterosis became a normal quality among mixed offspring. What is more, the competitive atmosphere of American history has never ceased since the arrival of the Spanish. Perhaps, during times of peace or in the cities, competition has been expressed in another way: in the form of hierarchies of status among so-called castes placed in a permanent search for status promotion precisely on the basis of racial mixing.

That is, if, on the one hand, apart from having their own social stratification, the Spanish—peninsular or criollos—held higher position than those exercised by the so-called castes or people of color, on the other hand, the individuals of the castes who competed among themselves and, through filtering, provided new members to the Spanish layer of society also signified, from the biological viewpoint, products of greater energy who were also led toward dominance and toward the intelligent control of the strategies and of the energy necessary to obtain it.

It even becomes necessary to think that when we speak of heterosis, the social conditions that allow individual dominance in competitive situations also constitute a process of synthesis in the sense that mestizos were gradually led to power as their social aggressiveness grew, and with it they developed their adaptive intelligence. Adaptation, in such a case, consisted of wanting the same things as the Spanish and joining them in their cultural styles.

Mestizo women played an important role in the social promotion of their children when the latter were the products of mixture with Spaniards and were born outside of a native context, since in the reality of these situations, the nature of dominance by the Spanish included the fact that their mestizo or descendant generations came closer to power, or at least increased their competitive possibilities to the extent that the latter were a function of the role that individuals played within the structure according to their different racial qualities. In such circumstances, heterosis approached its optimization because muscular vigor was being added to the manipulative intelligence of its social reality.

From the beginning, racial heterogeneity constituted a factor of permanent mixing because it not only dealt with joining racial contrasts but, once the mestizo varieties had been created, widened the spectrum into a greater diversity. When this heterogeneity appeared—and with specific laws, social stratification was quite rigid—selection for heterosis was established more by chance than it had been before, precisely because the formal obstacles erected against racial mixture, although they did not prevent it in actual practice, led to casual unions in many cases. When they got to casual unions, unions between greatly contrasting racial stocks declined, while unions between closer ones increased. Mestizos played a connecting role in this juncture. Now selection, governed by the laws of statistical chance, was manifested in a relatively more complex form, and while in the rural areas there were more direct controls with regard to the identification of the progenitors, in the cities the very weakness of social control made the fortuitous nature of heterosis all the more probable.

If genetic elites are usually social elites when there is a combination of environmental and selective conditions that are based on competition and make this superiority possible, it appears that although those elites are accustomed to stability as a ruling group, a certain number of their individuals, nonetheless, is susceptible to a loss of energy or of competitiveness, which then makes them subject to the pressure exerted by others who seek to dislodge them from the positions that they are incapable of maintaining within the demands of social energy necessary to the continuity of the group. These are losses based on the existence of biological or social (demographic) weaknesses that, when subjected to the dynamic of adaptive selection, can be covered either by the group itself, by means of a greater reproductive capacity and sufficiency by some individuals more than others, or from outside through the entry of individuals who stand out from inferior groups in the same society, or through the entry of foreign individuals or groups ideally suited to take on ruling functions. It is thus apparent that each racial group produces and renews elite individuals, which means that in the history of racial mixing in Ibero-America, the first stages—conquest and colonization—were characterized by being racially exogamous and biologically more competitive with regard to selection for hybrid vigor than were the second stages, corresponding to the stable institutionalization of Hispanic culture.

In this sense, the competitive atmosphere of that first stage not only included racial confrontation, but introduced social competition into each racial group. As a consequence, the best in this competition became the elites of the next stage, and additionally, the hybrid vigor resulting from interracial unions appeared with the genetic stamp of this first biological association. This included mestizo generations born of progenitors in their best reproductive years, but also in their best qualities of biological expression and of cultural expansion.

As the biological vigor of these progenitors was diminishing with age and with the social stability of their power, their mestizo offspring also constituted basically social selections, biologically less selective in that they were no longer products of biological competition, but rather products of circumstance and social opportunity often associated with chance. Thus, the simile of "psychological castration," applied generally to vertebrates who, because of their lesser energy for competition or power, choose their mate only from among those individuals disdained by those who hold that power, comes to mean that the emergence of hybrid vigor in the case of America would diminish as the progenitors aged in power and, because of the stratification of society into castes, were obliged to renounce crossbreeding with individuals of other races.

Within these circumstances, the most vigorous mixed populations continued to be those that emerged from individuals who took part in competitive selection, the ones from the "frontier" being the most likely to be produced in this sense. Nevertheless, European immigration, especially from Spain, continued to occur, and it was the humblest of these immigrants who mixed with the acculturated generations of natives and Africans, since the social consolidation of ruling groups at local levels, and politically in general, largely eliminated their participation in the normal processes of miscegenation. In the majority of cases, this role was undertaken in the context of a polygynous patriarchy on the basis of escapades and prohibited adventures that, by their nature, delegitimized the mestizo progeny that resulted, and degraded them—even biologically—because of their social deterioration.

According to this schema, these associations made a place for new social classes that, while they behaved as castes, were blended socially by the very diversity of the racial spectrum to the extent that their morphological characteristics were ambiguous. In any case, there was a gradual replacement of situations of racial conquest by others of ascent for social positioning. In this direction, the Spanish of the lower classes—and even middle classes, with regard to their condition as a formally endogamous racial group—replaced the upper classes as the habitual progenitors of mestizos.

A historical perspective of this type leads us to point out that so-called psychological castration was symbolized by the capacity—usually of men— to choose those women of other races who allowed themselves to be selected or adopted as a sexual mate without there being a counterpart among Spanish women for men of the other races, except, especially, in the cases of kidnapping in war. In this selection there was always a scale of distribution of the powers of disposition. This scale was manifested in the sense that, as whites and as persons ascribed to the dominant race, Spaniards and criollos assumed the power of decision on sexual mates, especially when the latter occupied a racial position socially invested with inferiority.

Here, we take up the dialectic indicated by Schwidetzky (1955, 283) when he states that crossbreeding between races, where one of them has defeated the other, is distinguished by the fact that the masculine part prevails over the feminine with regard to the decision to choose a sexual mate. This fact involves not only the factor of the dominance and sociocultural prestige of the victor, but also the latter's greater mobility, which acts as a seed that is spread over a wide territory on the basis of excluding, through his very expansive strength, every individual or group who might seek to dispute his decisions. Hence, the idea of psychological castration becomes applicable symbolically as it defines an exclusion of sexual competitors to the extent that the latter lack the power to compete for the objects of desire. Psychological castration came to mean the inclusion in this symbolic group of all those men who, during certain periods, lost the social ability to compete for the sexual objects that they desired and who were taken from them by the victors.

In any case, the most notable condition for heterosis continues to be organic health, but in the Ibero-American case we add the factor of the circulation and relative mobility of the parental groups placed in competitive activity. In this circumstance, the men were the carriers of this dynamic. And within this sense, it is particularly true that the fact of the racial exogamy practiced by the individuals of greatest geographical mobility—the Spanish—meant the expansion of the genetic repertoire of the population in contention, stimulating racial exchanges as Hispanic social structures were embracing an enormous variety of castes and classes whose definition acknowledged the biological range itself as a dynamic factor.

In the Ibero-American case, biological hierarchies were not the direct effect of the results of interracial confrontation in itself; rather, they were the effect of the fact that in the specific selection of each racial group for the exercise of social dominance, one group—the Spanish—appeared politically and culturally more cohesive and technologically more evolved than the native group and, of course, the African group.

Truly, if from the adaptive point of view the Spaniard was more energetic as well as more flexible during the first stage, and if his military confrontation with the native populations demanded that he possess a formidable competitive ability, the mixed descendants corresponding to the products of his sexual experiences exhibited greater degrees of heterosis than in the succeeding historical stages—that is, those corresponding to periods of institutional stratification when Hispanic-American society had reduced its levels of racial exogamy among the elites or ruling groups.

From the moment that a colonial system of castes formally closed to racial exogamy was established, heterosis retreated precisely because it became more a product of chance. In historical reality, heterosis is the product of masculine aggressiveness, and within it, of exogamy and of a dominance that excludes defeated competitors from power. In these conditions of racial exogamy, selective pressure is greater than on occasions of localized racial endogamy, even when we are dealing with a multiracial society such as colonial Ibero-America. Thus, the most possible heterosis would correspond to the first competitive generations more than to those that had been stabilized by means of a system of social stratification such as the later regime of castes.

The loss of interracial competitiveness in society during the period of stratification would be compensated, nevertheless, by interracial competitiveness and by the development of ecological adaptations that would diminish the role of climatic hostility, as well as cause the appearance of biotic equilibria and of specific resistances to diseases and epidemics on the part of the different offspring, in contrast to the vulnerability of the different racial progenitors to certain environmental adversities. In this sense, the nature of biological competition for survival and the adaptation to new environments took on the character of a social competition for dominance within the new political and institutional structures.

The role played by culture in these situations of time and space was a decisive one, at least in the sense of accelerating Hispanic dominance in strategic geopolitical areas, such as those corresponding to the civilized centers of America. Thus, culture as an instrument of social discourse and knowledge in the specific behavior of Ibero-America was not only predominantly Hispanic, but the emergence of this predominance must be considered as a selective phenomenon equivalent in symbolic meaning to a racial mixture where the parental strength of its "hybrid vigor" was essentially Hispanic in the civilized centers and their dependent outlying areas (such as the so-called Southern Cone and northern Mexico, also including the Greater Antilles because of their historical precedence and affirmation). Meanwhile, the marginal area of the Amazon, soon to become colonial Brazil, was Portuguese.

And in a certain way, as a sign of an environmental adaptation that was arising in response to the new needs—political, military, and economic— established on the basis of the Hispanic model, the tropical areas would foster the appearance of mixed offspring alternating between black and mulatto without their culture achieving dominance. That is, dominance would also correspond to Spanish culture. In reality, heterosis as a biological phenomenon in the tropical areas had an expansive nature that was limited to the extent that, historically, it did not constitute the master cultural model of colonial society. In this sense heterosis was restricted to being a localized phenomenon, often a marginal one, and generally a function of metropolitan power or of geopolitical necessities derived from economic strategies founded on the objectives of the new American societies.

Cultural mixing would not only have a Hispanic mode but the latter would be accentuated in the areas of Spanish colonization and settlement, whereas the areas of densest native population in pre-Hispanic times would represent the comparative maximum of native cultural participation in those proportions related to racial mixing or to the various syncretisms of culture that were produced. Still, these syncretisms did not mean the institutional and structural dominance of native forms. In reality, pre-Hispanic native culture was incorporated into the process of routines of daily behavior related especially to diet and to the arts, as well as to the inclusion of vocabularies in common speech that thus presumed the presence of a native influence in these contexts. The syncretisms that occurred in this sense were adapted basically by the lower classes of society. But in any case, these classes belonged to a single dominant cultural system and institutional structure—the Hispanic—that defined the culture and the organization of the new societies of colonization, settlement, and population. Where there was Spanish control, the sociocultural mode was also Spanish.

In these conditions, with the period of stratification, the mestizo biological phenotypes appeared as furtive products of a sexual repression based on rigid moral standards of ecclesiastical origin that, due to their co-active nature, not only inhibited the frequency of sexual interaction between different races, but also influenced the adaptation of personality types less open with regard to social behavior and also selectively less numerous.

The domesticating nature of a heavily stratified social structure includes here the praxis of a more conservative society that, because it is less aggressive, restricts itself to a maximum of formal endogamy and a minimum of racial exogamy. From this perspective, the hybrids of that society can be healthy, but because of an excess of specific localization they will end up exhibiting racial variability without necessarily producing general heterosis. Therefore, heterosis is more a question of first generations in periods of aggressiveness and bellicosity in pursuit of dominance than it is in the succeeding generations, when aggressiveness and dominance are more the result of a social competition for status within institutional limits themselves; these are the limits that encompass all the racial groups that before represented groups structurally and institutionally separated by status. In this sense the genetic repertory is more vigorous in hybrids of the first, competitive, stage than in those of the second stage, who are the results of a stabilized social relation lacking in the tougher biological trials implicit in the selection derived from open interracial confrontations.

The genetic repertory of the second stage is basically a selection of energy derived from social position. On this point we must stress that in Hispanic America, selection for hybrid vigor presents three historical circumstances, according to the nature of interracial competition and the position of the different races in it. Thus, we would have a first selection that takes place with the combatants and with the Indians who oppose them, as well as with the Africans who were recruited precisely for their qualities as vigorous individuals.

This first selection is biologically the most likely one for heterosis, precisely because, independent of whoever succumbs or survives, it is also the selection corresponding to a population socially chosen for competition. In this first stage, due to the select nature of their progenitors, the products of mixture were individuals especially endowed for heterosis in settings and circumstances that demand strength and adaptive capacity. With regard to heterosis, this first phase was above all the most biologically selective period, when we consider qualities of environmental endurance and survival as well as the application of intelligent strategies for the objective of social dominance.

A second selection occurs as a consequence of the determination of the existence of a common cultural system and of a single social structure, independent of the three existing races. We refer to the phase corresponding to Hispanic political and social dominance that followed their military victories, in some cases, to the missionary Indian reducciones in others, and finally, to the Spanish settlements founded on American soil with interracial participation, as occurred in haciendas, mines, villas, and cities.

In this second phase, and in the third historical circumstance, settlement, the different racial groups coexisted in a relationship within a single society— a multiracial one in this case—though it was organized structurally into castes. It is evident that during this period racial mixing was more intensive than it was in the first stage of combat. Nevertheless, the point of departure for racial mixtures was not the prior biological selection of the progenitors; rather, that selection functioned more by chance, in that individuals of different racial origin took part at the same time, often physically degraded by their social situation, along with others who were biologically spent through the persistence of effort. Additionally, it is true that the most socially and physically protected group was that of the Spanish, because it was the one that wielded political and economic dominance.

In these conditions, racial mixing itself did not guarantee hybrid vigor, precisely because the populations that took part as progenitors found themselves in unequal positions, not only socially but also biologically, at least with respect to the phenotypes or specific expressions of health and disease. This inequality is the reason why chance played a more important selective role in the second stage than in the first. And in this sense, prior selection wielded an influence on the vigor relating to the products of mixture, such that, given the lowly social situation of castes, many of the value judgments expressed about the physical and moral qualities of the mestizo or the mulatto varied enormously according to the environment and circumstances in which the persons they referred to lived.

Regarding this particular of judgments—sometimes favorable, sometimes negative—about mestizos, it becomes evident that no homogeneity actually existed, not only in the judgments about them, but also in the experience of their observable biological qualities.

Having established these two phases as selective and environmental conditions related to hybrid vigor, we think it clear that heterosis did not necessarily occur in every case, because the previous levels of health and disease were variable and inevitably affected the descendants. If the selective nature of the first populations was more severe, then it is more probable that more heterosis occurred in them.

Once stratification had occurred and was consolidated in the form of castes, the structure of Spanish society in America reduced competitive relations among those castes and even among the Spanish themselves. Even though there was a common cultural system and a single social and political structure, positions of status distributed social dominance more on the basis of governmental bureaucratic decisions in the light of royal interests than on the basis of a mobility founded on the merits derived from a true, open competition for status.

Within this setting and with a social structure consequent to a social organization stratified into castes, the value of biological selection did not reside exactly in competition, but in the seduction and induction of the mate, in some cases, or in the simple power of sexual disposition over her based on the exercise of dominance, in this case no longer necessarily a biological dominance in a racial sense. It was, however, social in a broader sense; that is, heterosis appeared representing the randomness that derived from the structure of the social milieu. This structure implied greater variability among the lower castes than among the upper castes, insofar as the latter protected their status by closing themselves off more than the former. On this basis, for reasons of prestige, the lower castes would always be more open to racial mixing than the upper because their opening appears as a condition for their social ascent, whereas the protective closing of the upper castes corresponds to the exercise of a historical function aimed at the survival of their status.

In reality, from this perspective those individuals who belonged to the subordinate races and who, by internal caste selection, stood above the others of their dominated racial group were also the ones who contributed hybrid vigor to the mixed offspring resulting from their union with individuals of the dominant races, but also from their union with selected individuals from other at least immediately proximate races. In this circumstance, in general, the first selections that occurred among races subjected to social degradation contributed hybrid vigor because they represented an adaptive take-off superior to that of their other companions in the group. In that sense, mixed offspring were climbing toward social equalization with individuals of higher castes, and were received into the higher castes when they approached, or rather reproduced, the cultural style of those castes.

The participation of mulattoes with military rank in the Spanish army, or their engagement in some economic triumph, could involve access to the sexual objects of the higher group, although at first mulattoes were forced to endure much social resistance and aesthetic scruples against their new status. Fundamentally, the conditions for access to the group of dominant castes or races—the Europeans—were highly selective because they involved at the outset the existence of a handicap greater than could be faced by lower-class Spaniards. In these cases, access to the dominant castes was in itself a severe test, usually of personal excellence, such as valor in battle at the service of the Spaniards, or economic success. On occasion it could be the exercise of attributes of strategic or political intelligence, or of leadership skills, ratifiable in terms of the values of accomplishment demanded by the dominant race or caste in a regime of little status mobility.

Of course, as the neo-Hispanic societies increased their racial mixing, the regime of stratification based on racial differentiation was weakening, because the stigma attached to color in such a mestizo racial spectrum lost its power to make distinctions. Thus, with the impossibility of making genealogical distinctions with a certain preciseness, only a small minority in each racial group could demonstrate clearly their exclusive differentiated anatomical origin, especially since the cultural style of the Spanish had been assumed totally by all the racial castes. At this point, the class system emerged, gradually replacing that of racial castes. Contributing to this replacement was the social subordination of natives, Africans, and mestizos in general, but the most significant role must be assigned to lower-class Spaniards who moved socially in intimate contact with the races and mixed offspring who occupied positions of inferior status. Further contributing to the dissolution of this system of racial stratification were the different pressures applied by egalitarian ideologies that were impregnating social routines and, within these, the endowment with cognitive and personality resources of those groups that previously had been stigmatized not only in the context of racial and cultural differences, but also in the context of economic differences and of those rooted in aristocratic principles of genealogy.

On the basis of these structural conditions, the greatest heterosis was contributed from below; and although the racial group situated in the upper layers of social stratification maintained its selective system, nonetheless, those from the lower racial groups who were contributing individual excellence and were assuming the cultural values of dominance were also assimilating the resources inherent in the practice and control of the strategies of pressure that their demographic growth allowed to them.

This means that the filter for racial passing in a highly stratified society is not only more rigid but is historically slower than that of an open society. In terms of hybridization, however, the greatest contribution within the structure came more from those individuals who demonstrated competitive excellence in conditions of social inferiority. In the American case, the competitive flow coming from the dominated castes accentuated their pressure as it increased their use of the cultural forms that had given rise to the dominant position of the Spanish peninsular groups. Meanwhile, in terms of biological selection, the most active ones in their contribution to heterosis were those who excelled from positions of inferior status and those peninsular Spaniards who maintained the flow of immigration.

This means that, in general, sexual and biological energy was more complete and spontaneous in the competitions of transition than in those of stratified periods, when the classes—or in this case, exclusive racial castes—have been stabilized, and therefore their relations of sexual exchange and formation of mestizo genealogies has decreased, that is, when racial endogamy is preferred to racial exogamy.

What is said above alerts us to the fact that if the period of transition signifying the phase of military struggle for control of space and for political power was a highly selective one and rewarded those who used more energetic and culturally more advanced strategies, we can also acknowledge that the most vigorous persons in that phase also devoted more energy to sex than is customary in more stable social situations, in this case, than those that came later. In the following periods, when society inhibited the energy applied to risk taking, then the limits of energy's action were also more restricted. It follows that, whereas the levels of heterosis were relatively sure in the first stages, in the following stages they were more dependent on chance.

By contrast, when a multiracial society had already been established, its genetic variability and its greater number of heterozygotic combinations contributed very frequent probabilities of hybrid vigor to its populations, specifically on the basis of more specialized cohorts in a given space. Even in this latter variant, we should recognize that, at the least, the geographical mobility of the populations, especially the Spanish, continued to be a common phenomenon. And in this sense, the successes and failures of their adaptive changes and the specific result of the mobility of their members constituted important aspects of competitive selection, assets that, in their social and biological fortunes, swept along with them the castes involved in the effort to participate in the never interrupted adventures of exploration and settlement.

In this way, at least an important fraction of American societies continued to be subjected to the test of environmental selection, precisely because during the Spanish period America represented the most active setting for racial filtering, a filtration that, through constant influxes of European immigration and the social ascent of races that occupied lower positions in the structure, has never been interrupted. Compared to other more racially homogeneous continents, America has had the most active, as well as the most diversified, history of racial mixing.

In regard to this particular aspect of American history, if there had not been a permanent environmental filtering, facilitated by the diversity of the racial spectrum and of the product of mixture acting within the same cultural system and same social structure, the populations would not have endured the impact of the permanent challenge of climatic hostility, on the one hand, and of the social and cultural aggressions that their people have experienced and continue to experience, on the other. In fact, if it is true that these three challenges constitute specific environments and have been manifested dynamically in the history of Ibero-American nations, it is also certain that the adaptive exercise of their different populations has constituted the most rigorous test of selective flexibility to which a cohort of descendants can be subjected. The overcoming of these rigors is manifested in the constancy of Ibero-American fertility and in the uninterrupted renewal through racial mixtures in first generations of racial groups who are constantly filtered and are carriers of heterosis. Without the existence of heterosis, the evolutionary selection represented by their ethnic types would not have been possible.

The Geographical Distribution
of Racial Mixing

Initially, the basic role in the development and expansion of racial mixing on American soil can be attributed to the Spanish soldier and the native woman; to the former, because of his vocation as a colonist and because of his pragmatic circumstance as a bachelor, and to the latter, for her receptivity to union with this man. In addition, although the acceleration of racial mixing has depended largely on the historical conditions in which the encounter of Spaniards with the natives took place, it is certain that the increasing demographic proportions attained by the mestizos and their identification of prestige with Spanish culture are what allowed the achievement of a swift colonization and acculturation of the continent, and therefore facilitated the conversion of American native life to the Spanish model.

When the process of racial mixing is placed within its specific historical and social scheme, we can establish certain special results of interest to our description of the phenomenon of the biocultural integration of racial mixture. Thus, we should refer to the historical situation of the mestizo itself in terms of his social frame of reference. According to that frame, we can state that, because of the cultural differences existing between Indians and Spaniards at the beginning of the conquest and in ensuing periods, as well as the political and military clash that they faced, the association and exchange that finally led to mestizo formation was a painful process. It is also certain that those unions that led to the formation of a mixed family group were rarely accepted. Thus, both the native and Spanish societies tended to reject the mixed grouping because with it, their own forms of culture and of traditional functioning were changed, and those who were born mestizos in each specific group were made uncomfortable. In many cases, at first, the sexual relations between Indians, Spaniards, and blacks were tolerated but did not receive the backing of institutionalization.

The casual union of the Spaniard and the Indian woman led to biological, but not cultural, mixing; the resulting hybrid was culturally socialized as an

Indian, although he or she would commonly develop strong resentment against that society, but most of all against the Hispanic group. By contrast, the lasting or definitive union of the Spaniard with the Indian woman produced a stable, biocultural racial mixture defined by a synthetic integration of the biocultural characteristics of both lineages. At any rate, in certain cases the integration shows facets of oscillation between the mestizo's emotional solidarity with the Indian society of the mother and with the Spanish. Nevertheless, what we could call this "pendulum of identification" occurred in those situations where the social groups of one of the progenitors lost prestige or presence during the process of socialization because of the social preponderance of one group over the other. While the general identification of prestige leaned toward the Hispanic, we should not forget that the specific influence exerted by the process of socialization—generally maternal— assumed that the mestizo would feel more linked to the culture and society of his or her mother than to that of his or her father, that is, of the Spaniard, especially in the cases of casual union between the two. In this sense, the mestizo's system of security was emotionally more protected through the social group of the mother than of the father. At any rate, it is also true that the social ascent of the mestizo would take place through his identification with the father's culture, such that if he identified basically with the mother, socially his aspiration for status impelled him to adopt the goals of the father's culture. In any case, we can say that the more rural was the social group in which the mestizo lived, the less European or Hispanic was the way of living in the culturally dominant group.

The cases of casual mixture, resulting from mere sexual impulse, are the ones that created a greater psychological problem for the personality structure of the mestizo because they often led him to a marginal position within the society, particularly in the urban centers. During this phase, the mestizo as a social group is largely an uprooted one, without decision-making power in its society and without prestige in the Indian and Spanish communities. This situation often moved the mestizo to the simultaneous formation of a certain evanescent and fluctuating character structure. In a certain way, since there was frequent irregular, or noninstitutionalized, sexual activity in the early periods of Spanish society in America, the mestizos came to feel like an illegitimate caste, resentful of the type of society and person who made them feel illegitimate. Nevertheless, the mestizos themselves were not seen pejoratively, except when they were the product of a casual or noninstitutionalized union. The trail left by this type of personality has often assumed a character, in the psychology of many mestizos, in the form of a fluctuating position (Zavala 1958, 888), especially before their cultural stabilization and full social recognition took place.

The cultural and biological differences between natives and Spaniards also led to social differences between the two that crystallized finally into class antagonisms. These differences created, first, a status situation where the Spaniard occupied the highest levels of the recently constituted Ibero-American society, and the native the lowest ones. In addition, we must not lose sight of an important fact. The Spanish themselves had a class structure in which the conquistadors of the sixteenth century formed a social group clearly superior to that of the immigrants who came to colonize, such that not all Spaniards were *caballeros* and *señores* (ibid.).

This situation suggests that the great majority of the first stable racial mixing took place in the rural or frontier areas, such that, once the conquest was accomplished, the process of urban racial mixing was less frequent and more problematical than was the rural for the mestizo and for the society from the viewpoint of the process of individual socialization. Thus, only when the rural mestizo is established in the national culture and political system and moves into the urban centers does a mestizo national consciousness appear in Ibero-American life. This appearance took place at the beginning of the present century, and later took form through the victories of the revolutions in Mexico, Guatemala, and Bolivia. In Mexico, for example, the Revolution of 1910 has been for the mestizo the platform, first, to attain political control of the country, and then, to achieve its economic and social domination.[1]

In reality, although these revolutions were influenced by a profound mixture of social resentment and protest, at heart they constituted a popularization of mestizo culture and were, paradoxically, instruments of propagation of Hispanic culture. They were so to the extent that their ideology was held by mestizo groups and by the masses of the indigenous population, and to the degree that this ideology was crystallized in institutions with strong Hispanic roots. Thus, Hispanic life in Ibero-America following independence was popularized more by the mestizo than by the Spaniard himself, especially to the extent that one part of Spanish society, the upper classes, had gradually become socially and culturally isolated from the Indian-mestizo society by means of a rigid social stratification.

The elements or features by which the mestizo or mestizo life has been recognized have been very fluid ones, but we must not forget that at the beginning of the Spanish settlement of America, the term *Indian* was applied to the rural peasant directly occupied in the cultivation of land (Kubler 1952). The concept of mestizo itself is relative in its practical expression; consider, for example, the fact that in Otavalo, Ecuador, ethnic identification is made according to the clothes that an individual may wear. Thus, the case may arise where two brothers are classified by the census, respectively, as an Indian and as a mestizo, because each of them dressed according to the customs of one ethnic group or another (Buitrón 1945, 191). In the case of the first Spanish settlements in America, those individuals who formed the urban proletariat were considered mestizos, along with those others living in the midst of rural society who had no direct ties to the land. This assumes that there were many mestizos who lacked a clear awareness of their culture and of their social role, although they did realize their position of status. Otherwise, according to this state of ideological confusion, the line separating whites and nonwhites was very fluid, much more so than is currently assumed, because every child of a Spaniard and Indian could be counted as a Spaniard just by the say-so of the father, and in some cases, even by just acting as a Spaniard. By contrast, a culturally Indianized mestizo could be considered an Indian, not for his color, but for his very ascription to an indigenous social group (Jara 1959). This means that the most important thing for the ascription of status was not racial difference, but rather belonging to a Spanish or Indian community. In this sense, the division of class and culture was harder to cross than that of race or color (Pierson 1942).

Halfway between the Indian and the Spanish, then, the mestizo emerged, historically a form of life that has had three decisive moments: (1) the group was defined, first, as a culturally confused ethnicity in its loyalties between the natives and the Spanish; (2) it then appeared as a middle rural and lower urban social class that in either case struggled to attain first economic then political power; and (3) it has since emerged, in our times, as a biocultural synthesis that is gradually eliminating the social differences between Indians and Spaniards, that were based on initially biocultural differences, and now has begun to constitute itself as the ethnic group that assumes consciousness of the present and future of Ibero-American society.

Thus, the mestizos are the transition through which ethnic and social leveling in the life of Ibero-American culture is facilitated. Therefore, they become the instrument for the achievement of a society more fit for social mobility. Their cultural role is similar to the social role of the middle classes in Western society. In the case of contemporary culture, the mestizos are agents of transmission and exchange between Indians and Europeans, but in turn, because they occupy a middle position, they constitute the main factor of equilibrium. Through the mestizo, Ibero-American society has become culturally more receptive and socially less rigid and more dynamic. This current role of the mestizos dominates the heart of Ibero-American society to the degree that their egos feel less frustrated as they gain confidence in their methods and in themselves. Thus, in a certain way, this role is developing parallel to their achievement of sociocultural stability. In this case, it assumes their consciousness of feeling at the same time as the creator and carrier of a new biocultural synthesis.

The evolution of Ibero-American culture and ethnicity has followed a process of gradual formation of mestizo consciousness whose most distinctive features revolve around the popularization—by the mestizo—of Iberian culture. Nevertheless, before arriving at the present situation, it is also true that Ibero-American society first aimed at the idealized reproduction of various regional Spanish worlds, hence, the names of New Andalucía, New Galicia, New Granada, and so on; but progressively, as the generations of mestizos and mestizoized criollos began to acquire the consciousness of their demographic and social importance, these ideals played out, to be replaced by others that represented the mestizo cultural and biological synthesis.

If we say that the social position of the mestizo at the end of the past century and the beginning of the present one was that of an enormous rural middle, proletarian, and lower-middle class situated halfway between the Indian and the Spanish, and in certain cases between the latter and the black and the mulatto, we will also be correct in stating that this social position has evolved until it is today defined as the nucleus of the basic personality structure of the Ibero-American, especially in the major populated centers of America.

In any case, the first stage of racial mixing as a form of living occurred in rural society. This was a stage in which the mestizo lacked organized political awareness. Nevertheless, later in the second stage, when the mestizo group emerged in Ibero-American cities in the form of a distinctive cultural model whose interests and functions eventually overcame those of the criollos, the third stage appeared: that of an ideological consciousness translated into political forms. This is the one that corresponds to the current period and is expressed by means of a victorious political capacity, which has already taken place in some countries, and is manifested as a promise of a similar triumph in other Ibero-American countries in the coming years. This is so to the extent that the cultural formula of racial mixing, in achieving awareness of its strength, has also become a dynamic force of transformation, which it derives from its political ideology and organization.

In this sense, we find such a mestizo character in the revolutions of Mexico (1910), Guatemala (1944), and Bolivia (1952), and we can venture to say that the renovating type of political movements that have occurred in Venezuela, Colombia, Ecuador, Peru, and other Ibero-American countries signal changes that are being led by the mestizos according to their formulas (Esteva 1961a). The revolutionary aspect in this case resides in the discovery and highlighting of sentiments and mestizo forms of life that now are taking on a determinant character through political consciousness, after having manifested themselves previously in the form of a cultural consciousness.

The difference between that incoherent world of the mestizos prior to this

century and the present situation is that now they have a political consciousness and have defined their objectives regarding the American future. This is
something that did not show so clearly before. Thus, it follows that racial
mixing is today a specific problem of the anthropological sciences, and the
conscientious research of it constitutes one of the most complex fields of
study of cultural anthropology.

Racial Identification

Considered racially, the classification or taxonomy of Ibero-American populations has been given emphasis in anthropometric studies based on the description of characteristics such as skin color, hair texture, the form of the
nose and related facial angles, the color of the eyes, and other defining phenotypes. The study of these characteristics has been accompanied by such
considerations as their statistical frequency and their relative geographical distribution among given ethnic groups. Up to now, the majority of racial taxonomy and of anthropometric terminology has relied on these types of morphological values.

Nevertheless, in recent years, and since 1900 with the discovery by Landsteiner of the blood groups pertaining to the ABO system, racial classification
has paid increasing attention to human serological data, to the extent of
constituting a raciology based on the relative frequency of certain genes or
sanguineal phenotypes in given geographically localized human populations.
The prime perspective of this racial taxonomy, working with serological
data, consists of indicating that certain genes occur more in some human
groups than in others. This greater frequency is also identified with a certain
geographical distribution, such that once certain anthropometric data are
known, such as those we have indicated—skin color, hair texture, thickness
of lips, shape of the nose, and so on—especially in their extreme values for
the purposes of racial identification, we can develop a certain raciological
classification. Thus, such a classification is useful when, as in our case, we
know the most characteristic frequencies of each gene or sanguineal phenotype in the populations that contributed and continue to contribute to racial
mixing in Ibero-America.

In this regard, Krogman (1966, 64–65) points out that in the human species we find 10 percent of characteristics that are definitely recognizable as
contributing to racial differentiation, while 90 percent of the total discernible
genes are common to the general endowments of human beings, whatever
their race. According to this, out of a total of forty-four thousand pairs of
genes constituting the genetic endowment of the human being, 10 percent

act in combinations that are distinguished by having a racial value. In addition, half of the latter work in hereditary combinations that establish differences in form and function.

In this way, furthermore, although these racial classifications require concepts of a morphological nature—such as skin color and eye color, hair texture, relative width of the nose, the shape of the lips, and other facial features especially—once these characteristics are determined, genetic research shows that it is possible to diagnose their relative incidence in large populations by turning to the study of frequencies with which they appear in human populations defined by blood groups. We must acknowledge, additionally, that racial classification considered individually, that is, according to the techniques specific to physical anthropology, contributes to the determination of the qualitative characteristics we must keep in mind in order to establish what constitutes the morphological differences that designate one race in comparison to another or others.

According to the above expectations, and knowing some of the statistical frequencies of these principles, we have developed a demographic estimate through which we can obtain a picture of racial distributions in America, by regions and by countries. In each case, these distributions represent the latest or current expression of the historical tendencies that we have observed throughout this work.

In this study, due to their greater phenotypic homogeneity in terms of frequencies, we have preferred using serological data to that of morphological anthropology. We agree in this case with certain postulates put forth by Boyd (1953, A95) to the effect that racial characteristics based on genetics offer certain advantages, especially because: (1) they have an objective value and are quantitative; (2) they largely eliminate elements that often turn out to be subjective, such as skin color; (3) they refer to frequencies; (4) they allow us to predict the proportion of genes in a given population, based on knowledge about the genes of certain human groups; (5) they develop taxonomy and, particularly, eliminate biases since the latter have not been manifested against genes; and finally, (6) they distinguish clearly between the influences of the environment and of heredity.

In addition, it must be clearly understood that a racial classification employing only blood-type systems as data would lack precision, since, in the first place, two progenitors of different races or ethnic origins but possessing the same genetic phenotype—let us say, O—will produce a mestizo not recognizable as such through purely serological data. Thus, there is a need for more complete morphological antecedents, which can be provided only by anthropometry.

It is also true that, once certain models for measurement have been accepted, visualizable characteristics are much more precise for the purposes of racial particularization, since in this sense we can have no doubt that a mestizo will exhibit visually, at least in one of his forms, mixed characteristics that represent the contributions of the two progenitors who differ genetically from the racial viewpoint. If the mestizo is seen serologically, he can exhibit only one of those characteristics. In the case where the parents' phenotype is the same, it is not possible to identify the mestizo by the genetic result, and therefore it will be necessary to turn to the anthropometric data supplied to us by physical anthropologists.

This is the main reservation we have against serology seen as an exclusive, or self-sufficient, method for classification. Nevertheless, if we define the problem in terms of the identification of large population groups, the serological method allows us to discern the genetic frequencies of the those groups. Knowing these frequencies in given racial populations also makes it possible to determine certain statistical tendencies that, in turn, reveal the relative participation in that population by the races under consideration.

In this sense, we are in agreement with Oschinsky (1959, 5) when he states that single-gene serological factors in themselves do not have importance for racial taxonomy. We would add that, in themselves, neither do they provide distinctive morphological data for racial classification, unless we complete the frequencies of blood type with the racial identifications made by anthropometry, ethnology, and cultural anthropology. On this basis, in our case, the serological results are valid for purposes of statistical frequencies applied to racially heterogeneous populations among which it would be impossible to carry out a separate measurement of each individual. The serological data thus take on a greater statistical than qualitative value, but in the case of racial mixing they help us to represent frequencies in terms of the relative participation of each known racial group.

Of course, we are not presenting here a biological process, but rather some results or phenotypes derived from some relative genetic frequencies or combinations. Information regarding mestizo groups is still very scarce, and in some cases the control of the components that are racially distinctive or differentiated is questionable or problematical. Nevertheless, the knowledge of certain genetic frequencies designated as characteristic, or highly frequent, in Indian, Caucasian, and Negro populations, as well as knowledge of their relative geographic distribution, allows us to contemplate with a certain accuracy the reality of racial mixing from this biological wellspring. In addition, we are certain that the difficulties presented by this problem are largely resolved through the help offered by ethnohistorical as well as census data.

In this sense, we can appreciate that the serological frequencies obtained through genetic research among the indigenous, Caucasian and Negro populations of Ibero-America, and mixtures of these, agree largely with the descriptions made by cultural anthropology, which follow cultural more than biological criteria of classification. This coincidence especially underlines the fact that mestizo populations exhibit different genetic and cultural combinations according to the different regions of America under study. According to this differentiation, in some regions the genes and cultural forms of one racial group predominate over another, whereas in other areas the respective proportions are more balanced and therefore produce a more harmonious racial mixture.

Additionally, the relative predominance of the genes and culture of some ethnicities over others indicates the different importance of the historical functions of those ethnicities as racial groups and as forms of life. At times, according to its historical circumstance, a racial group has remained relatively more pure in one region than in another, and the same thing has occurred with its forms of culture. Throughout, the variants that we may encounter are specialized responses that each racial group in general and each ethnic group in particular has made to its different historical and environmental circumstances. Consequently, we may speak of differential frequencies of mixture, both genetic and cultural.

From a biological perspective, the variants that emerge are the result of the intervention of several factors, among which four seem significant: (1) the number of individuals that each racial group contributed, and contributes, to the process of miscegenation; (2) the relative frequency of sexual exchange practiced by each of them; (3) the relative homogeneity of each racial group at the beginning of miscegenation; and (4) the geographical expansion of each racial group and its specific distribution into the components of racial mixture.

According to this perspective, the genetic composition of racial mixture in Ibero-American populations, obtained through the study of the frequencies of the phenotypes that form the ABO blood system,[2] brings out the relative participation of each racial group in the constitution of the various mestizo types. The mestizo population that results from miscegenation is different, therefore, in each geographical area, since the proportions of each formative racial group—the Caucasian, the Negro, and the Indian—will differ.

With regard to the population of the United States, we did not have sufficient serological and anthropological data available to make it possible for us to apply them to the racial estimates there according to the same method used for the Ibero-American countries. We have found the same problem with Canada, and therefore, we have decided to estimate the racial populations of that country through the consideration of their censuses, in combination with certain characteristics of their ethnic composition. We have examined the Canadian census of 1961, and on the basis of that census and other data that tend to classify the European, Indian, and Asian populations, especially by ethnicity and race, we have applied the resulting percentages to the mestizo and Negro populations.

As for the United States, we have made use of the data relative to the immigration that occurred in that country during the period 1822–1960. Since these migrations are classified by their countries and regions of origins, we can make approximate judgments regarding their racial composition. Thus, for example, the total number of Europeans entering into the United States during this period (Berthoff 1966, 499–500) was 38,130,030; those individuals coming from the Americas south of the United States numbered 2,397,818, while persons of Asian origin totaled 847,542. We make our estimates based, therefore, on calculations of the proportionality applied to the census of 1960, assuming a certain continuity in its trends and grounding the assumption on various critical considerations made by a physical anthropologist, Krogman, the sociologists Schmid and Nobbe, and a historian, Berthoff. Their contributions have helped us to make adjustments that are reflected in the corresponding demographic results.

We have taken certain factors into account for the United States: (a) that country's immigration policies during the period 1820–1960, on the basis of immigration quotas generally equivalent to the proportional numbers of the ethnic populations already residing in that nation, except for blacks; (b) the rates of immigration by geographical regions and by nationalities, which can be reduced to racial groupings based on the provenance of the ethnic groups of origin, in this case, populations representative of the internal racial distribution of the United States; (c) the statement by Krogman (1966, 65) that some 28 million whites in the United States have one or more Negro genes; (d) the fact that the population census of the United States classifies as white those persons coming from Ibero-America (Schmid and Nobbe 1965, 921), whom we consider instead to be mestizos in large measure, especially mindful of their high demographic impact in some states of that nation, such as New York and the Southwestern states of California, Arizona, New Mexico, Colorado, and Texas; and (e) the fact that the Negro groups classified as blacks, who, according to Schmid and Nobbe (ibid., 909), represent 94.3 percent of a population of 20,009,280 individuals considered as nonwhite—from whom the Ibero-Americans are excluded—amount to 10.5 percent of the total population census of the United States. To this percentage we have added the 28 million blacks who appear white, as indicated by Krogman.

Comparative ABO Phenotype Frequencies

In the analysis of the different genetic proportions involved in racial mixing in Ibero-America, certain significant phenomena stand out. The first is the great statistical weight of the phenotype or blood group O in the Indian population, which reaches up to 100 percent in some societies, especially the most isolated ones. Another highly significant phenomenon is the relative incidence of the Rh factor, which shows up as positive in the majority of native individuals examined, sometimes in up to 100 percent of the cases. According to this analysis, the incidence of the Rh factor in mestizo Indians turns out to be halfway between that of pure Indians and Caucasians (Landsteiner, Weiner, and Matson 1942, 77). The Diego factor is nonexistent in Caucasians and Negroes in Ibero-America (Layrisse and Arends 1958, 182). It is true, nevertheless, that the Diego factor has been little studied among Ibero-American populations, and therefore, there are scant data available for a systematic comparison of incidence in mestizo groups, as well as for a geographical distribution of this type. With respect to the MN system, among the natives there is an extremely high incidence of the M group (Matson and Swanson 1959, 52), especially when compared with that of Caucasians and Negroes.

The Caucasian population is distinguished genetically by a certain higher incidence of the A blood group. The latter, in many cases and in that of the population of greatest interest to us—the Spanish—shows a very high frequency, sometimes even statistically surpassing the O gene. With respect to the MN system, in contrast to the natives of Ibero-America, Caucasians exhibit a much lower frequency of M.

For the purpose of establishing the relative incidence of the ABO phenotypes among the Spanish, we have taken some of their frequencies in those regional types that interest us from the standpoint of their relative importance in Ibero-America (Mourant, Kopec, and Domaniewska-Sobczak 1958, 75–78), particularly those ethnic groups—Andalusians, Extremadurans, Castillians, Basque-Navarrans, Asturians, and Galicians—who have been most associated historically with that continent. For a general median for Spain we have taken the frequencies for Madrid, since, given its character as a migratory receptacle for the peninsula, it tends to give us a representative population, at least for the peoples of the south, center, northwest, and north in general, which are the ones who largely move to the capital. In addition, with a thought to this character of representative generality that we seek, we can make reference to sample populations of Spanish in Brazil and Mexico that, in each case, are strategically equivalent to mixed Iberian populations (table 12.1).

When we consider the particular values for specific phenotypes, we observe that the incidence of the O gene is less than 50 percent in most of the Spanish ethnic groups, except in the Basque-Navarra region. Madrid and Spaniards in Brazil give figures within, or slightly above 50 percent, except for Mexico. The values for Madrid thus would be valid for a modern Spanish population, in this case for the populations that are currently moving to America, as is shown by Brazil. Nevertheless, for the purposes of the formative racial groups of racial mixing, the most significant values are those for Andalucía, Castilla, and Extremadura. In any case, the high incidence of type A in Spanish populations is the most characteristic feature, an incidence that in several cases is higher than that of type O. The high incidence of A is greater still in Portuguese populations, which means that in Ibero-American racial mixing, this incidence of the A phenotype serves in general to determine the relative degree of genetic participation that the Spanish and Portuguese groups have had in their respective areas of miscegenation, Spanish America and Brazil.

These proportions are confirmed also in the Italian contributions, which are more recent and therefore of less formative influence in American racial mixing. They show similar incidences of the A phenotype. With respect to the O gene, the Italian populations manifest a somewhat lower incidence than do the Spanish. The O gene shows low incidences in German populations, which are also important in our case when we think of certain areas of Brazil and Chile. The German populations, being newer to America than the Hispano-Portuguese and less favorable to miscegenation with Indians and blacks, have contributed little to racial mixing. By contrast, they have given particular increase to the proportions of purely white or Caucasian groups in those Ibero-American countries where they have emigrated. In large measure, this pattern is also the case with other European and even Asian ethnic minorities, especially when the emigrations are made by family groups. In such cases the non-American ethnic groups become socially and sexually self-sufficient for at least two and sometimes more generations. For these reasons, the significant genetic proportions to consider in racial mixing, apart from the black and indigenous ones, are those that come from the Spanish and Portuguese. In any case, the Spanish are of greater importance when we consider that they operated on demographically greater and culturally more advanced populations than those of Brazil. In addition, an important distinction to be made in that mixture is that in general, because of the relative

Table 12.1 European Populations (ABO System)

Ethnic Type	Number	O	A	B	AB	Author or Source
SPANIARDS						
South	644	42.08	37.73	15.37	4.81	Miserachs Riglat, 1949.
Extremadura	1,409	36.48	45.92	11.36	6.24	Hoyos Sáinz, 1947.
Castille	1,452	38.91	45.25	11.36	4.48	Hoyos Sáinz, 1947.
Basque-Navarra	3,876	50.72	40.66	6.06	2.55	Hoyos Sáinz, 1947.
Cantabria	1,302	447.54	43.01	7.45	2.00	Hoyos Sáinz, 1947.
Asturias	359	47.91	39.83	10.03	2.23	Hors y Marcos, 1951.
Galicia	542	39.30	48.71	9.04	2.95	Hoyos y Sáinz, 1947.
Madrid	1,090	53.30	38.95	5.87	1.74	Carrión y Hdez., 1946.
Madrid	1,526	50.00	41.61	6.68	1.70	Hoyos Sáinz, 1947.
Spaniards (Brazil)	2,258	50.93	36.71	8.72	3.63	Mellone et al., 1952.
Spaniards (Mexico)	296	44.26	46.62	5.40	3.72	Salazar M. y Martínez, 1947.
PORTUGUESE						
All Portugal	9,830	39.78	48.38	8.23	3.61	Fânzeres y Morais, 1940.
Northern Portugal	707	441.73	46.96	8.91	2.40	Tamagnini, 1947.
Central Portugal	2,087	42.90	46.10	7.20	3.60	Lessa, 1956.
Southern Portugal	590	43.73	48.98	4.92	2.37	Tamagnini, 1947.
ITALIANS						
Italy (general)	1,830	42.68	41.04	11.86	4.43	Tranquilli-Leali, 1934.
Northern Italy	732	37.30	46.86	10.79	5.05	Viola, 1928–1929.
Central Italy	649	37.44	47.00	10.63	4.93	Viola, 1928–1929.
Southern Italy	288	32.99	42.01	15.97	9.03	Viola, 1928–1929.
Italians (Brazil)	6,169	46.81	38.60	10.88	3.71	Mellone et al., 1952.
Italians (Buenos Aires)	464	49.57	36.85	11.42	2.16	Etcheverry, 1949.
GERMANS						
Soldiers	20,000	38.81	43.51	12.25	5.43	Krüpe, 1942.

scarcity of native populations, the Portuguese produced more hybrids with blacks than with Indians, the opposite to what occurred with the Spanish. The same is true for cultural mixing.

The determination of the relative contributions of the black racial group to racial mixing in America allows us to observe certain differences with the Caucasian group. Most important is the lower incidence of the B gene in the Caucasian ethnic groups when compared with black ethnic groups, since in general the incidence of the B phenotype among the latter tends to be more or less double that of the Caucasian racial group. They both share, as we see, a lesser incidence of O with respect to indigenous Americans, although there are rare cases where the incidence among the latter is also quite low. This interruption of the phenotype *normality* of the O gene characteristic of the American Indian constitutes a problem to be solved through serological research. Although there are few Indian groups who fall below the normal incidence for the O phenotype, the study of this phenomenon represents a kind of touchstone for the discipline of genetics, an issue that it must face in the near future if it aspires, in this case, to be something more than a technique of genetic identification and of establishing geographical distribution of blood-type frequencies. We believe, nevertheless, that when the O gene has an incidence of less than 60 percent among the natives, this is due to mixtures whose scientific control has not been established.

In any case, the racial differentiation of the black group from the Caucasian becomes much clearer when we compare the relative incidence of the Ro(cDe) chromosome, which appears in 55 percent of African blacks and in less than 5 percent of Caucasian individuals (Layrisse, Wilbert, and Arends 1958, 311–12). We will not analyze here the phenomenon regarding the Ro chromosome because we lack sufficient data for their comparison. Of course, in black African populations the incidence of A and B genes is quite balanced, although the B phenotype often predominates. The incidence of the O gene, however, is always greater than the A and B, sometimes doubling them in frequency.

In the following table (table 12.2) we show some data on the relative frequency of phenotypic values of the ABO system in certain black populations in Africa, especially in some that, because of their geographical location, are near to or related to specific groups who developed in the New World. In general, the specific serological incidences among African groups tend to vary with respect to the O gene, but are quite similar with regard to the A and B genes.

Based on the assumptions we have put forth, we can make a quantitative estimate for the total mestizo population of Ibero-America. The specific blood-type frequencies allow us to calculate the degree of mixture present in

Table 12.2 Negro Populations (ABO System)

Ethnic Group	Number	O	A	B	AB	Author or Source
Haussa	98	35.71	31.63	28.57	4.00	Kossovitch, 1934.
Ashanti	113	51.33	23.01	21.24	4.42	Armattoe et al., 1953.
Ewe	161	47.20	21.74	24.84	6.21	Armattoe et al., 1953.
Ga, Twi, Ewe, Busanga, Fanti and Andagbe	107	47.66	24.30	26.17	1.87	Layrisse and Arends, 1957.
Yoruba	325	52.31	21.54	23.08	3.08	Müller, 1927.
Portuguese Guinea	139	51.80	20.86	25.18	2.16	Almeida, 1955.
Santo Tomé	215	50.70	17.21	30.23	1.86	Almeida, 1955.
Mandingas (G. Port)	94	35.11	27.66	29.79	7.45	De Azevedo et al., 1945.
Angola	2,000	48.60	23.35	24.55	3.5	Teixeira, 1946.
Bantú	8,000	47.87	24.26	24.72	3.14	Mayor, 1954.

some populations in those countries. In certain cases, we even have mathematical values that measure the incidence of racial mixing in certain regions, as well as the specific proportions or genetic flows of each blood-type component in given populations. Though these mathematical values cannot be generalized to all Ibero-American populations, we can consider them as frequencies that allow us to estimate the specific importance achieved by hybridization in certain areas. Consideration of these can lead us to some significant conclusions.

As can be seen in table 12.3, with regard to the populations of greater significance in Ibero-American racial mixing, the distances that separate Indians, Iberians, and Africans from the viewpoint of their relative genetic frequencies emphasize an important fact: the minimum values among the four ethnoracial groups are closest to one another in the phenotype O, because in the A and B phenotypes the distances are much greater and can show enormous differences. In addition, it is clear that the incidence of the O phenotype is basically equal among Spaniards and blacks for the minimum as well as the maximum limits, which gives us to understand that it is in the relative frequencies of A and B where we must establish the calculation of their contribution to racial mixing. In this sense, the A and B frequencies shown by Spaniards and by blacks are those of greatest importance for the consideration

Table 12.3 Minimum and Maximum Incidences of ABO Phenotypes
by Ethnicity or Specific Racial Groups

Degree of Frequency	Ethnicity or Racial Group	ABO System		
		O	A	B
Minimum	Indians	50	0	0.0
	Spaniards	36	36	5.0
	Portuguese	40	46	7.0
	Blacks	35	17	21.0
Maximum	Indians	100	36	7.5
	Spaniards	53	49	15.0
	Portuguese	44	49	9.0
	Blacks	52	31	30.0

of their relative incidence in localized mixtures. Furthermore, with regard to the distances that separate one group from another, we shall highlight certain phenomena.

With regard to the A gene, we see that in their minimum limit Spaniards are separated by a frequency of 19 percent over blacks, while in the maximum limit this difference is less, achieving a frequency of 13 percent more in Spanish than in blacks. As for the Indians, except for the North American Blackfeet, Blood, and Piegan, there is really only one case of a maximum A frequency, equivalent to 36.52 percent (Mourant, Kopec, and Domaniewska-Sobczak 1958), among the Colla of South America. In the rest, the maximum incidence in Ibero-America reaches 17 percent, and in only two cases—the Pilagá of Argentina and the Araucanians of Chile.

With regard to the B gene, in its minimum limit the black group shows a frequency 16 percent greater than the Spanish group, and a 15 percent greater frequency than the Spanish in the maximum limit. By contrast, among the Indians the usual maximum frequencies of B approach 5 percent. There are two important exceptions: one, the Tenetehara (Maranhão, Brazil), with an incidence of 16.67 percent, and the other, the Carajá (Maranhão, Brazil), with 50.82 percent. Both incidences of B constitute a unique phenomenon whose cause cannot be shown through available data. It must be mentioned, however, that the Maranhão region of Brazil has undergone heavy racial mixing through black individuals, which increases the likelihood that a large part of the high incidence of B that we have mentioned may be due to the participation of Negro components in the Indian genotypes. Nevertheless, in principle this would not be a sufficient participation, since the Negro groups in general do not achieve such a high frequency of B. For this case, we know of but two exceptions: the Swahili and the Boni, both from Kenya, with a 46 and 50 percent incidence, respectively, of the B phenotype (ibid.).

Genetic Distributions

When we examine the genetic values and their relative incidence among the natives of America, we can observe that the O phenotype exhibits a lower frequency in North America than in Central and South America. It is even true that in certain native groups of North America—the Blackfeet, Blood, and Piegan—the incidence of the O gene is less than 25 percent, while, by contrast, the incidence of the A gene is very high, as can be seen in table 12.4.

There are very few populations with an A incidence of higher than 60 percent. Mourant, Kopec, and Domaniewska-Sobczak (1958) present only 35 cases out of some 1,100 populations, which represents a sample world relative incidence of 3.18 percent. These frequencies of A among the Indians of North America, as we see in the previous table, are exceeded only by the Australian aborigines. Also, the populations with the highest incidence of A appear in the islands of the Pacific, but especially in Australia, with the exception of Kaiserstuhl, Germany. A high specific incidence of the A phenotype therefore constitutes a relevant problem of anthropology.

The high frequencies of A that appear among the Blackfeet, Blood, and Piegan constitute an exception to the high incidence of the O phenotype, which generally produces frequencies of greater than 60 percent. These facts pose an anthropological problem that, in principle, admits two causal possibilities: (1) that we are dealing only culturally with Indian populations that are biologically mestizo, or (2) that we are dealing with Indian populations both biologically and culturally. In the first instance, we would need to establish which ethnic groups have been in contact with those populations, as well as their specific phenotypes and the nature of their historicocultural relations. In the second, we would have to determine whether we are dealing with a phenotype system that has become differentiated through adaptive specialization based on genotypes similar to or different from those exhibited by the other native populations of North America. Nevertheless, the most important fact about the exception mentioned above is definitely the high frequency of the A gene, to the exclusion—when it is indicated that they are

Table 12.4 ABO System

	Number	O	A	B	AB
INDIGENOUS ETHNIC GROUPS:					
Blackfeet (Western Canada)	123	15.40	83.70	0.00	0.80
"Pure" Blackfeet (Montana, USA)	115	23.50	76.50	0.00	0.00
Blackfeet (Montana, USA)	394	23.00	77.00	0.00	0.00
Blackfeet (Montana, USA)	103	24.27	74.76	0.00	0.97
Blackfeet (Montana, USA)	176	20.50	78.40	0.00	1.10
Blood (Montana, USA)	69	17.40	81.20	0.00	1.40
Blood (Montana, USA)	24	16.70	83.30	0.00	0.00
Blood (Montana, USA)	105	19.00	80.00	0.00	1.00
Piegan (Alberta, Canada)	42	19.00	80.90	0.00	0.00
Slave (MacKenzie, Canada)	41	36.00	64.00	0.00	0.00
EXCEPTIONS[a]**:**					
"Pure" Indians of Alberta and Montana (except Blackfeet)	182	72.50	25.20	1.10	1.10
Beaver and Slave Indians (North of Alberta, Canada)	128	71.80	27.30	0.70	0.00
OTHER NON-AMERICAN GROUPS:					
"Pure" Australian Aborigines	28	14.29	85.71	0.00	0.00
Australian Aborigines	22	4.55	95.45	0.00	0.00
Australian Aborigines	36	11.11	88.89	0.00	0.00
Kaiserstuhl (Baden-Würtember, West Germany)	139	17.27	75.54	7.19	0.00

NOTE [a]We refer to exceptions among natives of the same region.

racially "pure"—of the B gene, although in some cases, such as those in Alberta and Montana, the latter character appears.

The extraordinary incidence of the A gene in the three native groups mentioned is what makes the genetic phenomenon that concerns us so distinctive; this is a unique phenomenon that few populations approach and only the Australians surpass.

Because of their anthropological importance, these phenomena call for methodological observations. In this sense, it is important to stress that in those cases where the incidence of the O gene among the native groups is very low, ethnohistorical research has played a very minor role when there has been an attempt to establish the degree of relative isolation and therefore of the purity maintained by the Indian tribes or populations under consideration. Thus, for example, when we consider the relative incidence of the O phenotype among some Eskimo populations, we also observe that the percentages of O increase in small and isolated groups, which alerts us to proceed with certain caution when estimating the specific question of racial purity. This seems to be indicated by the fact that when we consider other samples made from Indians in the same region, that is, Alberta and Montana, we can observe that the incidence of A is rather low, and in this case that of the O gene is high. We can confirm this latter phenomenon among the Beaver and Slave Indians of northern Alberta.

It is also true that ethnohistorical research has defined its problems better in Ibero-America than in North America, principally because historical concern and preparation are greater among Ibero-American anthropologists than among the North Americans. This is due to the fact that in Ibero-American countries there is a longer historical tradition, with support in the humanities, and that the supply of resources relating to these problems is more abundant. In addition, the Ibero-American countries have developed a greater interest in ethnohistorical reconstructions, not only in the field of anthropology itself, but also in history as a separate discipline. In the case of field serology, it is equally true that most researchers interested in human racial study are not truly ethnologists capable of conducting their own adequate appraisal of ethnohistorical data. Except for a very few cases of interdisciplinary collaboration, field serology has not shown a great interest in determining the cultural relations maintained by the human groups under consideration. In this sense, Ibero-American serologists have operated with more intensive concern for this type of data and have demonstrated this concern by using a certain amount of ethnological material.

In some serological studies of North America where the ethnic identification is accompanied by the additional observation of "pure" Indians, a detailed investigation of the problem would likely lead us to acknowledge the existence of a historical phenomenon fundamental to this type of inquiry: the racial mixture between Indians and Europeans that took place during the time of the "frontier." This would be a slowly declining type of mixture, especially as European colonization took hold, a colonization based on settlement by families, a type of settlement that made the Europeans self-sufficient. *Racial mixing on the frontier* has been obscured by a characteristic attitude, which we may call "racial hypocrisy," and which consisted of whites practicing a furtive sexual exchange with the North American Indians with the latter's approval or social consensus on this relation.

With the problem thus stated, it would be useful to turn to the study of the role played in racial mixing by unmarried European males, or those acting substantially as such, who carried out the sexual exchange with the natives of North America in the capacity of *men of the frontier* free from the institutional controls of their own society. This *racial mixing on the frontier* would be one where the mestizo was absorbed by the maternal culture, if we take into account that the mother represented the continuity or permanence of the native culture, since she almost never abandoned her own society when she entered into relations with a European. The latter, in contrast, because of his very situational instability, seldom took on the role of sustaining a mestizo family. In this way, while there were changes in the genetic factors of the Indian population through their mestizo descendants, the ways of life of these societies remained basically the same, at least in their aspects of structural or sociopolitical integrity.

For the purposes of scientific observation, and lacking systematic knowledge of these phenomena—as in the case of serological research about which we commented—we might conclude that these North American Indian societies could have seemed "pure" without being so, whether culturally or biologically. In that case, the sociocultural isolation of many North American Indian populations could have been greater than their biological isolation. According to this, there would have been thousands of European individuals who practiced their sexual exchange on the frontier with Indian women, by which, evidently, they modified the original genetic components of the Indian population, as did the Spanish and the Portuguese in their turn to the south of Anglo-America. In the case of North America, the genetic modification could have been quite large, especially if we consider the low density of the native population and the relatively considerable flow of sexually active European population that came into contact with it.

With regard to Ibero-America, to whose racial mixing we refer, there seems to be a significant relation between the high incidence of O and the specific nativeness of its population. In well-established cases of isolation, the

O gene reaches an incidence of 100 percent. Santiana (1953, 62) has emphasized, however, that even in the most isolated of native populations the three
genes of the cases in which the O phenotype has an absolute value are due
to the low number of individuals examined, as occurs with native populations on the verge of extinction; when a minimum of 250 cases are studied,
then the A and B phenotypes appear.

It is also true that, as long as we have not established sufficiently the problem of racial specialization in a given gene—the O in this case—based on
the occurrence of the A and B genes in native populations of Ibero-America,
we must be prudent in regard to postulating the thesis of a universal genetic
homotype as a serological distinguisher of the American Indian. In effect,
most of the larger native populations exhibit the three phenotypes, although
some of them, independent of whether a small number of races have been
examined and whether their relative biocultural isolation is greater or lesser,
give an absolute incidence of 100 percent of the O gene. Nor is it clear in
any case whether native populations with an incidence of A and B phenotypes constitute clusters isolated from all mixtures with Europeans and African for nearly four hundred fifty years.[3] This is still an unsolved question and
one that prevents us, at present, from being categorical in our affirmation of
a native genetic homotype. Nevertheless, when serological research turns to
cultural data and employs historical criticism, it tends to demonstrate that the
relative incidence of the O gene should be the point of departure for the
determination of specific racial mixture, while it also reveals that the native
populations have been affected enormously in the manifestation of their phenotype because of their contact with other racial groups. In Colombia, for
example, certain references (cf. Layrisse, Layrisse, and Wilbert 1963, 46–49)
to the degree of racial mixture in the population of certain native areas of
that country allow us to distinguish clearly the importance of the genetic
exchange that took place among the three base racial groups in racial mixing in Ibero-America, even in populations that are culturally indigenous
yet have maintained a specific genetic exchange with Hispanic and black
ethnicities. Table 12.5 illustrates the characteristics of this exchange and its
relative frequency.

At any rate, only in a few cases, which many experts[4] who share in the
thesis of this work attribute to the influence of racial mixture, does the relative incidence of the O phenotype remain below 60 percent. The proportions of the A and B phenotypes increase in mestizo groups and, of course,
are greater among Caucasians and Negroes when compared separately with
those established by the natives. In the turn of indigenous Americans, if it is
said that they present some type of acculturation, in the majority of cases
some degree of mestizo formation is implicit (Stern 1956, 546). Even some

Table 12.5 Colombia: Percentage of Genetic Components Contributed
by Each Racial Group to Racial Mixture

	Caucasian	Negro	Indian
ETHNICITY OR INDIGENOUS GROUP:			
Páez (Central Cordillera)	12.0	12.0	76.0
Ica de San Sebastián (Northeast)	12.0	0.0	88.0
Turebo (Eastern Cordillera)	5.0	0.0	95.0

of those who live in relative isolation, which could include the Fuegians
[Tierra del Fuego], manifest a high percentage of nonindigenous phenotype
incidences (Pourchet 1963, 144). In any case, perhaps we can never say the
final word on this problem of the relative purity of each racial group in Ibero-
America because we have not had available the historicocultural controls
similar to those that Shapiro (1954) could utilize in the study that he made of
hybridization on Pitcairn Island. Still, we can avail ourselves of a key point of
reference to determine the relative degree of hybridization in Ibero-America.
Such is the case when we turn to the comparative incidence of the O gene
in the racial populations that form the basis of racial mixing in Ibero-
America. The table of genetic frequencies relating to a certain number of
native societies—144 groups—distributed within a wide geographical spectrum, indicates precisely that the O gene constitutes the characteristic phenotype of those populations. The extraordinary incidence of this component
even leads us to consider it a racial specialization inherent in the American
Indians. Thus, it contributes to explaining the incidence of other phenotypes
of the ABO system in the natives as being due to genetic exchange with the
other non-Indian populations or ethnicities (table 12.6). This latter phenomenon would not have been controlled historically in the case of serological studies.

Because of these frequencies of the O gene in the native populations, and
as a consequence of the fact that its frequency is significantly different when
compared to those exhibited by European and African groups, we can state
generally that the higher the incidence of the O gene—from 50 percent on
up—the greater is the contribution made by that Indian group to the population of Ibero-America. In this case, when the incidence of the O gene is
greater than 65 percent the racial mixture is predominantly indigenous,

whereas when the incidence is close to or somewhat lower than that percentage, it can be interpreted to involve a miscegenation that is relatively balanced with regard to its genetic proportions. By contrast, when the incidence of the O gene is close to or below 60 percent, then we can make the initial conclusion that we are dealing with a racial mixture with a Hispanic or Portuguese predominance, according to the case (table 12.7).

According to the phenotype distributions shown in table 12.7, which refers to mestizo population clusters, we can draw a certain initial number of conclusions. The distributions for Mexico indicate that the incidences of the O phenotype increase from north to south, that is, as we pass from the areas of low native population density to others where it is greatly elevated. Actually, the most balanced genetic composition, from the viewpoint of proportions contributed, occurs in central Mexico, a region that biologically can be considered highly mestizo. By contrast, the north—because of its historico-cultural characteristics, notably its low population density in pre-Hispanic times and later heavy Spanish settlement—constitutes the region of greatest European racial mixture in Mexico. Southern Mexico and Guatemala are noted for a great native predominance in racial mixing; it is exceptionally high because the European settlements have developed little here in comparison with those of the center and north of Mexico. This low density of the European element in biological mixing would be due essentially to the meager attraction that the tropics offered to the Spanish, as well as to the lesser need to control the area geopolitically for the purposes of economics and power, as was the case in the central highlands and the north.

Although we had no specific serological data available for the rest of Central America, some of them are significant. One, relating to El Salvador, points toward the fact that this nation, along with central Mexico and Paraguay, is probably the region with the greatest harmony in the genetic balance of its population, since, as Fleischhacker points out (1962, 771–72), the O gene shows an incidence approaching 60 percent, although in the extreme cases represented by Spaniards and Indians the incidence is 37 and 93 percent, respectively. By contrast, Costa Rica, considered in terms of its general population, exhibits a Hispanic predominance, as shown by the fact that the occurrence of the O gene is 52.54 percent. This figure is closer to the Hispanic model than to the Indian.

Along the Pacific slope of South America we observe a genetic mixture with indigenous predominances, except for Chile, where the European genetic frequencies are greater than the native ones. In Santiago de Chile, nevertheless, the population, though heterogeneous, features strong native inputs that doubtless were greater in the times preceding the great influx of

Table 12.6 ABO Genetic Frequencies Among Natives[a]

	No.	O	A	B	AB
MEXICO:					
North	241	233	5	3	
		97.6%	2.2%	1.2%	
Center	544	474	50	15	5
		87.1%	9.2%	2.8%	0.9%
TOTALS	785	707	55	18	5
		90.1%	7.0%	2.2%	0.6%
SOUTHERN MEXICO AND GUATEMALA:					
Southern Mexico	1,728	1,636	64	23	5
		94.7%	3.7%	1.3%	0.3%
Guatemala	664	627	28	8	1
		94.4%	4.2%	1.2%	0.2%
TOTALS	2,392	2,263	92	31	6
		94.6%	3.8%	1.3%	0.2%
ANDEAN AMERICA:					
Colombia	4,565	4,173	234	136	22
		91.4%	5.1%	3.0%	0.5%
Ecuador	25,471	24,297	855	263	56
		95.4%	3.4%	1.0%	0.2%
Peru	2,832	2,509	258	62	3
		88.6%	9.1%	2.2%	0.1%
Bolivia	100	82	13	4	1
		82.0%	13.0%	4.0%	1.0%
Chile	587	467	86	30	4
		79.6%	14.6%	5.1%	0.7%
TOTALS	33,555	31,528	1,446	495	86
		93.9%	4.3%	1.5%	0.3%

Table 12.6 *(continued)*

	No.	O	A	B	AB
NORTH AND NORTHWEST ARGENTINA AND PARAGUAY:					
Argentina	2,502	2,303	163	23	13
		92.1%	6.5%	0.9%	0.5%
Paraguay	333	330	1	2	
		99.1%	0.3%	0.6%	
TOTALS	2,835	2,633	164	25	13
		92.9%	5.8%	0.9%	0.4%
MAINLAND TROPICAL REGION:					
Brazil	2,264	2,143	17	54	50
		94.7%	0.7%	2.4%	2.2%
Surinam	335	326	4	5	
		97.3%	1.2%	1.5%	
Venezuela	751	749	1	1	
		99.8%	0.1%	0.1%	
TOTALS	3,350	3,218	22	60	50
		96.1%	0.7%	1.8%	1.4%

NOTE [a] These are figures whose averages we have analyzed on the basis of the serological data available to us for their preparation, references for which are found in the bibliography.

European populations—that is, during the time when the genetic exchanges were manifested between the formative ethnic groups, the Araucanian and the Spanish. The native frequencies in Chile are less important than those in the rest of Andean America, particularly the high plains at greater altitudes. There, the frequencies of the O gene increase, which reinforces the idea that access or flow into the high plains by European populations has halted, especially because of the climatic rigors imposed on physiological adaptation by Europeans in those regions. In this sense, in what Monge termed "climatic hostility," the Andean high plains have constituted the greatest obstacle to mestizo formation significant on a biological scale. The climatic environment has overcome the relative capacity for penetration by the European.

Table 12.7 ABO Genetic Frequencies in Mestizos
and General Populations

	No.	O	A	B	AB
MEXICO (MESTIZOS):					
North	338	200	95	40	3
		59.2%	28.1%	11.8%	0.9%
Center	3,184	1,832	1,045	222	85
		57.5%	32.8%	7.0%	2.7%
South	1,810	1,453	259	84	14
		80.3%	14.3%	4.6%	1.4%
TOTALS	5,332	3,485	1,399	346	102
		65.4%	26.2%	6.5%	1.9%
COSTA RICA (GENERAL):					
	10,000	5,254	3,114	1,323	309
		52.54%	31.14%	13.23%	3.09%
ANDEAN AMERICA (MESTIZOS):					
Colombia	1,597	1,162	328	95	12
		72.7%	20.5%	6.0%	0.7%
Ecuador	2,495	1,580	680	185	50
		63.3%	27.3%	7.4%	2.0%
Peru	10,426	7,333	2,023	918	152
		70.3%	19.4%	8.8%	1.5%
Bolivia	392	245	119	26	2
		62.5%	30.4%	6.6%	0.5%
Chile	18,113	10,118	5,542	1,925	528
		55.9%	30.6%	10.6%	2.9%
TOTALS	33,023	20,438	8,692	3,149	744
		61.9%	26.3%	9.5%	2.3%

Table 12.7 (*continued*)

	No.	O	A	B	AB
PARAGUAY, ARGENTINA AND URUGUAY (NON-INDIAN):					
	845	470	289	73	13
		55.6%	34.2%	8.7%	1.5%
Argentina	120,617	59,375	45,248	12,378	3,616
		49.2%	37.5%	10.3%	3.0%
Uruguay	25,597	11,726	10,703	2,327	841
		45.8%	41.8%	9.1%	3.3%
TOTALS	147,059	71,571	56,240	14,778	4,470
		48.7%	38.2%	10.0%	3.0%
MAINLAND TROPICAL REGION [a] (MESTIZOS):					
Brazil	588	404	133	40	11
		68.7%	22.6%	6.8%	1.9%
Venezuela	12,776	6,796	4,027	1,514	439
		53.2%	31.5%	11.9%	3.4%
TOTALS	13,364	7,200	4,160	1,554	450
		53.9%	31.1%	11.6%	3.4%
ANTILLES (NON-INDIAN):					
Dominican Republic	2,063	1,088	616	283	76
		52.7%	29.9%	13.7%	3.7%
Cuba	527	241	201	70	15
		45.7%	38.1%	13.3%	2.9%
Jamaica	144	67	42	32	3
		46.5%	29.2%	22.2%	2.1%
Guadeloupe	2,530	1,231	735	485	79
		48.6%	29.1%	19.2%	3.1%
Martinique	2,173	1,120	622	384	47
		51.5%	28.6%	17.7%	2.2%
TOTALS	7,437	3,747	2,216	1,254	220
		50.4%	29.8%	16.8%	3.0%

NOTE [a] We have no data available for Surinam concerning the general population, much less its racial mixtures.

The few European types who have reached this milieu have been absorbed by the native ethnicity. As we descend from the Andean high plains toward the western coasts, the European and African proportions increase accordingly. Notwithstanding this fact, biological mixing in Andean America, as elsewhere in the civilized centers of America, is manifested principally in the urban areas.

When we contemplate the data for the Atlantic region of the Río de la Plata and the tropical zone to the north, we observe first that the numbers for the Europeans increase until they seem almost absolute, and the same occurs in Brazil and Venezuela, although in those countries we note a greater native contribution.

The European numbers remain high in the islands that constitute the Dominican Republic and Cuba, while we can observe a clear black predominance through the B phenotype in the other islands of the Antilles.

→   →   →

Of course, the consideration of biological mixing according to genetic incidences is an indicator of the relative proportion that each racial group represents in current ethnic aggregations, but such data are still insufficient. In this sense, it is very important to approach the problem from the perspective of the inputs or contributions made by each racial group to given populations, since in such calculations we appreciate the specific importance achieved by the process of mestizo formation. Some studies relating to this problem prove to be extremely interesting.

Thus, in Venezuela Layrisse has emphasized the following conclusions, upon consideration of the relative incidence of native blood in hybrid populations of Venezuela where the ethnic base is variable (table 12.8):

Table 12.8 Venezuela (1958)

Community	Proportion of Native Blood (%)
Curiepe (Negro base)	23.3
Ciudad Bolívar (Caucasian base)	22.3
Caracas (Caucasian base)	6.3
Fajardo, Margarita Island (Native base)	40.6

The results reflected by these authors point, above all, toward the fact that in Venezuela the Atlantic coast and urbanized areas constitute points of European concentration, with certain significant African inputs. In addition, the black proportion has continued to shrink as a consequence of the constant immigration of European populations in recent years. This phenomenon of shrinkage is also true in the case of the native proportions, which decline significantly when compared with the absolute numbers of the European population. Thus, in a gradual way, Venezuela is becoming a mestizo population, but one with a predominance of European genetic components. Additionally, in the small populations with a large initial native base, such as Fajardo, the latter components remain high, although there is important participation by Hispanics, 46.11 percent, and less by blacks—12.64 percent (Layrisse, Wilbert, and Arends 1958, 312).

With regard to Brazil, the specific proportions of each genetic characteristic that appear in the racial mixtures vary, owing especially to the different historicocultural circumstances of the ethnic settlements made in each region. In this case, although the settlements made by the Portuguese and Africans led to rapid and intensive miscegenations between the two and with the Indians, those created after the advent of the Republic maintain a slower pace of mestizo formation, and, by contrast, the European ethnicities take longer to adopt a psychology favorable to racial mixture. This psychology of reluctance toward miscegenation as a form of life is favored by the fact that the greater numbers of the European Caucasian populations allow their members to be sexually self-sufficient within their own racial or ethnic group. Furthermore, the numerical weight of each racial contribution is a most important factor to consider in the nature and biocultural qualities of each miscegenation.

Thus, the African influence has been important in the northeast and in Bahía. In the latter region, and in the interior of the country, there was also a considerable crossing of Indians with Africans, whereas in the South there is increasing miscegenation between blacks and Caucasians (Pourchet 1963). Saldanha (1957, 754, 113) has established the relative importance of each genetic contribution by considering the contributions made by each racial group to racial mixing in the northeast of Brazil, based on the base populations of Portuguese, Africans, and Indians. In his estimate there is a certain white predominance, though the black participation is considerable, as we can observe in the data in table 12.9.

The same author (ibid.) also calculated at some 40 percent the accumulation of non-African genes present in the black population of Porto Alegre (see also the work of Tondo, Mundt, and Salzano [1963, 330]). This would be due basically to the gradual increase in Caucasian participation in racial

Table 12.9 Northeastern Brazil

Ethnicity or Racial Group:	%
Caucasian	48.00
Negro	34.00
Indian	18.00

exchange. Collectively, the genetic contribution made by the white group to the mulatto population of that country is 40 percent after twelve generations (Saldanha 1957, 308), with an accumulation of Caucasian blood amounting to 4.5 to 5 percent per generation (Layrisse, Wilbert, and Arends 1958, 314). In addition, the proportion of Negro elements in the Brazilian mulatto has been estimated by Da Silva (Glass 1954, 116) at between 32.3 and 52.7 percent, although Boyd (1950) calculated it at 50.8 percent. There was also a calculation of the relative quantity of Caucasian components introduced into the Indian population of Mato Grosso, and among the "purest" population the result was between 13.8 and 23.3 percent, whereas among the most mixed it reached a much higher proportion: 76.7 percent (Glass 1954, 116–17).

The Indian component in Brazilian racial mixture is important from the State of Bahía to Amazonas, and it increases as we move from east to west (Saldanha 1962, 184). Meanwhile, the black component in the total Brazilian population is between 40 and 50 percent, and the white component, at 40 percent in the north and at 60 percent in the south is, on average, 50 percent. The contribution of the black component is largely a stable one, whereas that of the white component varies due to the fact that it is replaced by the Indian component, especially in the populations of the northeast (Saldanha 1962b, 185).

The mixture of blacks with Indians has been extensive in the states of the north, especially in Ceará and Maranhão, while in the southern states there is little miscegenation of this type, particularly because the Indian population is sparse (Saldanha 1962a, 115).

If we consider the fact that the European populations that have come to southern Brazil in recent years are initially hostile to racial mixing with blacks (Saldanha 1957, 302), we become aware that the European genetic proportions in the generations of the south will tend to increase in the immediate future, especially as a racial population considered separately from the others.

This is more true to the degree that they are sexually self-sufficient populations, as is the case today. In this sense, Saldanha (ibid.) has pointed out that in the states of the south racial mixing was very frequent until 1872, a date that marks the beginning of the great immigrations of other non-Portuguese peoples who were less favorable toward miscegenation. Of course, hybridization in Brazil is now greater than it was before the freeing of the slaves, although, as Saldanha emphasizes (ibid., 307), where there are Portuguese, hybridization reaches a higher frequency.

According to table 12.10, there is no doubt that contributions to Brazilian racial mixing are made in very balanced proportions by Caucasian and Negro groups, although their frequencies vary according to the region involved, since, as we have said, in the south the Caucasian proportion is smaller than that in the northeast.

As we can gather from the ethnological knowledge acquired up to now regarding the relative characteristics and distribution of the cultures and ethnicities that inhabit regions of Ibero-America, and depending on the relative frequencies manifested by the A and B phenotypes, that racial mixture can also have a Negro character in certain areas where black populations are known to be numerically important. In general, a decline in the values of the O phenotype causes an increase particularly in the incidence of the A, and this fact can be identified with the greater participation of the Iberian component in the majority of cases, although, as we have stated, the Negro racial component can be important in certain areas, especially when it is manifested through the B phenotype.

Apart from the specific regional densities exhibited by biological mixing

Table 12.10 Brazil: Percentage of Genetic Components Contributed by Each Racial Group to Racial Mixture

Population, Ethnicity for Racial Group	Cauca-sian	Negro	Indian	Author or Researcher
Brazil (total)	50	40.0–50.0		Saldanha, 1962b
Mulatto (total)		32.8–52.7		Silva, 1949
Mulatto (total)		50.8		Glass, 1954
Pure (?) Indians of Mato Grosso	13.8			Glass, 1954
Pure (?) Indians of Mato Grosso	23.3			Glass, 1954
Mestizo Indians of Mato Grosso	76.7			Pourchet, 1963

in Ibero-America, it is also true, according to our data, that in urban locales this density largely approaches the European, Negro, and Indian values, in each case according to the related historicocultural or settlement tradition, which we have already considered, although we can perceive that the European genetic proportions predominate, approaching hybrid equilibrium, in the Andean region. We can observe this characteristic by contemplating table 12.11.

For the purpose of having a theoretical model that will serve as a point of reference for the relative identification of racial mixing, according to the genetic values and terms of frequency, we have prepared a table that, although a provisional effort, offers the most probable frequencies for the purposes of appreciating the relative incidence of each ABO phenotype in given Ibero-American populations. The frequencies represent statistical elaboration obtained by means of the analysis of the data available to us from Brazil, since the studies made in that country are more precise, from the ethnic viewpoint, than those of other countries. The base populations considered were adjusted to a sample of 2,264 individuals in each case, since this was the most accessible number for our purpose of establishing statistical proportions. In this sense, analysis was made of the data available for each racial group. In addition, the maximum frequencies—such as that of the O gene among small and isolated groups of Indians, often with an incidence of 100 percent—have been reduced as a consequence of the proportional analyses. The same is true of the minimum frequencies, at times with values of zero. In any case, the "pure" theoretical values, analyzed for each race or racial variety, would be slightly different from the outset. Nevertheless, it is important to keep in mind that the racial exchange carried out in Ibero-America affects the genetic composition of each one of the racial groups considered as a whole, so that, except for some native populations, it is difficult to represent "pure" genetic compositions, even based on a theoretical model. In general, the relative incidence of such genes will vary by region, but we do not believe that the specific differences will be particularly large with respect to the incidences we give here (table 12.12).

Having now described the perspective and situation of the biocultural characteristics of racial mixing in its concrete data, we think it important to determine its quantitative distribution by countries. For that, we turn to estimates based on the available census or demographic statistical elements, but we support our results especially with analyses relative to the genetic frequencies considered throughout this work. In general, it can be seen that the resultant figures maintain a close relation to the relative geographic distributions that we have already indicated in the course of the present study, such

Table 12.11 ABO Genetic Frequencies in Ibero-American Cities[a]

City	No.	O	A	B	AB
Mexico, D. F.	1,604	935	510	113	46
		58.3%	31.7%	7.1%	2.9%
Bogotá	943	663	222	51	7
		70.3%	23.6%	5.4%	0.7%
Quito	757	461	223	55	18
		60.9%	29.4%	7.3%	2.4%
Trujillo (Peru)	1,133	775	246	102	10
		68.4%	21.7%	9.0%	0.9%
Lima	100	69	21	10	0
		69.0%	21.0%	10.0%	0.0%
Cochabamba	158	81	59	16	2
		51.3%	37.3%	10.1%	1.3%
Santiago de Chile	15,764	8,790	4,982	1,640	352
		55.8%	31.6%	10.4%	2.2%
Asunción	845	470	289	73	13
		55.6%	34.2%	8.7%	1.5%
Córdoba (Argentina)	74,250	37,438	27,272	7,602	1,938
		50.4%	36.7%	10.3%	2.6%
Buenos Aires	40,161	18,620	15,792	4,207	1,542
		46.4%	39.3%	10.5%	3.8%
Montevideo	25,597	11,721	10,699	2,326	841
		45.8%	41.8%	9.1%	3.3%
São Paulo	27,528	13,076	10,617	2,829	1,006
		47.6%	38.5%	10.3%	3.6%
Caracas	472	248	147	48	29
		52.6%	31.1%	10.2%	6.1%
Havana	527	241	201	70	15
		45.7%	38.1%	13.2%	3.0%
San Juan (Puerto Rico)	429	209	166	41	13
		48.7%	38.7%	9.6%	3.0%

NOTE [a] These are analyzed averages.

Table 12.12 Table of ABO Genetic Frequencies (Theoretical Model)

Ethnicity	No.	O	A	B	AB
Indians	2,264	2,143	17	54	50
		94.7%	0.7%	2.4%	2.2%
Whites	2,264	1,096	800	261	107
		48.4%	35.4%	11.5%	4.75%
Blacks	2,264	1,166	575	441	82
		51.5%	25.4%	19.5%	3.6%
Triple mixture		64.8%	20.5%	11.1%	3.5%
Mestizos		71.5%	18.0%	7.0%	3.5%
Mulattoes		50.0%	30.3%	15.5%	4.2%
Zambos		73.1%	13.1%	10.9%	2.9%

that, in reality, the figures end up confirming them (see table 12.13 and maps 12.1, 12.2, 12.3, 12.4 and 12.5). As a whole, we can see that the mixed ethnicities or hybridizations between whites, Indians, and blacks represented the majority of the ethnicities on the continent, since they add up to something more than each of the other Ibero-American ethnicities considered separately. Nevertheless, the white group is in itself the most numerous one, and we may consider it to have the greatest sociocultural influence at present. Of course, the regional distribution of these influences is diverse, as we shall point out at the proper time.

Considered regionally, this ethnic distribution gives us the results shown in table 12.14 and fig. 12.1.

As we gather from the estimates made here, each one of the regions considered presents a different proportion of racial mixture. Most noteworthy is the presence of a predominant Indian-Spanish mixture in the Mexico-Central American region, not only from the viewpoint of the ethnicities taking part in it, but also with regard to the fact that the mestizos of that union constitute the majority population in those countries. These countries represent the most harmonic balance achieved by racial mixing, precisely because there, the racial exchange has been more open or receptive since the beginning of contacts between their formative ethnicities. They also constitute the countries with the greatest mestizo consciousness, and in this sense are the ones who have integrated their cultures into a mestizo melting pot.

In Andean America, the mestizo population is also the predominant

Table 12.13 Ethno-Racial Proportions in the Population of Ibero–America[a]

	Indians	Whites or Europeans	Mestizos	Blacks or Negroes[b]	Various[c]	Total
MAINLAND						
Mexico	3,030,254	1,821,525	29,393,240	34,625	346,259	34,625,903
	8.75%	5.27%	84.88%	0.1%	1.0%	
Guatemala	1,497,261	128,496	1,162,054	2,793	2,793	2,793,397
	53.6%	4.6%	41.6%	0.1%	0.1%	
Honduras	107,800	104,756	1,657,359	77,994	1,949	1,949,858
	5.52%	5.38%	85.0%	4.0%	0.1%	
El Salvador	100,000	265,285	2,126,070	5,002	4,902	2,501,259
	4.0%	10.6%	85.0%	0.2%	0.19%	
Nicaragua	43,000	73,549	1,294,135	58,839	1,470	1,470,993
	2.92%	5.0%	87.98%	4.0%	0.1%	
Costa Rica	8,000	653,911	556,748	12,372	6,186	1,237,217
	0.64%	52.86%	45.0%	1.0%	0.5%	
Panamá	62,187	325,010	430,216	247,374	10,754	1,075,541
	5.78%	30.22%	40.0%	23.0%	1.0%	
Colombia	250,000	4,696,800	7,092,664	3,600,880	15,656	15,656,000
	1.59%	30.0%	45.3%	23.0%	0.1%	
Ecuador	2,076,152	386,860	1,577,531	214,922	42,984	4,298,449
	48.3%	9.0%	36.7%	5.0%	1.0%	

(continues)

Table 12.13 (*continued*)

	Indians	Whites or Europeans	Mestizos	Blacks or Negroes[b]	Various[c]	Total
Peru	4,834,093	1,293,640	3,078,292	518,231	10,364	10,364,620
	46.64%	18.56%	29.7%	5.0%	0.1%	
Bolivia	2,180,738	235,738	1,038,600	3,462	3,462	3,462,000
	62.99%	6.8%	30.0%	0.1%	0.1%	
Chile	240,000	3,978,739	3,322,436		9,816	7,550,991
	3.17%	52.7%	44.0%		0.13%	
Argentina	130,000	18,939,996	1,886,043			20,959,039
	0.62%	90.38%	9.0%			
Paraguay	53,053	45,980	1,662,342	5,305	1,768	1,768,448
	3.0%	2.6%	94.0%	0.3%	0.1%	
Uruguay[d]	16,250	2,225,000	200,000	34,500	24,250	2,500,000
	0.65%	89.0%	8.0%	1.5%	0.97%	
Brazil	100,000	33,500,000	5,226,000	27,504,000	670,000	67,000,000
	0.15%	50.0%	7.8%	41.05%	1.0%	
Venezuela	108,823	2,113,379	3,698,748	771,551	16,638	6,709,139
	1.62%	31.5%	55.13%	11.5%	0.25%	
TOTALS	14,837,611	71,418,664	65,402,478	33,091,850	1,169,251	185,919,854
	8.0%	38.4%	35.2%	17.8%	0.6%	

Surinam	3,700 1.71%	2,283 1.05%	3,241 1.5%	102,501 47.4%	104,399 48.3%	216,124
ANTILLES						
Cuba	2,750 0.05%	3,773,000 68.6%	275,000 5.0%	1,430,000 26.0%	19,250 0.35%	5,500,000
Dominican Republic	2,250 0.1%	1,548,500 68.8%	382,000 17.0%	308,250 13.7%	9,000 0.4%	2,250,000
Haiti	3,000 0.1%	3,000 0.1%		2,994,000 99.8%		3,000,000
Jamaica		14,679 1.2%		1,164,525 95.2%	44,037 3.6%	1,223,241
Martinique	500 0.2%	2,000 0.8%		245,000 98.0%	2,500 1.0%	250,000
TOTALS	8,500	5,341,179	657,000	6,141,775	74,787	12,223,241

NOTES: [a] These estimates, based on calculations made by various authors, are broken down by countries and ethnicities. In addition, in some cases we have applied to the general population censuses the genetic proportions that emerge from the available data. The figures were calculated to reflect the 1962 population.

[b] This includes blacks, mulattoes, and zambos.

[c] This refers to other ethnicities, especially Asians, who were very important in certain countries, particularly in the British and Dutch colonies.

[d] Estimate.

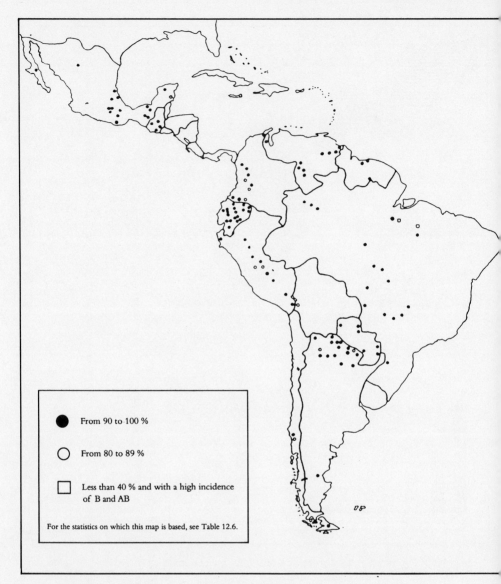

Map 12.1   Distribution of ABO genetic frequencies in native populations

From 90 to 100 %

From 80 to 89 %

Less than 40 % and with a high incidence
of B and AB

For the statistics on which this map is based, see Table 12.6.

Map 12.2   Frequencies of distribution of Indians by countries

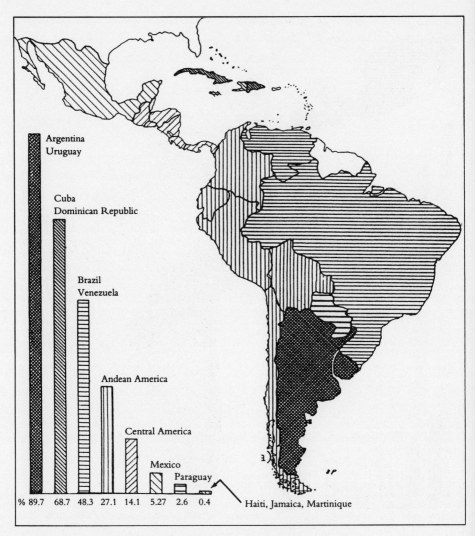

Map 12.3   Frequencies of distribution of Europeans by countries

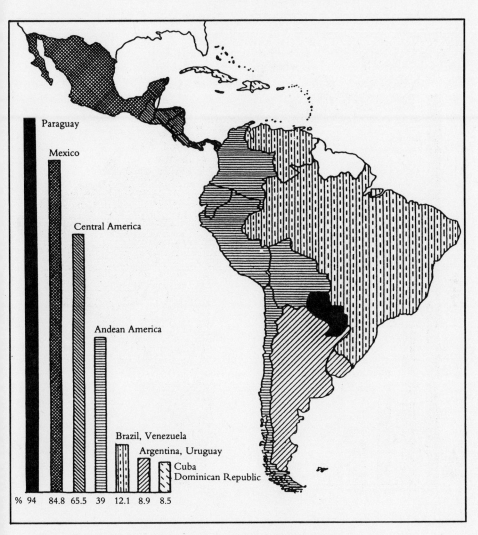

Map 12.4   Frequencies of distribution of mestizos by countries

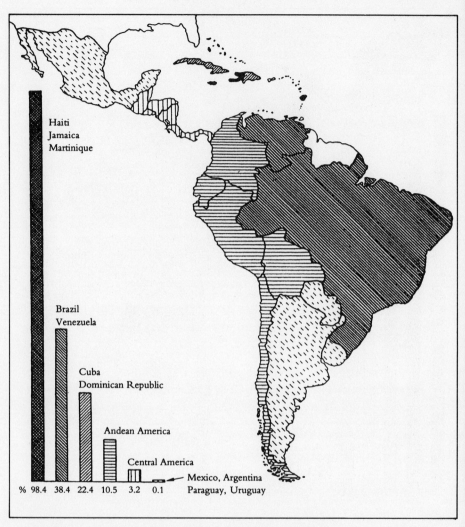

Map 12.5   Frequencies of distribution of blacks by countries

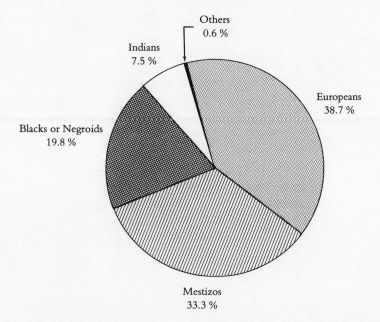

Others
0.6 %

Indians
7.5 %

Europeans
38.7 %

Blacks or Negroids
19.8 %

Mestizos
33.3 %

Figure 12.1   Ethnoracial proportions, Ibero-American mainland and Antilles

minority, but here both the European and the native minority constitute very important racial groups. In certain of these countries they seem to be the prevalent minorities. In general, Andean America has yet to integrate what we can call a mestizo model of life, and therefore it remains a region in the process of mestizo formation. This is a relatively slow process in the central high plains, especially in Ecuador, Peru, and Bolivia. Regarding this problem, we have already indicated the difficulties imposed upon biological mixing by the hostility of the climate, such that racial mixing in these countries will be produced, though slowly, through a process of urbanization that tends towards the intensive geographical displacement of great numbers of the population, mostly indigenous, and biological and cultural exchange between the various ethnic groups who make contact. In addition, the urbanization process in these countries assumes the launching of a demographic mobilization that will become the precipitator of racial mixture. We can further presume that the population exchange that that process foments will act as a dynamic agent with regard to racial mixing in the high plains. In this sense, the "climatic hostility" will be attenuated through the mestizo individuals who will be displaced toward the high plains and who will be the carriers of the national urban cultures. For the consummation of such an adaptive process, there can be no doubt that the mestizo of the intermediate areas is the most flexible individual, both culturally and biologically, and

Table 12.14 National and Regional Distribution of Racial Groups in America

Regions	Indians	Whites or Europeans	Mestizos	Blacks or Negroes[b]	Various[c]	Total
Canada	218,858	17,697,016	182,382	18,238	121,753	18,238,247
	1.20%	97.00%	1.00%	0.10%	0.70%	
United States	535,393	117,966,843	9,500,000	46,462,000	4,000,000	178,464,236
	0.30%	66.10%	5.32%	26.03%	2.24%	
Mexico	3,030,254	1,821,525	29,393,240	34,625	346,259	34,625,903
	8.75%	5.27%	84.88%	0.10%	1.00%	
Central America	1,818,248	1,551,007	7,226,585	404,374	28,054	11,028,265
	16.50%	14.10%	65.50%	3.70%	0.20%	
Andean America	9,580,983	11,221,777	16,109,523	4,337,495	82,282	41,332,060
	23.20%	27.10%	39.00%	10.50%	0.20%	

						Total
Paraguay, Argentina, and Uruguay	199,303	21,210,976	3,748,385	39,805	26,018	25,224,487
	0.80%	84.10%	14.90%	0.10%	0.10%	
Brazil and Venezuela	208,823	35,613,379	8,924,748	28,275,551	686,638	73,709,139
	0.30%	48.30%	12.10%	38.40%	0.90%	
Hispanic Antilles	5,000	5,321,500	657,000	1,738,250	28,250	7,750,000
	0.10%	68.70%	8.50%	22.40%	0.30%	
Non-Hispanic Antilles	3,500	19,679	[a]	4,403,525	46,537	4,473,241
	0.10%	0.40%		98.40%	1.00%	
TOTALS	15,600,362	212,423,702	75,741,860	85,713,863	5,365,791	394,845,578
	3.95%	53.79%	19.18%	21.70%	1.35%	

NOTES [a] Although there are populations of white and Indian mixture in the Lesser Antilles, we have not been able to discern them, precisely because they have been submerged within the total population. Nevertheless, their frequencies or percentages are rather significant.

[b] This includes blacks, mulattoes, and zambos.

[c] This refers to other ethnicities, especially Asians, who are very important in certain countries, particularly in the British and Dutch colonies.

therefore, it can be hoped that he will be at the same time the transmitter and the molder of mestizo creation in the high plains. The process in this case will be slower than that in the other regions of America. In this sense, Andean America is the region of most difficult access; but the development of urbanization and the expansion of national cultures from areas of lower altitude allows us to consider the expectation of intensive racial mixing in the future. At both ends of the region, Colombia and Chile, we behold an acceleration in the mestizo process, with a gradual European predominance in both countries, especially in the latter.

Racial mixing in Paraguay emerges as the most thorough of all that has taken place in the Ibero-American countries because the minorities found on its margins are quite small. By contrast, Argentina and Uruguay present a different perspective: in these countries, the European populations are expanding and tend toward the total absorption of the mestizo and native minorities within the next few years. Because of this, Argentina and Uruguay are the most characteristic examples of the transplantation of European ethnicities and their adaptation to a basically Hispanic culture. The absorption by this culture of the other European ethnicities, in this case, constitutes an example of its capacity for institutionalization.

The region of Ibero-America north of the Río de la Plata, represented particularly by Brazil and Venezuela, is predominantly white, but it is unquestionably influenced by a very significant black and Negro minority. This region has been favorable to the adaption of the latter racial group, but for historicocultural reasons that we have already mentioned—especially that of a policy of immigration with its growth into enormous proportions of European inputs—it is manifesting a process of absorption of black, Negro, and native ethnicities within a racial mixture in which the European input will continue in significance. In this sense, the white European group constitutes the most important minority, and its numbers can be expected to increase.

In the Antilles the process of racial mixing is clearly one with a European-African base, but as we have pointed out, there is a *Hispanic mode* in the Greater Antilles and an *African mode* in the Lesser Antilles. In the former, this process of Hispanicization has practically concluded, and the black minority is on its way toward mestizo integration in the biological sphere. By contrast, in the Lesser Antilles and Haiti there is an evident increase in Negroization, precisely because of the isolation to which the African ethnicities have been subjected. Given this situation, separate ethnic integrations tend to emerge—European, Asian, and African—whose simultaneous presence without fusion or racial mixture will lead to serious conflicts in the future. We can consider this aspect of social contradiction practically eliminated in the countries of Hispanic integration, although in Trinidad, for example, there are indications pointing toward the formation of a multiracial mixture (Crowley 1957, 820).

The most significant phenomenon of the ethnoracial figures that we are discussing is, then, the manifestation of a European-African development in the Atlantic regions, that is, in those areas facing the sea of European geopolitics. Meanwhile, this development assumes other qualities in the Pacific regions, because there, we contemplate a European-Indian biocultural version. For this reason, we can expect the development and expansion of different mestizo formulas along both oceanic slopes. In the Atlantic region, the lack of support for black-African cultures with regard to their continuity and historical vitality tilted the perspective in favor of the Ibero-European. On the Pacific shore of South America the situation is different, because this development appears as a Hispanic-Indian biocultural combination, where the continuity of the native traditions and ethnicities lends important support to the creation of mestizo ways of life, ways in which both the Hispanic and the indigenous share prestige and cultural elements that act as functional integrators. The socialization of the individuals who live along the Pacific slope of South America thus involves the amalgamation of Hispanic-Indian cultures, operating at different intensities according to the areas of their milieu of action (see map 12.6).

Accordingly, it can be expected that, once the process of racial mixing along the Pacific slope has concluded, the resulting institutions and ways of life will have an integration that is culturally more mestizo than that of the Atlantic slope. The sure reason for this phenomenon is likely given by that historicocultural fact that we emphasized at the beginning: that the civilized centers of pre-Hispanic America were located in that region, and therefore, that the content of the biocultural alloy that resulted had to be mestizo. By contrast, on the Atlantic slope the ethnic melting pot is Iberian and revolves around the integration of its cultural contents. Racial mixing with Negro ethnicities is the distinguishing feature here, but the cultural influence of the latter in the ways of life of today's populations is comparatively much less than that exerted by the natives on the other coast. As a consequence, the development of the Iberian model would be more vigorous in the Atlantic and relatively weaker in the Pacific, especially as the native substratum continues to emerge in the latter area, and as the members of that substratum take on the aggressivity engendered by confidence in their own means and continuity in their own population numbers.

As we see, racial mixing will continue acquiring different proportions in each of the regions considered. The geopolitics of this mixture will be more European in the Atlantic area than in the Pacific, except in the southern part of the latter. This difference will be true for biological as well as cultural

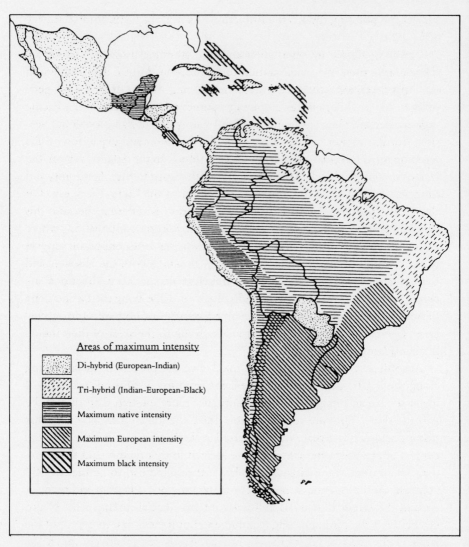

Map 12.6   Geographic distribution of ethnoracial intensities

mixing and will include the development of different political models that in each case can lead to peculiar philosophical developments. We interpret the process of mestizo formation within this perspective, and within that same perspective we can now begin to note a different integration, one significant for its ideology and concept of life, but especially for its historical and future creation.

NOTES

Translator's Note

1. For a key discussion of the full meaning of the term, see Gordon Willey, "The Prehistoric Civilizations of Nuclear America," *American Anthropologist* 57, no.3 (June 1955): 571–93.

Chapter 1: Concepts

1. For some of these problems, see Esteva 1957, 218, and Case 1948.
2. Esteva, *El biculturalismo como contexto del bilingüismo,* 1978.

Chapter 2: Acculturation and Racial Mixing

1. Studies by Redford, Linton, and Herskovits (1936); Herskovits (1938); Barnett (1953); Beals (1953); S.S.R.C. (1954); Siegel (1955); and Malinowski (1961), among others, are discussions that must be cited, but given their very general nature, they are insufficient for our purposes.

2. [*Encomenderos* were the grantees of encomiendas. See note below. Trans.]

3. Actually, they are the only social scientists who are doing this type of research. Thus, we maintain that the inadequacy is attributable to the problems of the scientific development of anthropology, where self-criticism attempts to minimize the relative deficiencies of the method used while increasing the volume of its analytical instrumentation. Additionally, anthropology is the first (social science) to have perceived the importance of studying social processes derived from the dynamics of cultural change.

4. This diffusionist focus is common among prehistorians concerned with cultural comparison, and among some ethnologists who subscribe to the historicocultural method.

5. [*Encomiendas* originally were royal grants of Indian tribute to Spanish colonists, who in turn were to Christianize and protect their native charges. In practice the system was much abused by the grantees, or encomenderos, and became an institution of virtual enslavement. Trans.]

6. The description and analysis of the Spanish institutional regime in America, as well as of those aspects related to some of the problems we are discussing, features an extensive bibliography, to which we refer the reader. Especially valuable are the stud-

ies of Céspedes (1957); Hernández Sánchez-Barba (1963); Ots Capdequí (1940, 1941, 1945, and 1959); Pérez Bustamante (1941); Pérez de Tudela (1956); and Zavala (1936, 1944).

7. In this macrostructural concept we should include the new religious organization of certain indigenous groups, with significant changes in the institutional order, theocratic and founded spiritually upon Catholicism.

8. [*Villas* were medium-size communities in the Spanish colonial system, larger than *pueblos* (towns or villages) but smaller than *ciudades* (cities). Trans.]

9. Of particular importance are the works of Adams (1956 and 1958); Beals (1953a); Gillin (1948, 1949, 1955); Nicholson (1955); Oberg (1955); Simons (1955); Wagley (1955); Willey (1955), and Wolf (1956). In each case they analyze regional aspects of Ibero-American and pre-Columbian society and culture with a tendency toward typification.

10. For example, *El Exilio español en México* (Mexico City: Fondo de Cultura Económica, 1982); Ascensión H. de León-Portilla, *España desde México* (UNAM), and others that have been published along these same lines.

11. For a discussion of these problems, see Steward 1958, 46ff.

12. Some of these methodological problems have also been discussed by Steward (1955, 9ff.).

Chapter 3: Historical Overview

1. [The term *nuclear America* is used by some authorities. Trans.]

2. [*Reducciones* or *Reducciones de indios* were concentrated settlements of mission Indians. Trans.]

Chapter 4: The Process and Context of Racial Mixing

1. [The Lucayan Islands were the colonial name for the present-day Bahamas. Trans.]

2. [*Altiplano* refers to the high plateaus of the Andes. Trans.]

3. [*Chicha* is a fermented corn drink. Trans.]

4. [*Ayllu* was the traditional kin group or subtribe of ancient Peru. Trans.]

5. See, specifically, Esteva, 1970, 1970a, 1970b, 1972. Bibliography.

6. [The *Bajío* is a fertile basin area of central Mexico, covering the states of Michoacán and Guanajuato. Trans.]

7. [*Cholos* is a term for mestizos in Bolivia and Peru. Trans.]

8. In my work, *El Indio como problema,* I have discussed at some length the problems arising from the classification of the Indian and of Indians; cf. Esteva, 1957.

9. For a discussion of the concept of mestizo ideology in the context of the contemporary revolutionary movement in Ibero-America, see my work, *El indigenismo en la política hispanoamericana.* See the bibliography.

10. [*Criollismo* is the adherence to the culture of criollos, or the Spanish born in America. Trans.]

11. The Portuguese colonial experience and the relations of white men with black

women has been admirably presented by Gilberto Freyre in his work, *Casa grande y senzala*.

12. We will concern ourselves on another occasion with the analysis and explanation of the specific problems of the cultural recombinations and the syncretisms that appear in the ideology and ways of life in Ibero-America.

13. In my works, *El Indio como problema* and *El Indigenismo en la política Hispanoamericana*, I provide an interpretation of the current political perspectives on the Indian problem and on the position that mestizo groups occupy within it. See the bibliography.

14. In my work, *Interpretación de México*, I have discussed the role of nationalist enthusiasm in the building of a unitarian Mexican identity with the Mexican Revolution. See the bibliography.

Chapter 5: Spanish Women

1. [*Estancias* are cattle ranches of southern South America. Trans.]

2. [*Hidalgos* were individuals of the lesser nobility. Trans.]

3. [Marcaida is a name taken from a place in Vizcaya province in Spain. Trans.]

4. [The *maravedí* was a basic sub-unit of the Spanish colonial peso; a *cuento de maravedíes* was a million *maravedíes*. Trans.]

5. [Cabildo de Guatemala refers, in this case, not just to a municipal council, but to the entire jurisdiction of Guatemala prior to its local administrative organization. Trans.]

6. [*Recopilación* refers to the *Recopilación de leyes de los reynos de las Indias* (or Compilation of Laws of the Kingdoms of the Indies), promulgated in 1680. Trans.]

Chapter 6: Indian Women

1. [*Yanaconas* in Peru were the hereditary Indian servitors attached to land and households. Trans.]

2. [*Soldaderas* were women combatants and soldiers' companions. Trans.]

3. [*Anaconas* is a variant of *yanaconas*. See note above. Trans.]

4. [The *alguacil mayor* was chief constable. Trans.]

5. [*Alcaldes ordinarios* were municipal magistrates. Trans.]

6. [*Naborías* were free Indian servants, allocated to the Spanish in the Antilles early in the conquest period. Trans.]

7. [The Carios were a Paraguayan tribe inhabiting the banks of the Paraguay River near Asunción at the time of the conquest. Trans.]

8. [*Aperúes* is a variant of Yaperúes, a sixteenth-century Paraguayan tribe near Asunción. Trans.]

9. [Antonio de Mendoza, viceroy of New Spain from 1535 to 1550. Trans.]

10. [The Achaguas apparently were a Paraguayan tribe, although the name also refers to a major tribe of Venezuela and eastern Colombia. Trans.]

11. [The Guarocoquis apparently were an Indian tribe of Paraguay, although no reference to them was found. Trans.]

Chapter 7: African Women, Zambos, and Mulattoes

1. They could also be Moorish women, but the context leads us to consider them specifically blacks.

2. [The *ducado* was a Spanish gold coin used through the 16th century. Trans.]

3. [*Regidores* were municipal councilors. Trans.]

4. [The Casa de Contratación, or royal Board of Trade, was established in Seville in 1503. Trans.]

5. [The *fazenda* is the Brazilian equivilant of the hacienda, or large agricultural property. Trans.]

6. [The *provisor* was a vicar-general. Trans.]

7. [*Cimarrones* were runaway slaves living in organized communities of resistance. Trans.]

8. [The *veedor* was an inspector or supervisor. Trans.]

9. [The Chiriguanos were a tribe of Paraguayan Chaco Indians, also known as the Guarayo. Trans.]

10. [*Alférez* is a military rank equivilant to second lieutenant. Trans.]

11. [Paramocaes is a variant of Promaucas, the Quechua name given by the Incas to their "wild enemies" in Chile south of the Maipó River. Trans.]

12. [The Albayas apparently were an Indian tribe of Paraguay, although no reference to them was found. Trans.]

Chapter 9: Population and Racial Mixing in the Cities

1. From *lépero,* a person of insolent speech, aggressive with women and given to vagrancy and to games of vice.

2. The concept of *savage Indians* is equivalent to the pre-agrarian, gatherer cultures, also designated by the name of *infidels* because they had not converted to Christianity.

3. In pre-Columbian Brazil there were no cities; we must keep in mind that their populations were of gathering, hunting, and fishing cultures, and some had incipient or grub agriculture.

4. In order to estimate the existing proportion between mestizos and mulattoes we have turned to the census figures for León, New Spain, which are, respectively, 70 and 30 percent.

5. The proportions between mestizos and mulattoes would be, respectively, 66 percent for the former and 34 percent for the latter. The numerical differences between mestizos and mulattoes living in cities of pre-Hispanic origin are very slight, which indicates that this factor could not be significant in that case. What really does vary is the indigenous base.

6. For Querétaro, New Spain, Alcedo reports 3,000 families of Spanish, mestizos, and mulattoes, and 3,000 families of Otomí Indians, creating a total of 47,000 inhabitants, which would give an approximate average of 8 persons per family.

7. For example, in San Lorenzo del Real de la Frontera, Peru, a population of 6,000 souls is specified, in addition to 15,000 individuals classified as servants.

8. We have applied a coefficient of 3.5 persons per family.

9. We have applied a coefficient of 4 persons per family. Additionally, since in the list of mining towns and localities no separate data appear for the mestizo group—their being accompanied always by other ethnicities—we have applied the proportion resulting from the calculation between Spaniards and mestizos, by which in the second half of the eighteenth century the latter represent, with respect to the former, 23.16 percent. In calculating the figures related to the "citizens," for the purpose of distributing them proportionally, we have applied the proportion of 10.8 percent of the Indians when the figures are listed under the heading of *citizens,* mindful that when distinctions have been made between Indians and citizens, this has been the percentage that has resulted.

10. We have applied the coefficient of 3.5 for each family.

11. We have applied the coefficient of 4 for each family.

12. Owing to the scant statistical significance, we have dropped the column referring to the Chinese.

13. In Cuba, according to Reynal (Humboldt 1960, 167), whites would represent 44 percent, and in Santo Domingo, according to the percentages resulting from the general figures given by Alcedo, the white would represent 22.5 percent.

14. We have applied the proportion between blacks and mulattoes in the census for Cuba done by Reynald (ibid.) in 1775. That would be 66 percent blacks and 34 percent mulattoes, considered among themselves, which would give a black and mulatto population breakdown in the Antilles that, aside from its numerical importance, would be the one given in Tables 9.9 and 9.10.

15. The notion of race has been used in a biological sense, and thus refers to a zoological type of classification. That of ethnicity defines a population that is culturally homogeneous and distinct in comparison to another.

16. We derive this percentage by excluding the savage Indians, insofar as the latter were not part of the institutional system of Ibero-American culture. Thus, the percentage includes the rural and urban populations.

Chapter 12: The Geographical Distribution of Racial Mixing

1. This problem has been discussed in my book, *El indigenismo en la política hispanoamericana.* See the bibliography.

2. There are also other blood-type systems with which this kind of special research deals, but because of the greater number of studies available for the ABO, and in the interest of homogeneity, we have prefered to use only the latter.

3. We must not lose sight of the possibility that a genetic exchange may have taken place between Indian—as well as black—individuals of the O phenotype and Europeans also possessing the O. Thus, this racial mixture would not be reflected differentially in the genetic components of their descendants.

4. According to Santiana (1962, 72) only 22 percent of the individuals were pure, since the rest were doubtless mestizos.

BIBLIOGRAPHY

Acosta Saignes, M. 1956. "Vida de negros e indios en las minas de Cocoroto durante el siglo XVII." Pp. 555–72 in *Homenaje a Manuel Gamio.* Mexico City: UNAM.

Adams, R. N. 1956. "Cultural Components of Central America." *American Anthropologist* 58:881–907.

———. 1958. "The Problem of National Culture in Central America." *Miscellanea Paul Rivet Octogenario Dicata* (Mexico City) 1:341–59.

Aguado, Fr. Pedro de. 1963. *Recopilación histórica de Venezuela.* 2 vols. Preliminary study by Guillermo Morón. Caracas: Biblioteca de la Academia Nacional de la Historia.

Aguirre Beltrán, G. 1972. *La población negra de México.* Mexico City: Fondo de Cultura Económica.

Alcedo, A. de. 1967. *Diccionario geográfico-histórico de las Indias Occidentales o América.* 4 vols. Biblioteca de Autores Españoles. Madrid: Atlas.

Allen, F. H., Jr. 1958. "Inheritance of the Diego (Dia) Blood Group Factor." *The American Journal of Human Genetics* 10:64–67.

———. 1959. "Summary of Blood Group Phenotypes in Some Aborginal Americans." *American Journal of Physical Anthropology,* n.s., 17:86.

Alvarez Nazario, M. 1974. *El elemento afronegroide en el español de Puerto Rico.* San Juan de Puerto Rico: Instituto de Cultura Puertorriqueña.

Arboleda, J. R. 1962. "La historia y la antropología del negro en Colombia." *América Latina* (Rio de Janeiro) 5:3–14.

Arce Larreta, J. 1929. "Contribución al estudio de los grupos sanguíneos en el Perú." *Revista de Ciencias* (Lima) 32:1–38.

Arcila Vélez, G. 1946. "Los Caramanta. Ubicación y serología." *Universidad de Antioquia* (Medellín) 80:445–52.

———. 1962. "Programa para un estudio de la raza de Colombia y un aporte inicial." *VIe Congrès International des Sciences Anthropologiques et Ethnologiques* (Paris) 1:405–9.

Arellano Moreno, A. 1964. *Relaciones geográficas de Venezuela.* Caracas: Academia Nacional de la Historia.

Azara, F. de. 1962. "Descripción e historia del Paraguay y del Río de la Plata." In *Viajes por América del Sur,* vol. 2, pt. 2 of *Bibliotheca indiana: Libros y fuentes sobre América y Filipinas,* compiled by Gaibros Ballesteros, 331–497, Madrid: Aguilar.

Azevedo, Thales de. 1953. "Indios, brancos e pretos no Brasil Colonial." *América Indígena* (Mexico City) 13:119–32.

———. 1957. "Panorama demográfico dos grupos étnicos na América Latina." *América Indígena* (Mexico City) 17:121–39.

———. 1966. *Cultura e situação racial no Brasil.* Rio de Janeiro: Civilizacão Brasileira.

Ballesteros Gaibrois, M., comp. 1962. *Viajes por América del Sur,* vol. 2, pt. 2 of *Bibliotheca indiana: Libros y fuentes sobre America y Filipinas.* Madrid: Aguilar.

Barnett, H. G. 1953. *Innovation.* New York: McGraw-Hill.

Barón Castro, R. 1942. *La población de El Salvador.* Madrid: CSIC.

———. 1946. "Política racial de España en Indias." *Revista de Indias* (Madrid) 7:781–946.

Barreto, C. 1959. *Povoamento e população: Política populacional brasileira.* Coleção Documentos Brasileiros, no. 68. Rio de Janeiro: José Olýmpio Editora.

Battegay, R. 1981. *La agresión.* Barcelona: Editorial Herder.

Bay-Schmith, E. 1930. "Blutgruppenbestimmungen bei Eskimos." *Acta Pathologica et Microbiologica Scandinavica* (Copenhagen) 7:107–16.

Beals, R. 1953a. "Acculturation." Pp. 621–41 in *Anthropology Today,* edited by A. L. Kroeber. Chicago: University of Chicago Press.

———. 1953b. "Social Stratification in Latin America." *American Journal of Sociology* 58:327–39.

Benedict, Ruth F. 1941. *Raza, ciencia y política.* Mexico City: Fondo de Cultura Económica.

Benoist, J. 1962. "Les groupes sanguines dans l'analyse anthropologique de la population martiniquaise." *VIe Congrès International des Sciences Anthropologiques et Ethnologiques* (Paris) 3:297–301.

———. 1966. "Anthropologie physique de la population de l'Ile de la Tortue, Haiti. Contribution à l'étude de l'origine des noirs des Antilles françaises." *Bulletin de la Société d'Anthropologie* (Paris) 3, no. 3:315–35.

Berthoff, Rowland. 1966. "Population Origins. Colonial and National Immigration: United States." *Encyclopedia Americana.* New York.

Birdsell, J. B. 1950. "Some Implications of the Genetical Concept of Race in Terms of Spatial Analysis." *Cold Spring Harbor Symposia on Quantitative Biology* 15:259–311.

Boas, Fanz. 1940. *Race, Language and Culture.* New York: Collier & Macmillan.

Borah, W. 1954. "Race and Class in Mexico." *Pacific Historical Review* 23:331–42.

Boyd, W. C. 1950. *Genetics and the Races of Man.* Boston: Little, Brown.

———. 1953. "The Contributions of Genetics to Anthropology." Pp. 488–506 in *Anthropology Today,* edited by A. L. Kroeber. Chicago: University of Chicago Press.

Brown, K. S., B. L. Hanna, A. A. Dahlberg, and H. H. Strandskov. 1958. "The Distribution of Group Alleles Among Indians of Southwest North America." *American Journal of Human Genetics* 10:175–95.

Buitrón, A., and B. Salisbury. 1945. "Indios, blancos y mestizos en Otavalo, Ecuador." *Acta Americana* (Mexico City and Los Angeles) 3, no. 3:190–216.

Cámara Barbachano, F. 1964. "El mestizaje en México. Planteamiento sobre problemáticas socioculturales." *Revista de Indias* (Madrid) 95–96:27–85.

Canals Frau, S. 1949a. "Algunos rasgos antropológicos de la población argentina." *Anales del Instituto Etnico Nacional* (Buenos Aires) 2:15–27.

———. 1949b. *Poblaciones indígenas de la Argentina.* Buenos Aires: Editorial Sudamericana.

Carvalho Neto, P. de. 1962. "Contribución al estudio de los negros paraguayos de Acampamento, Loma." *América Latina* (Rio de Janeiro) 5, no. 1–2:23–40.

Casas, Bartolomé de las. 1965. *Historia de las Indias.* 3 vols. Mexico City: Fondo de Cultura Económica.

Caso, Alfonso. 1948. "Definición del indio y lo indio." *América Indígena* (Mexico City) 8:239–47.

Céspedes del Castillo, G. 1957. "La sociedad colonial americana en los siglos XVI y XVII." Pp. 387–578 in *Historia social y económica de América,* vol. 3, edited by J. Vicens Vives. Barcelona: Editorial Vicens Vives.

Charlevoix, P.F.J. de. 1910. *Historia del Paraguay.* 2 vols. Madrid: Librería General de Victoriano Suárez.

Chiappe, D. H. 1962. "La Serología y su importancia en la determinación de los grupos raciales." *Notas del Museo de la Plata* (La Plata) 20:53–67.

Chiasson, L. P. 1962. "Gene Frequencies of the Micmac Indians." *Journal of Heredity* 54:229–36.

Chilton, J. de. 1963. "Notable relación de . . . acerca de los habitantes, costumbres, minas, ciudades, riquezas, fuerzas y demás cosas particulares de la Nueva España y otras provincias de las Indias Occidentales, 1561–1582." Pp. 33–51 in *Relaciones de varios viajeros ingleses en la Ciudad de México y . . . ,* edited by J. G. Icazbalceta. Madrid: Ediciones José Porrúa Turanzas.

Chown, B. 1957. "Problems in Blood Group Analysis. Letter to the Editor." *American Anthropologist* 59:885–88.

———. 1958. "The Diego Factor Among Blackfeet Indians of Western Canada." Personal letter to Layrisse.

Chown, B., and M. Lewis. 1959. "The Blood Group Genes of the Copper Eskimo." *American Journal of Physical Anthropology* 17:13–18.

Cieza de León, Pedro. 1962. *La crónica del Perú.* Madrid: Colección Austral, Espasa-Calpe.

Coca, A. F., and O. Deibert. 1923. "A Study of the Occurrence of the Blood Groups Among the American Indians." *Journal of Immunology* 8:487–91.

Cohn, E. J. 1946. "Blood and Blood Derivatives." *Annual of the Board of Regents of the Smithsonian Institution,* Doc. no. 3.817, 413–39, Washington, [D.C.].

Cold Spring Harbor Symposia on Quantitative Biology. 1950. *Proceedings*. Vol. 15. Cold Spring Harbor, N.Y.: Cold Spring Harbor Laboratory.

Columbus, Christopher. 1958. *Los cuatro viajes del Almirante y su testamento*. Buenos Aires: Colección Austral.

Comas Camps, J. 1941. "Aportación a la bibliografía y estadística serológica racial americana." *Boletín Bibliográfico de Antropología Americana* (Mexico City) 5, no. 1–3:29–37.

———. 1942. "Los grupos sanguíneos y la raciología americana." *Revista Mexicana de Sociología* (Mexico City) 4, no. 3: 69–73.

———. 1944. "El mestizaje y su importancia social." *Acta Americana* (Mexico City and Los Angeles) 2, no. 1–2:13–14.

———. 1957. *Manual de Antropología Física*. Mexico City: Fondo de Cultura Económica.

———. 1961. *Relaciones interraciales en América Latina, 1940–1960*. Mexico City: Cuadernos del Instituto de Historia, UNAM, Serie Antropológica, 12.

———. 1967. "¿Son los amerindios un grupo biológicamente homogéneo?" *Cuadernos Americanos* (Mexico City) 3:117–25.

Concolorcorvo. 1946. *El lazarillo de ciegos caminantes*. Buenos Aires and Mexico City: Espasa-Calpe.

Cook, S. F, and W. Borah. 1971. *Essays in Population History: Mexico and the Caribbean*. 3 vols. Berkeley and Los Angeles: University of California Press.

Corcoran, P., F. H. Allen, Jr., A. C. Allison, and B. S. Blumberg. 1959. "Blood Groups of Alaskan Eskimos and Indians." *American Journal of Physical Anthropology*, n.s., 17, no. 3:187–94.

Crevenna, T., ed. 1950. *Materiales para el estudio de la clase media en América Latina*. 6 vols. Washington, [D.C.]: Pan American Union. Social Science Section.

Crowley, D. J. 1957. "Plural and Differential Acculturation in Trinidad." *American Anthropologist* 59:817–24.

Davenport, Ch. D., and M. Steggerda. 1929. *Race Crossing in Jamaica*. Washington, [D.C.]: Carnegie Institution.

Díaz del Castillo, B. 1955. *Historia verdadera de la conquista de la Nueva España*. Buenos Aires: Colección Austral.

Díaz Soler, L. M. 1970. *Historia de la esclavitud negra en Puerto Rico*. San Juan: Editorial Universitaria.

Dobzhansky, T. 1950. "Human Diversity and Adaptation." *Cold Spring Harbor Symposia on Quantitative Biology* 15:385–400.

———. 1974. *Heredity*. London: Encyclopaedia Britannica.

Domínguez Company, F. 1978. *La vida en las ciudades hispanoamericanas de la conquista*. Madrid: Ediciones de Cultura Hispánica del Centro Iberoamericano de Cooperación.

Drapkin, I. 1950. "Contribución al estudio antropológico y demográfico de los pascuenses." *Journal de la Société des Américanistes* (Paris) 27:265–302.

Durán Ochoa, J. 1955. *Población*. Mexico City: Fondo de Cultura Económica.

Escobar, M. G. 1964. "El mestizaje en la región andina. El caso del Perú." *Revista de Indias* (Madrid) 95–96:197–220.

Esteva Fabregat, C. 1956. "Interpretación de México," *Cuadernos Hispanoamericanos* (Madrid) 83:147–62.

———. 1957. "El indio como problema." *Revista de Estudios Políticos* (Madrid) 95: 211–39.

———. 1961a. "El indigenismo en la política hispanoamericana." *Revista de Política Internacional* (Madrid) 56–57:49–63.

———. 1961b. *Estructura étnica y social de Iberoamérica.* Madrid.

———. 1964. "El método funcionalista en el estudio de la aculturación." In *Actes du VIe Congrès International des Sciences Anthropologiques et Ethnologiques* (Paris) 2, no. 2:583–87.

———. 1970a. "Algunas funciones y relaciones del compadrazgo y del matrimonio en Chinchero, Cuzco." *Universitas* (Salvador, Bahia) 6–7:55–90.

———. 1970b. "Medicina tradicional, curanderismo y brujería en Chinchero (Perú)." *Anuario de Estudios Americanos* (Seville) 27:19–60.

———. 1970c. "Un mercado en Chinchero, Cuzco." *Anuario Indigenista* (Mexico City) 30:213–54.

———. 1971. "La población de Chinchero (Cuzco) en el siglo XVIII." *Lima, Quinto Congreso Internacional de Historia de América (1971),* 3:318–40.

———. 1972. "Ayni, minka y faena en Chinchero, Cuzco." *Revista Española de Antropología Americana* (Madrid) 7, no. 2:309–407.

———. 1978. *Cultura, Sociedad y Personalidad.* Barcelona: Anthropos Editorial del Hombre.

———. 1984. *Antropología Industrial.* Barcelona: Anthropos Editorial del Hombre.

Esteve Barba, F. 1965. *Cultura virreinal.* Barcelona: Salvat Editores, S.A.

———, comp. 1968. *Crónicas peruanas de interés indígena.* Preliminary study by Biblioteca de Autores Españoles. Madrid: Atlas.

Fernández de Navarrete, M. 1954–64. *Colección de los viajes y descubrimientos.* Biblioteca de Autores Españoles. Madrid: Atlas.

Fernández de Oviedo, G. 1959. *Historia general y natural de las Indias.* 5 vols. Biblioteca de Autores Españoles. Madrid: Atlas.

Fernández Guardia, L., comp. 1907. *Colección de documentos para la historia de Costa Rica.* Vol. 6. Barcelona: Imprenta Viuda de Luis Tasso.

Firschein, I. L. 1961. "Population Dynamics of the Sickle-Cell Trait in the Black Carib of the British Honduras, Central America." *American Journal of Human Genetics* 13:233–54.

Fleischhacker, H. 1962. "Zur Anthropologie Zentralamerikas. Die indianid-europide Rassenmischung in El Salvador." *Akten des 34, Internationalen Amerikanistenkongresses,* 771–72. Vienna.

Forde, C. D. 1966. *Habitat, Economía y Sociedad.* Barcelona: Ediciones TAU.

Foster, G. M. 1962. *Cultura y conquista.* Xalapa: Universidad Veracruzana.

Freyre, G. 1943. *Casa grande y senzala.* Buenos Aires: EMECE Editores, S.A.

Friede, J., comp. 1955–. *Documentos inéditos para la historia de Colombia.* Vols. 2–4. Bogotá: Academia Colombiana de la Historia.

Fuente, J. de la. 1948. *Cambios socioculturales en México.* Acta anthropologica, vol. 3, no. 4. Mexico City.

Garn, S. M. 1971. *Human Races.* 3d ed. Springfield, Ill.: Charles C. Thomas.

Genovés, S., and J. F. Passy. 1976. "Introducción. Una visión general." Pp. 1–40 in *Comportamiento y violencia,* edited by S. Genovés and J. F. Passy. Mexico City: Editorial Diana.

Genovés, S., and J. F. Passy, eds. 1976. *Comportamiento y violencia.* Mexico City: Editorial Diana.

Gerheim, E. B. 1947. "Incidence of Rh Factor Among the Indians of the Southwest." *Proceedings of the Society for Experimental Biology and Medicine* 66: 419–20.

Gilli, P.F.S. 1784. *Ensayo de historia americana . . . ,* vol. 87. Bogotá: Biblioteca de Historia Nacional.

Gillin, J. 1942. "Mestizo America." Pp. 156–211 in *Estudio del hombre,* edited by Ralph Linton. Mexico City.

———. 1948. "The Cultural Area of Latin America in the Modern World." *América Indígena* (Mexico City) 8:31–43.

———. 1955. "Ethos Components in Latin American Culture." *American Anthropologist* 57:488–500.

———. 1961. "The Social Transformation of the Mestizo." Pp. 73–78 in *El mestizaje en la historia de Iberoamérica,* compiled by M. Mörner. Mexico City: Instituto Panamericano de Geografía e Historia. Comisión de Historia.

Ginsburg, B. E. 1968. "Breeding Structure and Social Behavior of Mammals: A Servo-mechanism for the Avoiding of Panmixia." Pp. 117–28 in *Genetics: Biology and Behavior,* edited by David C. Glass. New York: The Rockefeller University Press and Russell Sage Foundation.

Glass, B. 1953. "The Dynamics of Racial Intermixture: An Analysis Based on the American Negro." *American Journal of Human Genetics* 5:1–20.

———. 1954. "Genetic Changes in Human Populations, Especially Those Due to Gene Flow and Genetic Drift." *Advances in Genetics* 6:95–139.

Glass, David C., ed. 1968. *Genetics: Biology and Behavior.* New York: The Rockefeller University Press and Russell Sage Foundation.

Góngora Marmolejo, A. de. 1960. *Historia de Chile desde su descubrimiento hasta el año 1575.* Biblioteca de Autores Españoles. Madrid: Atlas.

Harrison, G. A. 1960. "The Biological Effects of Miscegenation." Pp. 33–47 in *Man, Race, and Darwin,* edited by Philip Mason. London: Oxford University Press.

Hart-Terré, E. 1973. *Negros e Indios. Un testamento social ignorado del Perú colonial.* Lima: Editorial Juan Mejía Baca.

Henckel, Ch. C. 1962. "Sobre el estado actual de las investigaciones sero-antropológicas en los indios mapuches de Chile." *Anthropos* (Freiburg) 57:509–13.

Henckel, K. O., A. Castelli, and J. D. Borgo. 1941. "Algunas observaciones acerca

de la producción de los grupos sanguíneos M y N en los indios mapuches."
Boletín de la Sociedad de Biología de Concepción, Chile (Concepción) 15:
37–41.

Hernández Sánchez-Barba, M. 1981. *Historia universal de América.* New ed. Madrid:
Alhambra Universidad, 1981.

Herrera, A. de. 1936. *Historia general de los hechos de los castellanos en las islas y Tierra
Firme del Mar Océano.* Biblioteca de Autores Españoles. Madrid: Atlas.

Herskovits, M. J. 1938. *Acculturation: The Study of Culture Contact.* New York:
J. J. Augustin.

Hoffstetter, R. 1949a. "Nota adicional sobre las características serológicas de la población de Quito." *Boletín de Informaciones Científicas Nacionales* (Quito) 2,
no. 15–16:20–23.

———. 1949b. "Las características serológicas de la población urbana de Quito.
Aplicación a la investigación de la paternidad." *Boletín de Informaciones Científicas Nacionales* (Quito) 2, no. 15–16: 47–73.

Hollanda, G. de. 1956. "Los españoles y las castas." *Historia paraguaya* (Asunción)
1:69–76.

Hooton, E. A. 1946. *Up from the Ape.* New York: Macmillan.

Hrdlicka, A. 1946. "Las razas del hombre." Pp. 193–224 in *Aspectos científicos del
problema racial,* by various authors. Buenos Aires: Editorial Losada, S.A.

Humboldt, A. de. 1960. *Ensayo político sobre la isla de Cuba.* Havana: Publicaciones
del Archivo Nacional de Cuba.

———. 1962. "Viaje a las regiones equinocciales del Nuevo Continente." Pp.
561–1120 in *Viajes por América del Sur,* vol. 2, pt. 2 of *Bibliotheca indiana:
Libros y fuentes sobre América y Filipinas,* compiled by M. Ballesteros Gaibrois.
Madrid: Aguilar.

———. 1973. *Ensayo político sobre el reino de la Nueva España.* Mexico City: Editorial Porrúa.

Humphrey, N. D. 1952. "Race, Caste and Class in Colombia." *Phylon* 13:161–66.

Iam L., P. 1958. "Expedición al territorio Amazonas." *Memorias de la Sociedad de
Ciencias Naturales La Salle* (Caracas) 18, no. 50:77–89.

Ianni, F.A.J. 1958. "Time and Place as Variables in Acculturation Research." *American Anthropologist* 60:39–46.

Imbelloni, J. 1944. "Las investigaciones serológicas del profesor A. Santiana." *Notas
del Museo de la Plata* (La Plata) 9:439–43.

Irala, D. de. 1962. [Title/pages missing]. In Azara, F. de. "Descripción e historia del
Paraguay y del Río de la Plata." In *Viajes por America del Sur,* vol. 2, pt. 2
of *Bibliotheca indiana: Libros y fuentes sobre America y Filipinas,* compiled by
Gaibros Ballesteros, 331–497, Madrid: Aguilar.

Jacobs, J. 1971. "Formación de las especies." Pp. 140–59 in *Del origen de las especies,*
by various authors. Madrid: Alianza Editorial.

Jara, A. 1959. *Los asientos de trabajo y la provisión de mano de obra para los no-encomende-
ros en la ciudad de Santiago, 1586–1600.* Santiago de Chile: Estudios de Historia Económica Americana.

Jiménez Moreno, W. 1961. "El mestizaje y la transculturación en Mexiamérica." Pp. 78–85 in *El mestizaje en la historia de Iberoamérica,* compiled by M. Mörner. Mexico City: Instituto Panamericano de Geografía e Historia. Comisión de Historia.

Johansson, I. K. "Breeding." *Encyclopaedia Britannica.* 1974.

Juan, J., and A. de Ulloa. 1978. *Relación histórica del viaje a la América meridional (1748).* 2 vols. Madrid: Fundación Universitaria Española.

Klineberg, O. 1951. *Race et Psychologie.* Paris: UNESCO.

Konetzke, R. 1945. "La emigración de mujeres españolas a América durante la época colonial." *Revista Internacional de Sociología* (Madrid) 9:123–50.

———. 1946. "El mestizaje y su importancia en el desarrollo de la población hispanoamericana durante la época colonial." *Revista de Indias* (Madrid) 23–24: 7–44, 215–37.

———. 1952. "La emigración española al Río de la Plata durante el siglo xvi." In *Miscellanea Americanista,* Homenaje a D. Antonio Ballesteros Beretta, 3:297–353, Madrid, CSIC.

———. 1961. "La legislación española y el mestizaje en América." Pp. 59–64 in *El Mestizaje en la historia de Iberoamérica,* compiled by M. Mörner. Mexico City: Instituto Panamericano de Geografía e Historia. Comisión de Historia.

Kraus, B. S., and C. B. White. 1956. "Microevolution in a Human Population: A Study of Social Endogamy and Blood Type Distributions Among the Western Apache." *American Anthropologist* 58:1017–43.

Kroeber, A. L., ed. 1953. *Anthropology Today.* Chicago: University of Chicago Press.

Krogman, M. M. 1935. The Physical Anthropology of the Seminole Indians of Oklahoma. Comitato Italiano per lo studio dei problemi della populazione, Publications, series 3, volume 2.

———. 1966. "Negro." *Encyclopedia Americana.* New York.

Kubler, G. 1952. *The Indian Caste of Peru, 1795–1940: A Population Study Based on Tax Records and Census Reports.* Washington, [D.C.]: U.S. Government Printing Office.

LaBarre, W. 1961. *The Human Animal.* Chicago: The University of Chicago Press.

Landsteiner, K., A. Wiener, and G. A. Matson. 1942. "Distribution of the Rh Factor in American Indians." *Journal of Experimental Medicine* 76:73–78.

Lang, J. 1951. "Espectro racial de Honduras." *América Indígena* (Mexico City) 11:209–17.

Laughlin, W. S. 1950. "Blood Groups, Morphology and Population Size of the Eskimos." *Cold Spring Harbor Symposia on Quantitative Biology* 15:165–73.

Layrisse, M., and T. Arends. 1950. "High Incidence Blood Groups Found in Venezuelan Indians." *Science* 123:633.

———. 1958. "Anthropological Considerations of the Diego (Dia) Antigen. Possible Application in the Studies of Mongoloid and Hybrid Populations." *American Journal of Physical Anthropology,* n.s., 16, no. 2:173–86.

Layrisse, M., and Z. Layrisse. 1960. "Blood Group Antigen Tests of the Yupa Indians of Venezuela." *American Anthropologist* 62:418–36.

Layrisse, M., Z. Layrisse, E. García, and J. Wilbert. 1961. "Blood Group Antigen Tests of the Yaruro Indians." *Southwestern Journal of Anthropology* 17:198–204.

Layrisse, M., Z. Layrisse, and J. Wilbert. 1963. "Blood Group Antigen Studies of Four Chibchan tribes." *American Anthropologist* 65:36–55.

Layrisse, M., J. Wilbert, and T. Arends. 1958. "Frequency of Blood Group Antigens in the Descendants of Guayqueri Indians." *American Journal of Physical Anthropology,* n.s., 16:307–18.

Lima, P. E. 1950. "Grupos sanguíneos dos indios do Xingu." *Boletim do Museu Nacional* (Rio de Janeiro) 2:14.

Linton, Ralph. 1942. *Estudio del hombre.* Mexico City: Fondo de Cultura Económica.

———, ed. 1949. *Most of the World: The Peoples of Africa, Latin America, and the East Today.* New York: Columbia University Press.

Lizárraga, R. de. 1968. *Descripción breve de toda la tierra del Perú, Tucumán, Río de la Plata y Chile.* Biblioteca de Autores Españoles. Madrid: Atlas.

López de Gómara, F. 1946. *Historia general de las Indias.* Biblioteca de Autores Españoles. Madrid: Atlas.

MacCann, W. 1962. "Viaje a caballo por la República Argentina." Pp. 499–560 in *Viajes por América del Sur,* vol. 2, pt. 2 of *Bibliotheca indiana: Libros y fuentes sobre América y Filipinas,* compiled by M. Ballesteros Gaibrois. Madrid: Aguilar.

MacFarlane Burnet, S. 1959. "Migration and Race Mixture from the Genetic Angle." *Eugenics Review* 51, no. 2:97.

Malinowski, B. 1961. *The Dynamics of Culture Change.* New Haven: Yale University Press.

Mansilla, Lucio V. 1962. *Una excursión a los indios ranqueles.* Buenos Aires: Colección Austral.

Manzanedo, Fr. B. de. 1918. *Memorial de . . . La Habana* (Academia de la Historia de Cuba), vol. 7, pt. 1:1512–78.

Mariño de Lobera, P. 1960. *Crónica del Reino de Chile.* Madrid: Biblioteca de Autores Españoles.

Marroquín, J. 1946. "Particularidades antropológicas del indígena puneño." *Revista del Museo Nacional* (Lima) 15:13–32.

Mason, Philip, ed. 1960. *Man, Race and Darwin.* London: Oxford University Press.

Mateus, A. de M. 1947. "Contribuição para o estudo da sero-antropologia." *Publicações do Instituto de Zoologia do Porto,* no. 33. Porto.

Matson, G. A., and J. Swanson. 1959. "Distribution of Hereditary Blood Antigens Among Maya and non-Maya Indians in Mexico and Guatemala." *American Journal of Physical Anthropology* 17:49–74.

———. 1961. "Distribution of Hereditary Blood Antigens Among American Indians in Middle America: Lacandon and other Maya." *American Anthropologist* 63:1292–1322.

McQuown, N. A. 1955. "The Indigenous Languages of Latin America." *American Anthropologist* 57:501–70.

Medina, J. T. 1956. *Colección de documentos inéditos para la historia de Chile.* Vol. 1: 1558–72. Santiago de Chile: Fondo Histórico y Bibliográfico J. T. Medina.

Meléndez, C., and Q. Duncan. 1981. *El negro en Costa Rica.* San José: Editorial Costa Rica.

Meléndez Ch. C. 1981. "Acerca del trabajo indígena en Costa Rica durante el siglo XVII." *Cahiers du Monde Hispanique et Luso-Brasilien* (Toulouse) CARA-VELLE 37:37–50.

Miscellanea Paul Rivet Octogenario Dicata, Mexico City, XXXI Congreso Internacional de Americanistas, 1958. 1958. Publicaciones del Instituto de Historia, 1st Series, no. 50. Mexico City: UNAM.

Molina, C. de (El Almagrista). 1968. "Relación de muchas cosas acaescidas en el Perú." Pp. 209:57–95 in *Crónicas peruanas de interés indígena,* compiled by F. Esteve Barba. Madrid: Biblioteca de Autores Españoles.

Monge, C. 1949. "Aclimatación en los Andes." *América Indígena* (Mexico City) 9:267–85.

———. 1953. "Biological Bases of Human Behavior." Pp. 127–44 in *Anthropology Today,* edited by A. L. Kroeber. Chicago: University of Chicago Press.

Montagu, A. 1959. *Human Heredity.* Cleveland: World Publishing.

———. 1960. *An Introduction to Physical Anthropology.* Springfield: Thomas.

———. 1972. *Statement on Race.* London: Oxford University Press.

Morales Padrón, F. 1974. *Los conquistadores de América.* Madrid: Colección Austral.

Mörner, M. 1961. "Informe preliminar." Pp. 11–51 in *El mestizaje en la historia de Iberoamérica,* compiled by M. Mörner. Mexico City: 1961.

———. 1964. "La política de segregación y el mestizaje en la Audiencia de Guatemala." *Revista de Indias* (Madrid), 95–96.

———. 1967. *Race Mixture in the History of Latin America.* Boston: Little, Brown.

Mörner, M., comp. 1961. *El mestizaje en la historia de Iberoamérica.* Mexico City: Instituto Panamericano de Geografía e Historia. Comisión de Historia.

Motolinía, Fr. Toribio de B. 1971. *Memoriales o libro de las cosas de la Nueva España y de los naturales de ella.* Mexico City: UNAM, Instituto de Investigaciones Históricas.

Mourant, A. E., C. Kopec, and K. Domaniewska-Sobczak. 1958. *The ABO Blood Groups. Comprehensive Tables and Maps of World Distribution.* Oxford: University Press.

Nash, M. 1957. "The Multiple Society in Economic Development: Mexico and Guatemala." *American Anthropologist* 59:825–33.

Neel, J., and W. Schull. 1958. *Human Heredity.* Chicago: University of Chicago Press.

Nicholson, H. B. 1955. "Native Historical Traditions of Nuclear America and the Problem of Their Archeological Correlation." *American Anthropologist* 57:594–613.

Núñez Cabeza de Vaca, A. 1962. "Comentarios." Pp. 17–87 in *Viajes por América del Sur,* vol. 2, pt. 2 of *Bibliotheca indiana: Libros y fuentes sobre América y Filipinas,* compiled by M. Ballesteros Gaibrois. Madrid: Aguilar.

———. 1957. *Naufragios y Comentarios.* Madrid: Colección Austral, Espasa-Calpe.

Oberg, K. 1955. "Types of Social Structure Among the Lowland Tribes of South and Central America." *American Anthropologist* 57:472–87.

Olien, M. D. 1980. *The Negro in Costa Rica.* Eugene: University of Oregon Press.

Ordenanzas. 1900. *Revista de Archivos y Bibliotecas Nacionales* (Lima) pt. 3, 5:3–31.

Ordóñez de Ceballos, P. 1947. *Viaje del mundo.* Madrid: Colección Austral, Espasa-Calpe.

Ortiguera, T. de. 1948. *Jornada del río Marañón.* Biblioteca de Autores Españoles. Madrid: Atlas.

Oschinsky, L. 1959. "A Reappraisal of Recent Serological, Genetic and Morphological Research on the Taxonomy of the Races of Africa and Asia." *Anthropologica* (Ottawa), n.s., 1:1–25.

Ots Capdequí, J. M. 1940. *Estudios de historia del derecho español en las Indias.* Bogotá: Editorial Minerva.

———. 1941. *El Estado español en las Indias.* Mexico City: Colegio de Mexico.

———. 1945. *Manual de historia del derecho español en las Indias y el derecho propiamente indiano.* Buenos Aires: Editorial Losada.

———. 1959. *España en América. El régimen de tierras en la época colonial.* Mexico City: Fondo de Cultura Economica.

Oviedo, B. de. 1930. *Cualidades y riquezas del Nuevo Reino de Granada.* Bogotá: Biblioteca de Historia Nacional, vol. 44.

Oviedo y Baños, J. de. 1965. *Historia de la conquista y población de la Provincia de Venezuela.* Biblioteca de Autores Españoles. Madrid: Atlas.

Palza, S. H. 1950. "La clase media en Bolivia." Pp. 3:1–17 in *Materiales para el estudio de la clase media en América Latina,* edited by T. Crevenna, Washington, D.C.: Pan American Union. Social Science Section.

Paulotti, O. L., and L. González Alegría. 1943. "Grupos sanguíneos de los nativos de la Puna Jujeña." *Anales del Museo Argentino de Ciencias Naturales* (Buenos Aires) 41:21–28.

———. 1948. "Los Toba. Contribución a la somatología de los indígenas del Chaco." *Runa* (Buenos Aires) 1:9–96.

Pérez Bustamante, C. 1940. "Las regiones españolas y la población de América." *Revista de Indias* (Madrid) 2:81–120.

Pérez de Barradas, J. 1976. *Los mestizos de América.* Madrid: Colección Austral, Espasa-Calpe.

Pérez de Tudela, J. 1956. *Las armadas de Indias y los orígenes de la política de colonización, 1492–1505.* Madrid: Instituto Gonzalo Fernández de Oviedo.

Pericot, L. 1962. *América Indígena.* Barcelona: Salvat Editores, S.A.

Perma, T. 1950. *World Atlas.* New York: Permabooks.

Pierson, D. 1942. *Negroes in Brazil: A Study of Race Contact at Bahia.* Chicago: University of Chicago Press.

Pinedo, V. M. 1953. "Formaciones humanas en la Hylea Amazónica Peruana." *América Indígena* (Mexico City) 13:87–101.

Pourchet, M. J. 1963. "Brazilian Mestizo Types." Pp. 111–20 in *Handbook of South American Indians*. Vol. 6. Edited by J. H. Steward. New York: Cooper Square Publishers.

————. 1968. "Aspectos genético-antropológicos de una comunidad Kaingang. Paraná-Brasil." *América Indígena* (Mexico City) 23:141–47.

Pribram, K. H. 1976. "Una carta de los derechos biológicos." Pp. 53–68 in *Comportamiento y violencia,* edited by S. Genovés and J. F. Passy. Mexico City: Editorial Diana.

Price, T. J., Jr. 1954. "Estado y necesidades actuales de las investigaciones afrocolombianas." *Revista Colombiana de Antropología* (Bogotà) 2, no. 2:13–36.

Rahm, G. 1931. "Los grupos sanguíneos de los araucanos (mapuches) y de los fueguinos." *Investigación y Progreso* (Madrid) 5:160–62.

Ramos, A. 1952. *Le metissage au Brésil.* Paris.

Ramos de Andrade, R., C. Lascano, and M. Zárate. 1959. "Grupos sanguíneos (sistema ABO) de los indios y mestizos de los alrededores de Quito." *Humanitas* (Quito) 1, no. 2:19–21.

Recopilación de Leyes . . . de los Reynos de las Indias. 1950–. 4 vols. Madrid: Ediciones Cultura Hispánica.

Redfield, R. 1944. *Yucatán. Una cultura de transición.* Mexico City: Fondo de Cultura Económica.

Redfield, R., R. Linton, and M. J. Herskovits. 1936. "Memorandum on the Study of Acculturation." *American Anthropologist* 38:149–52.

Remesal, Fr. A. de, O.P. 1964. *Historia general de las Indias Occidentales y particular de la gobernación de Chiapa y Guatemala.* Biblioteca de Autores Españoles. Madrid: Atlas.

Ribeiro, L. 1934. "Les groupes sanguines chez les indiens Guaranis du Brésil." *Société de Biologie* (Paris) 3:777–78.

Roberts, J.A.F. 1960. "A Geneticist's View of Human Variability." Pp. 48–55 in *Man, Race and Darwin,* edited by Philip Mason. London: Oxford University Press, 1960.

Romain, J. B. 1962. "L'homme haitien, ses origines ethniques, sa psychologie." *VIe Congrès International des Sciences Anthropologiques et Ethnologiques* (Paris) 2:243–46.

Rosenblat, A. 1954. *La población indígena y el mestizaje en Iberoamérica.* Buenos Aires: Editorial Nova.

Saco, J. A. 1938. *Historia de la esclavitud de la raza africana en el Nuevo Mundo y en especial en los países américo-hispanos.* Havana: Cultura, S.A.

Sáenz-Rico Urbina, A. 1967. *El virrey Amat.* 2 vols. Barcelona: Ayuntamiento de Barcelona, Museo de Historia de la Ciudad.

Sahlins, M. D. 1976. *The Use and Abuse of Biology.* Ann Arbor: The University of Michigan Press.

Salas, A. M. 1960. *Crónica florida del mestizaje de las Indias.* Buenos Aires: Losada, S.A.

Salazar Mallen, M., and R. Hernández de la Portilla. 1944. "Existencia del aglutinógeno Rh en los hematíes de 250 individuos mexicanos." *Revista de la Sociedad Mexicana de Historia Natural* (Mexico City) 5:183–85.

Saldanha, P. H. 1956. "ABO Blood Groups, Age and Disease." *Revista Brasileira de Biologia* (Rio de Janeiro) 16, no. 3:349–53.

———. 1957. "Gene Flow White into Negro Populations of Brazil." *American Journal of Human Genetics* 8:284–98.

———. 1962a. "Os componentes raciais das populações nordestinas." *Ciência e Cultura* (São Paulo) 14:115–17.

———. 1962b. "Taste Sensitivity to Phenilthiourea Among Brazilian Negroes and Its Bearing on the Problem of the White-Negro Intermixture in Brazil." *Human Biology* 34:179–86.

Salzano, F. M. 1965. "Race mixture." *International Social Science Journal* (Paris) 1:135–38.

Sanchiz Ochoa, P. 1976. *Los hidalgos de Guatemala.* Seville: Universidad de Sevilla.

Sandoval, L. 1944. "Los subgrupos sanguíneos A1 y A2 en la población de Santiago." *Boletín de la Sociedad de Biología de Concepción* (Concepción, Chile) 19:99–107.

———. 1945. "El factor Rh en la población de Santiago y los tipos del factor Rh." *Boletín de la Sociedad de Biología de Concepción* (Concepción, Chile) 20:3–9.

Sandoval, L., and M. Domínguez. 1945. "Los grupos, subgrupos, tipos y factores sanguíneos en la población de Santiago." *Boletín de la Sociedad de Biología de Concepción* (Concepción, Chile) 20:77–86.

Sandoval, L., C. O. Henckel, and L. Givovich. 1946. "Grupos, subgrupos y factor Rh sanguíneos en los indios mapuches de la provincia de Cautín, Chile." *Notas del Museo de la Plata* (La Plata) 11:283–99.

Sandoval, L., and O. Wilheim. 1945. "Comunicación preliminar sobre antropología serológica de los pascuenses." *Boletín de la Sociedad de Biología de Concepción* (Concepción, Chile) 20:11–15.

Santiana, A. 1944. "Los grupos sanguíneos de los indios del Ecuador." *Notas del Museo de la Plata* (La Plata) 19:431–38.

———. 1948. "Sobre los grupos sanguíneos de los fueguinos." *Boletín Bibliográfico de Antropología Americana* (Mexico City) 10:117–20.

———. 1953. "Los indios del Ecuador y sus características serológicas." *Boletín de Informaciones Científicas Nacionales* (Quito) 55:52–74.

———. 1962. "Antropología fueguina." *Humanitas* (Quito) 3:7–84.

Santillán, H. de. 1968. "Relación del origen, descendencia, política y gobierno de los Incas." Pp. 97–149 in *Crónicas peruanas de interés indígena,* compiled by F. Esteve Barba. Biblioteca de Autores Españoles. Madrid: Atlas.

Schmid, C. F., and Ch. E. Nobbe. 1965. "Socioeconomic Differentials Among Non-white Races." *American Sociological Review* 30, no. 6:909–22.

Schmidel, U. 1962. "Viaje al Río de la Plata." Pp. 267–329 in *Viajes por América del Sur,* vol. 2, pt. 2 of *Bibliotheca indiana: Libros y fuentes sobre América y Filipinas,* compiled by M. Ballesteros Gaibrois. Madrid: Aguilar.

Schwidetzky, I. 1955. *Etnobiología.* Mexico City: Fondo de Cultura Económica.

Service, E. R. 1955. "Indian-European Relations in Colonial Latin America." *American Anthropologist* 57:411–25.

Shapiro, Harry L. 1954. *La mezcla de razas.* Paris: UNESCO.

Siegel, B. J. 1955. *Acculturation.* Stanford: Stanford University Press.

Silva, E. M. da. 1948. "Absence of Sickling Phenomenon of Red Blood Corpuscle Among Brazilian Indians." *Science* 107:221–22.

———. 1949. "Blood Groups of Indians, Whites and White-Indian Mixtures in Southern Mato Grosso, Brazil." *American Journal of Physical Anthropology* 7 (1949):575–85.

Simmons, O. G. 1955. "The Criollo Outlook in the Mestizo Culture of Coastal Peru." *American Anthropologist* 57:107–17.

Simón, Fr. Pedro. 1961. *Tercera noticia historial de la conquista de Tierra Firme en las Indias Occidentales.* Madrid: Publicaciones Españolas.

Social Science Research Council (U.S.). 1954. "Acculturation: An Exploratory Formulation." *American Anthropologist,* n.s., 56:973–1002.

Solórzano de Pereyra, J. de. 1736–39. *Política indiana.* 2 vols. Madrid: M. Sacristán.

Solórzano Velasco, A. de. 1961. "Una historia inédita de los primeros ochenta años de Buenos Aires." *Revista de Historia Argentina* (Buenos Aires) (December, 1961):484.

Spindler, G., and W. Goldschmidt. 1958. "Experimental Design in the Study of Culture Change." *Southwestern Journal of Anthropology* 8:68–83.

Spiro, Melford E. 1955. "The Acculturation of American Ethnic Groups." *American Anthropologist* 57:1240–52.

Steggerda, M. 1946. "Características físicas y fisiológicas de los Mayas actuales." *Enciclopedia Yucatanense* (Mérida) 6:63–92.

———. 1950. "Mestizos of South America." In *Handbook of South American Indians.* Vol. 5. Edited by J. H. Steward, 655–68. Washington, D.C.: Smithsonian Institution, Bureau of American Ethnology, Bulletin 143.

Stern, C. 1956. *Principles of Human Genetics.* San Francisco.

Steward, J. H. 1955. *Teoría y práctica del estudio de áreas.* Washington, D.C.: Unión Panamericana.

———. 1958. *Theory of Culture Change.* Urbana: University of Illinois Press.

———, ed. 1950. *Handbook of South American Indians.* Vol. 5. Washington, D.C.: Smithsonian Institution, Bureau of American Ethnology, Bulletin 143.

———, ed. 1963. *Handbook of South American Indians.* Vol 6. New York: Cooper Square Publishers.

Thomas, W. L., ed. 1956. *Man's Role in Changing the Face of the Earth.* Chicago: University of Chicago Press.

Thompson, W. S. 1956. "The Spiral of Population." Pp. 970–86 in *Man's Role in*

Changing the Face of the Earth, edited by W. L. Thomas. Chicago, University of Chicago Press.

Tondo, C. W., C. Mundt, and F. M. Salzano. 1963. "Haptoglobin Types in Brazilian Negroes." *Annals of Human Genetics* (London) 26:325–31.

Torre, A. de la. 1947. "Contribución a la determinación de los grupos sanguíneos en Cochabamba." *Gaceta Médica Boliviana* (Cochabamba) 15–16:41–67.

Torre Revello, José. 1943. *Esteco y Concepción de Bermejo: Dos ciudades desaparecidas.* Publicacíon no. 85. Buenos Aires: Instituto de Investigaciones Históricas.

Urizar, U. 1942. "Grupos sanguíneos de autóctonos del Chaco paraguayo." *América Indígena* (Mexico City) 3:49–50.

Varallanos, J. 1962. *El cholo y el Perú. Perú mixto.* Buenos Aires: Imprenta López.

Various [authors]. 1946. *Aspectos científicos del problema racial.* Buenos Aires: Editorial Losada, S.A.

Various [authors]. 1971. *Del origen de las especies.* Madrid: Alianza Editorial.

Vega, Garcilaso de la. 1965. *Obras completas.* 4 vols. Biblioteca de Autores Españoles. Madrid: Atlas.

Vellard, J. 1934. "Quelques recherches sur les groupes sanguines chez les indiens du Paraguay." *Société de Biologie* (Paris) 2:471–72.

———. 1956. "Causas biológicas de la desaparición de los indios americanos." *Boletín del Instituto Riva Agüero* (Lima) 2:77–93.

Vicens Vives, J., ed. 1957–59. *Historia social y económica de España y América.* 4 vols. in 5. Barcelona: Editorial Vicens Vives.

Villaseñor y Sánchez, Joseph A. de. 1746. *Theatro americano.* 2 vols. Mexico: Imprenta de la Viuda de D. J. Bernardo de Hoqal.

Wagley, C., and M. Harris. 1955. "A Typology of Latin American Subcultures." *American Anthropologist* 57:428–57.

Wagner, P. 1964. *The Human Use of the Earth.* New York: Free Press of Glencoe.

Wetherill Shock, N. 1974. "Aging." *Encyclopaedia Britannica,* 1974.

Wiener, A., J. Preciado Zepeda, E. B. Sonn, and H. R. Polivka. 1945. "Individual Blood Differences in Mexican Indians, with Special Reference to the Rh Blood Types and Rh Factor." *Journal of Experimental Medicine* 81:559–71.

Wilbert, J. 1958. "Datos antropológicos de los indios Piaroa." *Memoria de la Sociedad de Ciencias Naturales La Salle* (Caracas) 18:155–83.

Wilheim, O., and L. Sandoval. 1956. "Genealogías y sero-antropología de los pascuenses." *Boletín de la Sociedad de Biología de Concepción* (Concepción, Chile) 31:119–39.

Willems, E. 1958. "Minority Subcultures in Brazil." In *Miscellanea Paul Rivet Octogenario Dicata* (Mexico City) 2:877–83.

Willey, G. R. 1955. "The Prehistoric Civilizations of Nuclear America." *American Anthropologist* 57:571–93.

Williams, G. D. 1931. *Maya-Spanish Crosses in Yucatán.* Cambridge, Mass.: Bureau of International Research of Harvard University and Radcliffe College for Peabody Museum of American Archaeology and Ethnology.

Wissler, C. 1920. "Opportunities for Coordination in Anthropological and Psychological Research." *American Anthropologist* 22:1–22.

Wolf, E. 1955. "Types of Latin American Peasantry: A Preliminary Discussion." *American Anthropologist* 57:452–71.

Zavala, S. 1935. *Las instituciones jurídicas en la conquista de América.* Madrid: Imprente Helénica.

———. 1938. "Los trabajadores antillanos en el siglo XVI." *Revista de Historia de América* (Mexico City) 3:60–88.

———. 1944. *Ensayos sobre la colonización española en América.* Buenos Aires: Emecé Editores.

———. 1958. "Vida social en Hispanoamérica en la época colonial." *Miscellanea Paul Rivet Octogenario Dicata* (Mexico City) 2:885–96.

ABOUT THE AUTHOR AND THE TRANSLATOR

Claudio Esteva-Fabregat

Claudio Esteva-Fabregat is Professor Emeritus of the University of Barcelona. From 1965 to 1968 he was the Director of the Museo Nacional de Etnologia in Madrid, he has served as a Fullbright Visiting Professor at the University of Arizona, and he is a member of various international societies and an advisor to journals in his field of expertise. Professor Esteva-Fabregat received the Malinowski Award from the Society for Applied Anthropology in 1994. He has published numerous articles and the following books in addition to *El mestizaje en Iberoamérica: Función y funcionalismo en las ciencias sociales; Antropología y filosofía; Razas humanas y racismo; Cultura, sociedad y personalidad; Antropología industrial; Estado, etnicidad y biculturalismo; La corona española y el indio americano;* and *Antropología industriale.*

John Wheat

John Wheat has been the archives translator at the Center for American History at the University of Texas at Austin since 1978. A professional archivist/librarian, historian, and Latin American area specialist, he has taught in the Graduate School of Library and Information Science at the University of Texas, has served as a translator and interpreter of Spanish, and has produced Spanish-language radio programs and concerts. Among his published translations is *Views from the Apache Frontier: Report on the Northern Provinces of New Spain,* by José Cortés, edited by Elizabeth A. H. John.